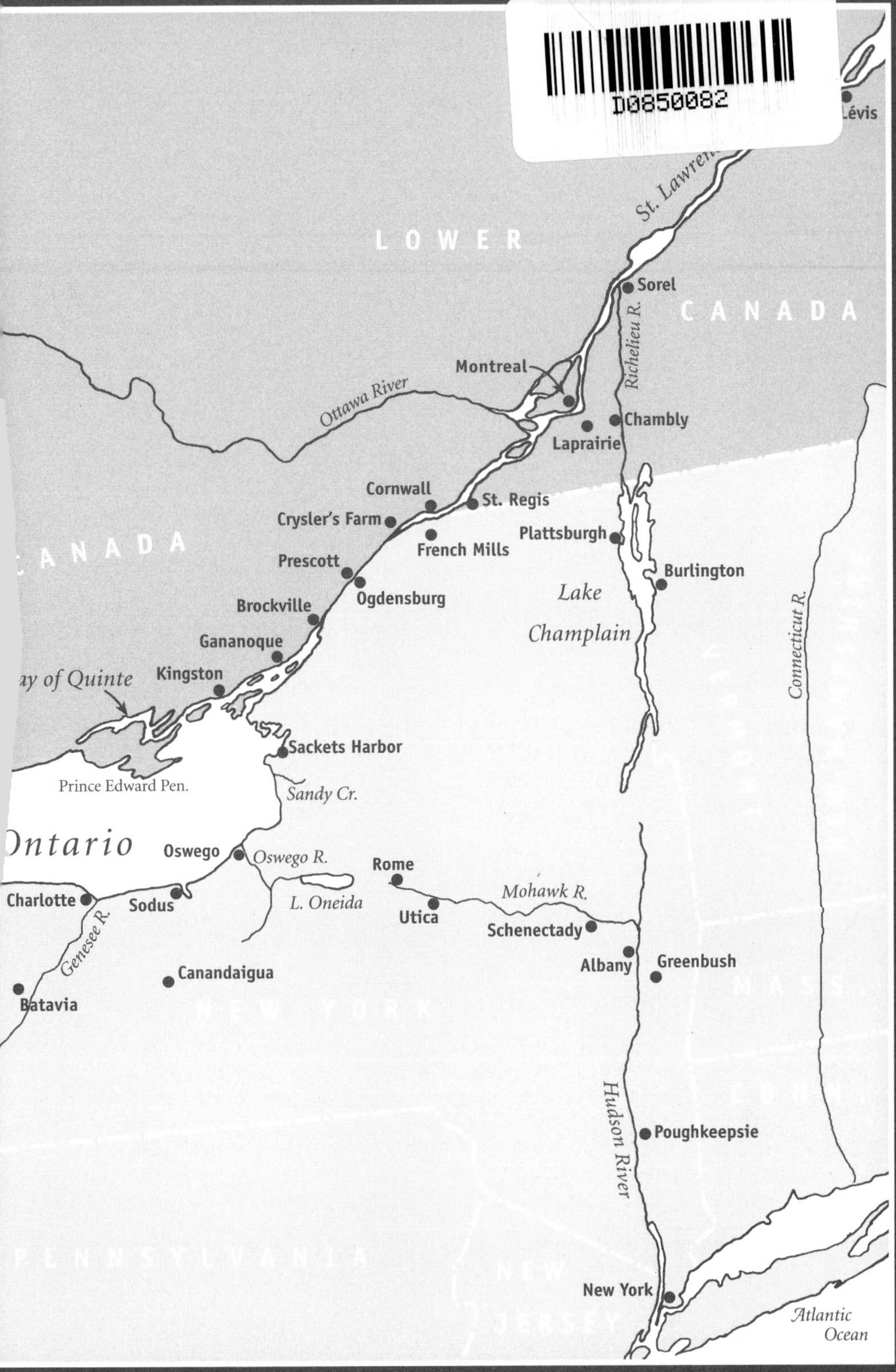

L O W E R

C A N A D A

*St. Lawrence*

Lévis

Sorel

*Ottawa River*

Montreal

*Richelieu R.*

Chambly

Laprairie

C A N A D A

Cornwall

St. Regis

Crysler's Farm

French Mills

Plattsburgh

Prescott

Ogdensburg

Burlington

Brockville

*Lake*

*Champlain*

Gananoque

Kingston

*ay of Quinte*

*Ontario*

*Prince Edward Pen.*

Sackets Harbor

*Sandy Cr.*

*V E R M O N T*

*Connecticut R.*

*N E W   H A M P S H I R E*

Oswego

*Oswego R.*

Rome

*Mohawk R.*

Charlotte

*Genesee R.*

Sodus

*L. Oneida*

Utica

Schenectady

*N E W   Y O R K*

Canandaigua

Albany

Greenbush

*M A S S.*

Batavia

*C O N N.*

*Hudson River*

Poughkeepsie

P E N N S Y L V A N I A

N E W

New York

*Atlantic*
*Ocean*

J E R S E Y

# A VERY BRILLIANT AFFAIR:
# THE BATTLE OF QUEENSTON HEIGHTS, 1812

OTHER TITLES BY ROBERT MALCOMSON

## Books

*Warships of the Great Lakes: 1754-1834* (2001)

*Lords of the Lake: The Naval War on Lake Ontario, 1812-1814* (1998)

*HMS Detroit: The Battle for Lake Erie* (with Thomas Malcomson) (1990)

## Edited Memoirs

*Sailors of 1812: Memoirs and Letters of Naval Officers on Lake Ontario* (1997)

## Monographs

*Burying General Brock: A History of Brock's Monuments* (1996)

*The Battle of Queenston Heights* (1995)

# *A Very* Brilliant *Affair*

THE BATTLE OF QUEENSTON HEIGHTS, 1812

ROBERT MALCOMSON

*Maps by Christopher Johnson*

ROBIN BRASS STUDIO
*Toronto*

Published 2003 by
Robin Brass Studio Inc.,
10 Blantyre Avenue, Toronto, Ontario M1N 2R4, Canada
Fax: 416-698-2120 • www.rbstudiobooks.com

Printed and bound in Canada by Friesens, Altona, Manitoba

**National Library of Canada Cataloguing in Publication**

Malcomson, Robert, 1949-
A very brilliant affair : the Battle of Queenston Heights, 1812 / Robert Malcomson ; maps by Christopher Johnson.

Includes bibliographical references and index.
ISBN 1-896941-33-8

1. Queenston Heights (Ont.), Battle of, 1812. 2. Canada – History – War of 1812. 3. Brock, Isaac, Sir, 1769-1812. I. Title.

FC446.Q4M343 2003 971.03'4 C2003-903254-X
E356.Q3M34 2003

*In memory of*

The days and nights
on Queenston Heights.

# *Contents*

## MAPS

# *Preface*

The Battle of Queenston Heights took place on Tuesday, 13 October 1812. The action, which lasted from dawn until dusk, proved to be a defining moment for everyone involved. From that day forward, Queenston Heights would forever be a benchmark in their lives.

For the British army, the victory was one more in a long line of military successes, earning promotion for veterans of warfare such as William Holcroft and James Dennis. It brought a taste of fame to Roger Hale Sheaffe while sealing the fate of others, most notably Isaac Brock, who was arguably the most admired figure in the society of Upper Canada at the time.

The Americans generally considered the outcome "a most mortifying and unexpected event," as one officer described it, a setback that needed to be retrieved as quickly as possible with another invasion attempt.[1] The engagement introduced many Americans to the realities of the battlefield. Jared Willson swore he would never go back, but John E. Wool and Winfield Scott and others were determined to return to "the hoarse clangor of the trumpets," eager to take advantage of the lessons learned at Queenston.[2]

The militia of Upper Canada ever afterwards pointed to 13 October 1812 as a date of great significance. For all of the 700 or so men of the province – the lawyers, merchants, tradesmen and farmers – who fought that day, it was the first time they had to stand in defence of their homes and families. They took their places in the line of battle and acquitted themselves well, and even on subsequent days of combat when the militia did not hold firm, the men who served at Queenston could point to their accomplishment with pride.

Among the Canadian militia were young officers who would soon rise to prominence in their society, men such as William Hamilton Merritt, John Beverley Robinson and Archibald Maclean. They, and others like them, were the ones who first proposed to honour Brock, their fallen hero, with a spectacular monument. They originated the idea of turning the old military reserve atop the Niagara Escarpment into a parkland and through the rest of their lives faithfully worked to see that it was expanded and maintained with reverence. Nearly two hundred years later the park and Brock's monument remain as the most popular memorial to the War of 1812 on the border between Canada and the United States.

I have lived nearly my whole life within half an hour's travel of Queenston Heights. I do not know when I first went there, but it must have been on one of our Sunday outings, when my dad packed the family into the '56 Chevy he was so proud of and headed down the road. I can see us looking for a parking spot, carrying the picnic basket, eating sandwiches near the great stone pillar, taking a hike to use up little-boy energies. There I am, clambering over the ornamental guns, charging up the hill, falling in mock death, jumping up to dream of battlefield glory.

I doubt that a year has gone by when the Heights has not known my footsteps. I was there as a student, and then a teacher, a lover, a husband and a father. I have trodden the paths as a guide and re-enactor, even addressed the assembled few at a commemoration. I have sweated in redcoat wool on a stifling day in July, and one time I gained the insight I needed while standing in the frigid October rain.

The place, and what happened there, has always fascinated me. I have talked about it, taught it, studied it, written about it, always trying to bring the scenes into sharper focus as much for myself as anyone else. There were always so many questions, so many loose ends. Where did Brock die? What was he doing there anyway? Who was with him? Who was against him? How did they get there? Why did the battle happen here? Why that day? What difference did it make? Who else was a hero? Who never went home again?

This book is a product of those questions and countless others. If I have accomplished anything, it is that I have satisfied myself in finding answers to just about everything. Actually, my goal is much loftier than this. More than a century ago E. A. Cruikshank published his pamphlet about the battle and since then no one has produced a thorough military study of the campaign and battle. My ultimate goal has been to fill that gap.

I have not changed the main plot of the story. The armies are still there on opposite shores, watching each other all summer. So are the river crossing and the capture of the redan battery and Brock's last charge, the failure of the New York militia and the commitment of its Canadian counterpart, the final phase on the Heights, the conquered and conquerors.

There was much more to be told, however. For instance, the American defeat at Queenston was almost a certainty from the time that President Madison and Congress started down the path to war. Their lack of preparation put a half-baked army in the field and left Governor Daniel Tompkins to scrounge resources essential to the defence of New York State. Tompkins's motivation for proposing Stephen Van Rensselaer as the general of the army on the Niagara was not as simplistic and self-serving as many have alleged. And Van Rensselaer's force was never intended to be anything more than a diversion in support of other military thrusts until things changed late in the campaign. Stephen was no general, but he was a man with character and so were his aide, Solomon Van Rensselaer, and secretary, John Lovett. I hope these pages reveal their personalities and predilections while also giving new insights into the actions of such previously shadowy figures as William Wadsworth and Nicholas Gray. To tell the stories of the lesser-known men, to give a glimpse of their origins and the essence of their days along the Niagara River in the summer of 1812 has been another of my goals. And I hope the reputation of the New York State militia is saved in some small part here since they were not as completely culpable for the defeat as has often been said.

This book shows the U.S. Army in its first major engagement with the renowned British redcoats. Led at a safe distance by the lethargic Henry Dearborn, the regular force on the Niagara comprised raw recruits and inexperienced officers who were for the most part poorly equipped and inadequately trained. Those young Americans in the field were imbued with a zealous patriotism and they did the best they could to prepare for war. Nearly every one of the regular troops available crossed into Canada and many of them bore the scars of that day for the rest of their lives. True, there seemed to be a fair amount of confusion about giving and obeying orders, but in the thick of the firefights men such as John E. Wool proved their mettle. The text describes in detail, for the first time, the critical role his regiment, the Thirteenth U.S. Infantry, played in establishing and holding the American beachhead.

Isaac Brock has usually been identified as the hero of Queenston Heights. There is no doubting his competence, dedication and awe-inspiring charisma, as his masterful defence of Upper Canada revealed, but he was not as infallible as legend would have us believe. When Brock died others quickly stepped forward to defend Canada as bravely as he had. The much-maligned Roger Hale Sheaffe coolly assessed the setbacks of the early morning at Queenston, concentrated his force and deployed it to win the day; it was his victory to celebrate, though, given the treatment he has received in most history books, one would hardly know it. And one would hardly know about men who have been barely mentioned over the years. There were William Holcroft and his guns and John Norton's Grand River warriors, the light company under William Derenzy, and James Dennis, his wounds bandaged, riding to join Sheaffe's column as it headed for the Heights. Young Hamilton Merritt was in the saddle too, and not far off were James Crooks and George Ridout marching with their companies. They were all loyal Britons and Canadians and they fought to protect the shore of a young Canada and for that reason alone each of them deserves to be remembered.

A note: as with most military stories, many regiments and other units are mentioned. To help the reader keep track of the opponents, I have followed the practice of identifying British units by using numerals while I have spelled the names of American units.

I have named this book *A Very Brilliant Affair* because such words were used widely to describe the events of 13 October.[3] This particular line came from the quill of Captain Holcroft of the Royal Artillery, who, in my view, epitomizes the career soldier – dedicated to his craft, devoted to his flag, "indefatigible" as Brock once called him. I have often imagined giving this book to Holcroft, sitting across from him at the mess table, with James Dennis at one end and Solomon Van Rennselaer at the other, Chrystie, Glegg, Mullany, Williams, the others, filling in the spaces. What would they say about it? Would it do them justice?

In the real world I succeeded in bringing a group of readers to a virtual mess table where they did me the honour of critiquing various stages of the manuscript as I laboured over it these past two years. They formed an ensemble of distinguished historians and friends: Carl Benn, Robin Brass, Dennis Carter-Edwards, Gary Gibson, Hugh Gilliland, Donald E. Graves, John Grodzinski, Donald Hickey, Janet Malcomson, Joy Ormsby and Wesley Turner. To my readers I am greatly indebted for their advice and encouragement. Ultimately, the telling of the tale is the writer's responsibility so any deficiencies found here are the result of my decisions.

The list of people who helped during the research and writing phases is a long one and to each of them I extend my sincere appreciation. They are: Margaret Dore, Susan Moskal and Annie Relic of the Interlibrary Loan Department at the James A. Gibson Library at Brock University in St. Catharines; John Burtniak, Lynne Prunskus and Edie Williams of the Special Collections and Archives at the Gibson Library; Lori Fisher, Maxine Lorang, Liselle France and Erin Christian at Historic Cherry Hill in Albany, New York; Mike Lawlor, Legal Surveys Manager in the Public Words Department of the Niagara Region; Elizabeth Putnam and Amy Rupert at the Rensselaer Polytechnic Institute in Troy, New York; Dianne Graves, who conducted research for me at the Public Record Office in Kew, England; Clark Bernat, managing director of the Niagara Historical Society Museum in Niagara-on-the-Lake; April Petrie at the Niagara Parks Commission; Heather McNabb at the McCord Museum of Canadian History in Montreal; Leslie Jensen of the United States Military Academy at West Point, New York; Peter Harrington of the Anne S. K. Brown Military Collection at Brown University Library in Providence Rhode Island; James Campbell at RiverBrink, Home of the Weir Collection, Queenston, Ontario; Linda Kennedy at the Buffalo Erie County Historical Society Research Library; David W. Parish of the Livingston County Department of History in Geneseo, New York; Brian Dunnigan and John Dann of the William L. Clements Library at the University of Michigan in Ann Arbor; Sarah Bennett at the Albany Institute of History and Art; Dennis Gannon in Washington, D.C.; René Chartrand; A.T. Holden; Greg Young; and Kiersten Hay, who gave me the Fanny Doyle print.

I conducted research at the following institutions and express my gratitude for the opportunities to explore their remarkable collections: the

National Archives of Canada in Ottawa; the United States National Archives in Washington, D.C.; the Archives of Ontario in Toronto; the New York State Archives and New York State Library in Albany; the Toronto Reference Library; the Niagara-on-the-Lake Public Library; Fort George Historic Site in Niagara-on-the-Lake; the Mills Memorial Library at McMaster University in Hamilton; the Lockwood Memorial Library at the State University of New York at Buffalo; the Geneva Historical Society at the Prouty-Chew House and Museum in Geneva, New York; the Ontario County Historical Society in Canandaigua, New York.

Peter Rindlisbacher has created another breathtaking cover illustration and Chris Johnson's maps are a great enhancement to my descriptions. I thank both of them for sharing this project with me. Robin Brass has encouraged me from the day I mentioned that I wanted to step ashore from naval activities for awhile. He has guided me and treated my drafts with respect and my writer's ego with kid gloves. I can barely begin to express the appreciation I have for his commitment to this project. In the same vein, I willingly tip my hat to my other mentor, the oracle of Wolf Grove.

My family has continued to be a vital source of support in all my writing projects. Janet, my research assistant, indexer and fellow tombstone detective, and our children, Melanie, Carrie, Geoff and Holly, christened me "Bookie" during this long campaign. It was one of those serendipitous events, and I want them to know that it made sitting down in this chair each day a lot easier.

ROBERT MALCOMSON
*St. Catharines, Ontario*
*29 April 2003*

# A VERY BRILLIANT AFFAIR:
# THE BATTLE OF QUEENSTON HEIGHTS, 1812

# PROLOGUE

## *"Do justice to the occasion."*

Thursday, 13 October 1853, the forty-first anniversary of the Battle of Queenston Heights, was the day selected for the re-interment of Major General Sir Isaac Brock and his aide-de-camp, Lieutenant Colonel John Macdonell. Their burial in the tomb of the new monument rising on the Heights had been long anticipated, but preparations for the event were bungled. The members of the organizing committee did not meet to plan the ceremony until Monday of that week, and only on Tuesday did they publish programs and begin mailing invitations around the province.

Nevertheless, by early Thursday morning, the middle of the work week, "the roads toward the frontier began to be thronged with horsemen, waggons, carriages, loaded with families of the happy and independent farmers of the old Niagara District, and the enterprizing merchants, professional men and mechanics of its numerous villages and towns."[1] Steamers arrived at the Queenston dock with crowds of passengers. The village filled up with young militia officers and aging veterans in the fading red coats they had worn in battles fought four decades before. The band of the Royal Canadian Rifles, a troop of the Toronto Light Horse, the Hamilton Independent Artillery and an informal platoon carrying "the old Colours of the gallant First York Infantry" took their places in the procession that slowly formed up on Queen Street. A light breeze carried the scent of ripe fruit from the nearby orchards. The air was mild and clear, the sun brilliant in a pristine sky, creating "one of those soft, lovely, golden mornings of our Canadian Autumn."

Just after 11:00 a.m. the procession got underway. The centre piece of the parade was the magnificent funeral car, designed by William Thomas, architect for the new monument. It was a long, wide carriage, with three tiers rising twelve feet off the ground and even taller pillars crowned with dark plumes and wreaths of laurel at its corners. Draped in black fabric, the car bore coats of arms, a military trophy made up of weapons from the days of 1812 and "the British Colours, folded in mourning bands." The two caskets rode high on the tiers where everyone could see them, Brock's bearing the plumed hat he had ordered from England which only reached Canada after his death. Six black horses drew the car.

By this time between twelve and fifteen thousand people had gathered. They lined Queen Street and covered the hillside up Portage Road, falling silent as the cortège approached. When it had passed they hurried to the hilltop to claim a place where they could see and hear the burial ceremony and speeches. The monument consisted so far of only the base and the tombs, beside which a platform had been built for the dignitaries and speakers. The crowd packed so tightly into this area that the correspondent for the *Niagara Mail* lamented that he found it "utterly impossible to take a note."

The Canadian Rifles led the way up the hill and to the monument with arms reversed, the band playing a dirge, its drums muffled. Beside the car walked the honorary pall bearers, among them James Crooks, who had been in the thick of the action on the Heights. The mourners followed, prominent among them Colonel Donald Macdonell, whose brother was making his final trek to the undisturbed resting place he deserved; and then came the representatives of the Grand River Six Nations, the files of veterans, William Thomas, the building committee, the clergy, the Grimsby Brass Band and the Chippawa Fire Brigade.

Among the mourners walked William Hamilton Merritt. At dawn on 13 October 1812 he had been a nineteen-year-old militia dragoon asleep in the town of Niagara when Isaac Brock galloped away from Government House to investigate the sounds of fighting coming from Queenston. Later, young Merritt had ridden with despatches for the commander at Chippawa and returned to the Heights to take his place in the final hour of battle, risking his life beside his comrades. He had lived a life of great accomplishment, and now he was marching up the hill on another perilous mission. The planning committee had begun its work too late to find a gifted orator to deliver the main address, so Merritt, as chairman, was "volunteered" to make the speech. An entrepreneur, an influential legislator, a builder of canals and railways and bridges, Merritt had every reason to feel confident and at ease in front of a large assembly, but the weight of his task was heavy, and he was nervous.

What went through Merritt's mind as he stood at centre stage, looking out over the mass of faces, upturned to hear his words? Did he think back to his call to duty, the exhausting days of the long summer of 1812, the miserable rainy nights of October, the sight of American flags flying above Queenston that morning? Did he pause to envision days ahead, decades, centuries in the future when distant families would meet on the Heights to renew acquaintances, when school children would line up to ascend the monument, when lovers would find silence in the shadows of the parkland?

Merritt shuffled his papers. He scanned the crowd again, cleared his throat and looked to his text. "There are few among us who could do justice to the occasion," he began humbly. "We have reason to be thankful, that so many, then Brock's compatriots, are still spared to witness this imposing ceremony. May its effects not be lost on the rising generation."

## PART ONE

# *War Is Declared, 1812*

*I had from my infancy listened to my father's recitals of the injuries sustained by this country and the violation of every principle of justice by Great Britain and [how] it had become a jest and byword in England that the country "could not be kicked into war;" but we were kicked into it, and totally unprepared for such a contest. After a peace of thirty years, and entirely engrossed in trade, every means had been neglected to prepare for war. Our treasury poor, our arsenals empty, fortifications in ruin, our Navy neglected, Military Science unknown, our Army nominally about 6000 men, the country divided in opinion....*

*[B]ut I had heard my father's opinion relative to the duty of defending our beloved country, and ... without any delay applied for a commission in the army.*

LIEUTENANT ISAAC ROACH, SECOND U.S. REGIMENT OF ARTILLERY[1]

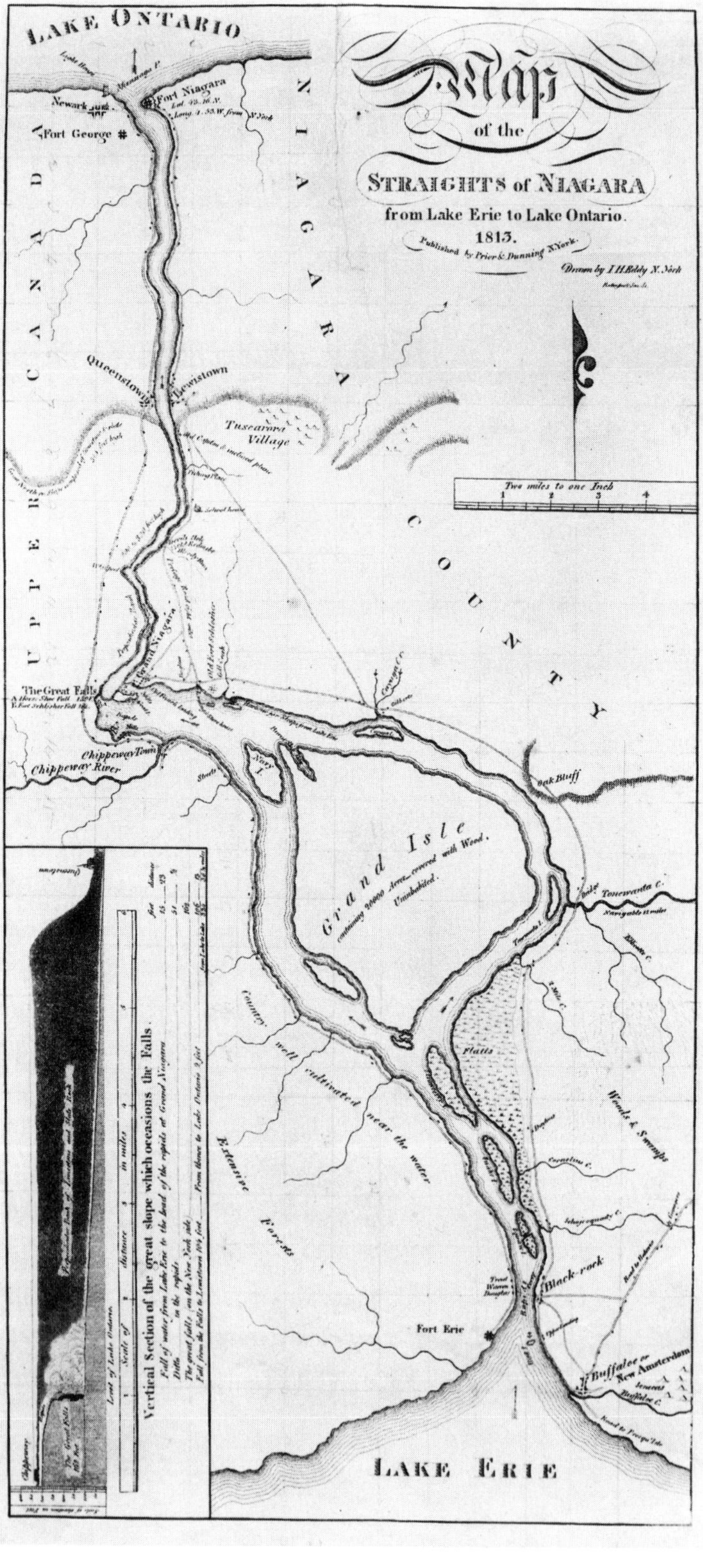

Map of the STRAIGHTS of NIAGARA from Lake Erie to Lake Ontario. 1813.
Published by Prior & Dunning N. York.
Drawn by I. H. Eddy N. York
LAKE ONTARIO
Fort Niagara
Newark
Fort George
NIAGARA COUNTY
UPPER CANADA
Queenstown
Lewistown
Tuscarora Village
Two miles to one Inch
1
2
3
4
The Great Falls
Chippeway Town
Chippeway River
Oak Bluff
Grand Isle
Tonewanta C.
Flatts
Country well cultivated near the water
Extensive Forests
Woods & Swamps
Black-rock
Fort Erie
Buffaloe or New Amsterdam
Buffaloe C.
LAKE ERIE
Vertical Section of the great slope which occasions the Falls
Level of Lake Ontario
Scale of distance in miles

# 1

# "In the midst of the labors of man"

## THE NIAGARA FRONTIER IN 1812

William Hamilton Merritt was eighteen years old when the War of 1812 began. He lived with his parents on a farm near the hamlet of Shipman's Corners about twelve miles west of the Niagara River. War with the United States had long been expected in Upper Canada, but the news that Merritt heard on 27 June (nine days after the Americans had declared hostilities) still took him by surprise. The next morning he rode into the hamlet and there, outside the tavern owned by Paul Shipman, Merritt found "the Captains of Companies assembled, collecting their men as fast as possible."[1]

The sight of the militia mustering made Hamilton Merritt (he preferred his middle name) realize that his life was about to undergo an abrupt change. Just weeks before he had been commissioned as a lieutenant in the 1st Troop of the Niagara Light Dragoons, under the command of his father, Major Thomas Merritt, so a call to service applied as much to him as it did to any other militiaman in Lincoln County. By 2 o'clock that afternoon, Merritt found himself on duty with his troop, watching for signs of activity on the American side of the Niagara River. "We kept patrol up and down the River," Merritt wrote, "momentarily expecting an Attack."[2]

*(Facing)* **"The Straights of Niagara from Lake Erie to Lake Ontario, 1813."** This is a rare contemporary map of the full 35-mile length of the Niagara River, showing settlements and roads. (J.H. Eddy, courtesy of the William L. Clements Library)

The shores of the Niagara River would become the setting for the events that led to the battle on Queenston Heights, where young men like Merritt would get their first taste of war. From the 1780s the river had formed part of the boundary between the United States and the British province of Upper Canada. It was thirty-five miles long and carried the waters of Lake Erie to Lake Ontario, 326 feet below, with the sharpest descent being the famous Niagara Falls, from which the river roared northward through a narrow, seven-mile-long gorge until it spilled out to form a wide stream, still full of eddies and back currents, at the village of Queenston.

The gorge cut through the Niagara Escarpment, a 300-mile-long ridge stretching from the vicinity of Rochester in New York State west and north to the tip of the Bruce Peninsula, the neck of land between Lake Huron and Georgian Bay. The escarpment was the most striking geologic feature on both sides of the Niagara River, "a sharp topographic break" between the seven-mile-wide lower plain extending to Lake Ontario and the upper plain stretching south to Lake Erie.[3] Rising roughly 300 feet above the river, the escarpment was in some places a sheer cliff of exposed layers of sedimentary rock and elsewhere a series of terraces densely covered with vegetation.

From Queenston, the Niagara River continued its northward course in a series of gentle curves down to Lake Ontario, varying in width from 300 to 700 yards. This stretch of relatively quiet water was navigable, but the wild rapids of the gorge and the great falls interrupted passage between the lakes and travellers had developed a portage route along the eastern shore. Its lower landing was the foliaged ravine on the current site of Artpark, a theatre located just south of Lewiston, New York, while the upper landing was about a mile above the falls.[4]

Control of the Niagara River route passed through the hands of the Neuter, or Neutral, confederacy, the Senecas, the French and the British until the outcome of the American Revolutionary War (1776-1783) left it in the hands of John Stedman and his family.[5] Stedman had monopolized the carrying business on the Niagara River since the 1760s, but the redrawing of the political map of North America led to his decline. By the late 1780s British merchants in Montreal complained to the government at Quebec about his rates and his preferred treatment of their American rivals and lobbied for the creation of a portage route on the western (Canadian) side of the river.

It was during this period that the British surveyed the Niagara Peninsula in preparation for the settlement of thousands of citizens, soldiers and native nations who had remained loyal to the Crown and were forced to abandon their properties in the Thirteen Colonies. As part of this undertaking, a thirteen-mile overland route was cut from the lower Niagara up to the mouth of Chippawa Creek, as this part of the Welland River was, and is, known. Its lower landing was located close to the escarpment where a wide pocket had been eroded into the forty-foot sandstone and shale banks, creating a spacious beach. About this spot a British engineer wrote, "the bank of the shore is lower than at any other place, and seems in all respects the most convenient spot for the Purpose, whether on this or on the other side of the River. There is good ground here for storehouses and other conveniences and it is close to the road leading through the settlements."[6] In 1791 the army constructed a wharf, a blockhouse and a two-storey storehouse there, later adding a stone guardhouse. When a row of huts was built to serve as barracks for a detachment of the Queen's Rangers, the place became known as Queenstown.

After the British parliament passed the Constitution Act in 1791, thereby dividing the old province of Quebec into Lower and Upper Canada, settlement on the Canadian side of the Niagara River progressed with relative ease and prosperity.[7] The first principal town, at the mouth of the river, went through a series of name changes in its early years, from Butlersburg (after Lieutenant Colonel John Butler, whose soldiers were among the first residents) to New Niagara, West Niagara and, simply, Niagara. Officials in Quebec originally referred to the town as Lenox and when Lieutenant Governor John Graves Simcoe chose the settlement as Upper Canada's first capital, he changed the name to Newark. In 1798, however, two years after Simcoe had returned to England and the capital had been switched to the village of York (today's Toronto) directly across Lake Ontario, the provincial legislature passed an act making the town's official name Niagara. Today it is known as Niagara-on-the-Lake.

Its selection as the capital caused Niagara to grow quickly. The twenty new houses mentioned in 1793 had become fifty the next year and in 1796 a visitor remarked that "Few places in North America can boast of a more rapid rise than the little town of Niagara, nearly every one of its houses having been built within the last five years."[8] When James Fenimore Cooper, then a midshipman in the U.S. Navy, visited the town in 1809 he noted "the transition was like that of suddenly quitting the forest to be placed in the midst of the labors of man."[9] By 1811 Niagara was an established community of eighty homes, a courthouse, churches and shops with a population of about five hundred people. Laid out in a carefully planned grid, Niagara was a pioneer settlement where ordinances allowed for hogs "to run at large," put portions of the public roads under the care of private individuals and ordered fences to be five feet high.[10]

A quarter mile east of the town was Fort George, the major British military installation on the peninsula. Situated on a plateau overlooking the river nearly three quarters of a mile from the river's mouth, the fort was garrisoned by detachments from various regiments after 1796 when its construction began. Wooden palisades connected its bastions and enclosed a large parade ground, several wooden blockhouses, a barracks for officers, kitchens, a bakery and oven, a powder magazine and a hospital. But the fort was ill-placed, being too far away to command the mouth of the river and vulnerable to a wide arc of fire from the American shoreline. In 1811 one British officer described Fort George as, "an irregular field work, consisting of six small bastions, faced with framed timber and plank. These bastions are connected with a line of picketing, twelve feet in height. The whole of this work is very much out of repair; its situation and construction very defective, and cannot be considered capable of much defence."[11]

A network of roads spread out from the town of Niagara, along the lake, to the interior and beside the river all the way to Fort Erie. River Road had been one of the first byways laid down by the British; Elizabeth Simcoe, the lieutenant governor's wife, wrote of making the seven-mile trip between Niagara and Queenston in a two-horse gig in forty-five minutes. "The Road is good," she noted, "but for the stumps of trees on each side which it requires attention to avoid."[12] By 1811 the road was well developed with bridges crossing the numerous, deep ravines that incised the steep banks of the river. Along the road stood prosperous and trim farms, "pleasant and well-cultivated, ... [with] plenty of young orchards of apple and peach trees."[13]

Queenston developed at the same time as Niagara, though less quickly. Situated directly across the river from the Stedman landing, Queenston

**Fort George, ca. 1807**
From a vantage point near Fort Niagara on the American side of the Niagara River, the artist depicted Fort George to the left on the opposite bank above the naval depot and the town of Niagara to the right. Note the roadway leading down to the river, dug out of the bank midway between the fort and the town. The location of Fort Niagara gave it control of the river's mouth and put the British town and fort within range of its guns. The British erected batteries along their shore to counter the American guns. (Engraving by Frederick C. Lewis of a watercolour by George Heriot, National Archives of Canada, C-12794)

owed its existence to the British portage route.[14] Robert Hamilton, a Scot who had arrived in Montreal in the early 1770s to work as a clerk in a trading company, was one of the group of merchants who won the first contract to operate the new portage. He was a founding citizen of Queenston and built an impressive two-storey dwelling overlooking the landing. When Mrs. Simcoe visited in 1795 she complimented the "very good stone house, the back rooms looking on the river. A gallery, the length of the house, is a delightful covered walk, both above and below, in all weather."[15]

The portage flourished; in 1799 an observer noted "four vessels of 60 and 100 tons burden unloading at the same time and sometimes not less than sixty wagons loaded in a day.... [T]he farmers ... carry from 20 to 30 hundredweight for which they get 1s. 8d., New York currency, per hundredweight, and load back with furs."[16] Profits for Hamilton and his associates rose steadily through the decade but began to suffer after 1800 as the fur trade and movement of military goods decreased. The situation worsened in 1807 when Porter, Barton and Company gained control of the American portage route, building a dock at Lewiston and improving the haulage service with the support of the New York State government. Despite this downturn, Queenston grew into a successful pioneer community by 1812. Hamilton's house, occupied by George Hamilton after his father's death in 1809, dominated the village, which consisted of about twenty houses, an inn where the stage coach running between Niagara and Fort Erie changed teams and took on passengers, several stores, warehouses and sundry enterprises such as a distillery, a smithy and a tannery. It was described as "a small but handsome village; most houses are built of stone or brick, large and well-finished. It is also a place of considerable trade, inhabited by a civil and rich people."[17]

From Queenston the road followed a long and steep incline up the Niagara Escarpment to Queenston Heights. The northern face of the escarpment and a wedge of land along its rim (200 yards across at its widest

**Hamilton House, Queenston, 1792-93**
Robert Hamilton's impressive home at Queenston was one of the first brick houses built on the Niagara River. It provided him a view of the Queenston landing and the carrying business that made him a commercial leader in early Upper Canada. (Watercolour by Elizabeth P. Simcoe, Archives of Ontario, F 47-11-1-0-65, 49)

**Chippawa Village and the King's Bridge, c. 1807**
Chippawa developed in the early 1790s as the southern terminus of the British portage on the Niagara River. Heriot depicted the bridge over Chippawa Creek just above the point where it flowed into the Niagara. (Watercolour by George Heriot, National Archives of Canada, C-12768)

point) was an area of Crown land held as a military reserve, the uppermost edge being covered with trees, mainly oak. It was in this area that the Queen's Rangers built a second cantonment early in the 1790s, from which they had a splendid view of the Lake Ontario plain below them on both sides of the river, and when the weather was clear, they could see the smoke plumes of York thirty miles north across Lake Ontario. The military reserve continued to the river's edge and along the bank all the way down to the town of Niagara. Close to Queenston the heaviest timber along the face of the escarpment had been cleared, leaving some brush and bracken behind. On the Heights, south of the reserve was the first range of lots in the township of Niagara, mainly cleared and cultivated land owned (north to south) by Samuel Street, Elijah Phelps and Daniel Rose. Part of Street's land was separated from the reserve by a fence made by a zigzag arrangement of wood rails, the ends of which were stacked one upon the other; this was commonly known as a "snake fence," but the locals preferred the term "worm fence."

Portage Road, as this segment of River Road was known, ran across Street's property and that of Phelps and Rose and south to the village of Chippawa, where a bridge crossed Chippawa Creek and wharves marked the limit of navigation on the upper reaches of the Niagara River. A traveller in 1810 remarked that Chippawa was "a mean village of twenty houses, three stores, two taverns, a wind-mill and distillery.... [as well as] barracks ... surrounded by demolished palisades, in which a lieutenant's guard is stationed."[18]

Fifteen miles upriver, past Grand Island and the widest stretch of the Niagara, lay Fort Erie. The original fort had fallen into ruin, and a new structure, begun in 1805, had never been completed as planned. It consisted of two sets of barracks and several gun positions and, as he had commented about Fort George, the British engineer Ralph Bruyeres wrote "Fort Erie cannot be considered a strong military position."[19]

American settlement along the Niagara River developed significantly after 1800 when the first surveys of the region adjacent to the river created townships and town sites; by 1810 the three counties directly east of the Niagara River (Niagara, Genesee and Ontario) had a population of 63,000. Two main roads entered western New York from the direction of the state capital at Albany, one from the south passing through the village of Bath and a more central route through Canandaigua. This latter village (about 170 miles west of Albany and eighty miles east of the Niagara) comprised 450 residents in 1810, clustered around a large brick courthouse, a jail, a school, six stores, six taverns, tanning yards, distilleries and half a dozen each of doctors and lawyers. Fifty miles west of Canandaigua was the village of Batavia with a population of 100 in 1810; from here two roads branched westward, one to Buffalo and one to Fort Niagara.[20]

Though it was surveyed in 1800, the mile-wide strip along the entire American shore of the Niagara River did not come into state ownership until officials finalized a treaty with the Seneca nation in 1802. In 1805 twenty-three of the 111 lots along the river were sold to individuals and partnerships, and the townsite of Lewiston, named after then-governor Morgan Lewis, was established about a mile below the escarpment. That

**Fort Niagara, July 1806**
This view of the American fort was drawn from the road dug down to the Niagara River beside Fort George. The old stone barracks (the French "castle") is located on the left inside Fort Niagara while a wooden stockade encloses other barracks, storehouses and shops. (Print by an unknown artist, National Archives of Canada, C-24291)

same year Peter B. Porter and his associates took over the American portage business, constructing a new landing at Lewiston and virtually ending commercial use of the traditional landing at the ravine south of the village. In spite of this improvement, Lewiston grew slowly; one traveller referred to it as "a shabby American settlement opposite Queenston" while another acknowledged that it had "a ware-house and wharf, a Post-Office and about twelve dwelling-houses, with a great amount of business."[21] A town equal to the British Niagara did not develop on the lower reaches of the American side of the river. The closest settlement to Fort Niagara was Youngstown, said to be "an inconsiderable settlement … of about 6 or 8 houses" just before the war.[22]

Near the upper end of the portage and about a quarter mile above the falls stood the village of Manchester, which Porter, Barton and Company established in 1807. It was an industrial centre, utilizing the power of the upper river, consisting of "a carding-machine, a grist-mill, a saw-mill, a rope-walk, a bark-mill, a tannery, Post-office, tavern and a few houses."[23] From there to the tiny settlement at Black Rock and to Buffalo (with a population of 508 in 1810), the road was frequently impassable so that many travellers went by boat.

There were two military establishments on the eastern (American) side of the Niagara River before the war. Fort Schlosser, at the upper end of the portage, appears to have been essentially a storehouse surrounded by a light palisade. Fort Niagara, though long established, walled, armed and more formidable in appearance, was in weak condition. Prior to the declaration of war a single company of artillery under Captain Nathan Leonard manned the fort, which was no better prepared for war than Fort George, its opposite number across the river. As one militia officer explained to Daniel Tompkins, the governor of New York State, the fort was "in a miserable and decayed situation, and can make but a feeble defence."[24]

Despite the presence of garrisons and troops on parade, there was no sharp divide between the communities along the Niagara River before the spring of 1812. Over the thirty years of settlement in the region a network of families, friends and commerce had developed, connecting the societies of New York State and Upper Canada with little regard for the international boundary line. True enough, the province inaugurated by Simcoe in 1792 had been a new home for refugees from the Thirteen Colonies, but twenty years later Upper Canada was no longer a bastion of loyalty to the Crown. It had evolved into a North American hybrid, still indisputably tied to England, but heavily influenced by the United States. Some of the hostility that the founding families of the peninsula felt after their expulsion at the hands of "rebels" had softened before the turn of the century.

Although the Americans had been slow in settling the eastern banks of the Niagara River, New York State far exceeded Upper Canada in population and resources in 1812. Its population had doubled in the preceding decade to nearly one million while the best estimate of the numbers inhabiting the British colony is about 77,000.[25] Even within the four largest provinces of British North America there were fewer than 500,000 people and the capital at Quebec had a population of fewer than 18,000. By comparison, a census of New York City showed 96,500 people living there in 1812, the population of the United States as a whole being about 7.7 million. It is no wonder that American influence upon the Canadian provinces was significant. Newspapers published in the states were important sources of copy for their Canadian counterparts, providing valuable information on agricultural matters, industrial innovations and educational practices. Travel across the border was commonplace and in the farming communities and cities of their neighbour to the south, Upper Canadians found models for their own development schemes.

British North America did not unconditionally approve of all things American, however, and while diplomatic relations between the colonies and the states were generally amicable in the decades before the War of 1812, many of the elite in Upper Canada were wary of threats posed by the United States. They had developed a certain respect for the Federalist policies of George Washington and John Adams and looked on with dismay when Thomas Jefferson and the Republicans gained power after 1800. Jefferson and Madison's policies were seen as promoting "unjust and unprincipled measures" that were dividing their nation and ruining an experiment in democracy that seemed to have some value, though it lacked the merits of the parliamentary system.[26] Some leading citizens in Upper Canada worried that republican principles would migrate north, a fear that seemed to come true after 1805 when the first opposition factions appeared in the provincial legislature. This radical element in combination with the presence of the numerous Americans who had settled in Upper Canada caused concern about where loyalties would lie if war broke out.

Talk of war that began in 1807 gained momentum in the late months of 1811 as the hostile words of President James Madison and other authorities filled the columns of newspapers at Niagara, York and Kingston. They created the impression that the United States was constructing a war machine that would easily roll over any defence the people of Upper Canada could mount.

At Shipman's Corners young Hamilton Merritt saw the growing anxiety among his friends and neighbours. "All were in Commotion," he wrote, "as we expected an Immediate attack from the Americans, who, we believed had long been prepared for it."[27] When the call to arms came, Merritt and his compatriots rode off to defend their homes, but with little hope of success. The men, he explained, "turned out with a desire and determination of doing their duty." But at the same time they "were acting under the impression of being eventually Conquered."

As they conducted their first wartime patrols along the Niagara River, Merritt and the other dragoons of his troop were understandably on edge, expecting the ferocious republican eagle to cross the stream and swallow them up, destroying the productive and peaceful lives that they were carving out of the wilderness. Little did they know that the eagle's wings were clipped.

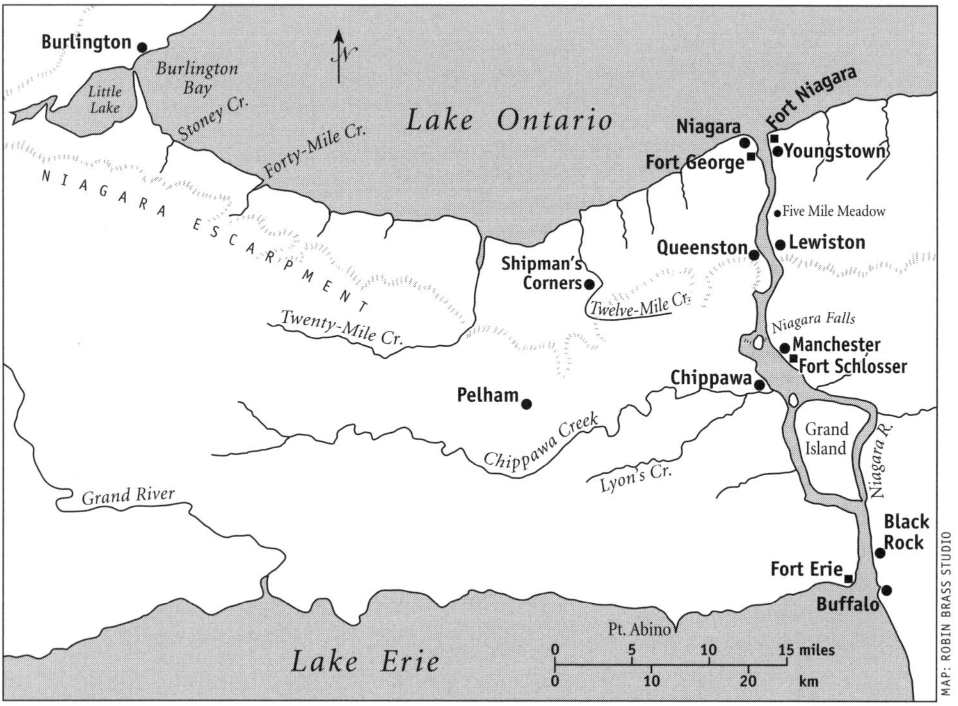


**"The Niagara"**
When contemporaries used the term "the Niagara," they referred to the British settlements on the Niagara Peninsula (west of the river) and the American settlements on the Niagara frontier (east of the river).

# 2

# "An armor and an attitude"

## WAR PREPARATIONS AT WASHINGTON AND QUEBEC

The international conflict that sent young men like Hamilton Merritt to war had been simmering for a long time. For nearly two decades Britain and France, and their respective allies, had been locked in far-flung warfare that eventually affected the United States.[1] Besides fighting on land and sea, the two adversaries had sought to injure each other by interfering with the free flow of commerce and supply. Embargos imposed by Napoleon's Continental Decrees and Britain's Orders-in-Council impeded the commercial relations of neutral parties, including American shippers who suffered the loss of vessels, cargos, capital and time. From 1807, various individuals and groups had urged President Thomas Jefferson and his successor, James Madison, to take hostile actions against the European powers, a position that received significant support when the congressional elections of 1810 and 1811 sent a covey of new representatives, the "War Hawks," to Washington. The matter of which nation to regard as the prime aggressor was undecided, however, as some politicians favoured war against France as much as war against Britain.

Other grievances, however, served to make Britain the focus of indignation. The Royal Navy, chronically short of men, impressed American merchant seamen suspected of being British citizens, forcibly removing them for service on board British vessels whether or not they carried a certificate of American citizenship. The incident on 22 June 1807 when HMS *Leopard* fired on and subdued the USS *Chesapeake* off Chesapeake Bay in order to remove four deserters was a flash point that sparked a temporary mobilization of troops and the framing of war strategies in Washington. In the wake of this event, American diplomats won modest concessions from the British, but the residual animosity was barely quelled. On 16 May 1811 when the USS *President* let loose its broadsides on HMS *Little Belt*, Washington celebrated; Secretary of the Navy Paul Hamilton wrote to Commodore John Rodgers of the *President*, "my sentiments towards, & estimation of you, go beyond what may be expressed by the words, esteem & respect."[2]

Although "Free Trade and Sailors' Rights" became the catch phrase for supporters of war against Britain, a third issue helped to make that nation the leading target for American wrath. The United States was spreading westward, a development that brought its settlers into conflict with native nations threatened by encroachment. Americans had long believed that the British surreptitiously supplied the aboriginal peoples with arms and ammunition as a means of inhibiting American expansion. From 1810, as clashes with the natives in the territories west and north of the Ohio River worsened, a call rose for Washington to sever the link between the British and native leaders such as the Shawnee chief Tecumseh and his brother, Tenskwatawa, The Prophet.

After years of perceived insult, the United States found itself at a crossroad late in 1811. It fell to President James Madison to choose a course of action that would show where the young republic stood in relation to the dominant powers of the time. Would the United States continue to be a supplicant for respect from Britain and France, or would the nation take action to redress the festering problems? It was a momentous and difficult choice for Madison as, despite the loud rhetoric of the War Hawks, there were many who were against hostilities and not just in the opposing Federalist party.[3] As well, Madison was facing a demanding electoral campaign in 1812 when he would seek the support of the various factions in the Republican party in hopes of winning their nomination for a second term during the protracted series of state caucuses. Concluding that diplomatic negotiations with Britain and France were making no headway, Madison convened the Twelfth Congress in November 1811, earlier than normal, and submitted his annual address in which he presented "evidence of [the] hostile inflexibility" of Britain and France and how they continued "trampling on rights which no independent nation can relinquish."[4] He expressed his aspiration that Congress would "feel the duty of putting the United States in an armor and an attitude demanded by the crisis."

Plainly meaning that the United States was on the road to war, Madison emphasized the improvements that were needed to prepare America's armed forces for active service. There was a lot to be accomplished if the nation was going to be able to meet the battle-hardened British or French, a point understood clearly by even the most ardent War Hawks.[5] In 1811 the U.S. Army numbered fewer than 5,500 officers and men divided among seven regiments of infantry and one each of artillery, light artillery, dragoons and rifles, plus a small corps of engineers. Officially, this "Peace Establishment" was supposed to number 10,000, but enlistments had never come close to that mark. The War Department, under William Eustis, was staffed by eight clerks who handled not only the army's business but Indian affairs and pensions. Its ability to supply the army was hamstrung by the lack of a quartermaster's department; responsibility for acquisition and delivery of all materiel had been assigned in the 1790s to an office in the Treasury Department. These conditions resulted in a bare-bones military establishment, spread among twenty-three different posts, that was further weakened by the appointment of too many officers who possessed little talent for their duties, although they were loyal Republicans. The U.S. Navy was hardly better in terms of men and materiel, consisting of seventeen vessels, although its leading officers were relatively young, skilful and ambitious.

Madison and his cabinet wanted Congress to pass laws that would allow them to reorganize and strengthen the army so it could take the field in short order, but this task was not easily achieved. After months of committee meetings and debates, and no small measure of backroom politicking, the legislators produced a series of measures that drastically augmented the army.[6] By the late spring of 1812 the old Peace Establishment was ordered to be filled up to its original total of 10,000 men while a new establishment was created to stand 25,000-strong, far more than the administration had requested and, in the view of many, impossible to recruit before hostilities commenced. The president also received permission to order detachments of the state militias into national service, and a 50,000-man volunteer forces was created to serve as a temporary regular army. Volunteers would enlist for one year and be fed, paid, armed and equipped out of the national treasury, and receive a $16 advance in lieu of a uniform.

On paper, the strength of the U.S. Army blossomed overnight and Secretary of War Eustis spread it around in March that "recruiting is going on well; and ... would be very much advanced in 6 or 8 weeks.... [and] in that time to have 10,000 to 15,000 regulars ready for service."[7] In truth his department was unable to obtain complete and accurate returns during the spring and early in June when Eustis again declared that enlistment was good, he was depending on word of mouth for his information. The best source available indicates that fewer than 2,100 men joined the regular army's rank and file between January and April 1812 and over the next four months the enlistments only rose to 8,140, far short of the authorized maximum.[8]

There were 700,000 militiamen on the state rolls, according to a return filed in February 1811, but their dependability was uncertain.[9] Several federal laws had been passed from the 1790s to cover militia activation, but no national standard for administering the militia had ever been established. Each state was required to muster most white males between the ages of eighteen and forty-five years and train, arm and equip them, but the diligence with which this was done varied from state to state. And, since the militia were state units, some governors did not welcome federal tampering with their administrative autonomy. In April when Congress authorized the president to call up a total of 100,000 militia, each state being assigned a quota, three New England governors (all Federalists) defiantly opposed the order.

There was another problem inherent in relying upon the militia as an effective auxiliary to the regular army, namely that its service was restricted to state boundaries. In New York, for instance, the troops could lawfully be used to repel an invasion, suppress an internal insurrection or back local marshals in quelling an obstruction of justice. There was no legal requirement for militiamen to cross into foreign territory or even neighbouring states. When Madison made his April call-up, governors were expected to arm and equip their quotas and hold them "in readiness to march at a moment's warning," but it was assumed their militias would only march to guard the borders, rather than carrying a war into British territory.[10]

The Volunteer Act of 6 February 1812 was intended, in part, to circumvent problems with the limitations of the militia.[11] In most states bands of

white worsted pompon
reported to have been issued blue, brown, drab and black coats
Shown in cotton pantaloons with-out gaiter bottoms. In colder weather they would have worn woolen overalls with gaiter bottoms
black Russia linen gaiters
Study for the 17th Infantry in the spring and early summer of 1813

**U.S. infantryman, 1812**

The uniform prescribed in 1812 for the infantry of the U.S. Army consisted of: a black felt cap with a white metal cap plate, white plume and cords; a dark blue, single-breasted coatee with scarlet collar and cuffs and white turnbacks on the short tails and white "lace" binding at the button holes, collar, cuffs and pockets; a white vest; white linen pantaloons; and dark blue half gaiters. A shortage of blue dye led to coatees being produced in grey, brown, black and "drab," a dull, light brown. (Watercolour by Frederick P. Todd, courtesy of the Anne S. K. Brown Collection, Brown University) patriotic citizen-soldiers had formed elite "uniform" companies of light infantry and riflemen, cavalry and artillery who took their training seriously and showed their style and precision at annual parades.[12] The February legislation was based on the premise that these bodies would be willing to serve under federal direction and not be limited by state regulations. As well, since volunteer units were meant only for temporary employment, the nation would be spared the expense of creating and maintaining a large standing army.

As with recruitment for the regular army, however, volunteers failed to step forward in numbers; a record kept by one of the War Department clerks showed the receipt of only twenty-three tenders from volunteer companies and regiments for service by the first week in June. One reason for such weak results was that the law was poorly communicated to the states, where most of the governors were occupied with activating their militia quotas and had little time to deal with the volunteer issue. For those who heard about, or read, the details of the law, there were few enticements in it to lure them away from militia service. In New York the period of enlistment for militiamen was six months, as in most states, while the voluntary recruits signed up for a year. Furthermore, enlistment as a volunteer meant that a soldier would "be under the same rules and regulations ... [as] the regular troops of the United States," and this, of course, could mean service on foreign soil.[13] Even the inducement of a 160-acre plot of land to be given to the family of a volunteer who died in the line of duty did little to attract men. In fact, many Americans viewed the volunteer program with derision; one Ohio citizen informed his senator of the popular opinion that "many wished every member of Congress had 160 acres of land stuffed up his...."[14]

Legislation was also passed to alter the internal workings of the Department of War, the most important of which concerned the creation of the Quartermaster's Department.[15] This act was intended to put the business of acquisition and supply within the hands of War Department officials, a change that had long been recommended. As with much of the other legislation, political wrangling complicated the final law, which became effective on 28 March and was slightly revised two months later. It combined the duties of a quartermaster general and commissary general into one department and required the appointment of officials from the top men down to the lowest deputy barrack master. These appointments took weeks, even months to complete; Secretary Eustis convinced Morgan Lewis, the former governor of New York, to take on the post of quartermaster general late in March, but it was not until August that Callender Irvine accepted the office of commissary general. Eustis was in the habit of issuing nearly identical instructions to both officials, which bred confusion over who was to do what. To this was added the time lost in working out a hierarchy of operation and opening new offices, where the various deputies and assistants often found they were expected to perform their jobs with little or no guidance from above and no end of belligerent demands from new regiments forming below.

Beyond the politics involved in organizing the new Quartermaster's Department, there were such practical dilemmas as the shortage of wool dyed in the traditional blue of American uniforms. In this case, the solution was to utilize whatever colours were available including black, brown, "mixed" (grey) or drab (a dirty shade of beige), but manufacture of even these outfits was delayed. Colonel Alexander Smyth, Acting Inspector General of the Army, reported early in June 1812 that nearly 7,400 "suits, deficient in some articles, [had been] issued at the depot in Philadelphia." But, delivery was slow due to the realities of transportation in 1812 and the War Department's tardiness in indicating the location of regiments, or detachments thereof, and what their needs were.[16] As a result, a number of the new regiments did not receive proper uniforms until the autumn of 1812, nor did they receive complete sets of accoutrements.

Congress allocated $1.9 million for ordnance and powder but this was considered barely adequate. The U.S. Army had never established standardized models of artillery, so there was an awkward variation in size of the guns and their equipment which confounded their employment. On the brighter side, the army was well supplied with muskets and rations. A prosperous small arms industry had developed in the United States and there was an abundance of weapons available for distribution. Similarly, the War Department had dependable connections with contractors who provided rations, but the actual delivery of food to the rapidly expanding army was a problem.

Other legislation established a corps of artificers, increased the engineers corps and made minor enhancements to the navy.[17] Nearly $9 million was appropriated for these improvements although little was done to reorganize or expand the Department of War, despite the avalanche of business that inundated Eustis and his clerks as the nation prepared for war. The topic of funding the war program provoked much debate during the early weeks of 1812 and ended up with Secretary of the Treasury Gallatin being permitted to borrow up to $11 million; imposition of a string of new taxes, sure to be unpopular with the electorate, was put off until after a declaration of war.

Six months after Madison's annual message, the U.S. Army was an altered institution, but it was a work-in-progress and not ready to face the demands of war. Where there had been only three brigadier generals, there were now six, (with seven more to be appointed during the summer of 1812), and two new major generals, Henry Dearborn and Thomas Pinckney.[18] Most of these senior officers were aged veterans of the Revolutionary War. What most of them lacked were active military careers in which they might have developed the qualities necessary for effective leadership. Because of previous reductions in the army, there was a shortage of trained junior officers. The United States Military Academy at West Point had graduated sixty-five officers, mainly artillerists and engineers, in the decade after its establishment in 1802, but few of these would play influential roles in the first campaigns of the coming war. Instead, during the spring of 1812 the army was dominated by the "old guard" who were by and large better suited for superannuation than for the rigours of command. Winfield Scott, promoted to lieutenant colonel in 1812, whose energy and competence set him apart from many of his peers, did not mince his words – he rarely did – when he described the majority of his contemporaries as "swaggerers, dependants, decayed gentleman ... *utterly unfit for any military purpose whatever.*"[19]

The "new" army created by Congress and the administration, the one that suddenly expanded from seven to twenty-five regiments of infantry, was largely filled with youth and promise. But the demands of appointing officers and filling up the ranks through enlistment slowed the formation and training of these units. The Thirteenth U.S. Infantry Regiment was a case in point. Authorized in January 1812, it was without a commanding officer until 12 March when Peter Philip Schuyler, a captain in the Regiment of Artillery with fifteen years experience, was appointed colonel. The lieutenant colonel was John Chrystie, who returned to the army from civilian life; he had held a commission in the Sixth Infantry for three years before resigning late in 1811. James Robert Mullany, the regiment's major, and the nine captains of the Thirteenth were all new to the service although most of them, and the flock of lieutenants and ensigns appointed that spring, had held militia commissions. Many of them were sons of New York State, where their appointments were directly related to their political affiliation, as seen in the recommendation that Governor Daniel Tompkins made to Secretary Eustis regarding Mullany. "Mr. Mullany," wrote Tompkins on 17 January 1812, "has held offices in the Militia of this State for ten years past ... [and] is also a well informed Republican, of a Military appearance and turn, and of gentlemanly manners."[20] Recruiting centres for the regiment were opened throughout the state, but not until late September 1812 were eight of the legislated ten companies filled sufficiently to join the march to war. Schuyler's regiment did enjoy advantages that other units lacked: it appears to have been properly uniformed and accoutred and was able to concentrate at the Greenbush military camp across the Hudson River from Albany early in the summer, where it was trained to a reasonable state of effectiveness.

While the army slowly expanded during the late winter and spring of 1812, talk of war dominated political circles in Washington and the states. There was no end to the debate about whether to declare against Britain or France, or both, while the nation's preparations were praised or condemned depending on the allegiance of the critic. Even the strength of James Madison's resolve to fire the first shot was questioned. "Our President tho a man of amiable manners and great talents," wrote John Calhoun, the representative from South Carolina, "has not I fear those commanding talents, which are necessary to controul [sic] those about him. He permits devision [sic] in his cabinet. He reluctantly gives up the system of peace."[21] It was true that Madison and his secretaries continued to hope for news from Europe that the British had relented on the Orders-in-Council and that France was living up to its promise to alleviate commercial restraints, but at the same time the administration actively promoted anti-British sentiments through various channels. By 1 April Madison's cabinet no longer entertained the idea of a war against France; if it came to hostilities, Britain would be the target, and to that end, the cabinet began to form a strategy for a summer campaign.

Some authorities advocated a war against Britain based on a maritime strategy alone but it became generally accepted that the best way to injure Britain, and extend the territory of the United States, was to invade Canada. Among those who counselled Madison, Eustis and the rest of the cabinet on this matter was John Armstrong, a veteran of the revolutionary period and former ambassador to France who would become one of two brigadier generals appointed to the U.S. Army early in July 1812. Armstrong supported the idea of invading Canada as the best way "by which Great Britain can be brought to a sense of justice."[22] He advised that the aim should be to capture Montreal, which would provide "control over all the portion of the Canadas lying westward of itself… . [and] Kingston, York, Fort George, Fort Erie and Malden, cut off from their common base must soon and necessarily fall." He stated further that for a "successful invasion of the Canadas … you must rely on a regular army." The militia, he wrote, were best employed for "the *protection of your own frontiers*," where they could act as threatening diversions "on the Niagara to keep within their walls the garrisons of Fort George and Erie, a second at Sackett's Harbor, to produce a similar effect and a third … on the eastern side of the Sorel [Richelieu River] as to menace the British posts on [the St. Lawrence]." Armstrong explained his campaign plan at great length but stopped short of operational details. These, he concluded, were "governed by circumstances as they occur in the camp or the field, [and] must be entirely left to the genius and judgment of your commanding general."

There were two candidates to provide the "genius" for Armstrong's plan, Major Generals Henry Dearborn and Thomas Pinckney. Pinckney, a resident of South Carolina, was given command of the south, while Dearborn, who lived in Boston, was to lead the northern campaign. Like many of his contemporaries, Dearborn had seen extensive action during the American Revolution, after which he settled in Maine (then part of Massachusetts), became a brigadier and then major general in the militia, held a seat in Congress as a Republican in the mid-1790s and served as Jefferson's secretary of war between 1801 and 1809. During his tenure in the War Department Dearborn is said to have "inserted himself immediately into every aspect of his department," making changes in the composition and organization of the army that ultimately "promoted inefficiencies."[23] Having turned that post over to William Eustis after Madison succeeded

**Major General Henry Dearborn (1751-1829)**
Dearborn began his professional life as a physician in New Hampshire in 1772. He raised a company of militia and participated in the Battle of Bunker Hill in June 1775. Later that year he joined Benedict Arnold's expedition to Quebec, where he was captured and detained until paroled the following spring. After the American Revolution he rose through the militia ranks and became involved in politics. (National Archives of Canada, C-10925)

Jefferson, Dearborn moved to Boston, where he was the collector of customs until the president summoned him to Washington in 1812. The energy of youth and commitment of a diligent secretary of war appear to have virtually disappeared from Dearborn's character by the spring of 1812. Although he accepted command of the northern army and, by implication, would direct the invasion of Canada, Dearborn showed little enthusiasm for his appointment. Augustus J. Foster, the British minister in Washington, described him as a"heavy unwieldy-looking man.... He has apparently accepted his appointment with great reluctance, having hesitated till within a few days His military reputation does not stand very high."[24]

In April when Dearborn finally presented his scheme for a campaign against the British, his line of thought closely resembled that of Armstrong. He advised that the main thrust be made by a strong army of regulars against Montreal to cut off the St. Lawrence River supply line, but he selected a more ambitious role for the militia. Seemingly oblivious to the laws restricting militia service to state defence alone, Dearborn intended to divert the attention of the British by sending militia brigades across the Detroit and Niagara Rivers and the upper St. Lawrence, rather than just massing large forces at border posts as Armstrong had suggested. If they understood this deviation from Armstrong's strategy, Madison and his cabinet did not find fault with it, since one of their pressing concerns was what the British might do in the west before Montreal could be captured. As the president later wrote, a single-minded march against Montreal "could not be attempted, without sacrificing the Western and N. W. Frontier, threatened with an inundation of savages under the influence of the British establishment near Detroit." And, he elaborated, "The multiplication of these offensive measures has grown out of the defensive precautions for the Frontiers of N. York."[25] This line of thought led to the adoption of a multi-pronged campaign against Upper and Lower Canada with regular forces deployed at each invasion point, supported by militia and volunteer units. The administration appointed William Hull, the governor of Michigan Territory, as brigadier general commanding the army of regulars and militia which would invade southwestern Upper Canada. Dearborn's area of responsibility was much more extensive since he was expected to establish his headquarters near Albany and then direct the attack on Montreal as well as its diversionary expeditions in Upper Canada. It actually stretched from Boston to Buffalo, the impracticality of which somehow failed to register in the minds of Madison and his cabinet; months would pass before brigadier generals would be sent to assist Dearborn on the several fronts. Even the old general was not fully aware of the extent of his command when he journeyed north to Albany, arriving by mid-May, and created the new military camp at Greenbush.[26]

Meanwhile, the twists and turns of international relations pushed the United States toward war. News from England in the third week of March showed no inclination on the part of the British government to remove its Orders-in-Council. With pressure on him to "give tone to public sentiment – [and] operate as a notification, … [for] the probable period of the commencement of hostilities," Madison proposed the imposition of a sixty-day embargo on shipment of goods out of the country which was approved on 2 April; its period was later extended to ninety days.[27]

On 19 May the U.S. Sloop *Hornet*, long expected to be carrying critical documents that might turn the tide, returned from abroad with no clear assurance the British government was about to alter its policies or change the attitude it displayed toward the United States; similarly, there was no evidence that France planned to reduce its commercial restrictions. On 1 June Madison sent a secret message to Congress reviewing the justifications for a declaration of war and asking Congress to make the final decision, as the constitution required. The Committee on Foreign Relations brought forward a bill declaring war on Britain, which passed the House of Representatives with a vote of seventy-nine in favour, forty-nine opposed. Debate in the Senate was protracted and included the proposition of numerous amendments, but on 17 June nineteen senators finally stood in favour while thirteen voiced their dissent. The total vote count, ninety-eight versus sixty-two, turned out to be the weakest support of a war bill in American history. Ironically, the declaration might have been avoided if news had reached Washington early enough of the assassination of Prime Minister Spencer Perceval on 11 May and the resultant change in the British government. Robert Banks Jenkinson, Lord Liverpool, became the new prime minister and convened a revised cabinet which, on 23 June, repealed the Orders-in-Council, a major stumbling block in Anglo-American relations. Word of the repeal would only reach North America late in July, long after Madison signed the declaration of war, making it law, on 18 June.

The inhabitants of British North America should not have been startled when word arrived late in June 1812 of the American declaration of war. Relations between London and Washington had been strained for years, but nonetheless a wave of surprise and apprehension swept through the provinces, especially Upper and Lower Canada. Despite dire reports in the colonies' newspapers of mobilization and armament to the south, many had hoped that "All of Jonathan's blustering will end in nothing of that sort" and that "the public voice restrained the United States government from commencing direct hostilities."[28] This was not to be.

When he read Madison's message to Congress, the commander-in-chief of the British forces in North America, Lieutenant General Sir George Prevost, wrote that it might be "full of gunpowder" but he saw "such a decided hostility toward England" in the president's words that he decided that it would best to put the provinces "in a state of preparation for that event."[29] Prevost made these observations late in December 1811 just three months after he had arrived at Quebec to assume his duties as the governor-in-chief. He was forty-four years old, the son of a Swiss-born, French-speaking officer in the British 60th Foot who was with his regiment in New Jersey when the boy was born. George joined the army at twelve and by

1794 had risen to the rank of lieutenant colonel in his father's regiment. Over the next seventeen years he was actively engaged in diplomatic posts and four separate campaigns against the French in the West Indies during which his skill as a commander in the field was recognized. From 1808 until 1811 Prevost served as the lieutenant governor and commander of the forces in Nova Scotia, which experience made him a perfect replacement for Governor-in-Chief Sir James Craig, whose failing health forced him to return to England. Fluent in French, skilled at diplomacy, battle-hardened, Sir George Prevost seemed an excellent candidate for the governor's chair at Quebec.[30]

Prevost's command extended over the provinces of Upper Canada, Lower Canada, New Brunswick, Nova Scotia, Prince Edward Island and Cape Breton Island as well as the stations at Newfoundland and Bermuda. The lieutenant governors of each of these colonies were responsible to Prevost, who in turn answered to the British cabinet. Besides performing their civil functions, Prevost and most of the governors were also military commanders within their jurisdictions, giving British North America a well-established chain of command which Madison and his subordinates lacked.

When Prevost suggested in December 1811 that it was time to make preparations against an attack from the states, the regular forces he commanded in Lower and Upper Canada alone numbered 5,700 officers and men, which was about equal to the number of men in the American Peace Establishment before the augmentations of early 1812. This force consisted of eight regiments of varying strength and a handful of Royal Engineers, with transport and support on Lakes Ontario and Erie provided by the Provincial Marine, which comprised two weakly-manned, army-run squadrons. These forces were mainly led by officers who had more than a decade of service and were accustomed to conditions in North America.

Possibly the best senior officer under Prevost's command was Major General Isaac Brock. Of all the people connected with the battle at Queenston, Brock stands out as the most competent. His strength of character and charismatic ease with friends and foes alike earned him great respect and admiration while he lived, and caused him to be elevated to legendary proportions thereafter.

Isaac Brock was born in 1769, the same year that saw Napoleon and the Duke of Wellington enter the world.[31] He was the eighth son in a family of

**Lieutenant General Sir George Prevost (1767-1816)** Prevost's term as governor-in-chief of British North America was marked by controversy over his handling of military and political affairs. While he was lauded in one quarter for his "vigilant foresight," others criticized "that indecisive conduct, which unhappily Sir George so steadfastly adhered to, during the whole course of the war."[1] (Artist unknown, National Archives of Canada, C-6152)

fourteen children whose parents, John Brock and Elizabeth De Lisle, lived in St. Peter-Port on Guernsey in the Channel Islands. In comfortable but not wealthy circumstances, Isaac Brock grew to be a strong and uncommonly tall youth (most Brock men appear to have been large of stature) who was said to have been gentle of spirit but skilled in boxing and swimming. He received his early education on Guernsey and at the tender age of ten years left home to complete his schooling at Southampton and later at Rotterdam. Four of Isaac's brothers served as officers in regular or militia corps and he followed this tradition when his older brother John purchased an ensigncy for him in his regiment, the 8th Foot, in 1785.

Transferring to the 49th Foot in 1791 with the rank of captain, Brock rose quickly through the ranks, purchasing at least two of his commissions, and six years later was the senior lieutenant colonel in that regiment with Lieutenant Colonel Roger Hale Sheaffe, who destiny also led to Queenston

**Major General Isaac Brock (1769-1812)**
Brock earned the respect and admiration of nearly everyone he encountered. In the words of Private Shadrach Byfield, 41st Foot, "Our general was very much beloved; he used to come out and talk very familiarly with us."[2] (M.G., National Archives of Canada, C-36181)

Heights, as his subordinate. Brock's combat experience was limited. The 49th Foot was part of the 10,000-man force that attacked the town of Egmont-aan-Zee on the shore of the North Sea twenty miles northwest of Amsterdam on 2 October 1799, during which battle Brock was knocked down by a spent musket ball. In 1801, the regiment was on board Vice Admiral Lord Nelson's fleet when it destroyed the Danish fleet at Copenhagen. Sailing in HMS *Ganges*, Brock spent weeks in the company of its captain, Thomas Fremantle, one of Nelson's band of brothers, and met the famous admiral, who was always ready to profess his adage that "the boldest measures are the safest."[32]

Unhappily for Brock, there were no immediate opportunities to emulate Nelson's style because in 1802 the 49th was sent to Canada, where it remained until the War of 1812.[33] The intervening decade provided Brock with experience in every aspect of army and civil society in the provinces as he commanded various posts in Lower and Upper Canada. In 1806 and 1807 he acted as commander-in-chief of the forces in the Canadas and by the winter of 1811 Brock was an established figure in Canadian society; he had been made a colonel in 1805 and a brigadier general in 1807. Affable and eloquent at a soirée, he had also shown himself to be a stern disciplinarian, a firm believer in drill and army regulation and, better yet, someone who understood the life of a soldier, knowing when to listen to a complainant and when to lock him in irons. He commanded respect and adulation wherever he served. Hamilton Merritt remembered him as "active, brave, vigilant and determined. He had a peculiar faculty of attaching all parties and people to his person: in short, he infused the most unbounded confidence in all ranks and descriptions of men under his command."[34]

Though an authenticated portrait of Brock at age forty-two does not exist, he was said to "have been six feet three or four inches in height; very massive and large boned, though not fleshy, and apparently of immense muscular power."[35] This was the remembrance of an American officer captured at Detroit in August 1812, although a second officer had a less complimentary view of the general, describing him as "a heavily built man, about six feet three inches in height, broad shoulders, large hips and lame, walking with a cane. One of his eyes, the left one I think, was closed and he was withal the ugliest officer I ever saw."[36] Somewhere between those two portraits lies the truth about the man who would lead the defence of Upper Canada in 1812.

In the years just before the war, Isaac Brock was troubled by two nagging problems. One was dissatisfaction with his seemingly endless tour of duty in Canada. Assigned to command in Upper Canada in 1810, Brock complained to his family about "the uninteresting and insipid life I am doomed to lead in this retirement," and he applied to Governor Craig for permission to return to England in search of assignment to a more active post, preferably on the continent in the war against Napoleon.[37] Craig refused the request but the next spring he informed Brock that he had been promoted to major general. Brock was at Quebec in the late summer of 1811 when Prevost arrived, and because Lieutenant Governor Francis Gore was departing Upper Canada on leave to England, Prevost appointed Brock to act as civil administrator of that province. This was hardly the type of employment the general yearned for, but it helped to solve a second problem that had lately arisen.

During the summer of 1811 Brock learned that the bank in which his older brother William had been a senior official was in default. William had loaned Isaac £3000 during his career to purchase commissions and had charged the amounts, under Isaac's name, against the company's books. The unfortunate result was that William's financial disaster turned Isaac and two other brothers into debtors, sparking a bitter family rift. Appealing to his brothers to make peace, Isaac pledged his salary as acting president in Upper Canada, worth about £1000 per year, to pay off his obligation, which meant he had to remain in Canada. In the meantime Brock had written directly to the Horse Guards, the British army headquarters in London, applying for a leave from Canada, but when permission arrived early in 1812 he turned it down. By then the Americans were making active war preparations and, as he explained to Prevost, "Being now placed in a high ostensible situation, and the state of public affairs with the American government indicating a strong presumption of an approaching rupture between the two countries, I beg leave to be allowed to remain in my present command."[38] So, debt-ridden and duty-bound, Isaac Brock remained in Britain's colonies to take part in a war that could be little more than a sideshow to the conflict in Europe.

Of the regular British forces mustered in the Canadas in the winter of 1812, only 1,150 officers and men were stationed in the upper province, including about 750 of the 41st Foot, about 300 of the 10th Royal Veteran Battalion and 95 officers and men of the Royal Artillery. This exceeded the usual number of troops in the province; since 1808 the 41st, 49th and 100th Regiments of Foot had alternated in doing tours of duty there, rarely standing more than 600 strong in total, a fact that some locals took to imply that the province would be given up without a fight against an invading American army.[39] In 1811, however, military stores had arrived on the frontier in ample quantities and the increased force in the colony had prompted what Brock referred to as "professions of a determination on the part of the principal inhabitants to exert every means in their power in the defense of their property and support of the government."[40]

To supplement the regulars there were 11,650 men ranging in age from sixteen to sixty years on the militia rolls, but Brock doubted their dependability. He was concerned about the "spirit of insubordination very adverse to all military institutions" that some elements of the population possessed, though he hoped that in an emergency "a large majority would prove faithful."[41] The native allies formed another source of potential support in the event of hostilities, but Brock was uncertain about the steadiness of their commitment, considering them to be, as he remarked on several occasions, "this fickle race."[42] Accordingly, in his reaction to Madison's message to Congress, Brock petitioned Prevost for a reinforcement of regulars. "Unless the inhabitants give an active and efficient aid," he explained to his chief, "it will be utterly impossible for the very limited number of the military, who are likely to be employed, to preserve the province."[43]

Prevost was unwilling to send up the kind of reinforcement that Brock wanted. As commander-in-chief, it was his responsibility to implement the strategy needed to counter the invasion that he believed the Americans were likely to undertake. From the Appalachian Mountains in Vermont to the village of Cornwall on the St. Lawrence and from there to the most distant garrisons in the northern regions of Lake Huron, the border between British North America and the United States was just over a thousand miles long. Most of the frontier was still a wilderness, "a country interjected in every direction by rivers, deep ravines, and lined at intervals on both sides of the road, by thick woods."[44] There were several well-trodden international crossings along the Lake Champlain/Richelieu River route and across the upper St. Lawrence, the Niagara and the Detroit Rivers. Some of the British posts at these points and places in between dated back to the days of the French, but most had been constructed following the American Revolution and as the international boundary was established during the 1790s. Prevost knew that the capture of Montreal and Quebec would likely be the object of an American campaign and that the St. Lawrence River and Champlain Valley would be the invasion routes as they had been during the Seven Years' War and the American Revolution. To that end, he decided to concentrate the bulk of his regular force in Lower Canada and could offer Brock little in the way of reinforcements.[45]

This was the same decision Brock had made in September 1807 while acting as commander-in-chief at Quebec. At that time the Americans had rattled their sabres and the military commander in Upper Canada had asked Brock for more men, to which he had answered that since "the means at my disposal are too limited... . I shall be constrained ... to confine myself to the defence of Quebec."[46] Whether he remembered this decision or not, Brock continued to request reinforcements throughout the first six months of 1812.

From early December 1811 Brock also tried to convince Sir George that pre-emptive strikes should be made against the American garrisons on the border before the Americans could strengthen them with men and arms. He was especially adamant about seizing Detroit and Mackinac Island because he felt such acquisitions would help to win the support of the aboriginal nations involved in the fur trade passing through these centres. Brock repeated these recommendations the following February, warning that if those two places were not captured immediately at the outbreak of war, "the whole country as far as Kingston must be evacuated."[47] He sketched out the composition of the forces needed and the methods they should employ, hoping, it seems, that the governor-in-chief would send up reinforcements as soon as possible so they could be prepared for lightning assaults, if and when news of war arrived from Washington.

In response Prevost told Brock clearly that he was not to undertake offensive action. He based his instructions on several factors. The home government, preoccupied with the war against Napoleon, had not advised an aggressive approach, nor had it seen fit to send large reinforcements. Receiving despatches from London that approved his defensive stance, and fearing that he lacked the strength to execute an offensive campaign, Prevost chose to establish his line and hold it as firmly as he could. The governor-in-chief did agree with his commander in Upper Canada "as to the advantages which may result from giving, rather than receiving the first blow," but he also believed the American government was waiting for an incident to occur on the frontier that could justify a quick declaration of war.[48] He argued that the American people were, in general, averse to war and so told Brock to "use every effort in our power to prevent any collision from taking place between our forces and the Americans."[49] The British ministers followed this same line of thought when they refrained from imposing a blockade of ports in New England in hopes of winning support among the American merchants.

Brock understood Prevost's reasoning but explained to his superior that, in practical terms, "the proximity of the two countries will in all probability produce collisions which, however accidentally brought about, will be represented as so many acts of aggression."[50] His point was proven in April when "an idle boy … wantonly fired with ball at the guard opposite Queenstown."[51] Such an uproar resulted from this one incident that Brock, busy with government matters at York, sent his aide Captain John Glegg to settle the controversy, wildly inflated news of which reached Quebec before Brock could transmit a despatch explaining the true details.

Showing that he was not deaf to Brock's requests, Prevost managed to make some additions to the regular forces in the upper province. Without confirming that he had the approval of the home government, he sanctioned the raising of a fencible regiment (a regular unit for service only in British North America) in eastern Upper Canada. This area fifty miles west of Montreal, had been settled by members of the Scottish Glengarry Fencible Regiment disbanded in 1803 and so was home to many experienced military men. Enlistments took place quickly, commissions were awarded and by May the new Glengarry Light Infantry Fencibles numbered 400 strong, providing Brock with an additional force for use on his left flank, the upper St. Lawrence valley.[52] Word arrived from England that the 41st Foot and the 49th Foot were both ordered home, but, given the state of affairs, Prevost elected to keep both regiments in Canada. He also decided to send up to Brock 300 recruits for the 41st Foot who had arrived at Quebec the previous autumn – "uncommonly fine young men and in good order" – and six companies of the Royal Newfoundland Fencible Regiment, some of whom were intended to fill out the complements of the Provincial Marine vessels.[53]

A report of the declaration of war reached Quebec on 25 June by the hands of a courier from the South West Company. Any hope Prevost had that the clamour for war could be stifled by American public opinion was dashed and he found himself facing the prospect of defending an extensive frontier. To the home government he expressed his disappointment that "the supply of arms and accoutrements shipped for Canada last autumn has not arrived."[54] And to Brock he sent word that he could not weaken his own garrisons in the lower province until some reinforcement arrived from Britain. The best Prevost could offer Brock was an assurance of "his cordial wish to render you every efficient support in his power."[55] Given that there was little "efficient support" available to bolster Brock's strength, his challenge would be to find ways to increase his force and prepare to meet whatever the Americans had planned.

# 3

# "We shall have our hands full."

## NEW YORK AND UPPER CANADA, SPRING 1812

No one had a more important role in preparing New York State for war than Governor Daniel D. Tompkins. Born in 1774, Tompkins was a Columbia College graduate and devoted Republican who practised law before being elected to the state assembly in 1803 and the House of Representatives the next year. He left the latter seat to accept the post of Supreme Court judge in New York, which paved the way for his election as governor in 1807 when he ousted the Federalist incumbent, Morgan Lewis. Married in 1797 to Hannah Minthorne, the daughter of a prominent New York City Republican, Tompkins was a dedicated family man and was said to be "gentle, polished and unpretentious.... [He] knew when to speak and when to hold his tongue, possessed a knack of getting along with men, and never forgot a name or a face that once had been brought definitely to his attention."[1]

Early in his term Tompkins learned his first lessons about war preparations. The embargo against trade with the British enacted by Congress at Thomas Jefferson's prompting in 1807 led to widespread smuggling in New York and Vermont, which grew so severe that the president asked Tompkins to call out the militia to support the small detachment of regular troops sent to the trouble spots. Hesitant at first to suppress his own citizens by force, Tompkins eventually acquiesced and activated various companies. During this period war with Britain seemed imminent and, concerned that his state would be open to attack, Tompkins persuaded the state assembly to purchase arms for the militia, build new arsenals at Canandaigua, Onondaga and Plattsburgh and erect batteries along the harbour at New York City. After the war clouds of 1807-1809 blew over, he continued to strengthen the state's defences and asked Secretary of War William Eustis for assistance. "In case of a war with Great Britain," Tompkins argued, "the northern frontier of this State and Vermont, extending from Lake Ontario eastwardly to opposite Montreal and Quebeck will require the greatest supply of warlike stores, and will be the principal theatre of war with Canada and that it is, therefore, highly proper to have an eye to the accommodations of that district."[2] Eustis's budgetary restrictions prevented him from fortifying New York, so the governor was left to his own devices. Early in 1812 Tompkins reported to the assembly that he had seen in the militia "flattering improvements in discipline and equipments, ... [which] have been universally exhibited both by the officers and privates."[3] At the same time, however, he called for more training, the purchase of additional muskets and ordnance and a better regulation of the storage and administration of the arsenals.

New York's first active involvement in the drift towards war in 1812 came in April when Congress passed the law mobilizing 100,000 militia. The state's quota was 13,500, but Secretary Eustis specifically requested that only 1,600 be immediately deployed "for the protection and defense of the northern frontier" at Sackets Harbor, Oswego and the Niagara River.[4] Tompkins responded by selecting three detachments for those posts: 600 to the mouth of the Black River at Sackets Harbor, 400 to Oswego and a further 600 to the Niagara. Lieutenant Colonel Philetus Swift, a veteran of the American Revolution and a state senator, commanded the Niagara detachment, which consisted of eight companies selected from the Seventh New York Division of Militia. This division, under the command of New York Major General Amos Hall, was from the counties of Genesee and Ontario with its concentration point at Canandaigua, just eighty miles east of the Niagara River. Since Swift had offered to form a regiment of volunteers under the law of 6 February, his unit was subsequently referred to as Swift's Volunteer Regiment.

The mobilization of the militia left Daniel Tompkins with a host of questions about its support and he wrote repeatedly to Secretary Eustis for clarification. Would volunteer units such as Swift's be considered part of

**New York Governor Daniel D. Tompkins (1774-1825)**
Although he knew his state was inadequately prepared for war, Tompkins believed a declaration against Britain was justified. "I hope ... we will forthwith gird on the sword rather than couch to insult any longer," he wrote in December 1811.[3] (Oil on canvas portrait by Ezra Ames, 1813, courtesy of the Albany Institute of History and Art.)

the militia quota, the governor wondered? Would the War Department supply tents and build barracks to accommodate the men? Would standardized forms be issued for muster and pay rolls, and instructions provided about the various allowances to be covered or about the regulations for courts martial? Eustis's answers were rarely definitive and often confusing, leaving Tompkins to fill whatever needs arose from the state's limited resources while he advised his commanders to wait patiently for further directions.[5] Eustis did specify that the militia was to arm and equip itself, and if the state could not provide all necessities of camp life, the federal government would at least pay for rations, the supply of which was to be arranged by Tompkins. Eustis was clear about another point, that the mission of the three detachments was to guard against pre-emptive British attacks; they were not to initiate offensive operations, and in time regular troops would arrive to take command at the border posts.

In anticipation of Swift's arrival at the Niagara River, Governor Tompkins contacted Peter B. Porter, the quartermaster general for the state, at Buffalo, sending him money and detailing how he was to provide for the housing and feeding of the troops. Porter, at thirty-eight years of age, was a Republican Congressman who held the influential chairmanship of the Foreign Affairs Committee in the Twelfth Congress. He was also a leading War Hawk, but his fervour for hostilities against Britain had been tempered through the early months of 1812 when he realized New York's vulnerability to attack. "It would, in my opinion," Porter wrote to Eustis in April, "be an act of madness to the administration to declare war at this time, when, so far from being in a situation to conduct offensive operations, we are completely exposed to attacks in every quarter."[6] Porter was in Buffalo at the time of the militia call-up and alerted Tompkins about conditions along the Niagara River, where the only established garrison was the crumbling Fort Niagara, manned by a company of regular artillery. The British were known to be actively preparing for war, and "the people of this place and from this to Niagara are very much alarmed," Porter revealed. Local militia from Niagara and Genesee counties, not officially deployed for duty, had stepped forward to volunteer their services but they were "deficient in arms and ammunition. … There is not five muskets that is fit for the use in this place."[7]

The last companies of Swift's detachment reached Niagara in the first week of June, where they took station at Black Rock and Lewiston and joined the garrison at Fort Niagara. In Albany the governor had been occupied in solving one problem after another relating to the call-up.[8] He forwarded money sent from Washington, endorsed other financing, arranged for the shipment of muskets, ammunition and field artillery, and asked Morgan Lewis, the quartermaster general for the regular army, to contribute tents, knapsacks and kettles from the federal arsenal. At the same time Tompkins answered requests from men seeking commissions, approved

**Quartermaster General Peter Buel Porter, New York Militia (1773-1844)**
Porter joined with Benjamin Barton, Augustus Porter and Joseph Annin in 1807 to form Porter, Barton and Company, which operated the carrying business from Lewiston to Fort Schlosser and other enterprises. From 1810 he sat on the Erie Canal Commission with his political foe, Stephen Van Rensselaer. (Oil by Lars Sellstedt, ca. 1870 from miniature by Anson Dickinson, 1817, courtesy of the Buffalo and Erie County Historical Society, C-19269)

defences under construction at New York, congratulated some officers for their efforts and reproved others. In short, he did the job of a secretary of war for New York State and, appropriately, referred to himself as the commander-in-chief in his general orders. In this work he was assisted by his aide-de-camp, Anthony Lamb, and the state's adjutant general, William Paulding Jr. His private secretary at the time was John McLean Jr., who was temporarily filling in for Nicholas Gray, who had been sidelined by illness. Gray would end up contributing to the Niagara campaign because of his military expertise; he was an Irish expatriate who, Tompkins wrote, "made Military matters his study and was Lieut General of the Irish patriots."[9] The governor relied upon Gray's advice and considered him to be "a Gentleman of a patriotic turn, [who] is ambitious of being useful to his adopted Country and is a man of modesty, information and amiable deportment."

Early in May Major General Henry Dearborn arrived at Albany where he began making arrangements to establish the military camp at Greenbush. Although Dearborn's orders stated clearly that he was to raise, concentrate, organize and discipline "the northern army," and then execute the campaign he had helped to formulate, the general did not focus on these critical preparations for long. Instead, when the governors of Massachusetts, Connecticut and Rhode Island declared their unwillingness to activate their militia as Madison had requested, Dearborn made a decision that would slow the preparations for war. On 21 May he announced to Eustis and Tompkins that he was going to Boston to confer with the reluctant governors, leaving Morgan Lewis to attend to the myriad supply problems. Dearborn advised the secretary of war that "Some Field officer ought to be here to perform the duties which have been assigned to General Gansevoort. The Service must suffer unless one is here soon."[10] Peter Gansevoort, a sixty-three-year-old brigadier and resident of Albany, was known to be on his death bed and no senior officer, other than Dearborn himself, was situated to assume command of the camp at Greenbush. But these circumstances did not alter Dearborn's intentions and off he went to Boston. When Eustis received Dearborn's letter, he immediately replied with his disappointment that arrangements in New York would suffer because of the general's absence. Dearborn was unfazed by the secretary's concern even when Eustis informed him that "it is the wish of the President that you should repair to Albany and prepare the force to be collected at that place for actual service."[11] The message was wasted on Henry Dearborn, who remained in Boston until late in July.

On 23 June news of the declaration of war reached Albany, leaving Daniel Tompkins and his staff to cope with preparing the state for imminent hostilities. They had already made plans to complete the state's quota of 13,500 militia by creating a new framework of detached units within the existing militia. They organized this detached force into two divisions containing a total of eight brigades, appointing officers to the various commands; each regimental commander formed his staff and unit from officers and men in his county. In this way Lieutenant Colonel Hugh Dobbin in Seneca County and Lieutenant Colonel Peter Allen in Ontario County raised the Eighteenth and Twentieth Regiments of Detached Militia respectively and were ready to respond when Tompkins ordered them to march for the Niagara frontier. They formed part of the Seventh Brigade of Detached Militia (the Nineteenth Detached Regiment under Henry Bloom of Cayuga County was yet to receive its marching orders) and were commanded by Brigadier General William Wadsworth. At fifty-one years of age Wadsworth, one of the founders of Geneseo in Ontario County, had long been a militia officer, but had never held command in the field. Tompkins's instructions to Wadsworth made it clear that he was "at liberty to act offensively as well as defensively" according to circumstances along the Niagara River.[12]

Problems of supply continued to plague Tompkins. The detached units

**Lieutenant Colonel Hugh W. Dobbin, Eighteenth Regiment of Detached New York Militia (1767-1855)**
Dobbin, a resident of Junius in Seneca County, received his appointment as militia captain in 1805. By 1811 he was the lieutenant colonel of the One Hundred Second Regiment of New York Infantry. He remained in the militia after the war, resigning as a brigadier general in 1818. (Artist unknown, courtesy of the Geneva Historical Society)

were to take what arms were available in local arsenals, but the men had to provide their own clothing and blankets and wait for tents and other necessities to be sent to them; on the Niagara frontier, where "there was not a camp kettle within four hundred miles of the post," the militia eventually bought some essentials from local inhabitants.[13] The small amounts of equipment that were available were locked up in a federal arsenal and Quartermaster General Lewis would not distribute them until he received orders from Eustis. On his own recognizance, the governor had some federal materiel forwarded to his troops, expressing frustration that Dearborn was not on hand to facilitate such arrangements. "I entreat you," he wrote to the general on 28 June, "to give orders to your officers here to furnish upon my order for the use of the militia detachments all needful weapons and articles, with which the United States are supplied and of which we are destitute."[14]

Reports arrived from the frontier about the British fortifying their positions, organizing their militia into select flank units, bringing up regulars from Lower Canada and arming their aboriginal allies. Alarms were sounded frequently in the border towns, and Lieutenant Colonel Daniel Davis stationed most of his Seventy-Seventh Regiment of New York Militia along the Niagara River in case the British invaded. Davis's men were there on an informal, volunteer basis, as were parts of the One Hundred Sixty-Fourth Regiment under Lieutenant Colonel Worthy L. Churchill and the One Hundred Sixty-Third Regiment under Lieutenant Colonel Silas Hopkins; a number of independent companies of infantry, artillery and cavalry also made camp at the river. Despite these additions to Lieutenant Colonel Swift's Volunteers, Quartermaster General Porter reported "the feeble force now on this frontier is not sufficient to inspire confidence, and families are moving back [from exposed positions near the river]."[15]

The chances of the militia being able to defend the state seemed even lower when William Wadsworth wrote Tompkins on 28 June to admit his own military incompetence. He graciously acknowledged receipt of his orders and promised to ensure "that the regiment and brigade which I have commanded should be distinguished at their reviews," but when it came to actual war service Wadsworth confessed that he was "ignorant of even the minor duties of the duty you have assigned me."[16]

Taken aback by Wadsworth's admission, Tompkins approached Major General Amos Hall about taking temporary command at Niagara. Under the normal organization of the militia, Hall commanded the Seventh Division of Infantry, but he had not been given a position in the new system of detachments. Tompkins offered Hall the pay, rations and subsistence expected for his rank and Hall agreed to go but with some apparent reluctance; it took him more than two weeks to make the four-day ride from his home in Bloomfield, just west of Canadaigua, to the Niagara River.[17] In addition to sending Hall to Wadsworth's aid, Tompkins ordered his private secretary, Nicholas Gray, to Niagara, with letters of recommendation. "You will find him a good Engineer and Artillerist," Tompkins informed Porter. "He has a manuscript compilation upon the duties and organization of staff officers and upon the arrangement of Pickets, guards, etc., in Garrison, Camp or March which you will find very useful."[18] "He is not assigned to any specific command or duty," the governor explained to Swift, "but repairs there at my request, with a view to be useful if his knowledge or experience will enable him."[19]

Although faced with difficulties, Daniel Tompkins remained optimistic about the eventual success of the summer campaign. Rumours had reached Albany about the resistance of the militia in Lower Canada to taking up arms. Tompkins predicted the same thing would happen in the upper province, and he declared, "I feel a confidence that we shall make ourselves masters of Canada by Militia only, if we maintain the spirit of union, perseverance and patriotism."[20] Adjutant General Paulding's attitude during the first week of July was similar. "We shall have our hands full," he wrote to Amos Hall, "but I calculate upon the energy and bravery of the officers and soldiers of the western country for the efficient protection of the inhabitants."[21]

Isaac Brock did indeed have problems in Upper Canada. Prevented by Prevost from launching pre-emptive strikes against the weak American garrisons, Brock had to content himself with spreading his regulars among his outposts as efficiently as possible and waiting for the other side to make the first move. Knowing that the strength of his regular force would be insufficient to oppose a determined invasion, he sought to supplement his regulars with militia and native warriors.

Brock knew that it was not possible to effectively train all of the 13,300 Upper Canadian men available for militia duty in the early months of 1812. As an alternative, he brought forward a bill when the provincial legislature convened in February which altered the Militia Act of 1808 to allow for the formation of two flank companies in each of the province's regiments. These men would be volunteers, "the best description of inhabitants," Brock hoped, who would be willing to assemble for training six times each month.[22] With a captain, two subalterns (a lieutenant and ensign), two sergeants, a drummer and thirty-five rank and file forming each company (more men to be added if hostilities began), Brock calculated that he would, in time, have 1,800 trained men available to augment his regular force. The legislature supported this idea but other changes that the general wanted were revised or deleted from the legislation; the militia were not required to take an oath of allegiance and the term of the flank companies' service was limited to the length of the current legislative session.

The lower house of the legislature, an elected body of twenty-four representatives, contained a strong element headed by Joseph Willcocks and others who found much to criticize in the policies of the Crown. Having to deal with dissenting voices frustrated Brock and he complained to Prevost that "The inordinate power assumed by the House of Assembly is truly alarming and ... [is] led by a desperate faction that stop at nothing to gratify their personal resentment."[23] Brock was not alone in his apprehensions about the influence of the political opposition. In reaction to their stinging protests, prominent citizens, steadfast supporters of the government, used the newspapers to call for unity in the face of the potential American aggression. One correspondent to the *Kingston Gazette* who signed himself "John Bull, Jr," wrote, "If we must fight, we fight *pro aris et focis*, as the Romans used to say, for everything that is dear and sacred to us.... Let us rally round the Standard and bid them defiance."[24]

Although legislative matters were a thorn in his side, Brock's change to the militia act, the formation of flank companies, proved to be popular, and by the end of April there were 700 names on the rolls with more being added weekly. In Niagara District, each of the five separate regiments from Lincoln County quickly filled up its flank companies with enough volunteers left over to form the Niagara Light Dragoons, two companies of militia artillery and a car brigade (artillery drivers). Brock was gratified to see the enthusiastic response to his militia plans, and when he made a tour of the Niagara Peninsula in May, he happily reported to Prevost that "an almost unanimous disposition to serve is daily manifested."[25]

**British private foot soldiers, 1st Foot**
British regulars on the Niagara Peninsula had uniforms very similar to those shown here. While white breeches and black knee-length gaiters were still commonly worn in 1812, the 49th Foot had been wearing grey trousers like these since 1811. The "stove pipe" shako was still in use, until replaced by the Belgic shako beginning in 1813. (Charles Hamilton Smith, aquatint from *Costumes of the Army of the British Empire according to the Last Regulations,* 1812-1815)

Securing the support of the aboriginal nations in and around Upper Canada was more difficult. Relations with the native peoples had been uneasy since Britain had failed to support them adequately during hostilities with the Americans in the early 1790s. The Indian Department had continued to work with the various nations, especially in relation to the fur trade, and military commanders had realized the importance of an alliance with the aboriginals, but the army and the Indian Department officers disagreed on how to achieve their shared goals and on occasion operated at cross-purposes. Following William Henry Harrison's attack on the native settlement at Tippecanoe in November 1811, thousands of warriors and their families under the leadership of Tecumseh, the Shawnee chief who had spent ten years trying to form a union of aboriginal nations, seemed ready to seek an outright alliance with the British. In trying to cement this agreement, Brock made sure traditional "gifts" were on hand in the spring of 1812, especially at Amherstburg where hundreds of the native peoples routinely gathered. Brock was also aware of the need for careful negotiations with the tribal leaders, fearing that a wrongly-worded statement might lead to open aggression against American communities and provoke war. "I am sensible this requires delicacy," he wrote to Prevost.[26]

The Six Nations of the Grand River formed an element of the aboriginal factor that was distinct from the western nations under Tecumseh.[27] Numbering fewer than 2,000 individuals in 1811, they were more intimately connected than Tecumseh's people to events along the Niagara since their forebears had crossed that river as refugees from the American government in 1784 to make new homes under British protection. They comprised families from each of the six Iroquois Nations (the Mohawks, Oneidas, Onondagas, Cayugas, Senecas and Tuscaroras) and other groups who had joined them during the eighteenth century. Over the years they had maintained relations with Iroquois who remained in New York State, their original homeland. Joseph Brant had been the dominant leader of the Grand River peoples until his death in 1807, after which his protegé, John Norton, rose to power.

John Norton, also known among the native peoples as Teyoninhokarawen, the "Snipe," was forty-two years old in 1812. His father was a Cherokee and his mother was a Scot, and Norton was raised and educated in Britain before enlisting as a foot soldier in 1784 and going to America. He left military life, was a school master, a fur trader and ended up as an

**John Norton, Teyoninhokarawen, the Mohawk chief (1770-ca.1830)** Among Norton's many involvements was his connection to the British and Foreign Bible Society. During a visit to England between 1804 and 1806, his Mohawk translation of the Gospel of St. John was printed in English and Mohawk. After returning to Canada, Norton had to shelve his plans for promoting Christianity in order to deal with the complex problems on the Grand River tract. (Watercolour by Mary Ann Knight, 1805, National Archives of Canada, C-1233841)

interpreter for the Indian Department. This brought him into Brant's realm, where he was soon involved in the fractious politics of the Indian Department and the Grand River people. As a war chief, he was seen as "honourable, vigorous, active," but in the autumn of 1811 Norton was fed up with conditions in Upper Canada and was planning to move to the American southwest, where he had recently visited his Cherokee family.[28]

It was Isaac Brock who changed Norton's mind. Shortly after assuming his position of administrator in the province, Brock queried Norton about long-festering problems on the Grand, most notably those involving the sale and lease of property. The chief was impressed with the general and saw him as a trustworthy ally. He admired "the decisive manner in which General Brock always spoke.... [W]hilst his discernment, candour and rectitude entirely confounded the spirit of Party, and exposed the Mystery of Calumny."[29] Norton resolved to remain in Canada and promote allegiance to the British cause, although many of the Six Nations people were hesitant about casting their lot with anyone. When Brock visited the Grand in May 1812, he was witness to this diffidence and was unable to secure a promise of Iroquois support. A few weeks later word reached the general that emissaries of the Six Nations in New York had visited their cousins on the Grand to debate alliances versus neutrality, prompting Brock to fear "that the Americans have been too successful in their endeavours to sow dissension and disaffection among ... this fickle race."[30]

When news of war reached Brock in the last week of June while he was at York, he immediately called out the militia and returned to Niagara. One hundred Grand River warriors soon arrived to make camp near Fort George, but the general continued to lack confidence in them, frankly voicing his apprehensions to Norton, who explained how his warriors needed "a regular stipend for their support" if they were to remain "steady and permanently serviceable."[31] Privately, Brock relayed this message to Prevost telling him that he would "have to sacrifice some money to gain them over. The appointment of some officers with salaries will be absolutely necessary."[32] Even John Norton referred to his contingent as "a small Party ... and many of these not the most steady men."[33] Steady or not, the sight of the Grand River warriors roaming along the banks of the Niagara River put fear in the hearts of the American settlers and militia.

Brock's most important asset was the 41st Regiment of Foot, numbering close to 700, lately reinforced by the recruits sent from England. The 41st traced its origins to 1719 when Colonel Edmund Fielding's Regiment of Invalids was formed from pensioned veterans still capable of performing garrison duties. Having long abandoned its "invalid" character, the 41st Foot arrived at Quebec late in 1799 and rotated through several tours of duty in Upper Canada. As with the 49th Foot, the regiment was ordered home in the spring of 1812, but Prevost chose to keep both units on hand in light of the rising crisis with the United States. Three hundred "very fine young men" had just arrived as fresh enlistments in Canada in November 1811 and marched to the upper province the following spring, raising the regiment's total strength to more than 1,000 (a portion of which was stationed at Fort Malden on the Detroit River).[34] Brock was pleased with the performance of the 41st Foot, which he considered to be "an uncommonly fine regiment" despite the fact that it was, in his view, "with few exceptions, badly officered."[35] Evidence shows that the regiment did have some ineffective and troublesome individuals among its "Gentlemen." Colonel Henry Procter, commanding the unit on the Niagara in July 1812, shared Brock's opinion to a degree, although the two men themselves did not see eye to eye on all matters. Still, officers such as Captains William Derenzy and Richard Bullock, Lieutenants William Crowther and Angus McIntyre were assets to the 41st and would demonstrate their worth as the campaign unfolded.

Also essential to Brock's defence was a company from the Fourth Battalion of the Royal Regiment of Artillery under Captain William Holcroft.[36] Only about sixty of Holcroft's unit were posted on the Niagara River, most of the rest being stationed at Fort Malden. The captain, who had been in the service since 1796, was a competent and battle-hardened officer. In May 1798 he had been part of an expedition against the French in Holland and participated in a raid that achieved its objective but was unable to re-embark on board the support vessels. The French attacked this force and Holcroft, then a lieutenant, was praised for the way he stood his ground when all but one of his men were wounded and, as his position was about to be overrun, cooly spiked his guns and pushed them over an embankment before he was captured. In 1807 he had been part of the Royal Artillery detachment that bombarded Copenhagen and contributed largely to its subsequent capture. During his time in Canada Holcroft had earned Brock's admiration, especially in the spring and summer of 1812 when he laboured tirelessly to set up the batteries on the river and train the militia artillery. "Captain Holcroft has been indefatigable," commented the general to Prevost.[37]

Not counted among Brock's regulars but significant to his preparations were the Provincial Marine squadrons on Lakes Ontario and Erie.[38] Created as a colonial naval force in the late 1770s, the Provincial Marine had been a mainstay of the British army on the lakes, evolving over the years into a transport service under the control of the Quartermaster General's Department at Quebec. There were three armed vessels on each lake, supplemented by hired private schooners and sloops, manned by the officers and seamen of the Provincial Marine and detachments of the Royal Newfoundland Fencible Regiment. The Americans had one 18-gun naval brig on Lake Ontario and a small army transport on Lake Erie which posed no threat to the British squadrons. The Provincial Marine was therefore free to carry men and materiel on the lakes faster than any army could march and so provided Brock with a valuable resource his opponents lacked. Similarly, the Quartermaster General's Department in conjunction with the Commissariat Department operated nearly190 batteaux between Montreal and Amherstburg in the spring of 1812.[39] These flat-bottomed rowing boats were usually about forty feet long and capable of carrying five tons of

**Royal Artillery men**
Popularly known as a "cannon," this heavy piece of ordnance, or gun, is mounted on a garrison carriage. The Royal Artillery men are dressed in white trousers with knee-high gaiters. The "royal" blue coats are trimmed with red facings on collars, cuffs and turnbacks, with white "lace" at the buttonholes and cuffs. (Charles Hamilton Smith, aquatint from *Costumes of the Army of the British Empire according to the Last Regulations,* 1812-1815)

goods or as many as three dozen soldiers. They formed a critical element in the British supply line between the garrisons and moved on the lakes with virtual impunity during the first summer of hostilities.

Brock deployed his force of 660 regulars and about 900 militia in what he termed four "divisions" of command along the Niagara: Fort Erie, Chippawa, Queenston and Fort George.[40] The troops were not concentrated at each of the centres but were spread out among its "dependencies," batteries lately erected at points within the area of each division. The dependencies at Fort George, for instance, consisted of several batteries closer to the mouth of the river and west of the fort along the lakeshore and others placed at roughly two-mile intervals up the river at Two Mile House,

Brown's Point and Vrooman's Point. A redan battery erected two-thirds of the way up the escarpment at Queenston was one of the new emplacements, and was described as "strong, built of stone and will probably mount two or three pieces."[41] Brock had sent some ordnance from Niagara to Fort Malden, so there were not enough guns available to arm each of the batteries until 12 July when the Provincial Marine ship *Royal George* and two smaller vessels arrived from Kingston with an assortment of artillery. Captain Holcroft saw to their installation and sent small detachments of gunners under non-commissioned officers to the divisions to assist in training the gun crews.

The thirty-five miles of the Niagara line was a considerable stretch of front to command, and one of Brock's tasks was to ensure that competent officers were in place to make quick decisions during local emergencies, especially if he was absent at York. To Colonel Procter he gave command of the district while Colonel William Claus of the 1st Lincoln Militia (and the Indian Department) commanded the troops at Fort George and Queenston and Lieutenant Colonel Thomas Clark, Lincoln Militia, had charge of Chippawa and Fort Erie. Another officer, Lieutenant Colonel Thomas Nichol, 2nd Norfolk Militia Regiment, served as the quartermaster general to the militia forces.[42]

Brock's personal staff consisted of Major Thomas Evans, 8th Foot, who was the major of brigade, and his aides-de-camp, Captain John Glegg, 49th Foot, and Lieutenant Colonel John Macdonell of the York Militia. Of the aides, Glegg was more closely tied to Brock and later wrote to one of the general's brothers, "I was intimately acquainted my dear Sir with your Brothers sentiments on the most private subjects."[43] Glegg entered the 49th as an ensign in 1797 when Brock became its senior lieutenant colonel, but the details of their eventual working relationship are absent from the record. Nevertheless, the responsibilities that Brock assigned to Glegg clearly showed that he relied upon his competence and judgement.

It was customary for a commanding officer to select a militia officer as an aide-de-camp and choosing John Macdonell to fill that appointment was a decision Brock did not regret. Macdonell was born in Scotland in 1785 and immigrated to Glengarry County, Upper Canada, with his family seven years later.[44] He studied law and began its practice at York in 1808, joining the society of other young men in the province's capital who were

**Lieutenant Colonel John Macdonell, Upper Canada Militia (1785-1812)**
Like anyone who rises to sudden prominence, Macdonell had his detractors. William Baldwin duelled with Macdonell at York in April 1812 and later wrote, "I can with the greatest indifference see him erect his crest and spread his spangled tail in the sunshine, and am only annoyed when I see him in his celestial adoration forget those around him and set his foot upon them."[4] (Toronto Reference Library, T-17053)

also called to the bar, such as John Beverley Robinson and Archibald McLean. From all accounts Macdonell possessed social grace in abundance, a bright mind and a quick temper that nearly cost him his life on the dueling ground in April of 1812 when his remarks in court insulted the sensibilities of a fellow barrister. From September 1811 Macdonell acted as the province's attorney general, bringing him into closer contact with Brock, who asked him to serve as his aide. Macdonell proved his worth by assisting Brock in all nature of situations with energy and poise.

As June turned to July Isaac Brock was content to wait and to see what would happen. When he heard of the declaration of war, he at first thought that offensive operations were justified, but then, after reflection, he acquiesced to Prevost's defensive strategy. Of the American posts on the upper lakes, he wrote, "the weak state of the garrisons would prevent the commanders from attempting any essential service," and Fort Niagara, the "only means of annoyance" immediately open to him "could be battered at any future period."[45] As a result, Brock assured the governor-in-chief, "I relinquished my original intention and attended only to defensive measures." Across the river the Americans were in the habit of parading their force, daily, which caused concern among the Canadian population, but the general confidently stated, "I consider myself perfectly safe against any attempt they can make."

# PART TWO

# *The Summer Campaign, June to October 1812*

*Did you ever expect to see me encamped on the Field of Mars, in my own Horseman's Tent, with my board slaw-bunk, 2 blankets, 1 trunk, a brace of Pistols, my valise stuffed with hay for a pillow, a large tin box at my feet and 12 round of cartridges for my pistols? Just so is the fact.... I am hearty, eat my allowance, do my duty, am first up, and last to bed. I am happy and respect myself but the Lord only knows what will become of home.*

MAJOR JOHN LOVETT, NEW YORK STATE MILITIA[1]

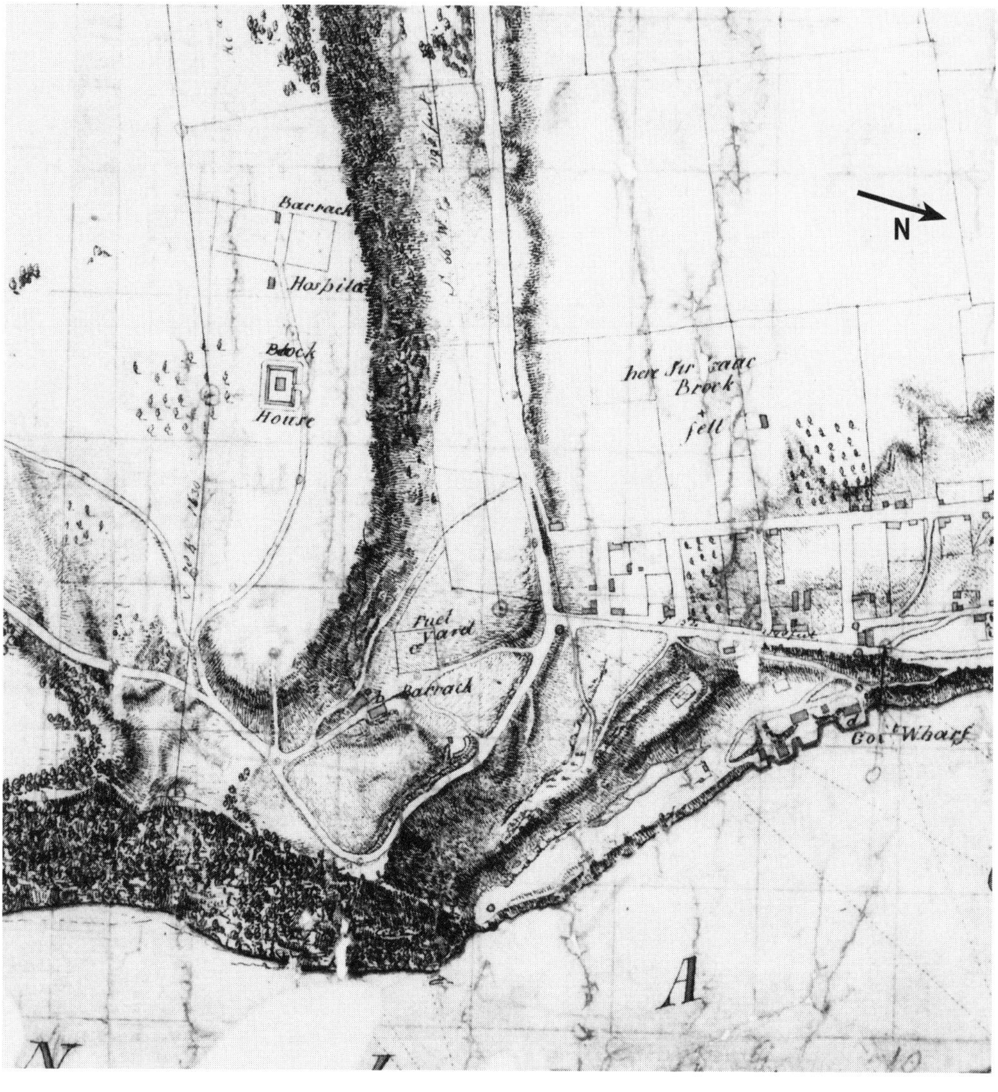


**Queenston and area, 1818**

The northern edge of Queenston Heights was reserved for military use. From the 1790s it was a camp for troops stationed there. By the end of the War of 1812 many of the oak trees on the reserve had been cleared and blockhouses built. (1818 map by Captain Vavasour, R.E., courtesy of the Niagara Historical Society Museum, National Archives of Canada, NMC-22750 1818)

# 4

# "A strictly amateur militia general"

## ENTER THE VAN RENSSELAERS, JULY AND AUGUST 1812

In the week that spanned June and July of 1812, the road from Canandaigua to Buffalo resounded with the tramp of armed men marching to the Niagara frontier. With William Wadsworth, the reluctant general, at their head, nearly 900 men had advanced to Batavia by 1 July.[1] They included the militia mobilized by Governor Tompkins on 23 June: 300 from Lieutenant Colonel Hugh Dobbin's Eighteenth Detached Regiment and 300 from Lieutenant Colonel Peter Allen's Twentieth Detached. These units had been joined by about 300 regular troops who had been enlisted in and around Canandaigua under the command of Major James Mullany, Thirteenth U.S. Infantry Regiment. Captain Myndert Dox, also of the Thirteenth, a resident of Geneva, New York, had formed the basis of his company as had Captain James McKeon, Third U.S. Artillery Regiment, who hailed from New York City. There was also a body of men lately recruited into the Twenty-Third U.S. Infantry, probably under the command of Lieutenant William Clarke. Mullany, Dox and McKeon owed their commissions in part to the patronage of Governor Tompkins, so when Major General Amos Hall asked them, on behalf of the governor, to march to the border and shore up the weak defensive line, the officers agreed willingly rather than wait for official instructions from the War Department. Mullany detached fifty of his men to escort a supply train proceeding ahead of Wadsworth's column.

Wadsworth's force reached Buffalo on Wednesday, 3 July, and advanced in stages to camps at Black Rock, Fort Schlosser and Lewiston, with the detachment of regulars taking up quarters in and around Fort Niagara.[2] Combined with Swift's Volunteers, who had been reduced from 600 to 400 by sickness and absences, the total strength of Wadsworth's brigade stood at about 1,600 (1,200 militia, Mullany's 300 and Leonard's 100). All but 100 men of the militia from Niagara and Genesee counties who had turned out at the alarm caused by news of the declaration were dismissed and went home soon after Wadsworth's arrival. About a week behind his main column were four more companies from Allen's Twentieth Detached, numbering in all about 185 men. Combined with a troop of twenty horsemen acting as express riders, this group brought Wadsworth's total strength, including invalids and absent, to about 1,900 men in arms by 10 July. He might have added warriors of the New York Iroquois to his numbers, but Erastus Granger, the federal Indian agent in that region, had already informed their leaders that the American army was so strong it would not need native assistance. Understanding the veiled threat contained in Granger's message – that the regular force could easily subdue native hostilities in New York – the Six Nations people retained their neutral status during the first year of the war.[3]

Brigadier General Wadsworth took several days to appraise the defences between Buffalo and Fort Niagara before he wrote to Governor Tompkins. His letter clearly showed that conditions along the Niagara were anything but conducive to the prosecution of an effective campaign. The men were living without enough tents to shelter them and had but one kettle or can per company for cooking their food. They "were able to draw but little bread," wrote Wadsworth, "and to draw flour seemed useless, for they had not any utensils to cook it in."[4] Wadsworth put his men to work erecting batteries, but this was nearly futile "without axes, hoes, spades, shovels or anything of this kind." Fort Niagara in the opinion of the general and others was "very much decayed" and possessed enough powder for only one hour of resistance by the six small guns it mounted. Wadsworth requested both heavy ordnance and field guns and the horses and harness necessary to haul them. From the industrious and orderly conduct of the British on the opposite bank and the information he could glean from various sources, the general reckoned there were up to 4,000 regulars, militia and

**Brigadier General William Wadsworth, Seventh Brigade of New York Detached Militia (1761-1833)**
With his brother James, Wadsworth founded the first American settlement on the Genesee River in 1789. He resided in Geneseo, Livingston County, for the rest of his life and did not marry. His obituary noted that "Few officers ... have been more universally respected and beloved by their soldiers."[5] (Artist unknown, courtesy of the Livingston County Museum)

native warriors (an exaggeration of that force) under Brock's command and that an attack might come at any time. "The great length of the river that must be guarded requires a great number of soldiers," explained Wadsworth and advised that his force should be increased to 4,000. This and the other improvements would help "to cease the prevailing opinion in Genesee and Niagara Counties that they are in danger."

By the time Wadsworth submitted his report, Daniel Tompkins had already ordered a shipment of 250 tents, muskets, accoutrements, ordnance and ammunition, but when his private secretary, the Irish engineer and artillerist Nicholas Gray, arrived from Albany on 18 July to assist Wadsworth, little of the materiel had arrived. "We have some fine companies of infantry here," Gray wrote to Tompkins, "without belts or cartridge boxes and all without uniform, except a very handsome company of light infantry raised by Captain Dox of Geneva."[5] After making a study of the terrain and British preparations, Gray recommended the construction of an additional bastion in Fort Niagara and batteries on the crest of Lewiston Heights and at Black Rock, but there were insufficient tools to do the work effectively and no heavy ordnance. Gray reported that the camps were relatively healthy and was impressed with General Wadsworth, who, he explained, had "ordered a military school, both for officers and soldiers...."

[and] pays unwearied attention to the troops, and [is forming] a system … which has as its object the organization of the staff and camp duties." The Irishman noted that the British militia were said to have left the Niagara front to tend to the July harvest, making it a good time to attack, were it not for the fact that the American force lacked strength and training.

New York Major General Amos Hall rode into Buffalo from his home in Bloomfield on 24 July, sixteen days after Tompkins had ordered him to replace Wadsworth.[6] Hall's arrival made no difference, however. No sizeable reinforcements were about to be added to the force and the supplies flowed at a thin trickle. And so the American army spent July struggling to establish itself along the Niagara River, lacking both the essentials for campaigning and a knowledgeable and active commander.

Henry Dearborn's absence from New York at the time of the declaration of war and in the weeks that followed aggravated the command problem on the Niagara. Wadsworth did what he could to establish a defensive line along the river and Hall offered his assistance as well. It was understood, however, that their commands were temporary since Governor Tompkins was expecting another officer to soon replace them. Without Dearborn or any other eligible regular officer present, Tompkins had already recommended to Secretary of War Eustis a third militia general for the task. This officer was Major General Stephen Van Rensselaer.

Most historians have agreed, and rightly so, that Van Rensselaer was "a strictly amateur militia general."[7] He was forty-seven years old at the time of his appointment and one of the most popular and influential men in New York.[8] His family had lived in New York since 1630 when Killian Van Rensselaer, a wealthy Dutch merchant and administrator of the Dutch West India Company, purchased a large tract of land near the confluence of the Hudson and Mohawk Rivers from local natives. The company had promoted the acquisition of land by promising the buyers that they would be granted baronial rights in return for colonizing their holdings, which made Van Rensselaer the first *patroon*, or baron, of Rensselaerwyck, a tract forty miles long and twenty miles wide spanning the Hudson.

Stephen Van Rensselaer was born on 1 November 1764 and when his father died five years later, Stephen became the eighth *patroon*. While his maternal grandfather managed the manor, Stephen was raised and educated amid aristocratic privilege, attending the universities of Princeton and Yale during the years of the American Revolution and graduating with a Bachelor of Arts degree in 1782. A devout member of the Dutch Reform church, Van Rensselaer joined the Masonic Lodge at the age of twenty-two and entered politics as a Federalist in 1789 when he won a seat in the state assembly. The next year he was elected as a state senator and in 1795 he accepted the nomination as lieutenant governor, the running mate on gubernatorial candidate John Jay's Federal ticket, with whom he served for two terms. The Federal Party's reign in New York ended in 1800, just as it did federally, and even Van Rensselaer's popularity could not win him a majority when he ran for governor, losing to George Clinton. Van Rensselaer returned to the state assembly as a representative in 1807 and remained there until 1810 when he joined the commission established to investigate the route for a canal across New York. Along with Peter B. Porter, Robert Livingstone, De Witt Clinton, Robert Fulton and others, Van Rensselaer made a tour of the proposed route and gave his enthusiastic support for what became the Erie Canal.

It was widely assumed in the spring of 1812 that Stephen Van Rensselaer would become the Federalist candidate opposing Daniel Tompkins in the 1813 gubernatorial election. With nearly a quarter century of public service behind him, Van Rensselaer had risen to prominence in New York with a reputation for being "noble and magnanimous"[9] in the opinion of J. B. Hammond, who documented the state's history in the 1840s. Van Rensselaer's memorialist, Daniel D. Barnard, lavished praise upon "the honest and true-hearted Dutchman," and alluded to a strength of will that Van Rensselaer could exert with force: "Being in the right, or thinking himself so, he would allow nothing to be wrung from him which would abate, by a feather's weight, the full moral force of the language he had used."[10]

Stephen Van Rensselaer's military career was essentially nominal, since he held the rank of an officer in the state militia during a relatively peaceful period, his service involving little more than semi-annual parades and inspections. It began with the acquisition of a majority in an infantry regiment in 1786 of which he rose to command as colonel two years later. In 1800, when Governor John Jay created a corps of cavalry within the militia, the commission of major general of cavalry went to Van Rensselaer, then thirty-five years of age and Jay's lieutenant governor. Although he wore the uniform of a high ranking officer, the truth remained, as one of his biographers admitted, that Van Rensselaer had "no training beyond the sanguinary prognosis of a dress parade, or a night attack on the café of the old Fort Orange Hotel at Albany."[11]

When Tompkins formally organized two divisions of detached militia brigades on 18 June, he split command of the divisions between Van Rensselaer and Major General Benjamin Mooers at Plattsburgh. Nine days later he asked Secretary Eustis to "send on a General Officer to take command of all the frontier detachments, or to authorize me to require Major-Genl., Stephen Van Rensselaer of this city to take the command until further orders."[12] Eustis replied with his approval of Van Rensselaer on 3 July and ten days later Tompkins made him the commander of the northern army. This put Van Rensselaer in a difficult spot since, as a Federalist, he was essentially opposed to the war policies of James Madison's Republican administration.

Daniel Barnard noted other factors that made Van Rensselaer's situation a perilous one, referring to his

> inexperience in the trade and business of war, the impracticable materials he had to deal with, and the very extraordinary extent of the exposed and defenseless territory committed to his immediate military care and keeping ... [that] must subject him, personally, to a fiery ordeal, which he might escape unharmed, and possibly with a burnished and brighter fame, but where the chances were fearfully prevalent that he would be utterly consumed.[13]

If he refused the command, Stephen Van Rensselaer and his party would be branded with "unpatriotic and odious sentiments" as Daniel Barnard attested, and his aspirations in the upcoming election would be crushed. So, lacking any real experience, Stephen Van Rensselaer found himself at war.

It has often been suggested that Daniel Tompkins had self-serving purposes in selecting his potential rival for this important command. Barnard chose not "to penetrate the motives which led to the selection of the General," but other commentators have suggested that Tompkins's goal was to win popular support for the war and himself by offering such a prestigious post to a prominent Federalist at the same time as he sent that individual, his adversary, to a risky situation far from Albany and New York.[14]

**Major General Stephen Van Rensselaer (1764-1839)**
Van Rensselaer was fully aware of his country's limited military resources when he accepted command of the army on the Niagara River. In 1810 he declared in the state assembly that it was a "lamentable truth that our country is unprepared to prosecute a war with either of the belligerents [Britain or France] however necessary the measure may be."[6] (T. Gimbrede, courtesy of the Rensselaer Polytechnic Institute Archives and Special Collections)

This explanation has a tempting ring to it, but fails to account for the fact that the complexity of the political scene in New York made it impossible to win an election with the movement of a single chess piece. The war with Britain was only one of the issues that raged in the legislature and committee rooms, the taverns and the soirées. Animosity between the Federalist and the Republican parties was sharp and dominated newspapers and pamphlets as well as the Assembly and the Council of Appointment, the most powerful instrument for patronage in the state.[15] As well, there was a faction in the Republican Party which threatened Tompkins's authority and that of President Madison. It was led by De Witt Clinton, the lieutenant governor of the state and the mayor of New York City, who intended to run against Madison in the presidential election of 1812. Clinton had great influence in New York and was promoted to the rank of major general by the Council of Appointment just before the declaration of war, whereupon he asked the governor for a prominent command in the field. Tompkins delayed a reply while he wrote to Secretary Eustis and put Van Rensselaer's name forward for the generalship of the army at Niagara. He later explained to Clinton that he could not overlook the older man – Clinton was forty-three years old; Van Rensselaer was forty-seven and had held his commission as major general for more than a decade. So, the governor had more than one rival with whom to contend in the spring of 1812 and picking one over the other to hold a prestigious command put him in a difficult position either way.[16]

Once Van Rensselaer was chosen to take charge at Niagara, Tompkins, it seems, worried that he might achieve some sudden success against the British and thereby enhance his popularity among the electorate. On 8 July when Tompkins asked Major General Hall to take command on the Niagara frontier, he urged him to go on the offensive against the British as quickly as possible, writing, "It would be a feather in your cap could you take the forts on the other side before Major Genl. Van Rensselaer arrives."[17] At one point during the summer, the governor even expressed an interest in replacing Van Rensselaer himself – since Tompkins also lacked any practical experience as a general, this would have exposed him to the "fiery ordeal." While discussing the relative status of militia and regular army commanders in a letter to Henry Dearborn on 14 August, Tompkins suggested that "should so large a body of Militia of this State be ordered into service as to render it suitable for me to take the command of them in person, ... or should the President assent to my taking command as in that case he ought, and I trust, will, it must not be expected that I can recognize any Military superior but the President."[18]

Beyond the convolutions of the New York political scene, however, it was understood at the beginning of the summer campaign that Stephen Van Rensselaer's command of the northern army was temporary; it was not thought that he would actually be responsible for a major invasion of Upper Canada. In granting his endorsement of Van Rensselaer on 3 July, Eustis wrote: "It should be fully understood ... that when General Dearborn shall have made arrangements for the Troops on that frontier he may find it expedient to entrust the Command to a Brigadier General of the [regular] Army. Should such be the arrangements, the services of the General ordered out by your Excellency may be not required."[19] Late in July Dearborn queried Eustis about who would command in Canada and then suggested that Colonel John Parker Boyd, Fourth U.S. Infantry, be made brigadier and sent to New York. Boyd gained that appointment in late August but did not become active until the next year. A few weeks later, it was even suggested that Brigadier General William Hull could "descend toward Niagara" after he captured Fort Malden, presumably to take charge of the invasion at that point.[20]

Tompkins made the formal announcement of Van Rensselaer's appointment on 13 July, informing him that he was "to assume Command upon our Northwesterly and Westerly Frontier," which covered the territory from St. Regis (near Montreal) to the border of Pennsylvania. "You are," the order continued, "... to consider yourself vested with liberal and ample discretion ... to adopt all such measures offensive and defensive as your own judgment may dictate." Tompkins finished by assuring Van Rensselaer of his "affectionate regard" and promised to do "everything in my power to render the services in which you are engaged agreeable."[21] There was no mention of any other officer who might supersede him and from all outward appearances it seemed clear that the *patroon* was on his way to war.

The general took to the road the same day Tompkins wrote his orders, proof that Van Rensselaer knew well in advance that his appointment was imminent.[22] His marquee and furniture, books and papers, uniforms, camp equipment, provisions and wagons were ready to roll but, more im-

**Lieutenant Colonel Solomon Van Rensselaer, New York Militia, (1774-1852)**
Ezra Ames, a prominent artist in Albany, painted this portrait of Solomon in the uniform of a major general in the New York militia, which he became in 1818, the same year he was elected to represent Albany in Congress. (Ezra Ames, 1819, courtesy of Historic Cherry Hill)

portantly, so were his two right hand men, Solomon Van Rensselaer and John Lovett.

The former was Stephen's second cousin, with whom he had only a passing acquaintance.[23] Solomon was born into the wealth and power of the Van Rensselaer family in 1774 and gained a commission as a cornet in the Light Dragoons of the U.S. Army at the age of eighteen. He went to war with General Anthony Wayne against the aboriginal nations and was in the thick of the fighting at the battle of Fallen Timbers in August 1794, where he was shot through both lungs and nearly killed. Having risen to the rank of major, Solomon was honourably discharged from the army when it was reduced in 1800; even an influential patron, James Wilkinson, could not save his military career. The next year Solomon began a term as the adjutant general of the militia in New York State, a position he held until 1811.

Like the general of the same name, Solomon Van Rensselaer was an avowed Federalist, but whereas Stephen appears to have had a relatively calm and magnanimous character, Solomon was opinionated, easily offended and impetuous, earning himself plenty of detractors, especially among Republicans. An example of how ardently he held his pride took place in 1807. Believing that he and his father had been slandered by political opponents, he sought a duel with his chief accuser, the Clintonian Republican Elisha Jenkins. The latter refused the challenge, so Solomon accosted him on State Street in Albany, knocking Jenkins to the ground with his cane. Later that afternoon, a group of Jenkins's friends attacked Van Rensselaer, beating him with clubs and kicking him senseless. So seriously injured was he that Solomon was bed-ridden for three weeks and, it was said, "for years afterwards he could not bear the motion of a carriage."[24] Lawsuits arising from the twin assaults cost Van Rensselaer $2,500 for his attack on Jenkins and won $4,800 for him in damages. Further proof of Solomon's unpopularity in certain influential circles was seen in a comment Tompkins made when he reviewed a list of men – one of whom was Solomon Van Rensselaer – put forward for appointment to the U.S. Army. "The State of New York," Tompkins wrote to an acquaintance, "scarcely contains five other men more distinguished by political intolerance or in whose capacity and fitness in other respects the Republicans of the State have less confidence."[25]

Stephen Van Rensselaer accepted Tompkins's offer to command on the condition that Solomon would serve as his aide on the campaign with the rank of lieutenant colonel. Solomon's daughter Catherine V. R. Bonney quoted her father's comment on the matter in her compilation of family papers: "That officer entered upon his command on the 13th of July 1812, having done me the honor to request my services as his aid. I was anxious to serve my country in the contest in which she was engaged, and I did not hesitate, therefore, to take the position thus offered me."[26]

Solomon Van Rensselaer's family problems at the time of his departure for war on the Niagara frontier may have affected the eagerness with which he responded to his kinsman's call to duty. Too often historical documents fail to provide much in the way of personal information about a soldier's life at home. In the case of Solomon Van Rensselaer a rich archive of correspondence with his wife, Arriet, has survived and allows a glimpse into their domestic setting. His love for her was evident, appearing not to have diminished since their elopement (her mother did not favour the impetuous young officer), soon after which military duty took him away from home in 1797. Arriet was by then pregnant with the first of eight children she would bear and Solomon wrote to apologize for his absence: "never did I know how sincerely I loved you until this cruel separation."[27] July of 1812 brought a similar situation since Arriet was six months with child when her husband left Mount Hope, their home near Albany, for Niagara. To make matters much worse, scarcely a month before, a deranged man had shot and killed their six-year-old son, Van Vechten, while he played in the woods near his home. Solomon had carried the boy's lifeless body back to the house, where Arriet collapsed in a state of grief from which she had not recovered by the time of Solomon's departure. Begging his wife to focus her attention on the other children and to rely on their devout Christian beliefs, Solomon cloaked himself in his gold lace and braid and rode off to the Niagara with a heavy heart.

With the Van Rensselaers went fifty-one-year-old John Lovett. Although he had not attained the prominence of Stephen and Solomon Van Rensselaer, he was a faithful Federalist and a gifted raconteur who was given to literary pastimes; "he was remarkably pleasant," wrote Catherine Bonney, "and his sparkling wit and flashes of merriment would set the table in a roar." Lovett had taken up the profession of law at Yale, but "he never excelled in the argument of a question of law and did not obtain that distinction as a counselor.... One of the errors of his life was a passion for a change of employment, not often the road to distinction or success." He had been a land steward and a representative in the state assembly, and it appears that at the outbreak of war he was the clerk of the common council in Albany. Though perfectly willing to accept Stephen Van Rensselaer's request to join him on the campaign, Lovett confessed, "I am not a soldier." The general is said to have replied, "it is not your *sword*, but your pen that I want."[28]

**Arriet Van Rensselaer (1775-1840)**
One of Arriet's descendants wrote that she "was very lovely but refused to have her portrait painted." Solomon commissioned Fink to create this image after her death, using their children as models for Arriet's features. Such methods were considered "never satisfactory to family."[7]
(Oil painting by Frederick Fink, 1840, courtesy of Historic Cherry Hill)

In a caravan, comprising a carriage for Stephen and his staff and wagons carrying their servants and the necessities of their offices, the Van Rensselaer party set out from Albany on 14 July. "If flying through the air, water, mud, brush," wrote Lovett, "over hills, dales, meadows, swamps: on wheels, or horseback, and getting a man's ears gnawed off with musquitoes and gallinippers make a *Soldier*, then I have seen service for – one week."[29] The turnpike was crowded with cavalry, artillery and troops of foot soldiers. At Utica, Little Falls and Herkimer there were salutes fired as Van Rensselaer approached, escorts to guide them through the streets, bands playing and invitations to dinner. It was a propitious start to an uncertain campaign. Impressed and exultant over the public's reception, Lovett exclaimed, "We *were all* SOLDIERS!!"[30]

It appears that Van Rensselaer's intention was to travel directly to the Niagara, but a rumour he heard on 16 July at Utica about an imminent British attack at Sackets Harbor prompted him to go there instead. This small post turned out to be safe and in the capable hands of Lieutenant Melancthon Woolsey, USN, of the brig *Oneida*, and a detachment of militia. Another distressing report then reached Van Rensselaer that citizens in the neighbourhood of Ogdensburg were "panic struck, and flying off in shoals" so the general rode there "to quiet them, to give them confidence and constancy to keep their homes."[31]

Ogdensburg *was* under threat of attack, or so it seemed, when Van Rensselaer's party rode into the village. The Provincial Marine schooner *Duke of Gloucester* and the ship *Earl of Moira* were anchored across the St. Lawrence River at Prescott, where a stockade was being erected and the militia was assembling. Almost immediately Solomon Van Rensselaer formulated a scheme for seizing the schooner after dark one night. He gathered 400 militia for the expedition, but when the hour came to cross all but sixty-three of his force lost their pluck and Solomon cancelled the expedition. "Never did I see a man more mortified and disappointed than is Col. Van Rensselaer," wrote Lovett to a friend. He added, as if in a whisper, and with an unwitting touch of foreshadowing, "This single fact of the Men's refusing to volunteer, if published, would raise a bobbery."[32]

The general and his companions did not get away from Ogdensburg until 29 July with a two-week ride ahead of them.[33] Given the weak state of the American formation at the Niagara, Van Rensselaer's delay in reaching that post did not prevent any serious attempt to invade Upper Canada. It did, however, allow weeks to pass during which the army on the Niagara waited without firm leadership, in its inadequately supplied camps, growing impatient for activity or permission to return home. Meanwhile, other events unfolded that would directly affect Van Rensselaer's army and he would face some difficult challenges when he finally made his appearance.

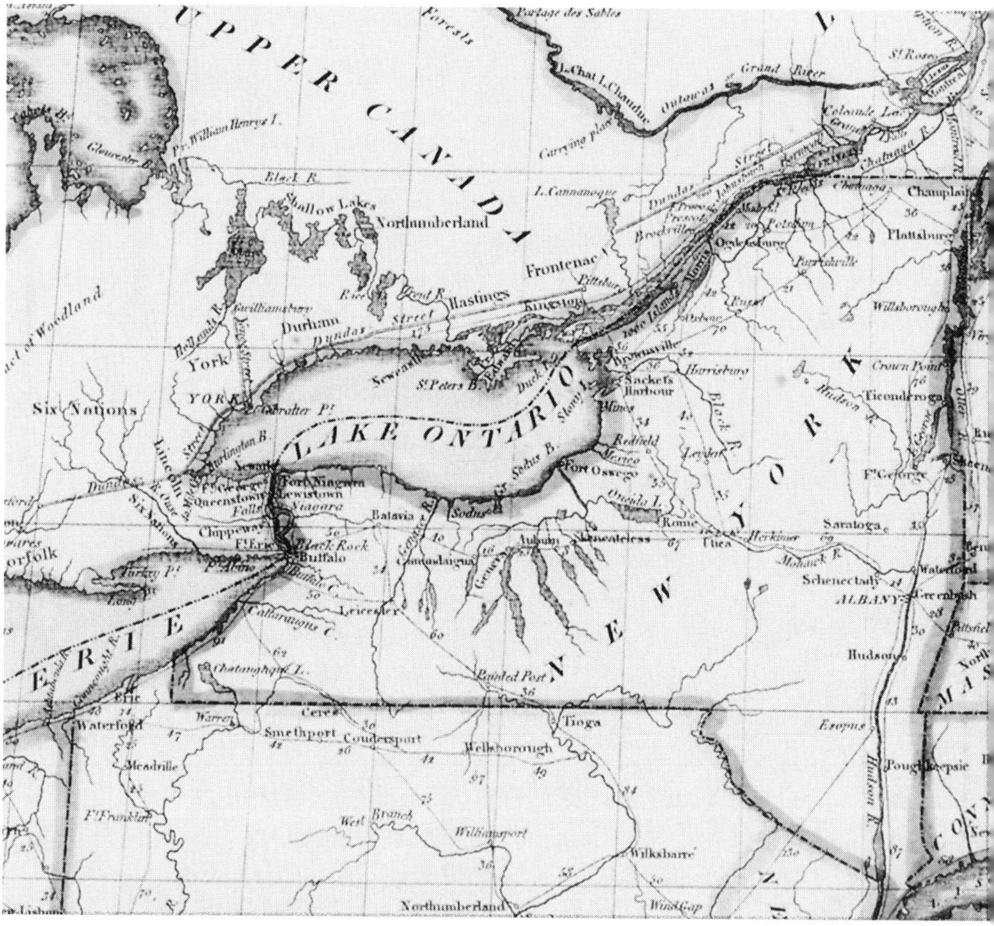


**"Seat of the War [of 1812]"**
This detail is from the map published by the American John Melish in 1813. The popularity of this map and his book *Travels in the United States of America* led Melish to become a leading publisher of cartographic and geographic material. (National Archives of Canada, NMC-6760)

# 5

# "A cool calculation of the *pours* and *contres*"

## DETROIT AND THE ARMISTICE, JULY AND AUGUST 1812

Major General Isaac Brock felt confident about the defence of Upper Canada during the first two weeks of official hostilities, but his peace of mind did not last. The Niagara River front seemed secure but the posts along the St. Lawrence and at Kingston and Fort Malden and at Saint Joseph in the northern reaches of Lake Huron were constantly on his mind while government business required his frequent presence at York. With despatches taking days or weeks to arrive, Brock could never be sure of the province's safety beyond what he could view along the Niagara. Still, this was exactly the kind of activity for which Isaac Brock had longed during the tedious years of "uninteresting and insipid life" he had endured on the frontier.[1]

Although the Lincoln militia turned out in numbers when mobilized, by the first week of July they were already showing "a spirit of impatience."[2] Brock praised "their ardent desire to acquire instruction" in a general order on 4 July and reminded them of "the great stake they have to contend for," but his words were not enough to maintain a consistent *esprit de corps*.[3] Time for the July harvests of fruit and grain arrived and the men were anxious to return to their homes rather than endure the army's "hurry up and wait" routine. Brock understood this concern and allowed half the militia to go home, beginning on 10 July, although some had already left by then.[4] A plus for the general was that the two companies of the 2nd York Militia

Regiment, under Captains John Chisholm and William Applegarth, and numbering about ninety men in all, arrived in the first week of the month and made their camp at Queenston.

The detachments along the river suffered from the same problems as their American counterparts.[5] There were shortages of kettles, tents and other camp equipment. The men were told to bring their own blankets and it was their officers' responsibility to find homes or barns in which to billet them. Uniforms, even haversacks, for the flank companies were non-existent, leaving Brock to lament about the militia's "wretched state in regard to Clothing, – many were without shoes, an article which can scarcely be provided in the Country."[6] The army was at least able to issue rations to the militia and arrange their pay for the time spent on duty. Another advantage, at least from the general's point of view, was that having the remaining militia at their posts provided the opportunity for drill under the direction of experienced non-commissioned officers of the line. Nevertheless, Brock was uneasy about the dependability of his civilian soldiers. "There can be no doubt," he wrote to Prevost on 12 July, "that a large portion of the population in this neighbourhood are sincere in their professions to defend the country, but it appears likewise evident to me that the great part are either indifferent to what is passing or so completely American as to rejoice in the prospect of a change of government."[7]

In the third week of July reports reached Brock of the American invasion of southwestern Upper Canada.[8] The army of Brigadier General William Hull, governor of Michigan Territory, comprising 300 regulars and 1,200 militia, had cut a road from Urbana, Ohio, to Detroit, arriving there on 5 July. Hull's instructions had been to advance into Canada, and a week after reaching Detroit he crossed the river, quickly occupying the settlement of Sandwich. The locals offered virtually no opposition as the Canadian militia withdrew ignominiously and many inhabitants offered their assistance to the Americans. Under Lieutenant Colonel Thomas St. George, 41st Foot, the British formed their line of defence on the southern bank of the Canard River, five miles north of Fort Malden and Amherstburg, their numbers including 300 regulars, 450 militia who had remained under arms and about 400 native warriors under Tecumseh. Hull received reinforcements and he sent a squadron of cavalry to ransack the countryside for supplies, and several skirmishes took place at and near the Canard, but the general did not press his attack. Instead, he waited through the rest of July for more troops, heavy ordnance and supplies to arrive by the new military road.

At Niagara, Isaac Brock fretted over the lack of information forwarded by Colonels St. George and Procter, the latter of whom he had sent to Fort Malden in the *Queen Charlotte* on 20 July. He contemplated going there himself, but the pending legislative session required his presence at York. Hearing that Hull's cavalry was penetrating the valley of the Thames River, Brock sent fifty men of the 41st Foot under Captain Peter Chambers from Niagara to unite in a patrol with two hundred militia near Moraviantown. He received what he considered to be an inadequate amount of assistance from the Grand River Iroquois and once more complained to Prevost about "this fickle race" and the absurdity of its professed neutrality.

On 22 July Brock ordered the recall to the Niagara line of all the militia who had been given leave in case the Americans launched a diversionary attack in this quarter. His concern over the failure of much of the militia in the southwest, and reports about local companies near the Lake Erie shores refusing to assemble, prompted him again to plead his case to Prevost for regular reinforcements. "Without strong re-inforcements, I fear the Country cannot be roused to make exertions, equal, with support, to meet the present crisis," he wrote on 26 July.[9] Brock had waited for some positive instructions from Prevost since the war was more than a month old, perhaps a change in the defensive policy that would allow a strike against the Americans along the Niagara. None arrived and his growing impatience revealed itself when he mentioned, "I should have derived much consolation in the midst of my present difficulties had I been honored, previous to the meeting of the Legislature, with Your Excellency's determination in regard to this Province."[10]

There was no consolation from Quebec, however, and less to be found in York when General Brock arrived there on Monday, 27 July, to open the new session of the provincial assembly. He hoped to win approval for a suspension of *habeas corpus* and for additional funds from the treasury, but nothing of the sort was about to happen. There had been an election in June without a noticeable shift in political balance and Brock met the same kind of opposition he had encountered during the winter session. Hull's invasion had shocked the public, nurturing a cynical attitude among the people, reflected in the demeanour of some assemblymen, "that this Province must inevitably succumb."[11] Brock complained to Prevost that "the population, believe me, is essentially bad.... Legislators, Magistrates, Militia Officers, all, have imbibed the idea [of defeat] and are so sluggish and indifferent in all their respective offices.... They dread the vengeance of the democratic party, they are such a set of unrelenting villains."

Even despatches that reached Brock on 29 July barely seemed to lift the pall of hopelessness and anxiety at York and elsewhere. They told of the capture, on 17 July, of the small but significant American fort on Mackinac Island at the confluence of Lakes Michigan and Huron by Captain Charles Roberts, the commander of the British fort on Saint Joseph Island, forty-five miles northeast of Mackinac. Roberts had landed at Mackinac with a force comprising forty-five men from his 10th Royal Veteran Battalion, 180 fur traders and 400 natives prepared to attack the weakly-held American fort. He undertook the expedition in response to orders from Brock advising him to protect his own position by seizing Mackinac and thereby securing that trade route for British native allies. This was a simple but ultimately important accomplishment because possession of Mackinac would influence American strategies for the balance of the war. Brock was delighted with Roberts's "zeal and judgment" but he was disappointed with the public reaction to the success of his expedition.[12] Realizing he would accomplish nothing more at York, and that action akin to what Roberts had accomplished was needed, the general prorogued the legislature on 5 August and turned his attention to the Detroit region.

Captain Roberts had seized Mackinac Island in violation of instructions he had received at Saint Joseph from Sir George Prevost, which the governor-in-chief pointed out to Brock when he heard of the capture. Prevost was relieved to learn that Roberts's assault had come after Hull's invasion and could not then be used as a flash point for sparking anti-British feelings among the American populace. Roberts's actions were not without authorization, however, because Brock had ordered him to take Mackinac on 26 June. The next day the general countermanded that order for reasons that can only be speculated. There is no doubt, however, that the next set of instructions he issued on 4 July telling Roberts "to adopt the most prudent measures either of offence or defence which circumstances might point out" prompted the captain's ultimate actions.[13] Hull had yet to cross the

Detroit River at the time Brock wrote to Roberts, so such aggression on Lake Huron might have provoked Americans to rally around their flag, which is what Prevost had recommended for six months should be avoided. Brock knew this, but at the same time he was assuring his superior that he was following a non-offensive policy by resisting a predilection to flatten Fort Niagara, the general gave Roberts the green flag for action. In the modern jargon, Brock "rolled the dice." Perhaps, after calculating the probable strength of Mackinac compared to the size of Roberts's force, and considering the capture of the American post as one of the keys for cementing native support, Brock concluded that the risk of defying Prevost's instructions was worth taking. Events proved him right and the governor-in-chief looked past his misgivings about Roberts's conduct and admitted that the seizure of Mackinac would strengthen an alliance with the native nations and put pressure on Hull's army.

The Mackinac incident revealed something of Brock's decision-making processes, showing him ready to take calculated risks. It was this same sort of cool reasoning that Brock displayed when he ignored potential protests from the public and dismissed the provincial legislators. He applied these tactics to the situation on the Detroit and resolved to take the initiative rather than waiting for Hull to make his next move. His speculation was that "part of [Roberts's] force might descend to Detroit," and, if General Hull heard about this at the same time as he learned that a British reinforcement was on the move from Niagara, he might decide to withdraw his army from Canada.[14]

Brock began organizing an expedition to Detroit before he prorogued the assembly. Fixing Long Point on the north shore of Lake Erie as a rendezvous, Brock sent about ninety officers and men from the 1st Flank Company of the 1st York Militia Regiment and the two flank companies from the 3rd York in that direction on 30 July. Captain Stephen Hatt received orders to muster part of the 1st Flank Company of the 5th Lincoln Regiment and the two companies of York flank companies at Queenston, numbering in all about sixty-five, to join the expedition. Here again Brock relied heavily on the competence of his staff officers. Lieutenant Colonel John Macdonell and Captain John Glegg prepared and issued orders and saw that they were put into effect; at Amherstburg, James Givins, a retired veteran of the 5th Regiment of Foot, was appointed a provincial aide-de-camp with the rank of major and later received his commander's praise. As the quartermaster general for the militia, Lieutenant Colonel Robert Nichol was instrumental in arranging transportation, rations and housing for the expedition. Similarly, Major Thomas Evans organized the detachment of the militia on the Niagara, outfitting them with cast-off uniforms from the regulars, but remained at the river, where Lieutenant Colonel Christopher Myers, 70th Foot, who had recently joined Brock's staff, assumed command in the general's absence. Under Brock's command, 300 militia, including companies from districts along the north shore of the lake, and fifty regulars embarked in batteaux at Long Point on 8 August, while others moved on land. They arrived at Amherstburg five days later after a difficult journey.

Brock found the situation on the Detroit front much improved. Procter had sent parties to intercept the American supply train with devastating effect and Hull had heard of Mackinac's capture. Fearful of being cut off in Canada, Hull withdrew to Detroit on 8 August to the dismay of his officers, who by then had lost faith in their commander. The British held a council to discuss their tactical options and, against the opinions of Procter and others, Brock chose to force the issue. He had read American correspondence captured late in June which told that Hull was not well supported by his followers, and he resolved to make a decisive move. He ordered a force of 700 regulars and militia, supported now by 600 natives fighters under Tecumseh, to cross the Detroit River early on 16 August. With what seemed to be a formidable formation of redcoats in place within a half mile of the town, intimidated by the menacing presence of a large body of warriors and under bombardment from British batteries, Hull lost his composure and abruptly surrendered.

Hull's regulars and militia, 2,200 in all, with 2,500 muskets, thirty-three artillery pieces and a vast supply of stores fell into British hands, giving Brock a nearly bloodless but resounding victory. The general was exultant. The defeat of Hull's army and the capture of Detroit greatly reduced the threat of invasion in that sector for the balance of the 1812 campaign. It lifted the sagging spirits of the citizenry and Brock proudly wrote to his brothers on 3 September that he had "received so many letters from people whose opinion I value ... that I begin to attach to it more importance than I at first inclined ... some say that nothing could be more desperate than the measure; but I answer that the state of the province admitted of nothing but desperate measures … [which] proceeded from a cool calculation of the *pours* and *contres*."[15]

Beyond the operational advantages gained by the victory, Isaac Brock was due to profit personally from the government's acquisition of the captured materiel as was the custom. "It is supposed," he wrote, "that the value of the articles captured will amount to 30 or £40,000."[16] His family's financial distress was very much on his mind and Brock admitted that if his share of this money eased their problem "I shall esteem it my highest reward." He was anxious about the rift between his siblings. Likening this situation to "the want of union" that he believed had nearly caused the loss of Upper Canada, he warned that "it operates in the same degree with families." Brock felt confident that the news of his success would be well received in England and would keep him from "the horror of being placed high on a shelf, never to be taken down."

Brock sent Glegg to Prevost's headquarters at Montreal with his report on the victory at Detroit. In the final paragraph of his despatch he expressed, in formal terms, a wish that his aide be allowed to carry the news home; "I shall esteem myself highly indebted to Your Excellency," he wrote, "to afford him that protection to which his merit and length of service give him a powerful claim."[17] Tradition allowed that the officer who delivered this kind of good news could expect immediate promotion in recognition of his commander's success. Brock was probably hoping that Glegg's description of the battle to the senior officers at the Horse Guards would also promote his own reputation; as well, Glegg would have been able to meet with Brock's brothers and return to Canada with the latest news about their hardships. Contrary to the general's wishes, Prevost gave the assignment to one of his own aides-de-camp, Captain Foster Coore, 3rd West India Regiment, explaining that Coore's recent mission to Washington had reaped information that the British cabinet would find of great interest. In Upper Canada the selection of Coore over Glegg was seen by some as an insult to "a brave General who had just saved the Province" and a bald attempt at "promoting a favourite," as John Strachan described it. "Capt. Glegg," Strachan added, "would open the eyes of the Ministry to the true Situation of the Province and how it has been neglected."[18] As it turned out, Coore was promoted to the rank of major upon his arrival, but Glegg was not forgotten and was likewise given a majority; Coore also made a point of meeting with Brock's brothers. As for Brock, his actions were "highly appreciated and acknowledged by His Royal Highness" and he was made a Knight of the Order of the Bath.[19] The announcement of this honour, however would not reach Canada until months after the general's death.

Leaving the Detroit frontier in the hands of Henry Procter, Brock sailed from Amherstburg on 17 August and, delayed by contrary winds, arrived at Fort Erie six days later. Almost as soon as he stepped ashore he heard that Major General Stephen Van Rensselaer had finally pitched his marquee at Lewiston.

The American general and his suite rode into Buffalo on Monday, 10 August, and immediately began to familiarize themselves with their new surroundings. Solomon Van Rensselaer conferred with Quartermaster General Peter Porter, who relayed rumours that General Hull's army was depleted, nearly cut off by 1,500 natives, and attempts to get supplies to him from Buffalo had failed. Despite having heard from Dearborn that Hull had probably captured Fort Malden, Stephen Van Rensselaer and his friends concluded that the Detroit campaign was in jeopardy.[20]

The general's first impression from what he saw and heard at Buffalo was that the army on the Niagara frontier was far from ready to "take the forts on the other side" as Governor Tompkins had suggested to Major General Amos Hall.[21] Hall had been busy since his arrival late in July distributing troops along the river, but desertion, furloughs and sickness had reduced his numbers to 1,400, he estimated, with only twelve light dragoons to serve as express riders.[22] Nicholas Gray had overseen the erection of three batteries, two at Black Rock and another on the edge of Lewiston Heights meant to subdue two British batteries recently set up at Queenston. This breastwork, soon to be referred to as "Fort Gray," stood empty because heavy ordnance had yet to reach the Niagara. As well, the army had no way to cross the river in force, although Porter was directing the construction at Manchester of batteaux large enough to carry thirty-five or more armed men each and hoped to have forty of them ready by the end of August. Short of labourers, Porter employed fatigue parties from the militia to help build the boats.

Van Rensselaer met with Hall and Wadsworth and the other principal officers when he made an inspection of the Niagara on 11 and 12 August, hearing their evaluations, seeking their opinions. The next day he formally assumed command by issuing a general order in which he assured the troops that "they may expect his unremitting exertions to render their situation at all times as eligible as possible."[23] He then settled down to prepare his army for war. In this endeavour his second cousin Solomon played a critical role, as he had been intended to do, advising the *patroon* on every detail. John Lovett remarked, "Nothing could have been more fortunate for the General than the man he has at his elbow, for Solomon in *fact and truth* does know everything which appertains to the economy of a camp."[24] As for Major Lovett, like nearly everyone else around him, he was up and active from dawn to dusk, doing his general's bidding. "I am a perfect machine," he wrote without a tinge of regret, "go just where I am ordered."[25]

One of the first things Van Rensselaer did was concentrate most of the militia units at a camp just south of Lewiston. Leaving Lieutenant Colonel Philetus Swift's regiment at Black Rock, he called in Lieutenant Colonel Hugh Dobbin's Eighteenth Detached Militia and Lieutenant Colonel Peter Allen's Twentieth Detached from their camps at Fort Schlosser and the clearing north of Lewiston known as Five Mile Meadow. Small detachments were left as guards at those places, while the regulars were at Fort Niagara and in Youngstown, where some had found lodging. Major Mullany continued to be the senior regular officer although he was about to be transferred from the Thirteenth U.S. Infantry to the Twenty-Third with the same rank, probably due to a shortage of officers in that regiment. Next Van Rensselaer instructed Porter to supply 100 cartridge boxes and belts, half a dozen horseman's tents and 100 common tents to the Lewiston camp.[26]

The general agreed with his subordinates that his force on the Niagara was too small to undertake an invasion of Canada, so he used his authority as commander of the north and western division of the state militia to activate several units.[27] The largest was the Nineteenth Regiment of Detached Militia under the command of Lieutenant Colonel Henry Bloom of Genoa in Cayuga County. Part of Brigadier General Wadsworth's Seventh Brigade, this unit numbered about 400 officers and men. From the militia encamped at Fort Oswego, Van Rensselaer also summoned the "battalion" of volunteer riflemen commanded by Major Charles Moseley, but this comprised only two companies of men, totaling fewer than 100 effectives. Lastly, he called up a troop of horse, the appointment going to Captain

Herman Camp, who was soon on the road with twenty-five dragoon-volunteers.

When the outlying militia detachments had established themselves in the camp at Lewiston, it became possible to regulate their training and in this undertaking Solomon Van Rensselaer played a central role. The general and his aide formed a list of standing orders for the efficient operation of the camp from week to week and distributed it to the unit commanders and their subordinates.[28] Strict adherence to these rules, as Solomon must have stressed to the *patroon*, formed the roots of a strong army and such would be needed if they were to succeed in Canada.

Beginning in the third week of August *reveille* would sound at daybreak, rousing every officer and man to form by company on the parade ground, after which the officers, under the watchful eyes of the general and his staff, would drill the men in individual sub-units; a second hour of drill would take place at 4:00 p.m. with full battalion drills at that time on Tuesdays and Fridays. "The dress of the officers and soldiers," Van Rensselaer's orders dictated, "is to be clean and their arms and accoutrements bright and in perfect order.... The General flatters himself that the Troops will vie with each other in the cleanliness of their dress, as well as their soldierlike and orderly conduct when on, or off duty." An eye would always be out for exemplary deportment and "refractory" conduct, the one being praised and the other subjected to the harshness of military law.

The *tattoo* would send everyone to his tent at 9:00 p.m., after which the guards, numbering about 160, in a ring around the camp, would begin to challenge passers-by. Guard duty, twenty-four hours of "on-call" as sentries, was taken in turn, company after company, with muskets loaded after sunset and twenty-four rounds of prepared cartridges for each man. To introduce incentive into this dreary chore, the men were allowed to fire off their rounds in the morning "at a target the size of a dollar at 100 yards distance." To the musketeer with the best aim, or the most luck, went the prize of a quart of whiskey, while the second and third marksmen earned a pint and half a pint of liquor respectively.

Cleanliness in the camp was considered another priority. Officers were to inspect their soldiers' tents to make sure they were aired, collapsed occasionally, cleaned and realigned as necessary. The ground behind and in front of each company's sector was to be cleared and levelled. "Two vaults, or sinks … [were] dug in the rear of each Company at least 100 yards in a line parallel to the tents," the orders explained and then warned that anyone found defiling any other part of the camp would be severely punished.[29]

The militiamen were unaccustomed to the rules and rigours of military life. The weather was oppressively hot and humid, with violent storms of rain and lightning. Drill and fatigue duty was tedious and exhausting, camp life less than exciting.[30] Under these conditions, not even a detailed description of the general's expectations could breed efficiency and decorum overnight. On 22 August, three days after issuing his order, Major General Van Rensselaer announced that the careless discharge of muskets was strictly forbidden. This was done in an attempt to stop his sentries and others from taking pot shots at British guards on the opposite bank. The British sentries eagerly returned the favour, which prompted the issuance of general orders for them also.[31]

Van Rensselaer also had to remind his officers that they were to sleep on site near their men in order to deal immediately with any misconduct. He praised the majority of his sub-units for prompt assembly at *reveille*, but he indicated his plain displeasure with the companies that failed to appear on time and a captain who had not even shown up one morning. Lastly, he harangued the guard for having allowed a prisoner to escape in the night.

Stephen Van Rensselaer saw it as his duty to be ever present among the troops. "Encamping in the midst of the soldiers," wrote Major Lovett of his general's activity, "and being every hour in their view pleases all." He seemed on his way to becoming "the favourite of the whole Camp," and tried to promote this view by demonstrating his genuine concern for the good treatment of his men. One morning while on the parade ground he saw a private collapse and hurried over to him, telling one of the men who huddled around the fallen soldier to go to his own tent and bring back a tumbler of wine to revive the fellow.

Solomon Van Rensselaer maintained a more remote and austere stance on the parade ground and so earned his own brand of respect. "Col. Van Rensselaer kept the troops every day at close drill and field duty," recalled one of the rank and file, "he was constantly among them; … he was generally feared and loved; and it was owing to his unflinching firmness that there was not a mutiny in the camp."[32] John Lovett watched how Solomon strode confidently through each day's events and remarked to a correspondent, "Those who know Solomon Van Rensselaer in civil life, know but very little about him. He is all formed for war; the whole economy of Camp is to him familiar as Pot-boiling."[33]

The lieutenant colonel's stern demeanour fell away when he sharpened a quill to write to his wife and express his anxiety and frustration over her continued silence. "What under the Heavens is the reason you do not write to me," he blurted out in the first line of a letter to Arriet on 21 August. "I have written from almost every place I have been at, without receiving a line from you."[34] New arrivals in the camp had brought Solomon reports of his family's good health, but that hardly appeased him. Still, the lieutenant colonel managed to put his plaints aside and tell Arriet about the camp and what he had been doing, adding that "I am everything to all, and as for my General, he is much pleased with me," before closing his letter with his best wishes and a request for his wife to remind the children of their absent father with a kiss.

Beyond the camps on the Niagara, larger events unfolding to the west and east would directly affect Van Rensselaer's army and his plans for it. Despatches that arrived at Quebec at the end of July announced the June repeal of the Orders-in-Council, the policy that most injured American shipping. Unaware of what Brock was about to accomplish at Detroit, Prevost saw an opportunity to provide some relief for that distant frontier and perhaps secure an end to hostilities *in toto*. Through Adjutant General Colonel Edward Baynes, Prevost quickly negotiated an armistice with Major General Dearborn (who had returned to Albany), beginning in the second week of August, ostensibly to give President Madison and his cabinet time to appraise the implications of this change in British policy.[35]

Word of the Prevost-Dearborn armistice reached Lewiston on 18 August and Van Rensselaer promptly sent the British the copies of instructions from Baynes that had been carried by the American courier. Major General Roger Hale Sheaffe arrived at the town of Niagara that same day and assumed command of the Niagara District. He acknowledged Van Rensselaer's note on 19 August and agreed to meet with Van Rensselaer's representatives to negotiate the particulars as they related to the situation at Niagara. The terms upon which Baynes and Dearborn had agreed confined operations of their frontier commanders to "defensive measures" only with hostilities being resumed four days after the official announcement of the termination of the truce. Both Baynes and Dearborn admitted that they had reinforcements and supplies in motion which could not be recalled and so they allowed those detachments to continue on their way, but not to advance west of Fort Erie. The wording of their agreement was ambiguous about how those detachments moved, by land or water, and this sparked some conflict between the opposing commanders on the Niagara.

Stephen Van Rensselaer wanted to expedite the transportation of some heavy ordnance from Oswego and urged Solomon, his delegate, to make sure water travel was permissible under the armistice terms. According to the Van Rensselaer family historian, Catharine Bonney, this issue led to a delay in arrangements as some heated words were exchanged in the several meetings that took place at the two headquarters.[36] During the most contentious discussion, in Queenston on 20 August, the British general asserted that the American request exceeded the limits of the original agreement, as he read it. In response, Solomon declared that there could be no armistice if Sheaffe did not comply with his request. According to Bonney, the officers then abruptly stood up and "Sheaffe clapped his hand upon the hilt of his sword, and in a hostile attitude said, '*Sir, you take the high*

**Major General Roger Hale Sheaffe (1763-1851)**
Sheaffe was a proponent of regular and strict drill. When Isaac Brock inspected the 49th Foot at Quebec in 1806, he reported its "good order and discipline ... much to the credit of Lieut-Colonel Sheaffe."[8] (National Archives of Canada, C-111307)

*ground!*'" Van Rensselaer answered in kind, "I do, sir, and will maintain it." Sheaffe is said to have then paced the room before withdrawing to consult with Lieutenant Colonel Myers and Major Evans. When he returned, he assented to the American's request "for amicable considerations" and the resolute lieutenant colonel returned triumphantly to Lewiston having achieved what many on his side thought impossible.

Meanwhile Sheaffe and his aides congratulated themselves at having played what they considered a sly game with their adversaries. They had received word of Brock's victory at Detroit and, keeping it from the Americans, had stretched negotiations out to give time for Brock to return to Niagara. Sheaffe also seems to have feared that Van Rensselaer might have ignored his orders from Dearborn and sent reinforcements to Detroit. Content with the delay and the fact that they had managed to get the Americans to agree not to gather boats at any place along the river, the British waited for the arrival of their commander.

Whether the charade at Niagara bore any significance in the larger picture is a moot point. The Prevost-Dearborn armistice, in limiting operations to defensive measures only, opened Lake Ontario to the Americans whether the local commanders disputed the issue or not. Under the protection of a truce, flotillas of batteaux could make the trip from Oswego to Fort Niagara without fear of interception by the Provincial Marine, just as the merchant vessels blockaded at Ogdensburg soon sailed, untouched, for the Niagara River. These vessels would eventually form the kernel of a U.S. Navy squadron on Lake Ontario. The waterways were also open to the unrestricted flow of British men and materiel, but this had always been the case, so the British gained little. Clearly, the armistice gave the Americans a reprieve when their fortunes were barely afloat. Prevost's goals in allowing this to happen were to facilitate the strengthening of his force in southwestern Upper Canada and promote the cause of peace, in the hope of ending a seemingly needless and certainly unpopular war. Inadvertently, he assisted the American army on the Niagara frontier.

When Brock returned to Niagara on 23 August and heard about the armistice he agreed in part with its arrangements. "Should peace follow, the measure will be well," Brock told Prevost.[37] But knowing that the Americans had been crushed at Detroit and that their position along the Niagara River was weak and that a new, optimistic mood was growing in Upper

Canada, Brock regretted that the armistice kept him from immediately challenging his enemy for control of the Niagara. He was anxious about the advantage the Americans had gained and remarked privately in a letter to his brothers that, "If hostilities recommence, nothing could be more unfortunate than this pause."[38]

The pause brought relief and disappointment to Lewiston. Solomon Van Rensselaer crowed to his wife about his coup in negotiations being "to the Army and the Merchants ... of incalculable value for future operations."[39] John Lovett remarked later, "We worked John Bull in the little Armistice treaty and got more than they expected."[40] But others were surprised by the sudden turn of events. "We are knocked on the head in consequence of this news of the armistice," wrote a disgruntled Nicholas Gray. Along the line there had been an expectation that General Van Rensselaer would order an invasion of the Niagara Peninsula as a way of tying up the British forces and offering some relief to Hull's army, still thought to be in Canada. Despite the repeated claims about the lack of training, ordnance and other essentials in the American camp, the general and his council of officers do indeed appear to have made firm plans to cross the Niagara River at several points simultaneously in the latter half of August. The truce snuffed out such intentions and left Gray complaining on 19 August, "Had we a General Hull here when I arrived, the United States should have been in possession of Upper Canada, and we should have our quarters in Montreal instead of playing ball on the banks of the Niagara River."[41]

Immediately after signing the truce with the British, the Americans learned of Detroit's fall and heard the truth about William Hull. Within days they witnessed the majority of Hull's wretched troops marching under guard along River Road from Fort Erie to the town of Niagara, where they boarded vessels for delivery to York and eventual detention at Quebec. Officers sent to inquire about the state of their friends returned with tales of disbelief and despair, allegations of Hull's treachery, admissions of ineptitude. All the American militia had been allowed to return to their homes on parole while the regulars, many of them destitute, lacking even jackets and shoes, could look forward to weeks, months maybe, of privation. At Lewiston and the other camps, the news of the disaster at Detroit and the price of defeat struck a sobering blow. The improvements made in the weeks following Stephen Van Rensselaer's arrival on the Niagara paled in importance now, fed by the whispered "insinuations that Gen. Van Rensselaer would do the like," that is, allow his army to be "*Hulled*."[42] The general was uncomfortably aware of a rising disharmony and wrote to Henry Dearborn on 26 August, "The surrender of General Hull's army excites a great deal of alarm in this vicinity. I shall, however, as far as in my power check and keep it under."[43]

As August turned to September Stephen Van Rensselaer, his aides and senior officers renewed their efforts to prepare their army for an invasion of Canada. At Albany Governor Tompkins and Henry Dearborn did what they could to support the force on the Niagara. With the fall of Detroit, the Niagara gained a new and urgent importance.

# 6

# "Redouble our exertions"

## MARCH AND DRILL ON THE NIAGARA, JULY–SEPTEMBER 1812

Unaware of developments in August on the distant Detroit frontier, the key American decision makers in Washington and Albany continued to try to carry out the proposed multi-pronged invasion of the Canadas. A stumbling block to this enterprise had been Major General Henry Dearborn's prolonged stay in Boston, where he had gone late in May to try to convince the New England governors to mobilize their militia. Unsuccessful in that mission, he returned to Greenbush on 26 July, after considerable urging by Secretary of War Eustis. Even President Madison wrote to emphasize the importance of Dearborn being closer to the northern line: "Your presence will aid much in doing all that can be done for the reputation of the campaign."[1]

Having re-established his headquarters at Greenbush, Dearborn revealed that he had not previously been aware of the extent of his command nor the role he was supposed to have been playing in support of Hull's army. Although he had proposed the current campaign plan in meetings with President Madison, Secretary of War Eustis and others in April, Dearborn inquired of Eustis on 28 July, "Who is to have the command of the operations in Upper Canada; I take it for granted that my command does not extend to that distant quarter."[2] How Dearborn could have misunderstood his responsibilities is bewildering, given the instructions he had received along with his commission in April and in the subsequent letters sent to him by Eustis in June and July. Waiting for him at Greenbush was another despatch from the secretary of war, dated 20 July, telling him to make arrangements with Governor Tompkins for putting the militia on the frontier under his direct control. As if that was not clear enough, on 1 August Eustis explained the importance of coordinating offensive operations in New York with those of Hull: "You will make a Diversion in his favor at Niagara and at Kingston."[3] Two weeks later, Eustis amplified his orders, this time with executive emphasis: "The President thinks it proper that not a moment should be lost in gaining possession of the British Posts at Niagara and Kingston, or at least the former and proceeding in cooperation with General Hull in securing Upper Canada."[4] It was not until early August that Dearborn finally acknowledged that the management of northern operations was his responsibility and that he was to coordinate his movements with those of Hull, although he continued to insist that before returning to Albany he had not "considered any part of the borders of Upper Canada as within the command intended for me."[5] And the suggestion by Eustis that he should execute diversionary operations in support of Hull at Niagara and below was something he admitted to having not even considered.

Dearborn's lassitude as commander in the north went beyond his orders from Washington. While at Boston he had not maintained regular contact with Albany, so when he arrived there, to find Governor Tompkins absent on business in New York, Dearborn was at a loss as to what to do. He did not know the command organization of the state troops, but figured Stephen Van Rensselaer was in charge of the region opposite Kingston and asked him on 29 July to comment on the size of force needed to begin offensive operations in that quarter.[6] Dearborn was uncertain whom to contact over a want of powder, or how to track down the field pieces said to have been ordered for thirty carriages expected soon from Boston. Congress had revised the organization of the army early in July, but the general had yet to see the plan on paper and was unsure how the new regiments were to be arranged. With these shaky hands holding the reins of operations designed to secure winter quarters in Canada, the prospects of American military success were indeed dim.

Nevertheless, news of the fall of Detroit did not lead to a sharp revision of the overall American strategy for 1812. Despite the fact that the army at

Niagara was hardly ready to advance into Canada and that the forces meant to cross the St. Lawrence River were even less prepared for taking the offensive, Madison and his cabinet were still committed to the original plan. Just days before word of Hull's defeat reached Washington, the president rejected the Prevost-Dearborn armistice and ordered a renewal of hostilities. Instead of retracting that hard line and buying some time, the administration escalated its efforts to seize Upper Canada, along the same invasion routes chosen in the spring, with one new initiative. Secretary of the Navy Paul Hamilton issued orders on 31 August for Captain Isaac Chauncey, USN, to create naval squadrons on Lakes Ontario and Erie and gain possession of those critical bodies of water. In the Northwest, Brigadier General James Winchester received instructions to recapture Detroit with help from Brigadier General William Henry Harrison. Dearborn began sending thousands of regulars and militiamen to Niagara, Sackets Harbor and Plattsburgh. "We have only to redouble our exertions and retrieve as soon as possible, this instance of an unfortunate beginning," Dearborn wrote to Eustis on 2 September, seeming to reflect the optimism of his superiors in Washington.[7]

In the deployment of troops General Dearborn finally demonstrated some administrative energy. The camp at Greenbush, a rough piece of ground three miles in circumference, was filled with 3,000 men, divided into regimental areas. "General Dearborn does not quarter in camp with us," observed a young officer. "He is a fine old gentleman and makes a very soldierly appearance."[8] Hoping that the Secretary of War would order "at least seventeen of the twenty-five regiments of infantry, one full Regiment of Artillery and three squadrons of cavalry" and a brigadier general or two to New York State, Dearborn sent to the various frontier posts most of the detachments at Greenbush and hurried forward any others who arrived.[9] These included one company of the Regiment of Light Artillery under Lieutenant Colonel John Fenwick and two companies of the Sixth Infantry along with heavy ordnance that Dearborn ordered to the Niagara on 8 August.

Through the authority of the president, and with the approval of William Eustis and Governor Simon Snyder of Pennsylvania, Dearborn also arranged for 2,400 militia from that state to be detached for duty on the Niagara. Near the end of August, the order went out from Harrisburg

**Regimental Colour of the U.S. Regiment of Light Artillery, 1812**
The regimental flag of the Light Artillery was buff, or yellow, silk with red lettering, highlighted with black. The scroll was also buff, its borders of a darker yellow and a green wreath surrounded the "U.S." (Courtesy of the West Point Museum Collection, U.S. Military Academy)

for the elements of a brigade to rendezvous at Meadville on 25 September.[10] In New York two more militia regiments received notice of assembly and departure for Niagara from their respective counties on 8 September, Lieutenant Colonel Farrand Stranahan's Sixteenth Regiment of Detached Militia and Lieutenant Colonel Thompson Mead's Seventeenth Detached. A long roll of independent companies of light infantry, rifle, artillery and cavalry would follow soon in their tracks.

Dearborn consulted closely with Daniel Tompkins in these and other matters, benefitting from the governor's energetic support. As he had all along, Tompkins played a crucial role in managing the details of these mobilizations. Illness and absence had left him short-staffed and he complained "that the transportation of Quartermasters' stores, and the payment of all the troops on the Frontier is somehow or other imposed on me."[12] His patience with Dearborn's lapses in understanding and military administration grew short, however, and on 14 September Tompkins wrote to an officer at Plattsburgh, "as the Commander-in-chief [Dearborn] seems willing to have the Command, without taking the responsibility of exercising it upon disagreeable occasions, I have concluded to assume the responsibility of exercising it, upon such occasions only."[13]

Despite what the thirty-eight-year-old governor might have felt, the old veteran from Revolutionary days believed he was overworked. When Brigadier General John Chandler arrived at Greenbush in the second week of September, Dearborn kept him on station to oversee the administration of the military camp. He might have sent him into the field, especially in light of the new urgency to regain what Hull had lost, but Dearborn believed he could not run the camp and everything else too, let alone take an active command himself. Of the responsibilities he shouldered, Dearborn wrote to William Eustis on 14 September, "I have never found official duties so unceasing, perplexing and fatiguing as at this place." He then sought to commiserate with the secretary of war by adding, "I presume you are not on a bed of roses."[14]

Along the Niagara River, the Prevost-Dearborn armistice officially ended on 8 September. The three-week hiatus had allowed time for Van Rensselaer's army to have many of its supply needs filled. Under the command of Lieutenant Colonel Fenwick, a flotilla of batteaux brought 200 regulars from Oswego, including half the company of light artillery (Captain James Gibson had taken the overland route with some of the men and the field guns) and two companies of the Sixth Infantry.[15] A native of South Carolina, Fenwick was a career officer who joined the U.S. Marine Corps in 1799 and rose to the rank of captain before resigning in 1811. The next winter he was given a commission as a lieutenant colonel of the Regiment of Light Artillery and outfitted a company under Gibson with artillery and horses at Lancaster, Pennsylvania. Fenwick headed for Greenbush late in June, arriving there on 30 July, and a week later the Light Artillery was en route for Fort Niagara via Oswego. They took with them their two iron 6-pdr. field guns and two 18-pdrs. and two 12-pdrs intended for use in fortifications. With the artillery went two companies from the Sixth Infantry under Captains George Nelson and John Machesney, which had been training at Greenbush. The vanguard of Fenwick's detachment, forty men with some of the guns commanded by Lieutenant Benjamin Branch, arrived by boat at Four Mile Creek just east of Fort Niagara on 2 September. The remainder reached this place, known locally as Johnson's Landing, the next day, with an additional pair of 18-pdr. guns apparently taken from the fortifications at Oswego.

The addition of Fenwick's command brought the total number of regulars on the Niagara line to about 800. As the senior ranking army officer present, Fenwick assumed command of the regulars from Major James Mullany. His arrival was greeted with pleasure by the Van Rensselaers and he soon formed plans to improve Fort Niagara rather than abandon it. His men strengthened the walls of the fort and removed the roof of the French castle, where they installed two brass 9-pdrs. and a howitzer. At the hamlet of Youngstown, directly opposite Fort George, the Americans erected a battery for four of the recently arrived pieces of heavy ordnance; it became known as the Salt Battery after the hundreds of barrels of salt over which earth was heaped to form the position. But the artillery officer had grave doubts about these preparations. "If [the British] throw over two hundred men, they can carry the Fort," Fenwick warned Major General Van Rensselaer. "The defense of this place is precarious outside of the storehouse."[16] The new battery rose too slowly for his liking and he blamed the incomplete works on a lazy contractor. Solomon Van Rensselaer agreed that progress on these projects was inadequate but he attributed this in part to Fenwick himself. "We have no one as fit for this all important service as Col. Fenwick, if he was at all times himself," wrote Van Rensselaer. "Unfortunately Col. Fenwick and Capt. Leonard are too much addicted to liquor to attend to this duty as they should."[17]

The day after Fenwick's party reached the Niagara, Major Charles Moseley's two companies of New York State volunteer riflemen arrived.[18] And about the same time Lieutenant Colonel Henry Bloom's Nineteenth Detached New York Militia reached the frontier and took up camp near Manchester; instead of the 700 men General Van Rensselaer had been led to expect, Bloom's unit numbered only 400. Shortly thereafter the gloom that had prevailed since word of Hull's defeat at Detroit reached Niagara lifted a bit when good news from a surprising source spread along the front. Isaac Hull, nephew of the disgraced general and captain of the USS *Constitution,* had achieved a remarkable victory over the British frigate *Guerrière* on 20 August near Bermuda. This singular achievement was celebrated along the American line – now the term "Hulled" could be taken two ways.

The British paid close attention to the arrival of reinforcements on the American side, scrutinizing the activity around Fort Niagara and along the eastern bank of the river. Brock surmised that his enemy's force had been considerably increased during the armistice and he expected a direct attack under cover of the new battery at Youngstown or a flanking movement on the Lake Ontario shore west of Niagara some dark night when the lake was calm. He had some of the heavy ordnance captured at Detroit positioned in the bastions at Fort George and he increased the exterior batteries he had ordered erected between the fort and the town and along the lake shore. Never far from his thoughts, however, was the concern that the posts at Queenston, Chippawa and Fort Erie were susceptible to attack and could expect little in the way of immediate support. Brock reasoned that he needed a large reserve of regular troops camped at a central location on the peninsula – Pelham was the spot he mentioned to Prevost – which could be rushed to repel an invasion at any vulnerable point. With this in mind, he suggested that the entire garrison at Kingston should be sent up to Niagara. "I stand in want of more artillerymen and a thousand regulars," he explained to Prevost on 7 September; this was in addition to the reinforcements he had recently received.[19]

The arrival of the 1st Battalion of the Royal Scots (the 1st Regiment of Foot) at Quebec early in August allowed Prevost to send about 650 officers and men of the 49th Foot to Upper Canada; six companies of them, just over 400-strong, arrived at Niagara by water in the first week of September.[20] It was a comfort to the general to have officers of long acquaintance with him again, among whom were Captains James Dennis and John Williams. They had joined the regiment in the mid-1790s and had served with Brock at Egmont-aan-Zee and Copenhagen, where Dennis had been wounded. As lieutenants, they arrived with the regiment at Quebec in 1802 and gained their captaincies while they rotated through various tours of duty in the upper and lower provinces. Their seniority in the regiment rose and they took command of the two flank companies, Dennis taking the grenadiers and Williams the light infantry. Not long after their arrival at Niagara, Brock posted their companies to Queenston while the other companies were dispatched to Fort Erie.

Major General Roger Hale Sheaffe was also an old acquaintance of Isaac Brock's. Sheaffe was born in Boston on 15 July 1763, one of eight children fathered by William Sheaffe, a customs collector. William died when Roger was eight years old so his widow established a boarding house to support her family. Shortly thereafter the British general, Earl Percy, later the Duke of Northumberland, hired rooms in Susannah Sheaffe's boarding house and took an interest in her family's situation. He offered to set Roger up with a career in the armed services, getting him, at first, a berth as a midshipman and then sending him to attend Lewis Lochée's academy in London, where George Prevost was also a student. In 1778 Percy purchased an ensigncy for Sheaffe in his own regiment, the 5th Foot, and the next year arranged his advancement to lieutenant, again by purchase. The influence of a patron such as Percy was helpful for the advancement of a young gentleman's military career, especially for someone of relatively common birth; Sheaffe benefitted from this "interest" through the 1790s.

The 5th Foot was stationed in Ireland from 1781 until 1787 and then sent to Canada, where it remained for ten years. Following the well established pattern, the 5th rotated through a series of posts, giving Sheaffe wide exposure to the Canadian frontier. He served at Detroit and Fort Niagara under Lieutenant Governor Simcoe, who considered him a "Gentleman of great discretion, incapable of any intemperate or uncivil conduct."[21] Sheaffe purchased a captaincy in 1795 and, back in England, transferred to the 81st Foot in 1798 by purchasing a majority in this unit. The next year he moved to the 49th Foot as lieutenant colonel, junior to Isaac Brock, and was with the regiment in the Netherlands and at Copenhagen before returning with it to Canada in 1802. Through another decade of various commands in the provinces, Sheaffe advanced to the rank of colonel by brevet in 1808 and then major general in 1811. Just before the war, Sheaffe received orders from Prevost to take command of the area around Three Rivers but in August Prevost send him to join Brock at Niagara to relieve some of the administrative pressures on that officer.

There is nothing in Brock's correspondence to show that he was pleased to be reunited with Sheaffe. There is, however, a comment he made to his brothers that reveals that his opinion of his old colleague was somewhat clouded: "General Sheaffe has lately been sent to me," he wrote home on 3 September. "There never was an individual so miserably off for the necessary assistance." What Brock implied with the words "the necessary assistance" is open to speculation as he did not expand on these private thoughts. It seems unlikely that he referred to Sheaffe's financial situation as the latter had always been amply supported by his patron and appears to have been well established in his station in 1812 and not lacking in funds.[22]

More likely, Brock was referring to Sheaffe's deficient leadership qualities, his lack of subtlety and social grace, and the fact that he was a frequent target of criticism among his peers. One unfortunate event that has figured largely in the handful of biographies dealing with the man was the near-mutiny at Fort George in August 1803 while Sheaffe held command. Brock was at York at the time and rushed to Niagara when he received word of the pending insurrection, where he quickly and efficiently arrested the perpetrators of the plot; they were tried at Quebec, the guilty parties being executed or transported. Early in 1804 Sheaffe's role in the affair became a subject of discussion, and Brock was required to give his assessment to then-lieutenant governor Peter Hunter. Brock acknowledged Sheaffe's strength, writing that "no man understands the duties of his profession better" and that he had "shewn great zeal, judgment, and capacity."[23] He was prone, however, to exercise the men of the 49th too rigorously, berate them without mercy, expect the highest level of perfection in every manoeuvre and abruptly reduce sergeants in rank if their men failed to meet his standard. His "rude manner of speaking" and "disagreeable ways," wrote Brock, have led to "many instances [when] he has been very indiscreet and injudicious." To Brock, it was plain that Sheaffe "possesses little knowledge of mankind" because "he did not sufficiently study the character of the men."

Brock spoke privately to his colleague about the mutiny and his manner with the men; Sheaffe soon left Fort George to take command of the post at York. Although Brock clearly considered Sheaffe to be at fault for the incident, he could not reveal this opinion publicly lest the lieutenant colonel "become the scoff and ridicule of the whole Regiment." As it was, Sheaffe had already earned "many enemies who have been in the habit of propagating reports highly injurious to his character as an officer." In this instance, Brock was referring to non-commissioned officers, but similar comments came from other quarters late in 1812 and during the following spring. Calumny, a favoured term of the time for malicious representation, seemed to follow Roger Hale Sheaffe wherever he went although he was not entirely without friends. William Dummer Powell, a judge of the Court of the King's Bench at York, and others regarded him highly, but they were aware that Sheaffe had many critics, blaming this on a prejudice arising from the fact that he had been born in Massachusetts rather than Britain. How pervasive this prejudice was when Sheaffe acted as Brock's second in command during the summer and autumn of 1812 is not apparent, but that it must have been an element of interpersonal relations at the Niagara headquarters seems undeniable

During the armistice Brock had allowed four-fifths of the militia to return to their homes, but they were soon recalled to fill out the four divisions along the Niagara. And to their numbers were added the flank companies of the 3rd York Regiment under Captains Duncan Cameron and Stephen Heward, who were ordered to Niagara during the first week of September. The victory at Detroit had greatly heartened the militia and Brock noticed the change: "The disaffected are silenced," he wrote.[24]

The flank companies of the Royal Newfoundland Fencible Regiment arrived in mid-September along with a twenty-five-man detachment from the 10th Royal Veteran Battalion, which Brock soon sent on to Mackinac.[25] Expecting that Prevost would not be able to reinforce his men quickly enough, Brock considered withdrawing troops from Amherstburg, but Colonel Henry Procter's position was too perilous. At Brock's suggestion, though counter to Prevost's preferences, Procter had sent a detachment to destroy American forts on the Maumee River while he remained at Detroit to ensure that the American residents did not fall prey to vengeful attacks by elements of Tecumseh's force. Retaining the loyalty of the natives was a grave concern for Procter and he explained to Brock that "a respectable force is requisite to give them confidence and render them effective."[26] So heavy was the press of business on the Detroit front that it took nearly two months for all the American prisoners and the captured ordnance and ammunition to be shipped by the Provincial Marine to Fort Erie. Rather than send part of the 41st Foot to support Brock, Procter hoped that Brock's recent reinforcements would allow him to transfer men to Detroit.

In the first week of September 500 warriors from the Grand River made camp near the town of Niagara. In part, their attendance in such large numbers was due to the efforts of Joseph Willcocks, the former voice of dissent in the provincial assembly. At the request of Brock, Willcocks had visited the Grand to try to persuade the chiefs of the nations to declare their full support of the British. Their poor showing in the Detroit campaign had confirmed the general's belief that they were not dependable, but after several councils with Willcocks, the Grand River chiefs committed their strength to the defence of Upper Canada. With John Norton at their head, the warriors arrived at the Niagara River, where they roamed up and down the banks, crossing to Grand Island, watching enemy movements, ready to go to the scene of action when needed. Brock's wariness about having the Grand River people on hand was not changed by the fact that "they appear ashamed of themselves, and promise to whipe away the disgrace into which they have fallen by their late conduct," as he reported to Prevost. He added, "They may serve to intimidate, otherwise expect no essential service from this degenerate race."[27]

The general's view of his enemy's ability to launch an attack changed as the September days passed. A week after petitioning Prevost for a 1,000-man reserve, Brock hinted at his growing desire to strike while the Americans appeared weak and vulnerable. This change of heart had been fostered by reports of desperate conditions on the other side, rampant sickness, frequent funeral services and numerous desertions. Brock described to Prevost one incident in which seven men from the Sixth U.S. Infantry stripped off their uniforms and attempted to swim across the Niagara. Six of them drowned, the lone survivor being followed the next night by two other deserters, one of whom turned back and was roughly hauled ashore. The successful pair of deserters then complained "of bad usage, bad and scanty food, and a total want of pay." Their companies had numbered sixty each when they reached Niagara on 4 September, but thirty of the men had already succeeded in deserting and half the others planned to follow them. "Nothing can be worse than the state of discipline existing among the [American] troops," wrote Brock.[28]

Discipline was at the core of daily training on both sides of the Niagara River throughout the summer of 1812. Without it, soldiers could never perform effectively in the closely packed formations that marched across battlefields of the period.

The basic infantry tactical unit was the battalion, a term often used synonymously with "regiment," although some British regiments had two battalions and others had up to four. In theory, a battalion numbered ten subunits, or companies, of about 100 officers and men each, but in practice the strength of a battalion often fell short of this mark.[29] Two of the companies were deemed the "elite," or flank, companies: the grenadiers, traditionally manned by robust veterans, who took their place on the extreme right of the battalion when formed in line, and the light infantry, composed of skilled, independent fighters, who stood on the left flank. In between were the eight battalion companies. A British battalion arranged its men in two ranks (like the horizontal rows on a chessboard) while the official American

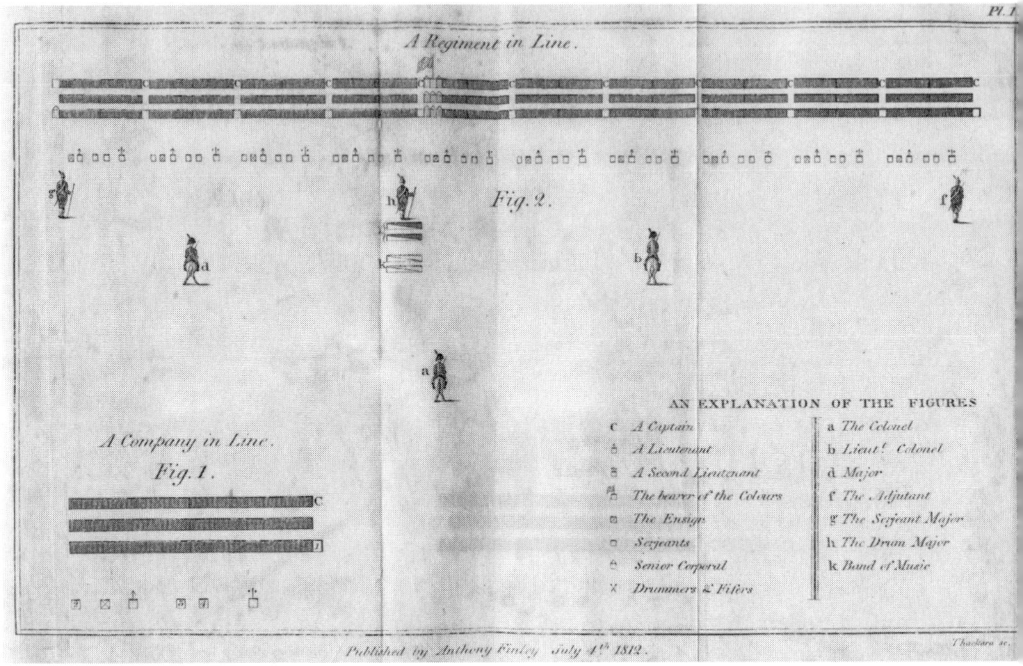


**A regiment in line**

Smyth's manual illustrated the formation of an American battalion in line of battle, showing three ranks of men in each company and the position of the various commissioned and noncommissioned officers. (From Alexander Smyth, *Regulations for the Field Exercise, Manoeuvres and Conduct of the Infantry of the United States*, 1812)

manual of 1812 preferred the three-rank system.[30] A commanding officer had the option of firing all his muskets at once in a mass volley, or by company from one flank to the other, creating a rolling fire effect, or from both ends toward the middle. Similarly, they could fire by rank or by file (men standing one behind the other), or platoons within each company could alternate their fire. An option to the double- or triple-ranked lines of battle was the two-company wide column featured in the American manual and based upon French tactics. It is uncertain, however, if the American units stationed on the Niagara in 1812 achieved a level of proficiency with basic line of battle evolutions to incorporate column tactics into their drill.

The idea of long lines of men firing away at each other on the open battlefield seems foolhardy by modern standards, yet such tactics were essential since the primary weapon of the period was the smooth bore, muzzle-loading, flintlock musket.[31] Its inaccuracy was legendary. One expert explained: "A soldier's musket, if not exceedingly ill-bored (as many are), will strike the figure of a man at 80 yards; it may even at a hundred. . . . [But] as to firing at a man at 200 yards with a common musket, you may as well fire at the moon and have the same hope of hitting your object."[32] Long before 1812, musket barrels had been "rifled" which means their bores were scored with a series of spiralling grooves, which gave a ball the spin it needed to maintain a true trajectory, but manufacturing costs restricted the supply of rifles to only a portion of the troops. Given their tendency to be inaccurate, the mass volleys of conventional muskets maximized their effect especially as an enemy came into closer range. When it struck home a one-ounce musket ball was lethal; it flattened and shattered upon impact and could even kill a man at three hundreds yards.[33] Beyond this range, the impact of a ball could knock a man down and leave him senseless; Napoleon and Wellington were both struck by spent shots, as was Brock at Egmont-aan-Zee.

The loading and firing of a musket was relatively easy and quick, which was another reason for its wide use. The musket ball and powder were packaged in tubes of greased paper and held in cartridge boxes fixed to a belt slung over the soldier's left shoulder to rest on his right hip. When ordered to load, the soldier withdrew a cartridge, bit off the end of it and, holding the musket horizontally at chest level, poured a small amount of powder into the pan of the firing mechanism. He covered this by snapping the base of the frizzen over the pan. Then he pulled the hammer, or lock, to half-cock and stood the musket on its butt, pouring the rest of the powder from the cartridge down the bore. The bullet went next, followed by the cartridge paper, all of which the soldier rammed tightly into the base of the bore with a ram rod stored in a fitting underneath the barrel. He raised the musket to his shoulder, levelling it toward the target, pulled the lock to full-cock and waited for the order to fire. When the order came and he pulled the trigger, the hammer, which consisted of a vise into which a piece of flint was locked, snapped sharply forward, striking the curved vertical arm that formed the top of the frizzen, forcing it to uncover the pan. Sparks produced by the collision of flint on steel dropped into the pan to ignite the powder, the flash of which was conveyed through the touch hole, or vent, adjacent to the pan and to the main charge at the base of the bore. In battle, the formal step-by-step drill was often abbreviated to increase the rate of fire, which could reach four or five shots per minute. At this rate, however, the soldier's cartridge box, holding as many as sixty cartridges, would empty too quickly, so a slower rate was maintained under most circumstance. Besides being inaccurate, muskets were prone to misfire between 15 and 25 per cent of the time due to windy or wet conditions or the fact that the filth of black powder clogged the mechanism.

The armies on the Niagara in 1812 had weapons of slightly different designs. The British used the India Pattern musket which had a 39-inch barrel with a 0.75-inch calibre bore, and fired a ball that was 0.71-inch in diameter. The American weapon was the 1795 Model, copied from an earlier French musket known as "Charleville." Its barrel ran about 44.5-inches long, with a 0.69 calibre bore and a 0.65 calibre ball; three buck shot were often packed with the ball in American cartridges. Though produced at factories in Springfield, Massachusetts, Harper's Ferry, Virginia and elsewhere, the weapon was often referred to as the "French" musket because of its calibre.[34]

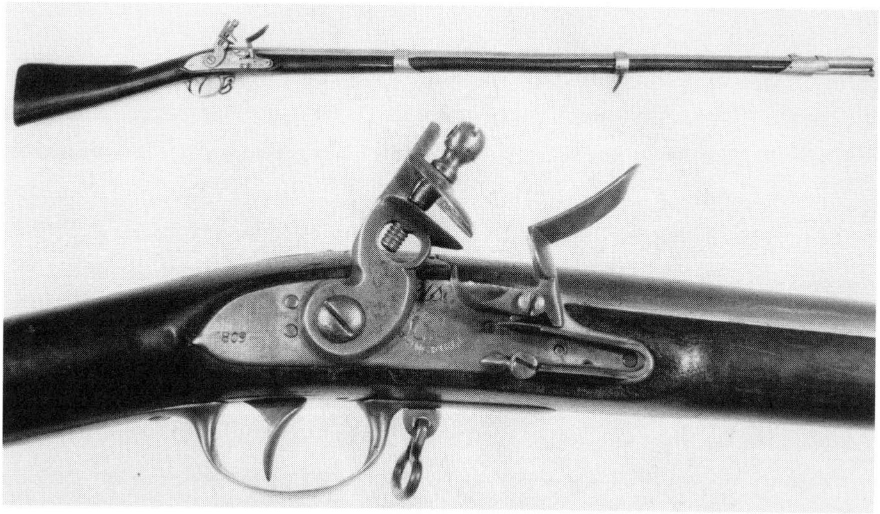

**U.S. Model 1795 musket**

The detail of this illustration shows a musket's firing mechanism. A piece of flint is missing from the hammer, revealing the vise-like grips that held it in place when it struck against the frizzen (shown here in the open position) creating sparks that dropped into the pan, igniting the powder there which caused the charge in the base of the musket's barrel to fire. (Courtesy of Parks Canada)

An infantryman also carried a bayonet in a scabbard attached to a belt slung over his right shoulder to sit on his left hip. It measured between fifteen and seventeen inches in length and was triangular in section so that it caused a wound that was difficult to close. In preparation for a charge, the soldier attached the weapon to the muzzle by means of a cylindrical socket that allowed the musket still to be fired. Bayonets were intended for use in face-to-face encounters with the enemy although this seldom occurred.

Recruits and veterans were drilled relentlessly for hours almost every day; young officers were expected to memorize all the evolutions and bark orders with clarity and poise. It was intended that a smartly stepping and precision-perfect unit would develop pride in its abilities, an *esprit de corps* that would help sustain it while facing the horrors of a battlefield. The 41st Foot was once observed exercising in Montreal, "continually on parade, marching, forming, filing, etc.... They made a very fine appearance."[35] A highly trained regiment with history as impressive as that of the 41st had a great advantage over the inexperienced units raised by the United States in the spring of 1812. The American officers on the Niagara were acutely aware that their men lacked sufficient preparation; one of them advised Stephen Van Rensselaer that "The regular force should be concentrated and organized.... They are all young and undisciplined, they may be cut up in detail."[36]

While the units trained to operate as highly coordinated wholes, a portion also drilled in light infantry tactics. This involved learning how to move ahead of the main body, fanning out in pairs or slightly larger groups and firing independently at the enemy, feeling out his strengths. Following the main encounter, the light infantry would provide a screen as the rest of the force regrouped. One British authority wrote that the men in this type of sub-unit must possess "vigilance, activity, and intelligence.... [and] must know how to gain upon an enemy along hedges, through corn fields, amongst gardens and ditches, almost without being perceived.... Light troops should all be expert marksmen. *To fire seldom and always with effect* should be their chief study."[37]

Artillery was the companion to infantry on the Niagara.[38] The calibre of most guns was determined by the weight of shot they fired, so an 18-pdr. weapon like the one in the redan battery at Queenston Heights fired an iron projectile that weighed eighteen pounds. When placed in a battery the guns were generally mounted on heavy wooden carriages while field guns were fixed to lighter carriages and equipped for rapid transport and positioning. A 6-pdr. field gun, for instance, had a limber and an ammunition wagon and was crewed by eight men excluding the drivers needed for its team of four to six horses.

The calibre of mortars and howitzers was expressed in terms of the diameter of their bores. Like garrison guns, heavy mortars were more or less fixed in one location. Smaller mortars, with calibres of 4.5 or 5.5 inches could be carried onto a battlefield. A howitzer of similar calibre had the advantage of being easier to manoeuvre since it was mounted on a large-wheeled carriage just as a field gun was. Because of the elevation of these weapons, the trajectory of their rounds had a significantly higher arc than that of the field or garrison guns.

A gun operated very much like a musket. The charge was contained in a flannel bag and sometimes came "fixed" with its ball, or shot, and charge combined in one package. The cartridge was rammed to the base of the gun's bore, followed by the shot. The gunner perforated the cartridge by inserting a brass wire with a sharpened tip down the vent of the gun, into which he then placed a quill or paper tube filled with mealed powder. Next a slow match or "port fire" was held against the upper end of the tube which instantly ignited the charge. With a ratio of about three-to-one in the weight of a shot to the size of its charge, a 6-pdr. had a maximum range of 1,200 yards although its effective range was about 500 yards.

Round shot made up between 70 and 80 per cent of the ammunition transported with each gun. Its purpose was to destroy buildings and barricades and cut bloody furrows through the ranks of massed troops, often relying on the ricochet effect on hard ground to increase the range of the rounds. For ranges of less than 600 yards, canister, or case shot, often incorrectly identified as grape shot (a common naval projectile), was used. It was essentially a tin can full of bullets that ruptured upon firing with an effect similar to that of a shotgun shell, fanning out to a diameter of just over 30 feet for every 100 yards traveled.

Shells, or bombs, were fired in mortars and howitzers. They were hollow iron spheres containing black powder and were equipped with a powder filled wooden fuse that ignited when the weapon fired. If the fuse was trimmed properly by the gunners, the shell would explode over the heads of the enemy or within a building that had been targeted.

The British alone used another type of projectile known as spherical case, the invention of Colonel Henry Shrapnel, R.A. A hollow, thin-sided iron sphere, this form of case was filled with gunpowder and musket balls and was fitted with a wooden wick for timing its detonation. It was fired from field guns and howitzers and was intended to explode in front of advancing or stationary troops, emitting a murderous hail that could spread out to well over 100 yards.

In battle, the artillery was usually placed on the flanks of the main infantry formation and fired at the enemy infantry, rather than at the opposing ordnance. They began with round shot, and changed to canister (and spherical case, for the British) as the enemy approached, managing up to

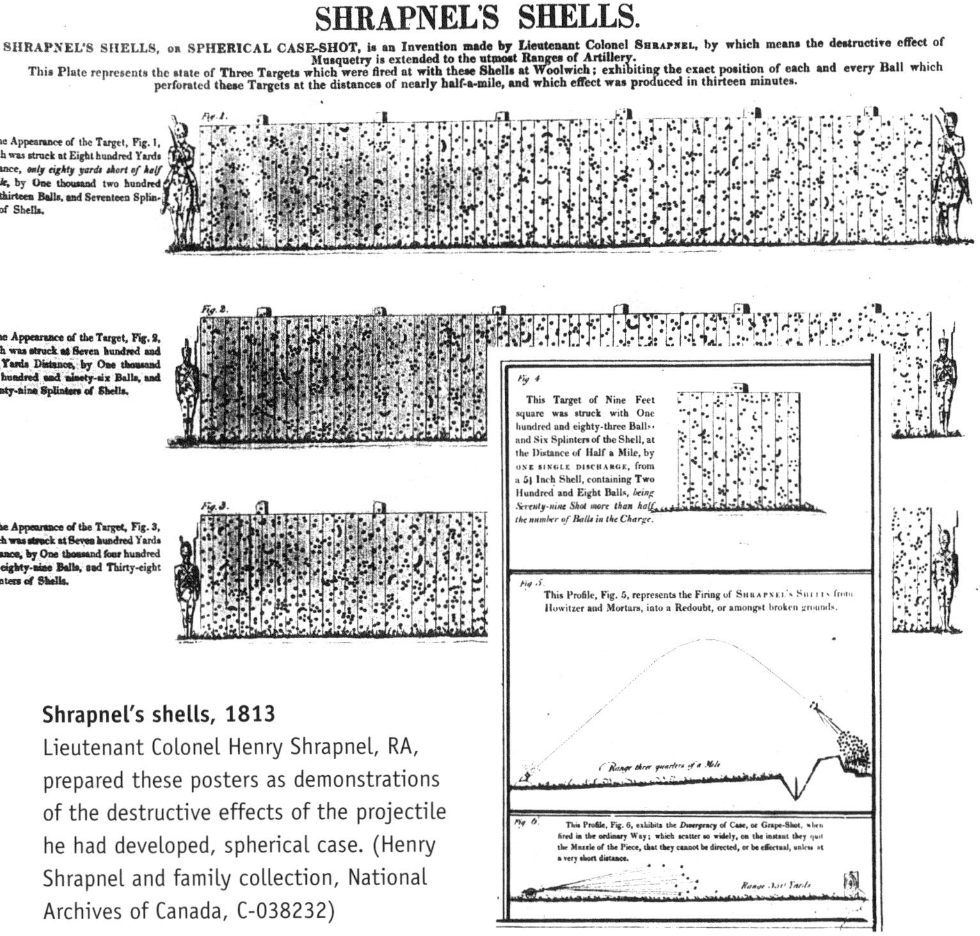

SHRAPNEL'S SHELLS.
SHRAPNEL'S SHELLS, or SPHERICAL CASE-SHOT, is an Invention made by Lieutenant Colonel Shrapnel, by which means the destructive effect of Musquetry is extended to the utmost Ranges of Artillery.
This Plate represents the state of Three Targets which were fired at with these Shells at Woolwich; exhibiting the exact position of each and every Ball which perforated these Targets at the distances of nearly half-a-mile, and which effect was produced in thirteen minutes.
Fig. 1.
The Appearance of the Target, Fig. 1, which was struck at Eight hundred Yards Distance, only eighty yards short of half a mile, by One thousand two hundred and thirteen Balls, and Seventeen Splinters of Shells.
Fig. 2.
The Appearance of the Target, Fig. 2, which was struck at Seven hundred and fifty Yards Distance, by One thousand two hundred and ninety-six Balls, and Twenty-nine Splinters of Shells.
Fig. 3.
The Appearance of the Target, Fig. 3, which was struck at Seven hundred Yards Distance, by One thousand four hundred and eighty-nine Balls, and Thirty-eight Splinters of Shells.
Fig 4.
This Target of Nine Feet square was struck with One hundred and eighty-three Balls, and Six Splinters of the Shell, at the Distance of Half a Mile, by ONE SINGLE DISCHARGE, from a 5½ Inch Shell, containing Two Hundred and Eight Balls, being Seventy-nine Shot more than half the number of Balls in the Charge.
Fig. 5.
This Profile, Fig. 5, represents the Firing of Shrapnel's Shells from Howitzer and Mortars, into a Redoubt, or amongst broken grounds.
Range three quarters of a Mile
Fig. 6.
This Profile, Fig. 6, exhibits the Divergency of Case, or Grape-Shot, when fired in the ordinary Way; which scatter so widely, on the instant they quit the Muzzle of the Piece, that they cannot be directed, or be effectual, unless at a very short distance.


**Shrapnel's shells, 1813**

Lieutenant Colonel Henry Shrapnel, RA, prepared these posters as demonstrations of the destructive effects of the projectile he had developed, spherical case. (Henry Shrapnel and family collection, National Archives of Canada, C-038232)

three rounds per minute, but more commonly two. As their own formation moved, the guns would be relocated, although this was a complicated task for the somewhat harried gunners, who had no means of responding to errant musket balls or to the deliberate bullets of sharp-shooting light infantry. If a gun was about to be overrun, there were several ways to disable it, the quickest being "spiking." Among a field piece's accoutrements was a rod of soft iron which one gunner could insert through the vent while a second would bend it over with several hard thrusts of a rammer. Removing the locked spike was a time-consuming task.

Guns were objects of great pride and ceremony and on the Niagara frontier two of them received some special attention. They were a pair of brass howitzers "of a size calculated to be carried on pack-horses, the wheels about as large as those of a wheel barrow."[39] They were captured at Mackinac and brought down to Fort George, where Solomon Van Rensselaer recognized them during one of his diplomatic visits. He recalled turning to John Macdonell and Thomas Evans and saying, "these at all events are old friends of mine." They had been used during General Anthony Wayne's campaign against the native nations in 1794, in which Solomon had participated. Van Rensselaer commented to Macdonell that he "felt partial to those pieces, and we must try to get them back." Then, answered Macdonell, it would be up to the British to defend them. As the days of September passed, the events that would bring Macdonell and Van Rensselaer, and perhaps the little howitzers, to the battlefield crept closer.

# 7

## "*We have but one object.*"

### FINAL PREPARATIONS, SEPTEMBER–OCTOBER 1812

The end of summer along the Niagara was marred by hard rains and high winds. On the American side the men became restless, calling for their pay, seeking furloughs, falling sick in droves. Shortages persisted with a lack of hospital supplies, shoes, camp equipment, mortar shells, canister and forage, and people looked increasingly at Quartermaster General Peter Porter as the culprit; Solomon Van Rensselaer considered him a "scoundrel." Major General Van Rensselaer relocated the Lewiston camp on Ridge Road about one mile east of the river in the first week of the month, well out of range of the 18-pdr. gun recently installed in the redan battery two-thirds of the way up the escarpment above Queenston. Work began on a new road between the camp and Fort Niagara. The Americans expected the British, still gloating over Brock's victory at Detroit, to attack at any moment. "I should say from present appearances, we must either fight or run, or both in a few days," wrote Major John Lovett.[1]

The sinking spirits in the American camp were reflected in the rising number of courts martial convened to deal with deserters, drunks and dissent."[2] Sentences for those found guilty varied from twelve days to four years of close confinement, sometimes attached to a ball and chain, rationed with bread and water alone and with stoppages of pay, as well as the charge for all expenses incurred by the arrest and trial. Three deserters were sentenced to be shot "on the Grand Parade at Fort Niagara. . . . [with] all the

Troops not on duty ... drawn up to witness the execution," but they were saved when the major general commuted their sentence in the hopes that his "act of clemency ... will make a lasting impression on their future conduct in life."[3] The rank and file were not the only ones who were summoned before the courts; Lieutenant Samuel Rathbone, First Artillery, was charged with striking a militia sergeant who sat down to rest under a tree and refused to bring his men back to their fatigue duties. Lieutenant Colonel Henry Bloom was accused by one of his own ensigns, Zelotus Sheldon, of neglecting his duty on guard and for "abusing ... Sheldon with profane and obscene language"; this dispute was settled out of court.[4]

Another controversy almost found its resolution on the dueling ground. The tension between Solomon Van Rensselaer and Peter Porter grew to a breaking point shortly after reports of the loss of Detroit reached the Niagara. Van Rensselaer had decided that the quartermaster general was lax in carrying out his responsibilities and outright treasonous in his behaviour. He finally accused Porter of causing "confusion and distrust among the Troops" by spreading it about that Stephen Van Rensselaer was "a traitor to his Country" who would surrender his army, as Hull had, the moment the British crossed the river.[5] Porter caught wind of Solomon's slander and challenged him to meet on Grand Island for a manly solution to the quarrel. According to John Lovett, the major general kept close track of the two firebrands and stifled the proposed duel by threatening to arrest them. Solomon Van Rensselaer's version of events confirmed the general's hand in the matter, but he blamed a disclosure of the arrangements on Porter's loose lips and demanded an apology for being "trifled" with, or else he would publicly declare that the quartermaster general was "a *poltroon*, a *coward* and a *scoundrel*."[6] Porter withheld any words of regret and Van Rensselaer lived up to his promise by having his comments published in several newspapers the following winter.

Solomon's temper was probably not improved by his wife's continued refusal to write to him. His exasperation increased when he heard from a family friend that Arriet's depression had not lifted but that she kept herself busy all day with her children and the responsibilities of running the farm. Someone else informed him that Arriet's reticence was due to "a sore finger" which prohibited her from picking up a quill. "I fear I am deceived by them," Solomon told her, "and until I hear from you in person I must remain in that unhappy state of suspense."[7] He wrote affectionately about their children ("kiss Matilda and my dear little Margaretta for me") and urged Arriet not to lend credence "to a thousand Idle reports" circulating in Albany about conditions on the front. He raised the matter of their murdered son, softly advising her that the "past events you must forget, it was the will of Heaven to give you cause of being distressed." "If I could only hear from you," he added, "and that you was well and happy, I should ask for nothing more." Another week passed with nothing from Arriet, leaving Solomon to pine for her. In the final week of September he took ill with a fever and removed himself from camp. "We bled him, and for three days filled him half full of salts, jalp, Castor-oil, Calomel, etc. etc., [but] his whole system resisted medicine so obstinately," wrote John Lovett.[8] During this time, Solomon again vented his misery to his still-silent wife: "I am heartily tired of this military life," he declared. "If I could desert I would do it for never in my life have I had such an anxiety to be with you, but it is otherwise decreed and we must submit to fate."[9]

As summer turned to autumn, the tempo of Major General Dearborn's correspondence increased; he wrote to Stephen Van Rensselaer on 17 September, "It is intended to have a force sufficient *to enable you to act with effect, although late*."[10] Midway through September, elements of the Fifth, Twelfth and Fourteenth Infantry Regiments and two units of the Second Artillery received orders to march for the Niagara frontier, followed soon after by the Thirteenth Infantry. Brigadier General Alexander Smyth arrived at Albany, petitioned Dearborn for a field command and was soon heading west. "I have concluded to give him the command of a Brigade at Niagara," Dearborn explained to Eustis, adding pointedly, "Maj. Gen. Van Rensselaer will command."[11] He ordered the batteaux on the Mohawk River and Lake Ontario sent to Fort Niagara and instructed more boats to be built at all the posts. Shortages prevailed at Greenbush, so much of the infantry sent up the road to Buffalo went without uniforms or sufficient ammunition.[12]

The strategy of the American campaign as established in the spring continued to guide operational planning late in September. Dearborn believed that a coordinated series of offensives by Van Rensselaer, Brigadier General Harrison and Commodore Chauncey was feasible but not likely to happen until 10 or 12 October. He explained his expectations to Van Rensselaer on 26 September, stressing "*At all events, we must calculate on possessing Upper*

*Canada before winter sets in.*"[13] How Dearborn conceived that widely separated formations could be coordinated when it was taking nine or ten days for letters to reach him at Albany from Lewiston is difficult to understand. Nevertheless, he repeated his ideas in a despatch to Van Rensselaer on 4 October and instructed him that "a correspondence by expresses be kept up between you and General Harrison" in order to have their forces move in concert.[14] Dearborn was also depending upon the quick seizure of control on Lake Ontario, although by the first week of October only some of Chauncey's sailors had reached Sackets Harbor, while a small detachment under Lieutenant Jesse Elliot arrived at Black Rock in mid-September.

Smyth reached Buffalo on 29 September, where he found Colonel William Henry Winder's Fourteenth Infantry encamped at nearby Black Rock. Smyth approved of this location as "an excellent piece of ground for exercise" and when detachments of the Twelfth and Fifth Regiments appeared a few days later, under Colonel Thomas Parker and Lieutenant Colonel Homer V. Milton respectively, they also took up quarters in the Black Rock camp.[15] Smyth lamented that "They are recruits without clothing and with little instruction" but he planned "to devote six hours daily in their instruction, in discipline and evolutions."

Alexander Smyth now proceeded to put his own stamp on the Niagara campaign. He was forty-seven years old and a native of Ireland who had taken up the practice of law in Virginia in 1791. Well respected there, he served as a representative and senator in the state legislature, and in 1808 he was commissioned a colonel in the Regiment of Riflemen, much to the annoyance of officers in that unit who were in line for promotion. His competence as an officer was suspect and one contemporary wrote that Smyth was "incapable of exercising a company."[16] Nevertheless, his political connections were secure and in 1811 he was ordered to Washington and given the task of writing a new drill book for the infantry. Smyth's *Regulations for the Field Exercise, Manoeuvres and Conduct of the Infantry* became the official training manual and he was appointed inspector general and then promoted to brigadier general.

From the start of his term on the Niagara frontier Smyth showed little respect for the chain of command and the need to obey orders. Dearborn implied in a letter to Eustis that he had told Smyth that Stephen Van Rensselaer would outrank him on the Niagara frontier, but whether Smyth understood his status is unclear. After assuming his post at Black Rock, he broke with military courtesy by neglecting to introduce himself in person to the major general. Instead, his first communication with Van Rennselaer included his hurriedly formed conclusion that the banks of the Niagara between Chippawa and Fort Erie offered the best points for invasion. Although he had never been in this region before and knew nothing of the river beyond what he could see from Black Rock or on maps, Smyth deemed it "proper to encamp the U.S. troops near Buffalo, there to prepare for offensive operations."[17]

Van Rensselaer answered with his own views of the operational assets offered by the river, his familiarity with its banks and the lengthy deliberations that had helped him form his decision about where attacks against the British should be made. He invited Smyth to a council of war, insisting "I trust we are both open to conviction, and we have but one object – the best interest of the service."[18] A more experienced and less tolerant field commander would likely have reminded Smyth of his subordinate rank and ordered the latest regulars to Lewiston or Fort Niagara, but Stephen Van Rensselaer was a politician and employed the only tools he possessed, those of diplomacy and consensus. Solomon Van Rensselaer was bed-ridden at this time and could not bring his strength of character and military knowledge to bear on the issue, leaving the major general to deal with the problem as well as he could. Stephen's mild rebuke had no effect on Smyth, who remained at Black Rock.

The arrival of reinforcements bolstered Van Rensselaer's force significantly, but shortages of all kinds continued to weaken the resolve of his army, especially among the militia. Many of them had been in camp for nearly three months and were fed up with military life. At one point a piece of birch bark was found bearing a scribbled note that if the troops were not paid by 25 September, they would desert. The bad weather through September and into October continued with torrents of rain and wind "eno' to make an Ox quake," as John Lovett observed.[19] Not surprisingly, the sick lists grew.

Lovett's optimism was not diminished by the difficult circumstances. In a letter dated 6 October, he continued to praise his chief: "General Van Rensselaer is in good health, firm as Atlas, actively engaged from dawn till dark, and often at night."[20] Solomon's place in camp was still secure: "You know that Solomon is often called *General* Van Rensselaer," Lovett noted.

As for himself, the major cheerfully claimed, "I take my duty as it comes, I do believe I can discharge it as well as any other man." The staff officers had read rumours about their campaign in newspapers and, trying to dispel the falsehoods, Lovett informed his correspondent, "Do not start if within three mails I date 'Canada.' I tell you we are going to work."

Through September the British maintained their close watch on developments along the American line. Brock knew that, despite some recent reinforcements, illness on the eastern shore was rampant and the fortifications were far from complete. To Prevost he suggested on 13 September that "A great deal could be effected against such a body at this moment," but assured the governor-in-chief that he was adhering to his instructions about not taking the offensive.[21] As for the lack of sufficient reinforcements from England, Prevost tried to explain to Brock "how entirely I have been left to my own resources in the event which has taken place.[22]

Through September and into October they kept up their back and forth discussion about reinforcements and defence, maintaining their gentlemanly manner with each other. At one point, however, Prevost pondered the possibility of Brock making a strong diversion from Upper Canada if the Americans invaded the lower province and the general snapped back with, "My force is so scattered and so immediately required for the defence of the different posts ..., that I am at a loss to know in what manner I can possibly act so as to produce the effect expected."[23] Brock expressed his frustration privately to his brother Savery on 18 September: "I have evidenced greater forbearance than was ever practised on any former occasion."[24] He did, however, grudgingly admit the wisdom in Prevost's defensive stance: "I firmly believe," he explained to Savery, "that I could at this moment sweep everything before me from Fort Niagara to Buffalo – but my success would be transient."

Although never satisfied with his resources, Brock was generally content with conditions along his line. He was pleased with the 41st Foot and 49th Foot and considered the fact that he had not lost a single individual on the Niagara from disease or wound for more than two months "certainly something singular."[25] Especially in comparison to what he heard was happening across the river, where "The militia, being composed of enraged democrats, are more ardent and anxious to engage, but they have neither subordination nor discipline. They die very fast."

Brock continued to modify his defences. The most ambitious project involved improvements to Fort George, where a curtain wall was built between bastions facing the river. A 12-pdr. and 18-pdr., each on a traversing platform, were mounted in one bastion, while a 24-pdr. went into the other; some of this work Brock directed personally. The exterior batteries were improved also and Major General Sheaffe noted how an 8-inch mortar had been set up to be "in a line with the big house [the French castle], commandants house, and North block house" of Fort Niagara.[26] Sheaffe mentioned "the transformation of the 'Big House' into a battery – the wheels of three carriages peep over the wall – of the roof there remain some of the rafters."

The four divisions of the Niagara command remained intact and district general orders were issued nearly every day reminding officers to check their men's ammunition and ensure that they were being drilled effectively and that officers themselves were doing their rounds punctually and thoroughly. The organization of troops in each quarter was fine-tuned as the weeks passed with a gradual increase of the force from Chippawa to Fort Erie. Lieutenant Hamilton Merritt spent most of his time in this area. He had just returned from a prolonged period of duty at Amherstburg and found that there was much anticipation of an attack by the Americans. Serving as a courier, young Merritt and his comrades in the Lincoln troop were constantly in motion; the hardships they suffered were "severe, up all Night, and slept in the day."[27]

The arrival of large numbers of Americans at Black Rock caught the attention of the officers at the upper end of the river. Brock rode up there during the fourth week of September to have a look and issued detailed orders on how that portion of his command was to be defended if the Americans launched an invasion. Although he had earlier predicted that an attack would centre on Fort George, Brock now believed lake conditions made expeditions intended "to turn either of our flanks extremely dangerous."[28] He warned his subordinates that "it appears likely to me ... that his principal attack will be made between Fort Erie and *Palmers* [a tavern opposite Grand Island]." To that end, the general made sure that his officers knew exactly what he wanted them to do if such an assault developed. Brock did not, it appears, issue similar orders for the steps to be taken in the event of an assault on the lower river.

While Brock was contemplating how to defend against a landing on the upper river, Stephen Van Rensselaer rejected Alexander Smyth's thoughts on the very same type of expedition. Certain that the time was quickly approaching when something significant had to be done, Van Rensselaer continued to meet with his senior officers and discuss plans of attack. These informal councils included Solomon Van Rensselaer and John Lovett, William Wadsworth, the militia lieutenant colonels at Lewiston and presumably Lieutenant Colonel Fenwick and other regulars from Fort Niagara, but no one from the Black Rock command appears to have attended them. Alexander Smyth stayed away, and so did Major General Amos Hall, Quartermaster General Peter Porter and the governor's advisor Nicholas Gray, all of whom had been on the frontier throughout the summer. It was obvious that in his hesitation to confer openly with Stephen Van Rensselaer about how to best employ the force at hand, Smyth was not alone. At the general's headquarters, the atmosphere of discord must have been almost palpable.

The scheme devised in the councils of war, as the general described it to Dearborn on 8 October, featured a two-stage attack. The operation would begin with the militia creating a diversion by attacking Queenston. Meanwhile the regular units would embark in batteaux near Fort Niagara, land on the lake shore above the town of Niagara and invest Fort George. To Dearborn, Van Rensselaer acknowledged that "Our best troops are raw; many of them dejected by the distress their families suffer by their absence, and many have not necessary clothing."[29] But he did not think success was unattainable and aspired to "wipe away part of the score of our past disgrace, get excellent barracks and winter quarters, and at the least be prepared for an early campaign another year."

Before Van Rensselaer could put these plans into effect, a combined force of American seamen and soldiers made a bold move at Fort Erie. The British brigs *Detroit* and *Caledonia* had come to anchor in the roads off Fort Erie just after sunrise on Thursday, 8 October. They were carrying the last of the captured arms, goods and prisoners from Detroit as well as a valuable cargo of furs; the *Detroit*, formerly the U.S. Army transport *Adams*, was itself a prize of war.

Among the Americans studying this scene was the headstrong and zealous naval lieutenant Jesse Elliott, who had reached Black Rock in mid-September with a small detachment of seamen and had begun modifying merchant vessels for naval service. As he watched, Elliott formed "a conviction that with those two Vessels added to those which I have purchaced and am fitting out I should be able to meet the remainder of the British force on the upper Lakes [and] save an incalculable expence and labour to the government."[30] He sought Generals Smyth and Hall and proposed a cutting-out expedition, manned from a larger detachment of seamen that had reached Black Rock at noon that day. They approved Elliott's plan, giving him weapons for the mission and ordering a body of regulars to join with the seamen. The lieutenant equipped two boats and under cover of darkness hauled them up to Buffalo Creek.

Elliott's attack on the *Caledonia* and *Detroit* was the baptism of fire for the Second Regiment of Artillery. Under the command of Lieutenant Colonel Winfield Scott, two companies of this unit, numbering about 160 men with four field pieces, had arrived at Buffalo on 7 October, having been on the march across the state from Greenbush for three weeks less a day.[31] Winfield Scott was easily recognizable in a crowd since he stood 6 feet, 5 inches tall and weighed in the neighbourhood of 250 pounds. With experience in both militia and regular units before the war, Scott received his commission as lieutenant colonel in July, just days before his twenty-sixth birthday. He recruited his command at Philadelphia and then hurried to Greenbush, where he sought active employment from Henry Dearborn. With him had come Captains Nathan Towson and James Barker, Lieutenants Isaac Roach and Patrick Mcdonogh.[32]

After Smyth approved the employment of the regulars in Elliott's raid, he gave Scott the nod to select volunteers from his companies rather than calling upon one of the infantry units at Black Rock. Lieutenant Roach was to have command of fifty men, but when Scott ordered volunteers to step four paces forward from the ranks of the assembled artillerymen, no one remained where he was. Scott and Roach were exultant and as the lieutenant walked down the line to select his men he found "every face was pushed forward with 'can I go, Sir?' 'I'm a Philadelphia Boy;' 'don't forget McGee.'"[33] The officers selected several dozen men and formed them in two detachments, one under Roach and the other under Towson.

Elliott's scheme met with success. After several wet hours in the dark, his two boats, crowded with more than 100 men, swept down on the brigs and

**Lieutenant Colonel Winfield Scott, Second U.S. Regiment of Artillery (1786-1866)**
A Virginian by birth, Scott trained to become a lawyer, but enlisted in a troop of militia cavalry immediately after the *Chesapeake/Leopard* incident in June 1807. Within weeks he found himself face to face with the enemy when he participated in the capture of a small British boat, manned by two officers and six men, who were suspected of having hostile intentions. (From *Portfolio Magazine*, 1816)

carried them. The plan had been, apparently, to escape onto Lake Erie, but the strong current of the Niagara River carried the brigs downstream past four British batteries that pelted them with shot. The *Caledonia* was towed to safety at Black Rock, where Scott had set up his guns, while the *Detroit* drove up hard on a shoal at Squaw Island. In the morning a party of the 49th Foot with some militia crossed in boats to attempt to recapture this brig, but failed, and shortly thereafter the Americans set it afire. It had been a sharply fought contest with casualties on both sides, but Roach and the others were thrilled by their victory. "Our brother officers on shore praised us extravagantly, and we were well satisfied to have brought ourselves back with a whole skin," wrote the lieutenant.[34] They were especially encouraged to have led raw recruits into a clash with the British veterans and to have come out on the winning side.

Isaac Brock heard about the attack on the *Caledonia* and *Detroit* late Friday morning and left the town of Niagara immediately to ride up to Fort Erie, attended by his aides and others. He arrived after sunset, when all that remained of the *Detroit* was a smouldering hulk, its cargo of heavy ordnance and muskets lost to him. He considered the incident "particularly unfortunate" and liable to cause "incalculable distress" to his position.[35] Now the Americans had four vessels outfitting for service above the Niagara and well protected at Black Rock, and Brock regretted that Prevost's "repeated instructions to forebear" had prevented him from making a pre-emptive attack on Black Rock. Hearing the reports of his officers, Brock learned that the guns at Fort Erie and the four remote batteries had not proven very effective during the action and this he blamed on the shortage of Royal Artillery personnel.

The strength of the American force continued to grow after the capture of the *Caledonia* and *Detroit*. Lieutenant Colonel Thompson Mead's Seventeenth Regiment of Detached New York Militia, about 400 strong, marched into Black Rock on 9 October and continued on to Fort Schlosser two days later. The Sixteenth Detached Regiment, numbering about the same, under Lieutenant Colonel Farrand Stranahan, also made camp near Niagara Falls at that time and a 400-man detachment of the Thirteenth U.S. Infantry Regiment arrived on 9 October at Four Mile Creek in a flotilla of thirty-nine boats brimming with supplies from Oswego. Engineer Captain Joseph G. Totten had made his appearance by this time and was ordering refinements to the fortifications built during the summer. In addition, a number of independent militia companies, summoned by general order, made their appearance, including Captain Andrew Ellicott with his unit of artillery, Captain William Sutton and his Light Infantry, and Captain William Ireland with his son Ensign William, Junior, and sixty riflemen. At its peak, Stephen Van Rensselaer's army consisted of about 2,350 officers and men from the U.S. Army and 4,050 New York militiamen. Across the river, the British line comprised roughly 1,230 regulars, 810 militia and 300 warriors from the Grand River; originally totalling 500 when it had come to Niagara in September, the native force had dwindled as individuals returned to the Grand River for the autumn hunting season.[36]

The arrival of so many men added momentum to events already under way at Lewiston, and one of the councils held by Stephen Van Rensselaer made the quick decision to mount a raid against a battery on the lower river on 6 October. This came about as a result of information from a spy that Brock had gone to Detroit with a large detachment, but when this proved false the expedition was abruptly cancelled. The deliberations continued daily, the general inviting Alexander Smyth to attend with Major General Hall and the commanders of the individual regular and militia units at Black Rock, but Smyth would not budge. Hall discussed the invitation with him and reported back to Van Rensselaer that Smyth "could not tell the day when he would attend at Niagara."[37]

When news of the capture of the *Caledonia* and *Detroit* reached Lewiston, it "began to excite a strong disposition in the troops to act."[38] And the word was passed to Stephen Van Rensselaer that the men "must have orders to act, or at all hazards they would go home." During Saturday, 10 October, the scheme of making a diversion at Queenston while launching a full assault on Fort George was put aside and a new plan was formed. Van Rensselaer had heard that Queenston was weakly manned and that Brock did not expect an attack there, so the objective of his first strike would be "to dislodge the enemy from the heights of Queenstown."[39] By doing this, the general hoped to "possess ourselves of the village where the troops might be sheltered from the distressing inclemency of the weather."

Coincidentally, the plan for attacking Queenston closely resembled the operation Henry Dearborn outlined in a letter he wrote to the general on 13 October. Dearborn recommended seizing detached batteries, occupying a strong position between Forts George and Erie, controlling the river and cutting off part of the enemy force.[40] Neither Van Rensselaer nor his chief identified, however, what the operational goals would become once the army occupied Canadian territory. Dearborn had reminded Van Rensselaer late in September about the importance of "*possessing Upper Canada before winter sets in*" but how they intended to quickly seize the province from a beachhead at Queenston was completely unexplained.[41] It was as if they expected the pieces of the invasion plan to miraculously fall into place once they had planted a national standard on Queenston Heights.

From the outset, the regulars at Black Rock were intended to be part of the column that would advance into Canada, and to that end Van Rensselaer issued instructions to Smyth on 10 October. "Immediately on the receipt of this," the note delivered to Black Rock read, "you will please to give orders to all the United States troops under your command to strike their tents, and march, with every possible despatch, to this place."[42] He had given the go-ahead for an assault on Queenston that night, Van Rensselaer explained to Smyth, and if this was successful he intended to cross over the next day and establish a fortified position.

Express riders flew up and down the river with instructions.[43] Lieutenant Colonel Van Rensselaer was to command the militia while Lieutenant

Colonel Fenwick was to bring up his unit of Light Artillery, some of Captain Leonard's First Artillery, McKeon's Third Artillery and most of the Sixth, Thirteenth and Twenty-Third Infantry, who had been at the river since July. This sparked instant indignation in Major James Mullany. He had carried despatches to Black Rock on the day of Elliott's cutting-out expedition and had just returned to the fort, where he discovered Van Rensselaer had failed to name him in his orders; the Irish-born officer could only conceive this as an offence to his honour. "I was the first Field Officer, of the U.S. Army arrived on these lines," he reminded the general. "And might in justice expect to be employed on the first expedition."[44] Van Rensselaer assuaged Mullany's grievance by informing him in a note that Fenwick would soon have orders for him. Later, Mullany would recall that part of his outrage had been provoked by the thought that Solomon Van Rensselaer, "an uncommissioned officer," might command the infantry that night.[45]

Another officer also felt sharp disappointment. This was Lieutenant Colonel John Chrystie, whose five companies of the Thirteenth Infantry (operating separately from Myndert Dox's company of this regiment under Fenwick), numbering about 400, had just reached the Niagara. When he announced his arrival at Johnson's Landing on Four Mile Creek to Fenwick on Saturday and learned about the intended operation, Chrystie immediately volunteered his battalion. His men were "full of ardour, and anxious to give their country a proof of their patriotism," as Fenwick explained to Stephen Van Rensselaer.[46] The general sent his permission for Chrystie's Thirteenth to head to Lewiston, but the message was delayed and the battalion remained in camp and was thereby saved a gruesome experience in the dark.

The detachment from Fort Niagara was on the move after sundown. They marched along the new military road accompanied by two cavalrymen who rode ahead to warn sentries not to holler their challenges, in the hope that the British would not detect their expedition. This concern became redundant, however, for it began to rain, not in intermittent showers but "in torrents and was freezing cold."[47] The wind whipped the frontier and soaked it from Saturday evening until midnight Sunday, turning the deeply rutted roads to mud. It took hours for Fenwick's force to trudge the seven miles to the embarkation point.

Thirteen batteaux, twelve of them big enough to hold twenty-five or thirty men and one somewhat larger, had been carted overland from Fort Schlosser and apparently launched on Saturday evening at the Lewiston dock owned by Barton, Porter and Co. General Van Rensselaer and his staff selected Lieutenant John Simms, of Captain Rufus Spalding's company of New York militia, to bring the boats up to the embarkation point, at the old portage landing, but in the dark and the rain Simms lost his way and went too far up the river. Then he secured his boat on the bank of the river and mysteriously disappeared from the scene. That boat, somewhat unbelievably, was said to have carried most of the oars needed for the remainder of the batteaux, which other supposedly experienced boatmen managed to beach near the landing. The story lacks credibility, but it was the explanation given by Stephen Van Rensselaer and others for how confusion disrupted the expedition, delaying it until the sky had lightened enough for the British to see what the Americans were up to. At this point, Solomon Van Rensselaer cancelled the assault, leaving the sodden troops to tramp back to their camps and recover as they shivered in their soaking tents.[48]

Alexander Smyth's brigade never made it to Lewiston. The general received Stephen Van Rensselaer's order and obediently followed it, heading down-river by a route that was "so cut up that empty wagons were seen sticking in the road."[49] Then it started to rain and the raw troops plodded through the black of night, ankle deep in muck. "The badness of the weather and roads harassed the troops yesterday more than can well be conceived," Smyth later wrote.[50] It was not until 10:00 Sunday morning that an express reached the column with a note from Stephen Van Rensselaer explaining that the attack on Queenston had been postponed, at which point Smyth turned his men around and began the slog back to Black Rock. As the counter march meant another ten or twelve hours of misery and exhaustion, it is no surprise that Smyth did not write again to Van Rensselaer until Monday, 12 October. He alluded briefly to the ordeal his men had survived and, stating that he expected the uniforms for his unclothed regulars to arrive on 13 October, he explained that his men needed time to clean themselves and their camp after the bout of tempestuous weather. After a short rest, he would outfit them in their new uniforms and prepare them to meet the enemy. "Next day [14 October]," he informed Van Rensselaer, "they shall march, to the number of 1200 effective men, but imperfectly disciplined."[51] Smyth ended with a conviction that the new reinforcements (Chrystie's Thirteenth Infantry) would provide good support and he stated "the time for your attack is favourable – and may you conquer is my prayer."

PART THREE

# *The Battle, 13 October 1812*

*It was on the fifth night successively, that I had been on guard, and tolerably wearied, when the universal stillness that reigned around me, was disturbed by the report of two 18 pounders, fired from the Mountain on the American side, upon Queenston, which was immediately returned by a discharge of Artillery and small-arms from our side; the distance from Queenston to our station here, is about three miles; all were immediately under arms, and we waited impatiently for marching orders; during the interval, I went down to our battery from whence the view was truly tremendous, the darkness of the night, interrupted by the flash of the guns and small-arms, was a scene I am unable to give you an idea of.*

LIEUTENANT GEORGE RIDOUT,
3RD YORK MILITIA[1]

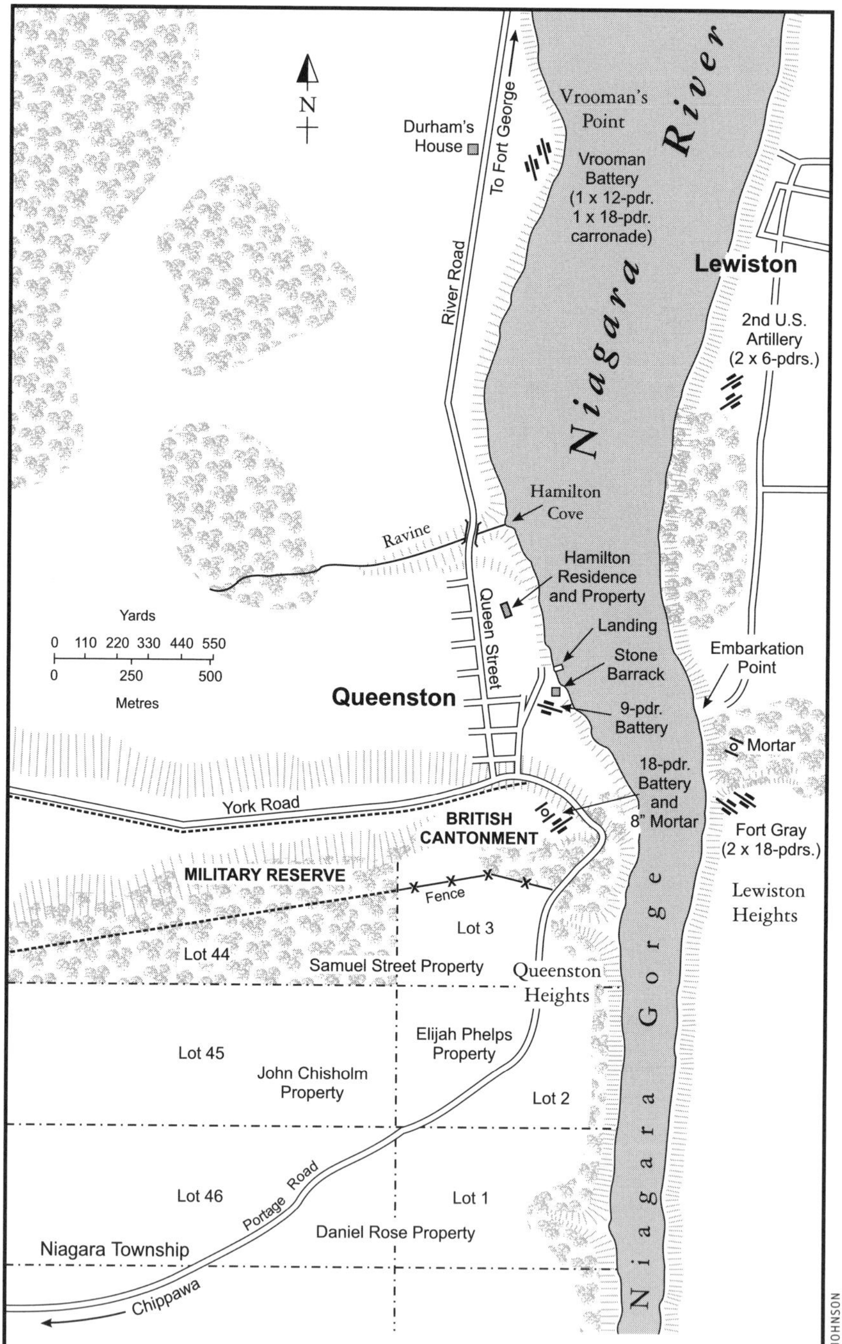


# Environs of Queenston Heights
## 13 October 1812

MAP: CHRISTOPHER JOHNSON

# 8

# "One incessant blaze from Musketry"

## LIEUTENANT COLONEL VAN RENSSELAER'S ATTACK

Isaac Brock and his entourage arrived at Queenston Heights on their rain-soaked ride from Fort Erie around noon on Sunday, 11 October. Here they were met by Captain John Williams with news of the failed American mission. Williams's light company of the 49th Foot, numbering about ninety officers and men, was stationed in the cantonment on the summit of the Heights. Sentries had detected the concentration of American troops near the ravine on the opposite shore and the captain informed Brock of this. Captain James Dennis, whose grenadier company, also ninety strong, was housed in the village below, probably rode up to meet Brock and an informal council took place as the officers scanned the American side with their telescopes from a vantage point at the edge of the escarpment.

Brock continued his muddy trek back to Niagara and wrote his despatches to Prevost. "I shall refrain as long as possible, under Your Excellency's positive injunctions," he assured the commander-in-chief, "from every hostile act, although sensitive that each days delay gives him [the enemy] an advantage."[1] The next morning Brock received information about the arrival of a thousand more men on the American side. He hurriedly penned a postscript to his despatch, predicting "an attack is not far distant," and for that reason he planned to activate all the available militia battalion companies. He ended with a hope of being able to "defy all their efforts against this part of the Province."

In the meantime a disturbing event had occurred at Queenston. The grenadiers, hunkered down out of the rain, got into liquor. At first this might have been a means to relieve their misery, but the drinking got out of hand and some of the company became boisterous and then mutinous and turned their frustrations upon their main accommodations, the old stone guard house on the landing. They tore up the insides of this building, "deliberately threatened to shoot their officers," and were only subdued by a firm resistance from Dennis and the remaining faithful in the company.[2] An express rider brought the news of the grenadiers' insurrection to Brock's headquarters at Government House later that evening. The general sent Major Thomas Evans up to Queenston to confer with Dennis and bring the worst of the culprits to Fort George for confinement. "I will make an example of them," Brock vowed.[3]

Evans reached the village early on Monday and met with Dennis at the Hamilton house, where the captain had his lodgings. Evans found the captain much distressed by the deplorable crisis in his sub-unit and Dennis agreed to parade a number of the guiltiest so they could be marched back to face the general. As the officers were leaving the house, musketry erupted on the opposite shore and a bullet zipped through the open door between them. When Evans jumped back in surprise, Dennis explained that the shooting had become so frequent as to make movement anywhere near the water dangerous. They left the house by the front door, and while Dennis went to muster his malcontents, Evans proceeded with the second part of his mission, which was to cross over to Lewiston and negotiate for the exchange of prisoners taken at Fort Erie on the previous Thursday night. The major, who had been across the river for one purpose or another several times, walked to the home of Thomas Dickson and asked for his assistance. Dickson's wife provided a white handkerchief, but warned that this would probably do no good. Holding the handkerchief aloft and taking Dickson by the hand, Evans walked down to the landing. Mrs. Dickson was right; while they launched a canoe and began to paddle across the treacherous river, bullets continued to whiz by until a loudly barked order stopped them. The two men reached the other side safely and tied up to the lower landing dock.

Major Evans was accustomed to being quickly escorted to Stephen Van Rensselaer's headquarters, but this morning affairs on the American side seemed disrupted. A guard, bayonet fixed and ready, instructed Evans to remain in the leaky canoe and to his formal request to see Solomon Van Rensselaer answered that the lieutenant colonel was ill and could not meet with him. The major asked to speak with someone else, and after a delay a man named Toock, who described himself as Major General Van Rensselaer's secretary, arrived. When Evans described the purpose of his visit, Toock (who might very well have been John Lovett, playing some misleading role) explained that nothing could be done for a couple of days at least. Evans insisted that his message be taken to the general and the secretary departed, leaving Dickson and him sitting in their canoe for two hours. When Toock returned with no change in policy, Evans decided to return to Queenston. To his eye, the American force "had been prodigiously swelled by a horde of half-savage troops from Kentucky, Ohio and Tennessee, which had evidently made it hazardous for their northern countrymen to show their accustomed respect."[4] And along the narrow beach near the landing he saw a line of batteaux drawn up and covered with brush.

When the major told Captain Dennis what he had seen, they decided that reducing the force by even half a dozen mutineers was dangerous. As a result, Dennis mustered the grenadiers and Evans addressed them, explaining why the prisoners would not be marched to Fort George that day and "appealing to them for proof of their loyalty and courage, which they were assured would be severely tested ere another day dawned."[5] Having received a pledge of loyalty from Dennis's company, the major then reviewed the defensive situation at the village with the captain, spoke with the militia officers on hand, and headed back to Niagara. Along the way, he stopped at the batteries at Vrooman's Point, Brown's Point and Two Mile House to alert the officers about the need for vigilance and finally reached Niagara after dark, exhausted from his long day.

The dining room at Government House was filled that evening. This seems to have been a customary occurrence; the previous Tuesday the senior officers had gathered there to celebrate Isaac Brock's forty-third birthday. Evans joined the group and described the situation at Queenston, speculating that Van Rensselaer would move quickly to gain what he had failed to achieve early Sunday morning. This was met with some good-hearted scepticism and bets were offered as to the depth of Van Rensselaer's boldness. Brock, however, went to his office with Evans to listen to the details in private and then returned to the dining room to instruct the officers that their units must be ready for immediate action. Riders from the Niagara Light Dragoons were soon in their saddles and spreading the word to the various militia commanders nearby. Just before midnight Brock and the others ended their gathering and went off to bed.[6]

After the failure of the planned assault in the early hours of Sunday, 11 October, the exhausted American troops returned to their camps expecting to have several days to recover from their unpleasant experience. Stephen Van Rensselaer also wanted to use the next few days to coordinate the larger attack he had described to Henry Dearborn five days earlier, namely a landing on the lake shore above Niagara of a formation of regulars preceded by a diversion thrown against Queenston by the militia.

But Stephen Van Rensselaer suddenly had run out of time. As the general later explained, "The previously excited ardour seemed to have gained new heat from the late miscarriage.... On the morning of the 12th, such was the pressure upon me from all quarters, that I became satisfied that my refusal to act might involve me in suspicion, and the service in disgrace."[7] Rather than wait for his men to recuperate, Rensselaer gave in to the clamour for action and ordered an attempt to be made again early on Tuesday, 13 October. Despite having received Smyth's note about the condition of his brigade, Van Rensselaer chose not to wait for the regulars to be available and informed Smyth that a new expedition was planned for that night and that he should await further orders. Where a more experienced field commander might have silenced those who demanded instant action and given his weary force the time it needed to assemble in good order, Van Rensselaer let urgent voices force his hand.

In the rush to undertake the attack Van Rensselaer and his council of officers failed to take into account a number of factors. For one, they paid no heed to the strategy of coordinating activities with those of either Brigadier General William Henry Harrison or Commodore Isaac Chauncey, which Dearborn continued to champion, impractical as this might have been. For this very reason Van Rensselaer may have overlooked Dearborn's directive, although in doing so he failed to follow orders. Of greater significance for the logistical success of the mission, Van Rensselaer did not use the days after the failed mission to bring more batteaux to Lewiston. In a letter written on 4 October (which Van Rensselaer might not have received by 12 October) Dearborn had advised the general to "have as many flat-bottomed Boats (and scows, if possible) as will be sufficient to transport Five thousand men, with field pieces and artillery horse at once."[8] The limit to the number of men that could be transported in thirteen batteaux, and the possibility that some of these craft might be lost under fire from the British artillery, caused Van Rensselaer and his staff little concern. Solomon Van Rensselaer played a key role in these decisions, as he had done throughout the campaign, and his belief was that "our boats were abundantly sufficient to have carried over our whole army ... before ten o'clock in the morning."[9] As a result of this decision, the thirty-nine batteaux that Chrystie's men had brought up from Oswego and dozens of craft that Peter Porter had built at Fort Schlosser remained idle through these hectic days.

Lieutenant Colonel Van Rensselaer, to whom the general had once more given command of the operation, was in and out of the camp all Monday. He went himself to Fort Niagara to discuss the attack with Fenwick, Mullany and Chrystie.[10] The first two were willing to participate, but they stated that their men were still recovering from the marches on Saturday and Sunday and that barely two thirds of them would be fit for service. Chrystie's infantry was raring to go into action, but their lieutenant colonel almost refused to participate. The sticking point was the fact that Chrystie could not, in all deference to his service, act in an inferior role to a militiaman, especially since his commission pre-dated Van Rensselaer's, making him the senior officer of the two. Van Rensselaer negotiated with him and at one point, according to a version of events that Chrystie gave later, offered him command of an attack on Chippawa; whether this was a hastily fashioned adjunct to the Queenston attack or a separate mission is unknown. After some discussion, the matter was settled with Chrystie agreeing "to take part without interfering with [Van Rensselaer's] arrangements for it," primarily because Chrystie admitted that he could hardly expect to lead an expedition in the dark on terrain he had never seen before.[11]

The decision to undertake another assault so soon after Saturday's disaster left John Chrystie shaking his head in dismay. He had gone to the Lewiston camp on Sunday to introduce himself to Stephen Van Rensselaer and to petition command of the next expedition, whereupon the general had told him not to expect anything to happen for ten or twelve days. Since the bad weather had passed, Chrystie issued instructions for the camp at the Four Mile Creek to be put in order, the tents struck and dried and all the firearms taken apart for cleaning. After speaking with Solomon, Chrystie returned to find his men in the middle of these tasks and still awaiting rations from Fort Niagara. They were hardly ready to march into action.

Chrystie called his captains together to explain the new situation.[12] The five of them, Henry Armstrong, William Lawrence, Richard Malcom, Peter Ogilvie and John Wool, had received their commissions in the spring and had recruited their companies in New York. Their commander was in his mid-thirties, a native of New York and a loyal Republican. He had joined the Sixth Infantry in 1808 as a lieutenant and had attained his captaincy before resigning this commission late in 1811 and resuming his studies in law. With the roll toward war suddenly gaining momentum over the next months, Chrystie changed his mind and sought a commission in the army. His offer, however, was not immediately taken up by Secretary of War Eustis even though there was a drastic shortage of officers to fill the vacancies in the new regiments. Chagrined by the secretary's apparent indifference, Chrystie sought assistance from several influential men. James Wilkinson, Chrystie's patron, wrote on his behalf to Eustis, and Albert Gallatin, the secretary of the treasury, made a strong plea for his nomination to the president himself, something Gallatin claimed he was not wont to do.[13] It was not surprising, then, that Chrystie was put into the Thirteenth, second only in command to its colonel, Peter Philip Schuyler, a regular veteran of fifteen years service.

The Thirteenth Infantry concentrated at Greenbush in July 1812 and trained there until sent to the Niagara frontier in mid-September.[14] Unlike the regiments under Smyth at Black Rock, the Thirteenth appears to have been outfitted properly, in arms, accoutrements and uniforms, wearing the regulation blue coats and white pantaloons. Chrystie's five companies formed what was termed the second battalion of the Thirteenth. The first battalion consisted of two incomplete companies and, under the command of Colonel Schuyler, reached Buffalo with Winfield Scott's artillery on 7 October; an eighth company, captained by Myndert Dox, had been at Fort Niagara since July.

Late in the afternoon of Monday, 12 October, Chrystie's detachment formed up in column and set out for Lewiston. He had told his captains to select their fittest troops since Solomon Van Rensselaer had stated that the whole battalion would not be needed. "After marching, or rather wading, by a new road through the woods," wrote Chrystie, "near[ly] 5 hours [I] reached Lewiston with 260 men most of whom rec'd their first meal of the day, but nothing for their haversacks."[15] Not long after, Major James Mullany arrived by the same route at the head of 240 men drawn from Captains John Machesney and George Nelson's Sixth Infantry companies, Myndert Dox's subunit of the Thirteenth under the command of Captain Hugh R. Martin of that regiment (Dox was carrying despatches to Dearborn at Albany and back) and Lieutenants William Clarke, John McCarty and Henry Whiting with a portion of the Twenty-Third Infantry.[16] The last of the regulars from Fort Niagara were about 110 artillery men under the command of Lieutenant Colonel Fenwick, who, it appears, though senior in rank to Solomon Van Rensselaer, also agreed to waive his right to command.[17] They included portions of Nathan Leonard's First Artillery (under Lieutenant John Gansevoort), James McKeon's Third Artillery (Lieutenant Robert M. Bayly) and the Light Artillery under Captain James Gibson.[18] The balance of the infantry and artillery units remained behind to garrison Fort Niagara and the Salt Battery at Youngstown; Van Rensselaer had instructed Captains Leonard and McKeon to open a bombardment on Fort George and the town of Niagara in support of the action at Queenston once it commenced.

The members of one more regular unit arrived at Lewiston later. These were Lieutenant Colonel Winfield Scott's two companies of the Second Artillery which had set out on the road from Black Rock on Sunday, 10 October, to join Van Rensselaer at Lewiston. Due to the horrid state of the route, Lieutenant Isaac Roach employed the two boats from the expedition against the *Caledonia* and *Detroit* to transport the field pieces by water to Fort Schlosser. He arrived on Monday morning, and after the men had remounted the guns, Scott heard a rumour of pending action and rode down to Lewiston to find out what was going on. He introduced himself to Stephen Van Rensselaer who informed Scott that an assault was about to be launched but that the plans had already been made and it was not possible to include him in the arrangements to cross. He did, however, give the lieutenant colonel permission to bring down his guns and support the landing, which Scott hastened to do, and well after midnight he led Towson and Barker's companies to take up a position with two guns near the dock in Lewiston, evidently thinking this to be the embarkation point.[19]

The general's orders also went to the militia, which probably numbered more than 3,000 strong at Lewiston by daybreak on Tuesday. The Eighteenth and Twentieth Regiments of Detached Militia were already encamped there while the Sixteenth, Seventeenth and the Nineteenth Detached Regiments marched down during Monday evening from their camps between Fort Schlosser and Manchester. Each of these regiments numbered about 400 officers and men, their strengths somewhat depleted by sickness and absence (explained and otherwise.) For instance, Hugh Dobbin was not present, since he had obtained leave to return home, and command of his regiment fell to Major John Morrison. Stranahan and Mead's units formed the Sixth Brigade of Detached Militia under Brigadier General Daniel Miller, who was also absent from Lewiston. William Wadsworth, "General Bill" as he was later called, commanded the Seventh Brigade composed of the other three detached regiments and, despite his admitted lack of military knowledge, was ready to do his duty and cross into Canada. Not so for Major General Amos Hall and Quartermaster General Peter Porter who, along with Nicholas Gray, the governor's special assistant, remained at Black Rock or Buffalo, obviously unwilling to participate in any expedition the Van Rensselaers had conceived. For these men, personal and political animosities prevailed over patriotism.

A number of independent militia companies were also on hand at Lewiston, loosely grouped under the command of Stephen Van Rensselaer, some of which probably came down from their camps at Manchester as the detached regiments had. The independents included riflemen under Major Charles Moseley and Captains William Ireland and Nathan Parke, artillery units under Captains Ellicott and John Pierce, and light infantry companies commanded by Captain William Sutton and Russel Nobels, as well as several troops of dragoons. No specific summons went to the approximately 600 militia at Black Rock and Buffalo, so Philetus Swift's regiment, which had been on the frontier since June, did not make the trek to Lewiston, nor did a number of other companies.[20]

As the militia tramped down to the assembly point the problem of supply threatened the expedition. Lieutenant Colonel Mead later wrote that his and Stranahan's units had virtually no ammunition and enough cartridge boxes for only half their men. This situation had more than just a practical effect on the militia rank and file. These regiments had finished their march to the frontier only days before and had crowded into dripping tents during the storm on the weekend. Mead told Stephen Van Rensselaer when they met at his headquarters that his men were worn out but that they would be ready for battle "if a day or two could be given for the soldiers to recruit, be furnished with ammunition and regain their spirits."[21] The general answered angrily that the mission would go forward as planned and that Mead should return at midnight for ammunition. This the lieutenant colonel did, but found no cartridges and no one with authority to explain where to find them. He then spent an hour searching for an officer who could help him, finally encountering Quartermaster Major Henry Wells who was supposed to be in charge of distributing the ammunition. There was none on hand, Wells told Mead, but assured him that a wagon was en route to an arsenal on Lewiston Heights and that full cartridge boxes would arrive in time for the attack. Here, as with the failure to provide sufficient batteaux, was another weakness in the logistical preparation for the operation against Queenston. How were troops, already miserable from the weather conditions, supposed to be willing to risk their lives in battle when the supply of such an essential as ammunition seemed so tenuous?

No one got much sleep at Lewiston that night while the hurried preparations continued. Solomon Van Rensselaer, still suffering the lingering effects of his recent illness, did not take time to write his wife a farewell letter. He had already done that two nights before when he had expected to be fighting the British in Queenston within hours. "My Enterprise this night will shorten our separation," he had assured Arriet, "if I survive I shall soon be with you, how pleasing the Idea and how Happy will be that moment."[22] He had finally received a letter from her five days before and though it mentioned only the hardships she suffered at home and how her "poor afflicted heart" still ached from the loss of their murdered son (made worse by his father's sudden departure, she noted), Solomon found some relief.[23] "The happiness I experienced at seeing your hand writing for the first time since I left home is beyond any power of mine to express," he wrote.[24] Now, with the battle fast approaching, Solomon Van Rensselaer did not take up his quill to record his thoughts. It would be more than a week before he received a letter from a friend with the news that on 12 October Arriet gave birth to "a fine young *Son*, large, fat and regular in all his limbs and features.... the image of your unfortunate son Van Vechten."[25] His mother named him Stephen; he survived less than a year.

Around 3:30 a.m. on Tuesday, 13 October, Lieutenant Colonel Van Rensselaer arrived at the spot where the Thirteenth Infantry had bedded down to wake Lieutenant Colonel Chrystie, who summoned his officers and read them their instructions. The plan was that the first wave of batteaux would carry 40 artillerymen, 150 militia and 150 of Chrystie's detachment. Lieutenant Colonel Fenwick would command the second wave with the rest of the Thirteenth and some of the detachment from Fort Niagara. Mullany would follow in the next wave with the remaining regulars and after that would come the rest of the militia. Chrystie formed his men for marching and, following a guide through the dark across the unfamiliar ground, headed for the river.

The embarkation point was the old portage landing at the foot of the ravine nearly a mile south of the hamlet of Lewiston. Solomon Van Rensselaer was already there and had seen the artillery detachment, under Lieutenants Gansevoort and Rathbone, into the largest of the batteaux. But from that point the loading went awry. No one had delegated an officer to marshal the detachments in a staging area and then send them to the boats in the prescribed order. As a result, Chrystie led all his companies down to the water, where they began to file into the batteaux with no obvious intention to leave room for the militia. Van Rensselaer wrote, "In this emergency it became necessary either to countermarch part of this force, a movement which we apprehended might arouse the attention of the enemy, or to fill the boats with regular troops in the first place, to the partial exclusion of the militia."[26] Choosing to leave the regulars where they were, Van Rensselaer hurriedly told Major John Morrison to bring over the 150 militia in the second wave. "I first walked along the line to see that all were ready, and finding they were so, leaped into the one containing the picked artillerists, and gave the word to push off."

In the pitch black of a moonless night, thirteen boats, carrying about 300 men, struck out to grapple with the eddies of the lower Niagara River and carry the war once more into Canada.

Queenston. Tuesday, 13 October 1812. 4:00 a.m. The scrim of night still hung over the village, the hill, the river, the opposite banks. It was windy, "one of those cold, stormy days that at this season of the year so strongly ... mark the changes of the season," as Captain James Crooks of the 1st Lincoln Militia described it.[27]

On the river, the Canadian shore stood like a shapeless wall against the slate-shaded clouds. Only an experienced boatman, familiar with the contours of the banks, could have found the prescribed landing place on such a night, all the while straining to dig his steering oar deep into the water to guide the heavily burdened batteau across the strong current of the lower Niagara. The Americans had selected a spot about 500 yards upstream of the Queenston landing. Here a narrow beach of broken sandstone and shale lay at the base of a steep bank rising forty feet above the water. The river curved at this point as it exited from the gorge and the beach was not wholly visible from the landing or the village even during the day, but it was a difficult spot to reach, since the current propelled boats downstream. There was, however, a back-current flowing up the Canadian side, and once the batteaux neared the shore, the steersman's work became easier as the river helped him to bring the troops to land.

About ten minutes after leaving the American shore, the first of the batteaux drove into the gravel of the beach, bumping against the rocks and tree limbs that erosion had tumbled down to the water's edge. Awkwardly, the men moved forward as quickly as they could to leap onto dry land without upsetting the boats. There was little space along the river's edge and it was soon crowded with scores of wide-eyed troops waiting for orders, expecting a counter attack. After they emptied, the boats pulled from the congested beach, taking the wounded and dead away.

Already the Americans had suffered casualties. Captain Wool remembered that "the guard stationed on the Bank discovered us and fired into our boats before we reached the shore, but fled on our landing."[28] There was a pause in this first exchange, but too late for Lieutenant John Valleau of Captain Richard Malcom's Thirteenth Infantry company, who had been killed outright, and for the uncounted others who lay bleeding in the boats.[29] Just offshore the Niagara was a mass of surges and transient whirlpools which grabbed the batteaux as they pulled away and whisked them down toward the embarkation point again.

"As soon as we left the boats we ascended the bank," wrote Wool. The lofty bank was blood red with flakes of shale and sandstone and covered in a tangle of trees, scrub, vines and brambles. The men struggled upward, slipping in the mud, grasping for handholds in the foliage and outcrops. Here and there eroded waterways incised the bank and some of the men filed upward this way, though the footing was treacherous and the jagged layers of bared rock tore their clothing. Valuable minutes were lost while the Thirteenth Infantry and the miscellaneous artillerymen struggled to the top of the bank, where their corporals and sergeants hurriedly pushed them into their ranks. They found themselves on a terrace below the shoulder of the escarpment and overlooking the landing; the lights of the village glimmered obliquely to their right.

The batteaux straggled to the landing place with Solomon Van Rensselaer impatiently waiting in one of the last to gain the beach. Already about 225 infantrymen had made it to shore and Captain Wool had taken charge, as he recalled:

**Queenston docks and Heights, 1915**

The old landing at Queenston was a thriving ferry dock in the early 1900s. This view, facing south, shows the little-altered shoreline between the dock and the point of land where the first wave of American invaders landed. The Thirteenth U.S. Infantry under Captain Wool advanced along the base of the escarpment, where a road was constructed in the 1850s to access a bridge across the Niagara River. (Niagara Falls Review Archives, care of the Niagara Historical Society Museum, NFR NF.26)

> [We] formed line fronting the heights. Being the senior officer in the absence of Lt. Col. Chrystie I took command of the detachment. At this moment judge Advocate [Major Stephen] Lush arrived and informed me of the landing of Colonel Van Rensselaer and his party, with orders from the Colonel to "prepare for storming Queenstown Heights." I informed him we were ready. In a few minutes he returned with an order to march. We proceeded a few rods when I received an order to halt. This was at the foot or base of the Heights – our right extending toward the Village of Queenstown.[30]

As they ran from the bank the British sentries spread the alarm, rousing the others on guard and the off-duty men who had lately been required to sleep in full kit. On the landing and in the village sergeants bawled orders for the men to form into platoons of regulars and militia.[31] Captain Dennis ran down from the Hamilton house trying to make out the location and size of the invading force as much as that was possible. In all, he commanded a force of nearly 420 this morning. The two regular companies comprised ninety officers and men each and they were supported by the two flank companies of the 5th Lincoln Militia under Captains Samuel Hatt and James Durand. These sub-units numbered up to eighty men each when fully mustered, but a rotation system appears to have been in effect that allowed one third of the local militia at a time to return to their homes; so the Lincolns probably added 100 more men to Dennis's line. Captain John Chisholm's flankers from the 2nd York Regiment were also on hand and brought forty men to the fight, as did William Applegarth's company from the same regiment. Many of the militia wore civilian clothing but some of them had cast-off uniforms from the regulars, making Dennis's force look stronger than it was, as Brock's brigade had at Detroit.[32] In addition to the infantry, some of the 1st Lincoln Artillery Company, nominally about forty-strong and commanded this morning by Lieutenant John Ball, were present to serve the artillery in the redan battery and the village. They were directed by six members of the Royal Artillery, with Sergeant Thomas Edlerton, at the redan battery, in charge. Lastly, a handful of men from the 41st Foot were also present in the village, among "the engineers employed at Queenston," as an officer in that regiment later revealed.[33]

Dennis peered into the pitch black of the night but from the landing there was little to see except for three batteaux heading downstream and when these were spotted the British opened fire, the flashes of musketry reflecting off clouds of dust-coloured smoke. On the lip of the Heights Captain John Williams's light company was peering into the night also and directing volleys down into the void. The 18-pdr. and the mortar in the redan battery on the hillside roared like thunder, as did a 12-pdr. gun and an 18-pdr. carronade nearly 2,000 yards downstream at Vrooman's Point, though without much effect at that great distance. On the landing itself a 9-pdr. mounted on a garrison carriage near the stone guardhouse was quickly discharging its shot into the dark.

To John Lovett, standing in Fort Gray atop Lewiston Heights, the scene below was frightening. "The shore was one incessant blaze from Musketry," he remembered, "three batteries pelted upon the Boats."[34] Stephen Van Rensselaer was there with Lovett, watching the enterprise. Though Lovett was in command of the two 18-pdrs., it was the general who directed the first shot from Fort Gray. These guns were supposed to support the landing by engaging the opposing batteries and firing into the masses of defending troops, but in the darkness Lovett feared that he might target his own men, so he gratefully allowed the general to take that responsibility until the sky began to lighten.

Although he never described his exact plan of action, Solomon Van Rensselaer appears to have intended to storm the redan battery by advancing up Portage Road or the slope at the rear of the battery. To this end, Wool had formed his men into a column and moved forward and was halted in line on the terrace at the base of the escarpment. "Whilst thus waiting further orders," Wool explained, "the detachment was attacked on its right by a party of British from the Village of Queenstown."[35]

James Dennis was not able to concentrate his force in one line of battle to oppose Van Rensselaer; Williams's light company was at, and above, the redan batttery while the main body of troops was in the village and on the landing. Even this latter division could not be brought to one point, since Dennis wisely detached a portion of it to guard the northern flank of the village at Hamilton Cove, where there was a wharf. This left Dennis to send the remainder of his troops in two groups to confront the enemy, one from the direction of the village and the other from the landing.

At the head of the American column, Wool immediately faced his men

**Captain John E. Wool, Thirteenth U.S. Regiment of Infantry (1784-1869)**
Born in Newburgh, New York, Wool went to work at twelve years of age for a merchant in Troy. He left the study of law to join the U.S. Army, rising to prominence after the War of 1812. Wool is shown here in the uniform of a major general, a rank to which he was breveted for distinguished conduct in 1847 during the Mexican War. (Engraving by Alonzo Chappel, 1858, courtesy of the Anne S.K. Brown Collection, Brown University)

around and ordered them to fire. In the American captain's words, it was "a short and severe contest." His men had their backs to the escarpment with the British advancing in their front and musket balls raining down on them from above when the light company could identify the column's location. At least they were immune to the power of the 18-pdr. in the redan battery, as they had been in its dead ground after touching land, and the other guns were not directed at them now, since they focused their fire on the river.

The fighting was furious and no sooner had it started when Wool was hit; "shot directly through both hips," as he later explained to his wife, although it was also reported that a ball deeply scored his buttocks causing him to bleed so heavily that the blood soon squelched in his shoes.[36] The shock of the wound made Wool dizzy and he stumbled to the ground, briefly leaving his company in the hands of Lieutenant Stephen Kearney. In the first skirmish Captains Malcom and Armstrong both received wounds serious enough to knock them out of the fight, as did Ensign James Lent. Ensign Robert Morris of the Thirteenth and Lieutenant Samuel Rathbone of the First Artillery were also hit; Morris died on the field while Rathbone lingered for two months. Of casualties suffered by the rank and file, little can be ascertained; the First Artillery had three men killed and three wounded at Queenston, some of whom probably fell during this stage of the battle. It is safe to speculate, however, that the casualties taken by the rank and file were not equal in proportion to those inflicted among their officers. Of about eleven commissioned regular officers in Van Rensselaer's wave, seven were killed or wounded during the first hour of the engagement.

And the most significant casualty of this phase of the battle was Solomon Van Rensselaer himself. As with Wool, the firefight had barely begun when the lieutenant colonel was wounded and then hit again and again, in his thighs, his calves, his heel, until he could barely stand, his white pantaloons splotched with blood. He asked his aide, Major Stephen Lush, for the loan of his greatcoat so he could cover the wounds from the men and then, realizing his plight, sent Lush to find Lieutenant Colonel Chrystie. The leader of the American attack knew that he could not maintain his command for much longer.

The British ranks also thinned during the firefight on the terrace, though not as drastically as the Americans. James Dennis might have received his wound at this time, although it did not stop him from remaining in command.[37] His grenadiers had eight killed and thirty-three wounded during the day, some of whom certainly fell in the early going. The Lincoln Regiment also suffered a portion of its fourteen casualties at this time. So sharp and effective was the resistance of the American force that the British line wilted and then fell back towards cover.

To Solomon Van Rensselaer's eye, the British got the worst of this initial exchange; he claimed that after a "severe engagement … with heavy loss on both sides … we were victorious, and the enemy gave way, and fled towards Queenstown, on our right."[38] Wool remembered it nearly the same way: "The enemy was repulsed.… Shortly after the enemy had retreated Judge Advocate Lush came and informed me that Colonel Van Rensselaer was mortally wounded, with orders from the Colonel to retire with the troops to the shore."[39]

Thus, the first exchange ended, with the British pulling back toward the village. The light was still dim. Van Rensselaer knew that the extent of his wounds would soon incapacitate if not kill him and, with Lieutenant Colonel Chrystie apparently nowhere in sight, he ordered the majority of his men to descend the bank to the beach, where they could recuperate and wait for Chrystie to arrive, if and when he did.

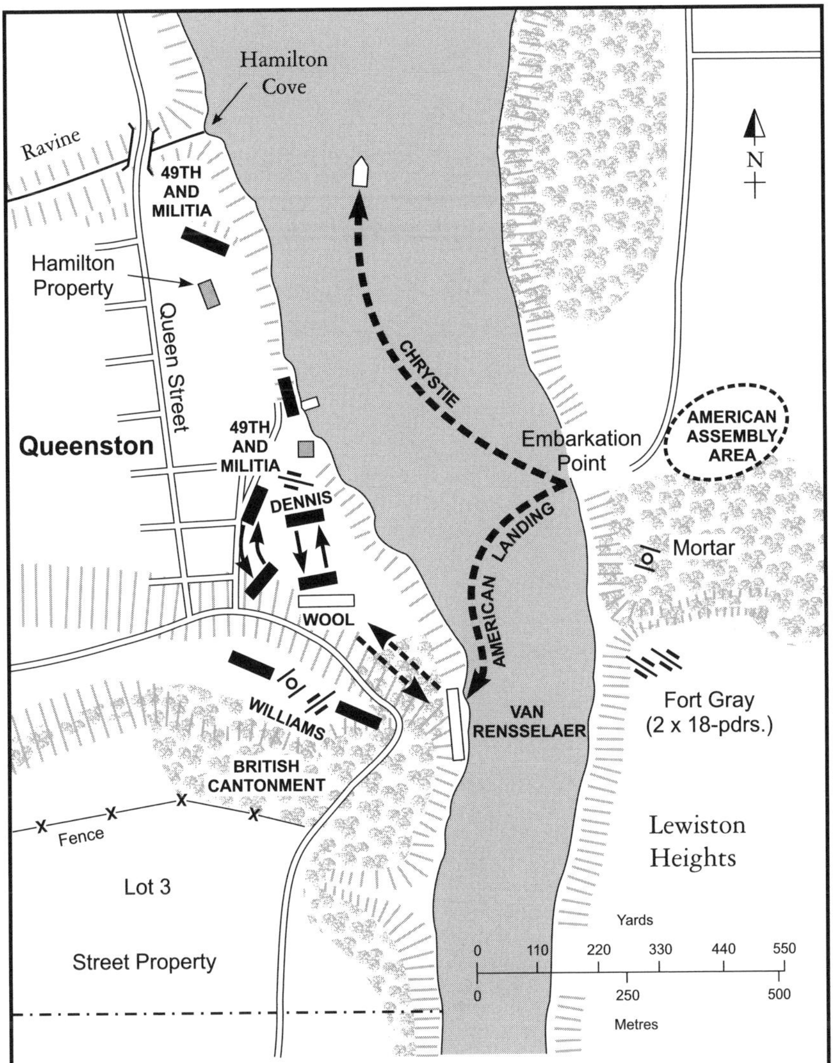


## Queenston Heights – 13 October 1812
### 1st Phase: c. 4:00 AM – 5:30 AM

1. The Americans land and Wool advances.
2. Regulars and militia under Dennis and Williams attack the American column.
3. Lieutenant Colonel Chrystie misses the landing point and returns to the American shore.
4. After a sharp fight, Dennis withdraws to the village and the Americans fall back to their landing point.

# 9

# "Are you much hurt, Sir?"

## MAJOR GENERAL BROCK'S LAST COMMAND

Instead of landing on the Canadian shore with the others, Lieutenant Colonel John Chrystie found himself a frustrated spectator. With Lieutenant John Fink at his side, he had climbed into a batteau at the downstream end of the line of boats and shoved off. From there everything went wrong. A rowlock broke on the right side and the boat veered downstream despite Fink's efforts to hold the unbound oar in place. The current seized the batteau and the pilot seemed incapable of turning it upstream in the wake of the other craft, obviously dumbfounded by the darkness and the riskiness of the job for which he had volunteered. To Chrystie's mortification, the boat soon came under fire from a party of British on the bank at the northern end of Queenston above Hamilton Cove. The helmsman turned away from this attack but Chrystie ordered him to land on the Canadian shore. After making an effort to comply and "*literally* groaning with fear," the pilot disobeyed the order and leaned on his steering oar to turn the batteau toward safety.[1] Chrystie appealed to a man named Hopkins who had been sent to guide the boat ashore, but when even he could do nothing, Chrystie, who by then had received a bullet wound in his right hand, gave up in his efforts to follow the main body of invaders, grabbed the steering oar and directed the craft back to the American shore. Two other batteaux were off course and Chrystie shouted for them to follow him to the east bank. Once there, Chrystie left the craft for the others to haul back to the embarkation point, and hurried up the shore. When he reached the foot of the ravine he found "a scene of confusion hardly to be described."[2]

The British had identified the embarkation point and were pouring shot and shell into the ravine. This narrow gap was crowded with the men of Lieutenant Colonel Fenwick and Major Mullany's detachments, but, as Chrystie stated, "no person being charged with directing the boats and embarkation or with the government of the boatmen, they forsook their duties."[3] This logistical oversight led to a free-for-all, with groups of men rushing forward into any batteau that returned with wounded and dead. As a result no organized second, third and fourth wave of regulars, followed by militia, crossed the river to reinforce the first landing at Queenston as originally intended and the operation's order began to dissolve.

Amid the confusion at the river's edge, Fenwick agonized to watch 18-pdr. shot cut swaths through his ranks while the shrapnel of spherical case (which many Americans erroneously identified as grape shot) sliced others up. He ordered his men to ascend the ravine and seek cover among the trees that still covered portions of the bank, but this order came too late for Captain George Nelson, who had just faced his Sixth Infantry company about when the explosion of a shell killed him.

The operation was barely an hour and a half old and it seemed already to have run amok. But not everything was in disarray. Up in Fort Gray, Lovett had covered the first wave of invaders resting below the opposite bank. "My Battery pelted alternately upon the Batteries, and upon Musketry on shore," he recalled, "while a snug little mortar near by complimented my battery liberally with shells."[4] This mortar appears to have been located near the embarkation point although who commanded it – either Captain James Gibson's Light Artillery or one of the New York militia artillery companies – is uncertain. "I directed both 18-Pounders against [the battery at the Queenston landing]," wrote Lovett, "we raked them severely; and at the eighth shot tumbled up a heap of men and I believe dismounted the Gun." This is probably the shot that severely wounded Gunner Henry Hunt, tore the leg off Gunner Robert Granger and killed Gunner William Birchell, thereby reducing half of the Royal Artillery detachment at Queenston. It also removed from the equation the spherical case and round shot that the 9-pdr. had been directing against the American embarkation place, and when Lieutenant Colonel Fenwick noticed this, he ordered his men down into the ravine again to find boats and row across.

How many batteaux remained in commission at this point is guesswork although some of them had made a return trip in good order, bringing over Captain Peter Ogilvie and the remainder of the Thirteenth who had not gone with the first wave. They found their comrades nursing their wounds and awaiting an assault by the British. By this time, Solomon Van Rensselaer had been laid in as comfortable a spot as the shaley beach would afford and he had given up hope of passing command to Lieutenant Colonel Chrystie. Captain Wool was still on his feet despite his painful wound and approached Solomon to ask what could be done. "He replied he did not know," wrote Wool. "I remarked that some thing must be done soon or we would all be taken prisoners. His reply was that he knew of nothing unless we could take Queenston heights."[5]

Solomon's recollection of the final order he gave on Canadian soil was that he put his faith in a group of "very young men, the highest of whom in rank were only captains, not six months in service."[6] To Wool and Peter Ogilvie he gave instructions to form up a detachment of the troops, head upstream along the beach "and ascend the heights by the point of the rock, and storm the battery." Wool and Ogilvie knew nothing of the topography, having never seen this part of the river before this morning, so Van Rensselaer instructed Lieutenant John Gansevoort, who had been posted with Nathan Leonard's First Artillery at Fort Niagara for some time, to guide the column. The detachment set out, numbering about 160, with Van Rensselaer's aide Major Lush bringing up the rear; his orders were "to shoot down the first man who offered to give way."

With the detachment gone, Solomon Van Rensselaer lay back. He listened to the booming of the opposing batteries, the rending of the air as the shot flew overhead and the crack of shells exploding. The river gurgled at his feet. The remaining troops muttered softly nearby. He had time to think about having finally succeeded in carrying the war into Canada, but now the fight was over for him. All he could do was wait and see what would happen next.

About this time Isaac Brock arrived in Queenston. The manner in which the general had learned of the American attack is unclear. Thomas Evans wrote that he was awakened by the sound of a distant cannonade as Brock was just leaving Government House and it has often been assumed that Brock's sleep was disturbed in the same way. But John Norton, in camp nearby with the Grand River peoples, remembered, "A firing was heard from Queenstown, although barely distinguishable from the high Wind blowing."[7] James Crooks referred to the effects of the wind also, noting that "so strong was the gale off the Lake.... [that] little was known of what had been going on at Queenston in the night."[8] Lieutenant Hamilton Merritt and Alexander Hamilton, captain of the dragoons, slumbered soundly in town also and did not stir until the guns at Fort Niagara opened up around dawn. Perhaps a rider brought the news to Government House (as Merritt claimed).

Whether awakened by the sound of battle or the message of a hard-riding dragoon, Brock rose before anyone else, dressed quickly with the assistance of his servant Thomas Porter and walked out of Government House into the chilly morning, leaving orders for Glegg and Macdonell to be roused out of bed and to follow him. He gave no specific orders for anyone else and did not take time to consult with Major General Sheaffe about what might be going on or the steps to be taken at Niagara in his absence. Evans claimed that "the impression on General Brock's mind ... [was] that the attempt on Queenston would prove only a feint to disguise his (the enemy's) real object from the creek in the rear of Fort Niagara."[9] Why he did not send Sheaffe, or one of his aides, to Queenston to assess the situation when he was expecting a larger attack on Fort George is a mystery. Perhaps he figured he could ride up to Queenston and get back to Niagara before anything more important could happen there, but the round trip alone, especially considering the con-

**Lieutenant William Hamilton Merritt, Niagara Light Dragoons (1793-1862)**
Following the war Merritt undertook a number of commercial enterprises which prompted him to propose the building of a canal to link Lakes Erie and Ontario. His interest in the development of the Welland Canal expanded to railways, bridges and politics, making him one of the most influential men in Canada during the first half of the 19th century. He is shown here in old age. (National Archives of Canada, C-29891)

dition of the road, would take more than two hours. A lot could happen at the town while he was absent. Still, Brock was a man of action who preferred to appraise things for himself rather than listen to a report and it must have been this trait that prompted him to climb into his saddle.

So away he galloped. And along River Road he unwittingly acquired a couple of legendary anecdotes that would be attached to his name nearly as often as the tales of his many accomplishments were repeated. The first concerned his horse, the famous Alfred, the subject of sculptors and poets alike. Some of Brock's biographers pictured him climbing into Alfred's saddle to make his ride to Queenston, but there is no documentary evidence to show that this was so. Sir James Craig, Prevost's predecessor, had owned a favourite mount named Alfred, said to be "ten years old, but being a high bred horse, and latterly but very little worked, ... still perfectly fresh."[10] When Craig decided that his poor health required him to return to England in the spring of 1811, he stated his desire for Brock to take ownership of Alfred. But whether Brock ever had the horse shipped to Upper Canada is not proven, nor is it likely that there would be only one horse in the government stable reserved for the general's use. As a result, Alfred's claim to being Brock's steed during the heroic ride to Queenston is questionable.

Another oft-repeated story is that Brock stopped at the home of Captain John Powell to bid "Good morning" to his fiancée Sophie Shaw (a daughter of Æneas Shaw, an influential citizen of York and the major general commanding the First and Second Divisions of troops on the Niagara River). This anecdote, as popularized by biographer Walter Nursey, had the twenty-year-old Sophie visiting her sister, who was Powell's wife, at their home off River Road.[11] Nursey depicted Brock stopping at the house, nearly four miles from Niagara, and being greeted by the amiable young miss with a cup of steaming coffee ready for him. This was the "stirrup" cup, as Brock did not leave the saddle, but drank up quickly before bidding his fair love *adieu* and charging off to his destiny. Once again, nothing beyond hearsay seems to confirm the "arrangement" between Brock and Sophie. The general's aide, John Glegg, later attested to being "intimately acquainted" with Brock's "sentiments on the most private subjects," and yet never alluded to Sophie Shaw's connection to his friend.[12] Not surprisingly, the story has been taken up by few of Brock's biographers, although it is still popular in oral histories.

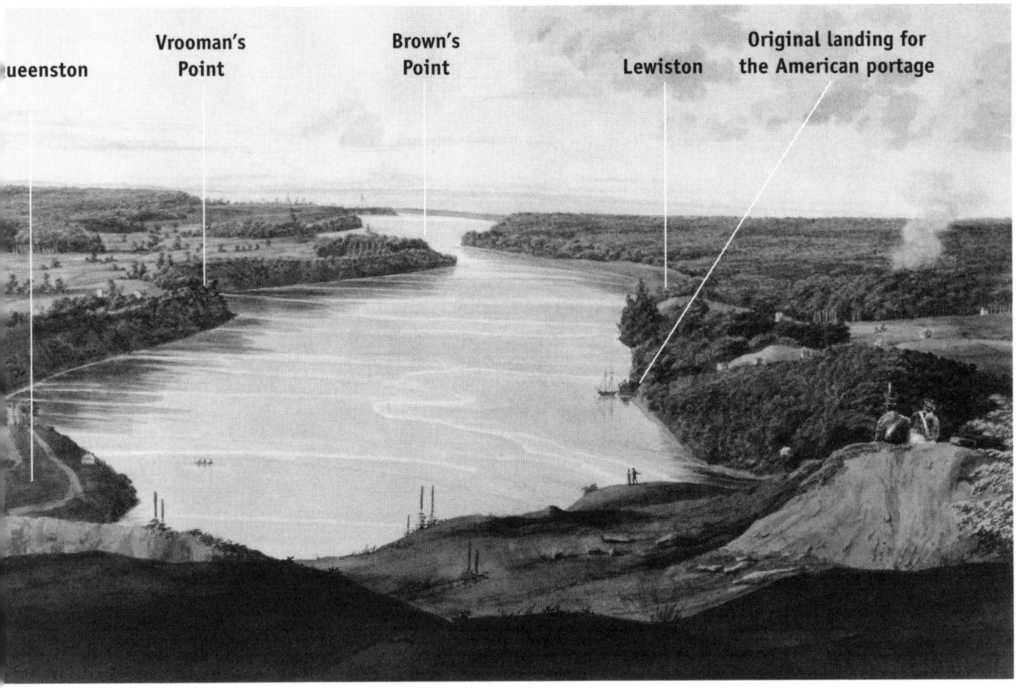


**Niagara River from Queenston Heights, ca. 1818-23**
Although the artist exaggerated the height of the bluffs on the British shores of the Niagara River as it winds down to Lake Ontario, he provided an image of how the American side of the river was still heavily forested after the War of 1812. As other views confirm, the slopes of Queenston Heights were nearly devoid of vegetation. A schooner is moored at the old lower landing where the Americans embarked for their attack on Queenston. (Watercolour by Thomas Smith, courtesy of the William L. Clements Library)

In reality, Brock's ride to Queenston must have been an exhausting ordeal, seven miles over a rain-ruined road in dim light. Though he no doubt pushed his horse as hard as he could, the general had to be mindful of its footing as they navigated the puddles and ruts, the quagmires of hock-deep muck. There were twists in the route, bridges over the deeper ravines and hollows to descend and then climb out of. He probably reined his horse off the main road at Two Mile House, the McCormick dwelling, to take a look toward Queenston from the battery there. After he viewed the fireworks up-river, Brock's ride became more urgent and when he reached the next batteries he barely slowed down to gather news or give orders.

A portion of the two flank companies of the 3rd York Militia was encamped at Brown's Point serving a 9-pdr. long gun on a garrison carriage and an 18-pdr. carronade mounted on a sliding naval-type carriage. Their captains, Duncan Cameron and Stephen Heward, had received no specific orders about what to do in the event of an attack at Queenston, so they watched and listened to the action going on less than three miles from their battery. One of Heward's lieutenants was John Beverley Robinson, a twenty-one-year-old son of a Virginian loyalist, who had been born in Lower Canada, educated at John Strachan's school and trained in the profession of law, as his friend John Macdonell had been. Robinson wrote of his experiences on 13 October and how the action began: "Day was just glimmering. The cannon from both sides of the river roared incessantly. Queenston was illuminated by the continual discharge of small arms."[13]

Cameron and Heward reasoned at first that they should keep their people at Brown's in case the Americans decided to attack that place also, but after some deliberation over the apparent severity of the fighting, they decided that a detachment should head for Queenston. Cameron rounded up thirty men and just as they got to the edge of River Road Brock came into sight "in great haste, unaccompanied by his aide-de-camp or a single attendant. He waved his hand to us, and desired us to follow with expedition, and galloped on with full speed to the mountain."[14] It might have been at

**Lieutenant John Beverley Robinson, 3rd York Militia (1791-1863)**
Robinson was among militia volunteers with Brock at Detroit in August 1812. "My short experience of soldiering was uncommonly lucky," he later wrote, "for the fort being full of stores of all kinds, my share of prize-money ... came to £90 and upwards."[9] Robinson is shown here in later life, (Print by Alfred Sandham, 1902, National Archives of Canada, C-111481)

**View of Queenston and Lewiston Heights from Brown's Point, ca 1836-42**
This landscape shows the Niagara River widening as it exits the gorge between the opposing heights. Lieutenant John Beverley Robinson initially viewed the battle from this vantage point. The first monument dedicated to Brock is shown here standing where the British cantonment was located in the copse of oak trees. (Watercolour by Philip John Bainbrigge, National Archives of Canada, C-11831)

this point that Brock called out his frequently quoted line: "Push on the brave York volunteers."[15] Macdonell and Glegg soon passed Robinson and the others, without taking a moment to slow their pace.

A few minutes later Brock arrived at Vrooman's Point and stopped briefly at the battery. Lieutenant Archibald McLean of Duncan Cameron's York Militia commanded the 18-pdr. carronade situated on the left of the 12-pdr. long gun and the stern-faced general called out to him, "Why don't you fire that gun?"[16] McLean, a friend of Robinson's and, like him, a twenty-one-year-old lawyer at York, hurriedly explained to Brock that they had stopped using the carronade because its shot all fell short. "It can't be helped," Brock confessed, and, as McLean remembered many years later, he "put his spurs to his horse and galloped away for Queenston. Soon after his ADCs Macdonell and Glegg came up as fast as their horses could carry them, and soon after them my companions of York Militia came trotting up from Brown's Point." The lieutenant asked Captain Cameron if he could join them but, much to his vexation, was told to stay where he was. A few minutes later John Robinson came running back down the road with orders for the remaining York militia at Brown's Point to cease firing. They had opened on a troop of dragoons across the river, which Cameron was afraid would lead the defenders at Queenston to conclude that the Americans were also landing further down the river also and redeploy their force to meet them. When Robinson approached Vrooman's Point on his return trip, McLean decided it was time to forget his orders and join his friend. "We made what speed we could," he recalled.

Brock's muddy ride probably took him an hour or more to complete and by the time he arrived in Queenston daylight was slowly spreading, so it must have been just before dawn broke at approximately 6:30 a.m. Solomon Van Rensselaer lay wounded on the narrow, rocky beach out of sight 500 yards to the south of the village. Lieutenant John Gansevoort was leading a detachment further south along the river's edge searching for a pathway up the face of the gorge in order to outflank the redan battery. Major Lovett's battery in Fort Gray had put the 9-pdr. battery in the village out of action, taking some of the pressure off the American embarkation place opposite Queenston, so down to the river filed a detachment of regular troops under Lieutenant Colonel Fenwick to board several boats that had returned from the Canadian side.

The Americans, rowing and piloting themselves, set out across the Niagara and, caught in the current, followed the same misdirected course that Lieutenant Colonel Chrystie had taken earlier, their bows aimed at Hamilton Cove. Four boats were said to be in this wave and another one or two might already have landed at the mouth of the creek just below the Hamilton house. There is a possibility that Fenwick deliberately took this course in order to relieve Van Rensselaer's force collected in the shelter of the bank upriver. Whether accidental or by design, Fenwick's imminent attack on the north of the village was perceived as a grave threat to the British defences in the village. The first exchange had weakened this force and to reinforce it Brock or Captain Dennis ordered a bugler to call Captain Williams's light company down off the summit of the escarpment, leaving the south flank completely uncovered. In this chain of events can be seen one of the

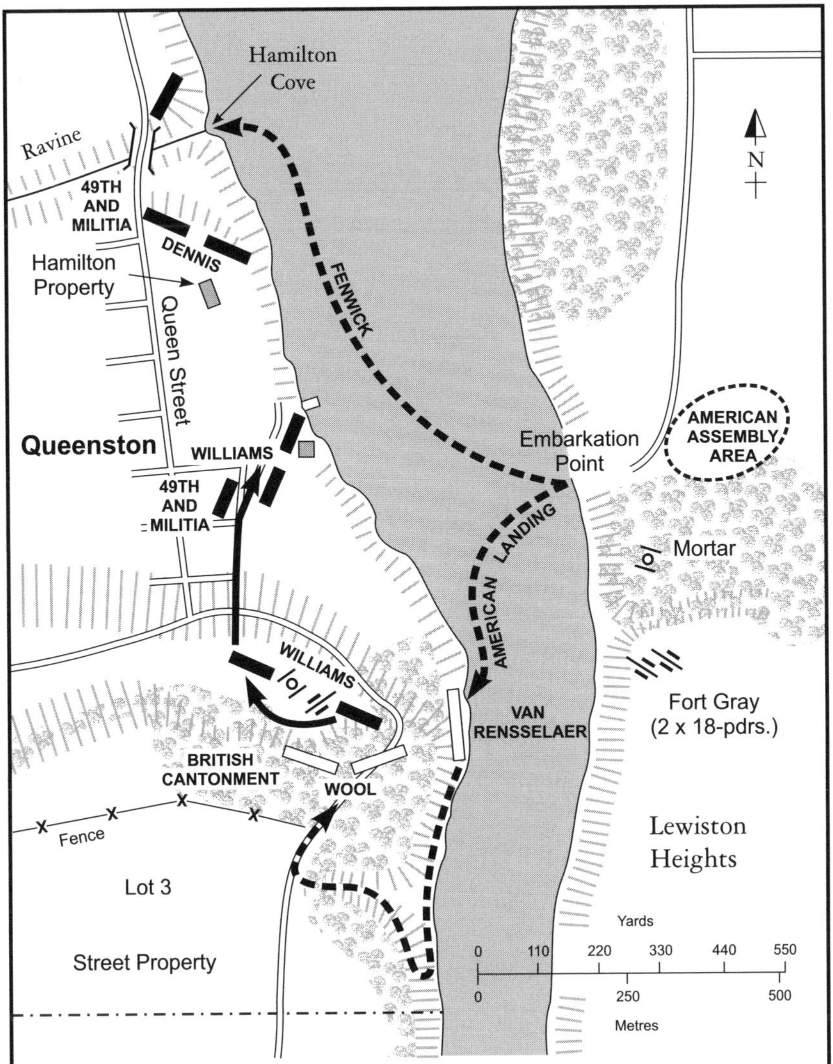


## Queenston Heights – 13 October 1812
### 2nd Phase: c. 5:30 AM – 7:00 AM

1. Lovett's battery at Fort Gray puts the British 9 pdr. on the Queenston landing out of commission.
2. While more Americans land at the intended spot, Lieutenant Colonel Fenwick's boats land at Hamilton Cove. A fierce skirmish erupts.
3. Dennis deploys troops to contain Fenwick's force.
4. Williams's company is called to reinforce the village.
5. Wool's detachment scales the gorge wall and captures the redan battery.

most blatant omissions in the tactical planning done by Stephen Van Rensselaer and his council of war. Had they planned to put more pressure on the defences of Queenston by doubling or tripling the number of boats available and sending waves against Queenston from the north and south simultaneously, the day's events might have turned out differently.[17]

The second major contact of the morning occurred as Fenwick's detachment landed at Hamilton Cove and found itself in a murderous firefight. Captain James Mullany was in charge of one of the boats and ordered his men to fire at the British who lined the shore, but the defence of the village was sharp and, as Mullany noted, "nearly half my men were killed or wounded."[18] One of the British claimed that Captain Dennis himself sighted a field gun that killed and wounded fifteen Americans in one boat while Lieutenant Colonel Chrystie reported the men in the batteaux "being cut to pieces."[19] Soon after stepping ashore Fenwick was severely wounded, "*clothed* with bullets," wrote Major Lovett, "one in his eye – one in his right elbow – one in his side ... nine ball holes in his little cloak."[20] A British platoon closed upon Fenwick and some of his men and captured them. Lieutenants Alfred Phelps, Thirteenth Infantry, and William Clarke of the Twenty-Third were also knocked down. Gamely, the Americans fought to gain ground and at one point Ensign George Grosvenor of Captain Charles Bristol's militia rifle company (some of whom had joined the regulars in Fenwick's wave) managed to recapture the wounded Fenwick, but the British resistance was too strong and soon most of the Americans still standing surrendered, among them Lieutenants Robert Bayly, Third Artillery, and Israel Turner, from Dox's Thirteenth Infantry. Captain Mullany had joined the battle on shore and he refused to yield. The batteau that had carried his men to Queenston sank upon landing, so the captain waded into the river, grabbed hold of another batteau drifting by, and pulled it ashore. Into it went six of the wounded and five volunteers. "It was a desperate alternative," Mullany wrote. "I took an oar, the whole of the enemy's fire continued on this Boat and yet I crossed [back to the eastern bank] without a wound."[21]

There was plenty of evidence to substantiate the bloodbath at Hamilton Cove. After he and Lieutenant McLean caught up with the men from York, John Beverley Robinson witnessed the American captives being marched under guard from Queenston. "The road was lined with miserable wretches," he wrote, "suffering under wounds of all descriptions and crawling to our houses for protection and comfort."[22] Late in the day James Crooks came upon one of the boats lying beneath the bank where there "were two wretches on the shore severely wounded one through the groin and the other had his bowels shot out." In the boat sat a third man, seemingly asleep, but when Crooks tried to stir him, "I found he was dead, a ball having entered his forehead."[23] At Fort George Ensign John Smith, 41st Foot, wrote, "Some of their Boats drifted down here with six or 7 Corpses in them who had been destroyed by the shot from our batteries."[24] John Chrystie estimated "that *at least* one hundred regulars were killed, wounded and taken prisoners on the left of the village, before or about sunrise."[25]

Meanwhile, Isaac Brock had conferred with Captain Dennis and assessed the situation and he had probably dispatched one rider to Fort George with orders to send up reinforcements and another to Chippawa; being downwind of Queenston, this latter force had probably already heard the sounds of battle. Brock is said to have ridden up to the redan battery to advise the gunners there to increase the charge in the 8-inch mortar mounted near the 18-pdr. so that its shells would carry farther. [26] Before more than a couple of rounds could be lofted over to the opposite shore, however, the American infantry suddenly appeared on the crest of the escarpment.

After struggling along the uneven shoreline, the detachment had found a path leading up the face of the gorge. It proved a hard climb, and when the first men reached the top they spread out to provide a protective screen for the others, who soon formed up into impromptu ranks. Lieutenant John Gansevoort, being familiar with the terrain, had led the way, but Captain John Wool now resumed command of the detachment and, though still bleeding from his wound, marched it toward the edge of the escarpment above the redan battery.[27] Their movement was covered by the oak copse and undetected since no guards had been left on the Portage Road or at the cantonment of Williams's company. When Wool and his men came out of the trees at the top of the escarpment, the gun crew saw them immediately and fled. The Americans quickly occupied the battery and Wool deployed the infantry so that it faced the village and covered the rear of the battery. The 18-pdr. and mortar were now silenced, making the embarkation point at the ravine safer for the next waves of troops, but of equal significance, the Americans held the high ground above Queenston. It would only be a matter of minutes before the artillerymen from the first wave of the assault rotated the 18-pdr. ninety degrees and prepared it for use against the British. The time was about 7:00 a.m.

The capture of the redan battery revealed the error of withdrawing Williams's entire company from the Heights. Had even a portion of the light infantry been left at its post, the American plan to scale the gorge wall would have been stymied and possibly defeated. Whether or not Captain Dennis ordered the entire company down to the village before Brock arrived, the general was certainly in the village for a period of time before Wool's detachment attacked and, therefore, the responsibility for leaving the redan battery and the right flank undefended was his.

Realizing this mistake, Brock made a second critical error. He resolved to recapture the battery by making a dash up the hill with whatever party of men he could gather around him without determining the strength of Wool's detachment. For all Brock knew, the Americans might have been sending men across the river during the night to scale the gorge well south of Williams's cantonment and wait, undetected, for an attack on the redan battery at dawn. Wool's force might very well have been the vanguard of a strong column, but Brock does not appear to have taken any time to reconnoitre his enemy's strength. His assessment of the tactical situation surrounding the loss of the redan battery revealed a weakness in Brock's ability as a commander. Perhaps with Nelson's motto – "the boldest measures are the safest" – in mind, he chose the most desperate of alternatives, a weakly-manned counter attack up a hill into the face of an enemy of uncertain strength.

The general rode to the north end of the village, where he found part of the light company and the flank companies from the 5th Lincoln and 2nd York with Glegg and Macdonell. Brock called out, "Follow me boys" and trotted up the hollow of Queen Street (the village's main thoroughfare, an extension of River Road) to the foot of the escarpment near the intersection of the road to St. David's, a village two miles west of Queenston.[28] Here he dismounted and without hesitation climbed over a stone wall and waved the men forward, his sword in hand; his force numbered fewer than fifty, most of them Williams's men. "Placing himself at the head of the light company of the 49th," wrote one of those soldiers, "he led the way up the mountain at double quick time in the very teeth of a sharp fire."

Now Isaac Brock made his third and fatal error. Rather than send Glegg or Williams (who were both present, or shortly thereafter on the scene) to lead this classic charge of a forlorn hope, Brock saw his place at the head of his troops; it was his nature to act boldly. He must have stood out like a signal beacon to the Americans, who recognized him immediately. His height and build, the obvious uniform of a commanding general, his sword drawn to rally and urge the men on, this could only be the Isaac Brock who had made such a fool of poor old William Hull. What Brock was doing leading such a charge must have been a question more than one American asked himself. Perhaps they concluded that this confirmed what they had heard about this brilliant British general, this man of action. If they felt awed by his presence, the American infantry did not show it. Instead, they eagerly levelled their fire in his direction.

A musket ball grazed Brock's left hand, but he continued his climb, intent on regaining that which had been carelessly lost. Striding near him was a fifteen-year-old lad named George Jarvis. He had joined the 49th Foot in September to serve as a "gentleman volunteer," which was an avenue taken by some young men who aspired to become officers to gain experience in the hope of acquiring the earliest available commission. On this day Jarvis found himself facing fire for the first time, following on the heels of the heroic and popular Isaac Brock, and fate made him a witness to the general's last moments. "Ere long he was singled out by one of them," wrote Jarvis, "who, coming forward, took deliberate aim and fired; several of the men noticed the action and fired – but too late – and our gallant General fell on his left side, within a few feet of where I stood. Running up to him I enquired, 'Are you much hurt, Sir?' He placed his hand on his breast and made no reply and slowly sunk down."[29]

Stunned by the sight of Brock collapsing, some of the rank and file gathered around their fallen leader. "One of them," Lieutenant Robinson insisted, "was severely wounded by a cannon ball and fell across the General."[30] The cry went out to avenge the general and the British continued their attack, while several men, supervised by Captain Glegg, carried Brock's body into the village to hide it in a house.[31] Captain Wool's infantry were too numerous for the British, however, and when some of them retreated to the village, others, including Captain Williams, appear to have sought cover among the trees at the top of the escarpment either near the cantonment or farther west across the clearing.

At the northern end of the village the thirty or so men from the 3rd York

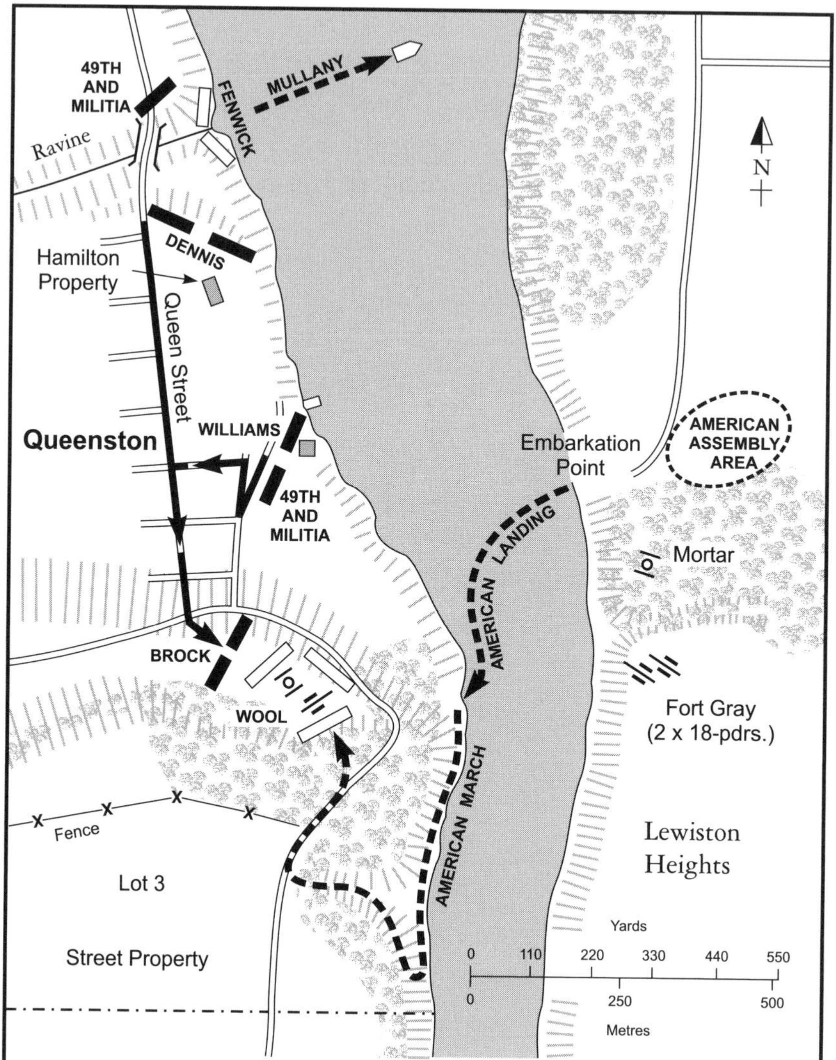


# Queenston Heights – 13 October 1812
## 3rd Phase: c. 7:30 AM

1. More Americans land. Wool reinforces the redan battery.
2. Fenwick's force is beaten and captured. Some Americans escape with Mullany.
3. Brock gathers a small force of regulars and militia and attempts to recapture the redan battery. Brock is killed. The British withdraw.

companies, who followed Captain Cameron to Queenston, had reached the Hamilton property and spread out in its garden. Here they were exposed to the fire of Fort Gray and the two 6-pdrs. in Winfield Scott's Second Artillery battery just above the main landing at Lewiston and suffered their first casualties. A single 18-pdr. round shot tore off Andrew Kennedy's leg and ripped open Thomas Major's calf; others too were wounded here as the remainder ran for shelter. Orders then came for the Yorks to march to the escarpment and join the light company at its crest, so along Queen Street they hustled, as shots fromLovett's 18-pdrs. tore swaths through gardens and bounced harmlessly down laneways. They turned onto York Road toward St. David's until they found a good path up the escarpment and ascended to the top, where they were brought forward to the position among the trees that Captain Williams had established. Along their route they had heard the news that Brock was dead and, though they could not believe it at first, the hard truth sank in.[32]

The anecdotal accounts of the next phase of the engagement are unclear, but it seems that Williams placed himself near the edge of the escarpment to the west of the now-American redan battery and its skirmish line. Wool's men were deployed below him in an oblique line to the rear of the battery, roughly facing the village. Instead of charging straight up the in-

**General Brock's uniform coat**
Brock's descendants, Henrietta and Emily Tupper of Guernsey, presented this coat to the National Archives of Canada in 1909. It was among the few belongings of the general that were preserved. Their family history maintained that Brock wore the coat, with markings of a brigadier general, when he died. A forensic examination in 1979 revealed that it would have fit Brock's large frame and that the hole in the middle of the chest was probably made by a projectile the size of a musket ball. (Photograph by B. Collenette, 1896, Notman Photographic Archives, courtesy of the McCord Museum of Canadian History, Montreal, MP-1978.41.4)

cline as Brock had attempted, Williams's plan appears to have been to advance downward from the Heights, pushing the enemy before him back toward the battery. He set his men in a line part way down the hill under cover of brush before giving the word to advance. He had about twenty men from the 49th and a few of the 41st with him, plus Cameron's thirty and another twenty brought by Macdonell, who came riding up the slope on his horse. The Americans, recently reinforced by regulars and some militia, most notably the rifle companies, numbered about four hundred.

The British slowly advanced through the shelter of trees on the terraces of the upper slope, and when the distance between them and the first of the Americans was about thirty yards, the fight was on. Macdonell anchored the lower left end of the British line "animating the men to charge." Williams cried out, "Feel firmly to the right, advance steadily, charge them home and they cannot stand you."[33] As John Wool later admitted, the strength of the British attack, a force more than half composed of militia, was so potent that it "drove us to the edge of the bank, when, with the greatest exertions, we brought the troops to a stand."[34] In this panicky scene, someone in the redan battery, thinking the fight was lost, spiked the 18-pdr., rendering it useless. Wool's detachment was now low on ammunition and about to make a desperate charge when the tide suddenly turned.

A musket ball hit Macdonell's horse, which reared up and twisted around, and a second ball hit the rider in the small of his back and exited through his abdomen. He fell from his mount and lay motionless. About the same instant, Captain Williams was wounded in the head so severely that it looked as if he had been scalped and he too collapsed. Macdonell, who actually suffered four wounds in all, came to and tried to get to his feet. Captain Cameron ran forward to rescue him, but a musket ball struck his elbow and he stumbled back. Macdonell could not get to his feet and seeing Lieutenant McLean, one of his friends from York, he cried out, "Archie, help me."[35] McLean scurried to his side and then was spun off his feet when a bullet hit him in the thigh. Cameron recovered himself and gallantly helped the two stricken officers off the field, despite the blizzard of lead that engulfed them. Williams suddenly rose, as if from the dead, and struggled out of the action just as the British attack collapsed completely and the Americans advanced. They pressed forward and soon captured twenty-one of their enemies, Private Jarvis standing unhurt among them.

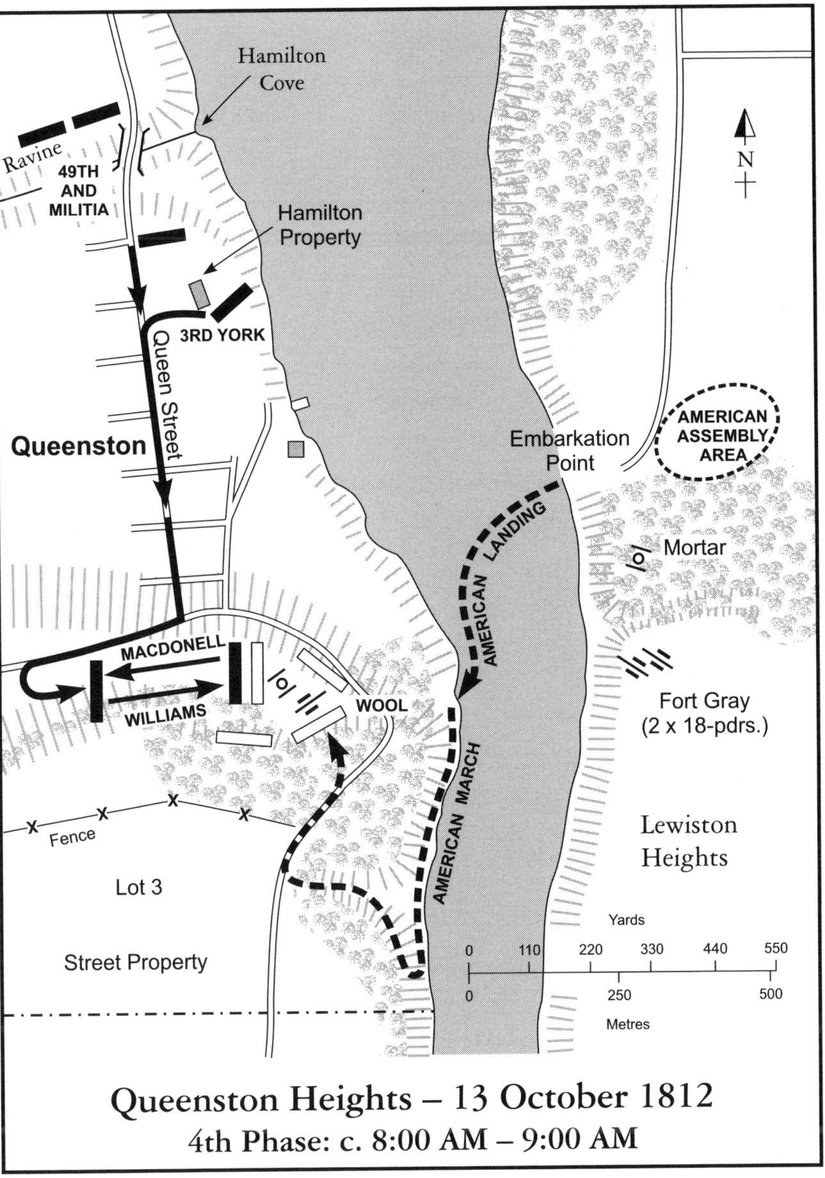


Queenston Heights – 13 October 1812
4th Phase: c. 8:00 AM – 9:00 AM

1. More Americans land and strengthen Wool's position in the redan battery.
2. Elements of the 3rd York arrive. Macdonell gathers men to join Williams in a second counterattack on the redan battery. It fails and the British withdraw.
3. The Americans have captured the high ground above Queenston.

The British who escaped from the disaster of the second counter attack fled toward either St. David's or the northern end of Queenston. With Brock dead, Captain Dennis was once more the senior officer commanding in the village and he made the decision to withdraw his force completely and reorganize it at a safer distance.[36] Accordingly, carrying the wounded as comfortably as they could and collecting the prisoners who remained on hand, the British marched north about one mile to the home of James Durham, roughly opposite Vrooman's Point. The village sat abandoned shortly after 9:00 a.m.

American regimental colours greeted the next reinforcements to reach the Heights, prompting one of them to term the preceding events "a splendid victory in the morning."[37] It was indeed a victorious moment for the officers and men of the U.S. Army. They had encountered the renowned British regulars and held their own. Now, except for the rather ineffective battery at Vrooman's Point, the river was safe for crossing, and militia and regulars were soon arriving in numbers. Among them was Lieutenant Jared Willson, from Captain Nathan Parke's rifles of Canandaigua, one of the independent companies called up by Van Rensselaer in September. John Wool had been an ensign in this outfit before joining the army, so as he stood the conquering hero on the rampart above Queenston he was greeted by old friends. Captain John Machesney arrived with his Sixth Infantry and went with the riflemen to guard the flanks of his line while Lieutenants Gansevoort and Randolph attempted to drill out the spike in the 18-pdr.

Sometime before this, the seriously wounded Solomon Van Rensselaer was evacuated to the eastern shore. The fight was over for him and so was the influential role he had played in Stephen Van Rensselaer's army. His absence would prove significant. Victory or not, who would tell the general what to do next?

While the battle raged at Queenston, plenty was happening in and around the town of Niagara. Fort George was awakening about the time Brock departed from Government House. Under a district general order issued the week before, all regulars and militia were expected to be in uniform and armed before sunrise and "not to be dismissed till broad daylight and distant objects seen."[38] It was this order that Captain James Crooks tried to ignore when he rolled over and went back to sleep, hoping to avoid an early, routine muster in the raw weather. But the urgent call of one of his men awoke Crooks to his duty and he was soon hurrying to the rendezvous point behind Fort George.

The whole town was awake by this point, "Women and Children running in all directions, and Soldiers repairing to their posts," as Lieutenant Merritt recalled.[39] He and Captain Hamilton hurriedly dressed and ran down to the stables where their horses were. "We received orders," Merritt wrote, "to repair to Queenston as fast as possible, as the Enemy had landed."

A gun had been fired in one of the fort's bastions while a blue pennant was hoisted on the flag staff, the signal for assembly. "It was most gratifying," wrote Crooks, "it being then broad daylight, to see each Company from their respective quarters in town vieing with each other which should cross the plain which separates the town from Fort George first."[40] Once the militia had gathered, normal army routine took over – that is, they had hurried to get there and now they could wait. Stacking their arms, they stood at ease, expecting further orders at any minute.

Major General Sheaffe was in command and had already made deployments, having heard from Thomas Evans that there was no sign of an American assault by water along the lake shore.[41] One anecdote of the day told of Brock sending a hurried message by dragoon for Sheaffe to commence a bombardment of Fort Niagara, and this order might have also included a request for reinforcements at Queenston. Whatever the circumstances may have been, around the break of day, 6:30 a.m., Sheaffe instructed three separate detachments to head up River Road. The two regular components of that force included the light company of the 41st Foot under Captain William Derenzy, numbering about ninety officers and men, and the whole of Captain William Holcroft's Royal Artillery based at Fort George. Holcroft had less than half a company stationed at the fort but that did not stop him from putting together a respectable artillery train of two brass 6-pdrs. and a 5.5-inch howitzer. His bombardiers and gunners lifted each gun onto its limber wagon, to which they harnessed a team of six horses; one or two pair of horses drew each gun's ammunition wagon. When the drivers had mounted the thinly padded seats, Holcroft gave the order to advance and the artillerymen headed up the muddy, rutted road to the scene of the battle. Those who were left without a ride went on ahead or behind to avoid the splatter of muck thrown up by hooves and wheels.

Along the way they would use their brute strength to get the guns over the worst spots in the road; their trek would take more than two hours.

The third detachment comprised about 160 men from the Grand River Six Nations. John Norton had been out and about before dawn and saw Brock gallop southward, followed soon after by his aides, but he remained in camp until he heard a rumour that the general had ordered the guns of Fort George to open fire on Fort Niagara. Realizing that something of consequence was happening, Norton sought out Major General Sheaffe and asked if his men were needed. Sheaffe at first advised Norton to have his force ready, but before the chief reached the camp Major Thomas Evans rode up with orders for him to take his men to Queenston immediately. About that time the batteries on both sides of the river's mouth began a furious cannonade "which roused the Spirits of the Warriors," recalled Norton, "and shouts re-echoed from one to another."[42] On the road the Grand River men saw Derenzy's light infantry on the march, "quick Time, in that regular order which increases confidence." Norton's people followed in a mad dash toward the action upriver.

Anyone in Niagara who was still unaware of the day's events was awakened by the artillery duel that erupted shortly after dawn. Stephen Van Rensselaer's plan of attack had included instructions for Captain Nathan Leonard to bombard the town and Fort George as soon as there was light enough to identify targets and this Leonard did with a vengeance. From the battery atop the old French castle in Fort Niagara, Leonard directed the operation of two guns, a 6-pdr. and a 12-pdr., while in a blockhouse in the southern part of the fort Captain James McKeon's Third Artillery served a single 6-pdr.[43] The Salt Battery also appears to have commenced fire at this time. Unknown to the British, the garrison possessed a shot oven that had been heating projectiles since before dawn and these were soon falling upon Niagara with devastating effect, setting fire almost instantly to the Court House and the adjoining jail.

Confusion spread as fast as the flames did. Thomas Evans thought at first that some of the prisoners in the jail had escaped and set fire to the building, but as the minutes passed a set of barracks, a storehouse, a block house and other public and private buildings began to smoulder. While bucket brigades formed throughout the town and at the fort, the British turned the guns in the bastions and the outlying batteries on the source of the menace. With

**An aide-de-camp and brigade major of cavalry**

Mounted, and in a hurry to relay Brock's orders, Captain John Clegg and Lieutenant Colonel John Macdonell (the general's aides) and Major Thomas Evans would have appeared very much like these figures. One exception might have been that they wore plain round hats, said to be the favourite style among British officers on the Niagara in 1812. (Charles Hamilton Smith, aquatint from *Costumes of the Army of the British Empire according to the Last Regulations,* 1812-1815)

**A British 6-pdr. field gun**
Field guns were made of iron or "brass" which was also known as "gun metal," an alloy usually fabricated from ten parts of tin to ninety parts of copper. Compared to iron guns, brass weapons were lighter and stronger although they were more expensive to cast and more likely to suffer deformities as they heated up during prolonged use in battle. (Photo by the author)

Holcroft's artillerymen gone and the regular troops preparing to march, however, there was a hectic scramble to man the ordnance effectively. Captain Henry Vigoreux of the Royal Engineers, whose living quarters were at that moment going up in smoke, took charge of one of the batteries. William Claus of the Indian Department, also the colonel of the 1st Lincoln Militia, was sent to command a battery, while Captains John Powell and Alexander Cameron of the 1st Lincoln Artillery efficiently directed the work in other emplacements. Those hands not employed in fighting the fires or forming up to march – the non-commissioned clerks, invalids and aged militia – provided the manual labour, carrying cartridges and shot, hauling on tackle and then covering their ears against the deafening detonations.[44]

The weight of the British cannonade (there were more than a dozen heavy carriage guns and several mortars in and around the fort) eventually took its toll on the Americans. McKeon's blockhouse "was shivered almost to splinters" by round shot and then peppered with "bombshells."[45] The 12-pdr. in Leonard's battery burst because of a defect in its barrel, killing two men outright and wounding others, which caused McKeon to order a retreat to the rear of the fort. At the town of Niagara the vast plumes of dense, black smoke were thinning as the residents and soldiers managed to extinguish the last of the fires. Where the courthouse, the brewery and several private residences had stood, there were now only cracked and charred chimneys rising above mounds of black and reeking debris.

While the town and fort were under attack, a dragoon arrived with the devastating news that Brock was dead and Queenston taken. Without hesitation, Roger Sheaffe rode to the battle, after turning over command of the garrison to Major Evans and instructing him to have every available man march for Queenston.[46] It seems likely that Lieutenants George Fowler, 41st Foot, and Walter Kerr, Glengarry Light Infantry, rode with Sheaffe in addition to his aide-de-camp Nathaniel Coffin. This left Lieutenant Angus McIntyre as the senior officer remaining in the 41st Foot at Fort George, but soon after Sheaffe departed, McIntyre advanced with 140 rank and file from his regiment, while the body of militia prepared to march from the fort.

About one third of the militia available at Niagara were on duty in the town and the various batteries, leaving another third free to go to Queenston. This portion was a patchwork brigade, a blend of flankers from five separate units. They were from James Crooks's 1st Lincoln and his brother William's 4th Lincoln, plus John McEwan's 1st Lincoln, Abraham Nelles's 4th Lincoln under Lieutenant Thomas Butler, and John Selby's 1st York under Lieutenant Barnet Vandenburgh. In all, 130 militia officers and men comprised the second relief column. Command of this detachment should have gone to William Crooks since he was the senior officer present, but his brother James contested this point on the grounds of familial need. "I represented to him," wrote the younger Crooks, "that we ought not to risk both our lives on the same chance, that we both had married about two years before and had each one child, and that if anything befell either of us the survivor would take care of the other's family."[47] This was a compelling explanation, but the argument that clinched the arrangement was James's firm belief that "the attack at Queenston was a mere *ruse de guerre* to draw the force from Niagara" and that William would probably see the real fighting there in town. With the deal between brothers made, the militia tramped away from Niagara and soon discovered how wrong their captain's idea about a ruse was.

# 10

# "Beneath the stride of death"

## MAJOR GENERAL SHEAFFE'S VICTORY

Before 10:00 a.m. on Tuesday, 13 October, the Americans had accomplished two of the objectives underlying their operation, namely "to dislodge the enemy from the heights of Queenstown and to possess ourselves of the village."[1] They had seized the redan battery, where the mass of troops was slowly growing, and the village was abandoned and vulnerable.

Inadequately restrained, some of the invaders crept into the village and, according to one report, "they plundered the houses of everything they could conveniently carry away."[2] The Americans, it was said, had been "allured over by the hopes of plunder." From the scant information available in damage claims made by village residents, it is evident that James Secord, John and Joseph Brown and George Hamilton all sustained losses to their homes and businesses. The Hamilton house suffered damage as one anecdote noted: "thirteen eighteen pound shot struck it [and] the two south chimneys [were] knocked down, several went into the kitchen, a number struck fair against the upper story and bounced back ... [the] stables are famously peppered and several went through the shop."[3]

Queenston landing was now open to the Americans, which allowed reinforcements to come ashore more easily in the few boats that were still in commission.[4] Captain James Gibson of the Light Artillery took advantage of this situation to embark, in pieces, an iron 6-pdr. field gun, its accoutrements and ammunition wagon. He might have taken his second gun but found only one boat available at the time. On the Queenston landing his artificers and gunners reassembled the train of artillery, then manually hauled it up Portage Road to the crest of the escarpment.

The rest of the regulars remaining from the original 600 who had gathered at Lewiston crossed over before noon, but this process took time due to a shortage of batteaux. Confusion continued at the ravine and any scheme for one organized wave to follow another was long since lost. And with it went the impetus that might have led to a better showing by the New York militia. Solomon Van Rensselaer had originally intended to include 150 militia, selected from the Eighteenth and Twentieth Detached Regiments, in the first wave of boats, but when Lieutenant Colonel Chrystie's Thirteenth Infantry took the places reserved for the militia, Van Rensselaer ordered Major John Morrison to follow in the second wave.

Morrison was acting as commander of the Twentieth Detached since Lieutenant Colonel Hugh Dobbin was absent on leave, but he apparently stood back as regular army officers hurried their men to battle. Furthermore, the batteaux that managed to return came back in ones and twos whereupon regulars hastily filled them up and departed. Morrison never succeeded in following Solomon Van Rensselaer's order and, in fact, he seems to have disappeared from the scene, the lieutenant colonel later wryly alleging that Morrison "suddenly found himself taken too unwell for the duty."[5] The outcome of this failure was that, right from the beginning of the day, the New York militia was unable to establish its place in the battle line at Queenston. This left the men waiting for hours during which they could begin to second guess their commitment to the operation and reconsider the legal limits of their militia duty, namely, that they were not required to fight beyond their native soil.

This does not mean, however, that the more than 3,000 militia between Manchester and Fort Niagara were universally reluctant to join the fight because more than 700 of them did cross.[6] The rifle companies, some of which were volunteers under the law of 6 February, were among the first to find space in the batteaux. For years they had formed elite "uniform" companies that had elicited praise from state officials and now, given an opportunity to prove their mettle, they joined the regulars and headed for Queenston. Charles Moseley's battalion and the companies of Captains

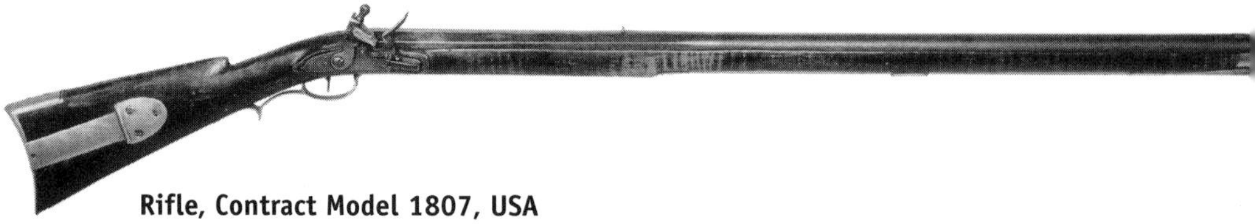

**Rifle, Contract Model 1807, USA**
Some of the American militia may have been armed with this weapon. All fittings were brass, including the patch box, which held the pieces of greased patches used to tighten the fit of the ball as it was rammed down the grooved barrel. (Courtesy of the West Point Museum Collection, U.S. Military Academy)

Nathan Parke and William Ireland crossed over. Having finally received their allotment of ammunition, the men in the Sixteenth and Seventeenth Regiments who had arrived on the Niagara just days before, crossed in numbers by noon. Eventually, members of each of the other three regiments advanced on Queenston, the four lieutenant colonels present, Farrand Stranahan, Thompson Mead, Henry Bloom and Peter Allen, leading the way. Following them were company commanders such as Eli Bacon, Peley Ellis, Stephen Clarke and Elisha Saunders, the latter two of whom lost their lives on the Heights.

There were many fine examples of individual leadership among the Americans, but missing from the attack on Queenston, after the first phase of the engagement and the removal of Lieutenant Colonel Van Rensselaer from the action, was a guiding hand. This was Stephen Van Rensselaer's role, but he appears to have stood back from the action; his presence at any of the crucial locations on either shore during the morning was never recorded. He is known to have been in Fort Gray before dawn, but his whereabouts thereafter are uncertain. Stranahan's Seventeenth Detached Regiment did not begin receiving its ammunition until after 7:30 a.m. and the general might have concerned himself with tasks of this nature. Dependent upon Solomon throughout the campaign, the general was now left on his own and proved incapable of taking charge.

Into the leadership void stepped a number of senior officers. Lieutenant Colonel John Chrystie appears to have spent the time after his aborted crossing trying to organize the embarkation and was witness to the disastrous landfall that Lieutenant Colonel Fenwick's detachment made at Hamilton Cove. He finally crossed to Queenston after the second counterattack on the redan battery failed and assumed command from Captain John Machesney, Sixth Infantry; Captain John Wool was still present but greatly weakened by loss of blood and Chrystie ordered him to return to the eastern shore to have his wounds treated. The Americans had formed a line at the redan battery and along the crest of the escarpment, fronting the village, and had established a second line, facing south along the snake fence that separated the military reserve from the property of Samuel Street.[7] Chrystie inspected these lines and issued orders to each of the various detachments as they arrived, including Lieutenant Colonels Mead and Stranahan with what Mead described as two hundred men. A Canadian dragoon stumbled into the American position with a message from the force at Chippawa, making Chrystie think an attack might come from that quarter at any minute. Accordingly, he reinforced the detachment at the snake fence and deployed a party of riflemen to scout for any enemy approaching from the south.

Brigadier General William Wadsworth then made his appearance and took command, hoping, as he told Chrystie "that his example might have a better effect than his orders in making the militia cross."[8] By this time it had become apparent that all of the regulars had crossed into Canada but that many of the militia were hanging back even when there were boats available to take them, a concern that Wadsworth and Chrystie discussed. They decided that the latter should return to the other side and explain the situation to Major General Van Rensselaer, so, rather than sending a message with one of the captains or subalterns, John Chrystie descended to the river, climbed into a boat and headed back.

It took a while to track down the general, but Chrystie finally found him "on the road about half a mile from the river."[9] He quickly explained circumstances on the Heights, to which Van Rensselaer responded that he had sent Captain Joseph Totten of the Engineer Corps over with orders to commence fortifying the position. This was an empty hope, however, because the lack of thought given to the logistics of the operation also included a failure to have suitable entrenching tools on hand, as Totten and the others soon found out. Obviously unaware that his intention to fortify Queenston Heights could not be achieved, Van Rensselaer told Chrystie that he had accepted Lieutenant Colonel Winfield Scott's offer to assume command at Queenston, seemingly unaware that Wadsworth was on the ground at the time.[10] Only Lieutenant Isaac Roach went with Scott, as his aide, as there was no order from Van Rensselaer for any part of the Second Artillery to join the force on the other side of the river.

An hour or so passed while General Van Rensselaer busied himself with orders to his remaining staff and then, around 11:00 a.m., the sound of sporadic fighting erupted on the Heights. Chrystie and Van Rensselaer, accompanied by Major Lovett, hurried to the ravine and down to the landing and there met "a company of men very handsomely equipped, which was just on the point of entering the boats when this firing was heard, but thereupon halted and now absolutely refused to cross."[11] Chrystie looked on with dismay as Stephen Van Rensselaer instructed the men to do their duty, but "neither the orders, nor threats, nor remonstrances of the General" could get them to change their minds. The unmistakable cries of native warriors echoing across the river startled the militiamen, making them more susceptible to the argument that they were not required by law to face the tomahawk's wrath in Canada. Perturbed by this scene, the three officers got into a batteau and ordered whoever was rowing to shove off; at the last moment Major John Mullany appeared and joined them.

After his safe return from the Queenston shore following Fenwick's attack, Mullany appears to have dashed from place to place, as John Chrystie did, assessing each situation and giving orders.[12] At one point he rode up to Fort Gray to advise Lovett on where to aim his guns, and later he was on Queenston Heights, where he noticed too many of his Twenty-Third Infantry rank and file were unaccountably absent. He returned to the other side, chanced upon Lieutenant Henry Whiting of his regiment, instructed him to round up any remaining regulars, and then he was at the ravine getting into the boat with Van Rensselaer and the others. Mullany's wanderings seem to be representative of how the American victory in the early morning dissolved into a helter-skelter operation, adrift without authoritative control.

The first clear signs that the British were about to take advantage of the disarray in the American camp were evident by 11:00 a.m. Lieutenant Colonels Mead and Stranahan had watched a detachment of British artillery arrive at Queenston and begin to fire on the remaining batteaux plying back and forth across the difficult current; they were discussing how they might dislodge this new menace when their attention was turned to the crack of small-arms fire south of the military reserve.

Captain Nathan Parke's company of riflemen was in that vicinity, having formed one of the patrols sent out to guard the flanks of the American line. As Lieutenant Jared Willson recalled, "We had not been gone long, when a party of indian Devils – about two hundred, attacked us in the woods."[13] And so came the turning of the tide in the battle at Queenston.

In the aftermath of 13 October, British ink flowed in effusive praise, and one individual particularly mentioned by nearly every participant, though given short shrift in later accounts of the battle, was Captain William Holcroft of the Royal Artillery. He acted "with the greatest Coolness," wrote Lieutenant Hamilton Merritt, "unmindful of consequences," added Major Evans; "exposed to the fire of Fort Gray over his head," noted Captain James Crooks. "Nothing could exceed the exertions of Capt Holcroft," wrote Ensign John Smith, 41st Foot, whose view of the day was blunt and critical.[14] Holcroft's conduct showed how a competent, experienced officer, leading veteran troops, could make a significant contribution to a larger enterprise.

After an arduous trek up from Fort George, the Royal Artillery train made its appearance near Vrooman's Point shortly after 10:00 a.m. Here Holcroft took time to examine the action and identify the positions of the enemy to determine where his guns would most effectively be placed. He quickly concluded that the two 6-pdrs. of Scott's Second Artillery across the river posed a threat to his intentions. This battery was located just south of Lewiston at a distance of 600 yards from the Queenston landing and operated in conjunction with a mortar nearer to the embarkation point. Although it was against doctrine in the British army for artillery units to engage enemy guns directly, Holcroft later admitted to having done just that. "Their ... six pounders were silenced three different times," reported Holcroft, "but the 18 pounder battery [Fort Gray] on the summit of the mountain was out of range."[15] Given the later deployment of the field guns he had brought up from Fort George, it seems reasonable to assume that Holcroft ordered the 12-pdr. gun and 18-pdr. carronade at Vrooman's (which had proven ineffective in stopping the American boats because of the range) to focus their fire on Scott's battery and the mortar.

After making his observations at Vrooman's Point, Holcroft hastened forward to Queenston, riding across the bridge over the stream that flowed

**Queenston Heights from River Road, ca. 1900**
This photograph of Queenston was taken just north of the stream winding down to Hamilton Cove, facing south to the escarpment about two thirds of a mile distant. It is the view seen by Derenzy's light infantry and Holcroft's gunners as they moved forward to retake the village. (Courtesy of the Niagara Historical Society, 984.5.235)

down to Hamilton Cove, and onto the Hamilton property. The village was in the hands of the looters going from house to house, which would have made the work of the artillery more perilous had it not been for the support it received from the light company of the 41st Foot under Captain William Derenzy. Selected for their ability to fight efficiently without the need for close supervision, the light infantry spread out in small groups to sweep slowly through the village, flushing out the marauding troops, firing upon them with restraint and accuracy and gradually forcing them back toward the escarpment and up to their position near the redan. As Holcroft's gunners set up each of their guns, they augmented the movements of the light company and within an hour the village was cleared of the enemy and the guns could be turned toward other targets.

One of Holcroft's 6-pdrs. was situated in the shadow of a "milk house" on the Hamilton property. It was normal artillery practice to separate the guns in a battery by at least twelve yards, so other protected locations were chosen for the second 6-pdr. and the howitzer from where they could fire at the American embarkation point, the batteaux or the line of infantry on the side of the escarpment. Many of the rounds were solid shot, but as Holcroft enthusiastically wrote, "our spherical case was of great use."[16] Although the

Americans discussed making an attack on the British artillery, nothing of the kind developed, leaving the three guns to pelt their enemy's positions through the rest of the day, ably protected by Derenzy's light company.

The main reason why no detachment descended the hill to confront Holcroft's artillery is that shortly after he opened fire, John Norton's warriors appeared on Portage Road south of Queenston Heights. They had rambled up River Road through the morning, during which they saw Major General Sheaffe gallop by on his way to assume command of the Queenston force. A platoon of the 49th Foot passed them heading for Fort George with prisoners, and about two and a half miles north of Queenston the news of Brock's death reached them, along with the rumour that the Americans were fanning out in large numbers through the dense forest west of the line of farms along River Road. Norton doubted the veracity of these stories, but, thinking to cover his approach to the escarpment, left the road, crossed the fields into the woods, splitting his force into five or six files to thread its way through the forest. Soon, as Norton recalled, they came upon "a few Militia Men that had escaped from Queenston – they said in excuse for their flight, that Six thousand Americans had gained possession of Queenstown Heights; – Some Warriors answered, – 'The more game, the better hunting.'"[17]

The thought of a plentiful quarry did not appeal to all of Norton's followers as he discovered when he exited the forest on York Road about one mile west of Queenston. Of the nearly 160 men who had advanced from the encampment only eighty remained; the others, Norton concluded, had taken the rumours for truth and returned to Niagara to protect their families. A number of the chiefs had stayed with Norton, however, as had John Brant, son of the late Joseph Brant, and William Johnson Kerr of the British Indian Department. Confident that he could still make a contribution to the defence of Niagara, Norton rallied his men with an impromptu speech. "Comrades and Brothers," he said simply. "Be men." He then reminded them about their ancestors who had never backed away from a stronger foe and of their purpose for coming to Niagara. "We have found what we came for," he cried. "Let no anxieties distract your minds: – there they are, – it only remains to fight."[18] And turning, Norton led the way up a path that followed a cut in the escarpment, trailed by his men, hollering and crying out, looking like spirits in their red and black paint, the symbols of life and death.

The Grand River party moved south until it came to Portage Road. Along the way they encountered a young man who had just escaped from the Americans and warned that they were nearby. Then a Canadian militiaman on horseback appeared and John Norton urged him to ride to Chippawa to bring on reinforcements. The native fighters were at Lot One of Niagara Township, a piece of land originally granted to Daniel Rose and a good portion of which was cleared and under cultivation; a fringe of trees ran along the crest of the Niagara gorge. It was among the trees that they first saw the Americans "at the other end of a Field: – We doubled our pace to come up with them, – fired and ran, and fired again."[19]

The New York riflemen, surprised on their patrol by what Lieutenant Jared Willson called "savages, greedy for plunder and thirsting for blood," ran for their lives. The incident shook Willson to the core, prompting him to admit freely, "I thought hell had broken loose and let her dogs of war upon us… . I expected every moment to be made a 'cold Yankee' as the soldiers say."[20] The riflemen fled across the property of Elijah Phelps and Samuel Street toward the safety of their line behind the fence at the military reserve.

Had he survived, Isaac Brock might have modified his attitude toward "that fickle race" after witnessing what John Norton and his warriors accomplished on Queenston Heights in the next couple of hours. The Ameri-

**Grand River Six Nations warrior, 1804**
In preparation for battle, Iroquois warriors decorated themselves elaborately. This individual's face is painted in red, black and yellow. His ear has been cut and stretched and is painted red. He wears earrings, a nose bob, a gorget, a chief's medal and a crucifix.[11] (Ink drawing and coloured wash by Sempronius Stretton, National Archives of Canada, C-14827)

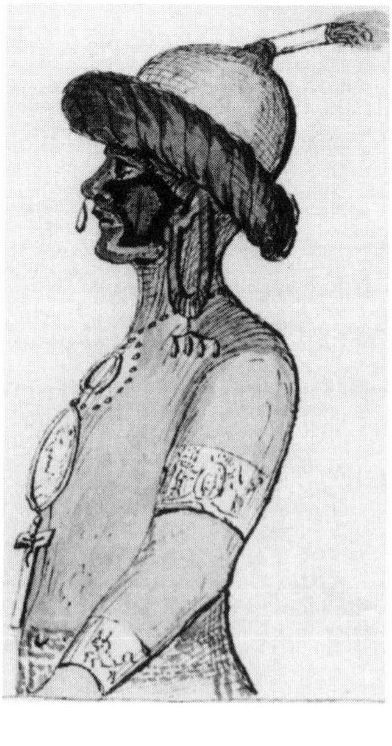

cans at the snake fence saw the riflemen running in full treat and a portion of the infantry near the west, or right, end of the line climbed over the fence and moved into the field to support them. Seeing the infantry advance, Norton led his people to attack them. The rest of the American line opened fire on the Iroquois, but they ducked into a hollow in the field and were unscathed. Individually, and in small groups, they lay down at the rise in the field to take careful aim at the Americans, who continued to send volleys flying harmlessly over their heads. In a short time Norton had crossed the field from east to west and disappeared into the forest on the western sector of Street's property and the adjacent military reserve.

From the shelter of the trees, the natives observed the Americans crouching behind the fence, under the cover of the copse of oak in which the southern front of their force was located. Between the two foes lay a clearing 200 yards wide, apparently an open field. It was unlike the Iroquois to risk their limited numbers in a frontal attack across such a space and Norton hesitated in the woods to reconnoitre the best way to get at the Americans. At this point spherical case from Holcroft's howitzer began to burst, spraying the American position with shrapnel and sounding like musket volleys striking the foliage, which caused Norton to think that the British were making another attempt to storm the Heights from the north. Intent on supporting the assault, Norton, with a small party of followers, descended the slope of the escarpment and sneaked through the undergrowth below the clearing until they closed on the American right flank. Here, as Norton remembered, "within a javelin's throw of the crowded [American] Ranks, ... they discharged Leaden death among them; ... [while] the Slight foliage of some Slender Oak concealed them from hostile view."[21]

Lieutenant Colonel Winfield Scott had just assumed command on the Heights, with Brigadier General Wadsworth's grateful approval, when Norton's detachment made its appearance. Their onrush across the cultivated field to the south produced a near-panic in the troops along the fence, but Scott, "in full dress Chapeau and plume," as Lieutenant Isaac Roach described him, kept the men at their posts and ordered the right flank to screen the retreating riflemen.[22] He then held firm, watching and waiting for the enemy's next move, and when Norton's group attacked, Scott retaliated in force. While his right flank fended off Norton, Scott ordered his men to cross the fence and wheel to the right to form a front facing west across the clearing toward the larger wood from where the main body of natives continued to fire. He then ordered a slow advance and the line moved forward, halting to deliver volleys by companies and platoons until they reached the verge of the trees. Rather than stop here, "the intrepid Scott" continued his advance.[23]

Under too heavy a press of musketry to remain protected even by dodging behind trees and fallen logs, Norton withdrew his warriors along the face of the escarpment until they were well in the rear of the larger stand of woods. Here they met a group of their compatriots "who lurked secure in a deep ravine."[24] Norton challenged them to join the fight near the leading edge of the woods. "Where are now those fierce Spirits that at the Village Feast, were wont to boast their prowess?" he exclaimed. With that, he ran forward, followed by most of the others, but they were stopped by the sight of a party of their men falling back, carrying wounded. Although numbering only twenty, this band had attacked the centre of the American line, instead of following their more effective and traditional hit-and-run, sniping tactics, and had paid a high price in casualties. Two of the Grand River chiefs and one of the warriors who were killed this day, as well as a number of wounded, fell in this phase of the battle. The sight of their comrades' suffering knocked the fight out of the Iroquois and many of them fled to an arranged rendezvous. Once more, Norton tried to rouse them to fight, managing to get some of them to join him as he rushed forward to see what effect their guerilla-style tactics would have on the Americans.

The skirmish in the woods was one of the better moments for the combined American regulars and militia. Under Lieutenant Colonel Scott's direction, the body of troops maintained its composure and, when he ordered a charge, it was "executed with bravery by our soldiers ... [and] the Indians fled with great precipitancy."[25] This was the observation of Lieutenant Colonel Mead, who marched under Scott along with Stranahan and many of the other militia officers and men (the exact strength of this detachment is unknown). Most of this force had missed the action in the morning, so the engagement with the men of the Grand River was their first experience under fire and they performed admirably, but, as Mead wrote, "We saw many brave officers and soldiers fall by the savage band."[26]

As the casualties mounted, the Americans realized they could not win against an enemy that was capable of appearing and disappearing at will, so

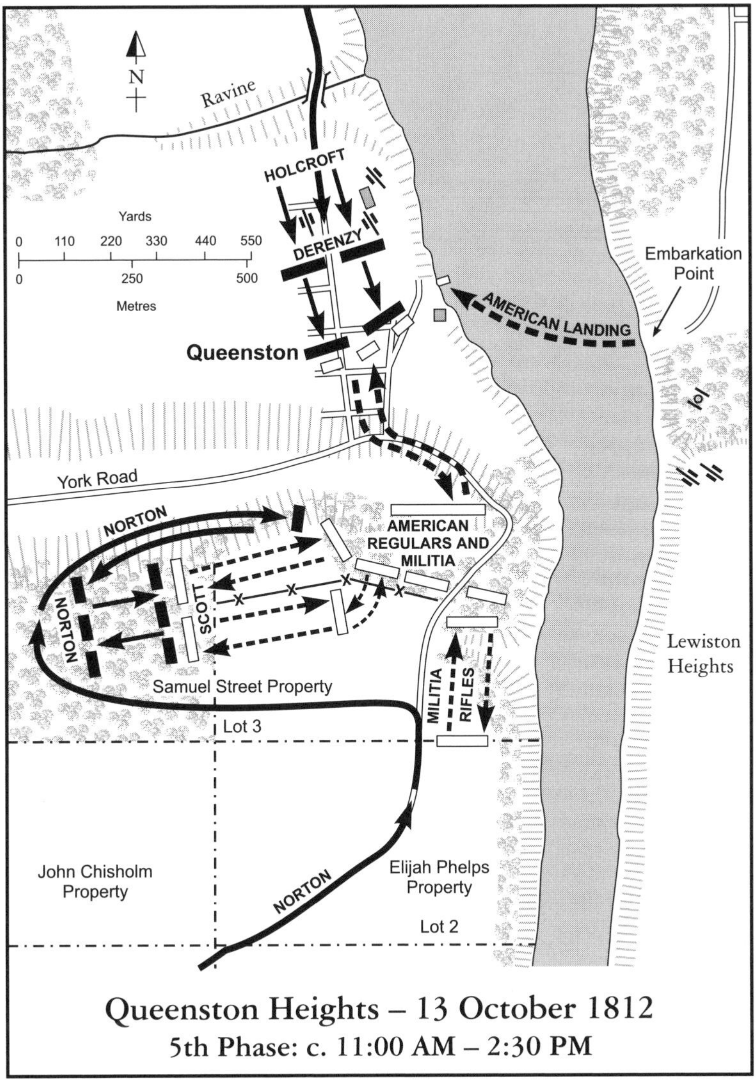


1. The British withdraw to a point north of Queenston.
2. The Americans land at the village dock and consolidate their position at the redan battery and in the British cantonment in the military reserve.
3. Looters infiltrate the village.
4. Derenzy's light company covers the advance of Holcroft's guns, which soon direct their fire at the American position on the escarpment and at any batteaux crossing.
5. Norton's warriors advance from the south, engaging a militia scouting party and then the main American force.
6. Scott leads an attack against the native warriors with some success and then withdraws to his original position.
7. Norton's warriors continue to harass the Americans.

**A 4.5-inch howitzer**
During this period all howitzers were made of brass. A typical 4.5-inch, or Cohorne, howitzer would measure 1 foot, 10 inches long and weigh 250 pounds. It is very likely that Captain William Holcroft used a 5.5-inch, or Royal, howitzer to fire spherical case at the American position near the redan battery since he could set the elevation of the howitzer higher than that of the 6-pdrs. (Photo by the author)

Scott called a retreat. Here also the new recruits of the regular units and the militia conducted themselves with order and confidence. Lieutenant Colonel Chrystie had arrived back on the Heights and had run forward to join the fight (his first direct action of the day) and noted how the withdrawal was effected "with care, small detachments being ordered to move to different points in rear, as with a view to meet other attacks."[27] Chrystie remembered that he and Scott were the last to leave the woods, slowly following the troops back to their previous line behind the fence. After this, the fire from the Iroquois became "less general and fatal," wrote Chrystie, "but it was never intermitted during the remainder of the day."

The efforts of Holcroft and Derenzy in the village and Norton's people on the Heights distracted the Americans from establishing a firm defence in the military reserve. The exhausted troops had no time to rest and little time to eat or drink, and a wave of despair probably washed over the regulars and militia when they noticed around 2:00 p.m. a column of British "Troops and Militia [was] passing obliquely through the Fields, at the foot of the mountain."[28]

These circumstances sparked a council of war with Stephen Van Rensselaer at its head. He had crossed the river with Lovett, Chrystie and Mullany, but unlike them, he had not hurried to join Winfield Scott's counter attack. Of the general's activities during this time, Lovett wrote that he "was taking a bite of bread and cheese in John Bull's barracks (for he had eaten no breakfast)" when Norton's assault began.[29] It was not until Scott had returned to the American lines that Van Rensselaer climbed the hill and met with the senior officers. The facts as they stood were clear: the British were preparing to mount a major attack; the defensive position in the military reserve was relatively strong, but the number of Americans present was insufficient to hold it; that number seemed to be shrinking as men skulked away from the line; the amount of ammunition available was inadequate to sustain a long engagement. There was, apparently, no talk of retreat or surrender, except from Chrystie who recommended that this was the best time to pull out.[30] Instead, the general decided to return to the New York shore himself to find men and ammunition to send over for the approaching battle. These were tasks that Van Rensselaer might easily have delegated to others (Lovett had already been sent back for these reasons), such as the lieutenant colonels of the militia units whose musters on the Heights were far from complete, but he chose to do them himself and left the battlefield after this one brief visit.

When Stephen Van Rensselaer reached the landing to board a batteau, a group of American soldiers suddenly swarmed the craft and shoved off, rowing as fast as they could to safety on the other side. Once on native soil, they ran away, a scene that was repeated continuously during the afternoon of 13 October; indeed, the batteau in which Van Rensselaer and the others had crossed earlier "returned immediately full of men, who had concealed themselves under the bank for the purpose of seizing opportunities to recross."[31]

The shocking spectacle of the battlefield, the cries of the wounded, the corpses dragged out of the way but not out of sight, sucked the fighting spirit out of many a would-be brave heart. And the caterwauling and wild antics of the Grand River warriors sprinting across the fields, their war feathers flapping around them, some of them half naked despite the cold and covered with paint, struck terror into the minds of the men who stood to repel them. As chances allowed, American regulars and milita left the lines and sneaked down the escarpment, or descended the path that Wool's men had used, to hide in the foliage below until they could get close enough to a boat to escape the horror above. The sounds of the battle and of the native attack carried clearly across to the American shore and many a soldier lost his resolve to fight and avoided any movement toward embarkation. When Stephen Van Rensselaer regained the eastern shore, he attempted to round up as many of the reluctant militia as he could find, assisted by Lieutenant Colonel Bloom and other officers who had returned wounded. It did not take long for them to realize that there would be no further reinforcement crossing into Canada that afternoon. Bloom found a boat and crossed the river again to stand with his men; Van Rensselaer stayed on the American side.

Roger Sheaffe established his headquarters at Durham's farm at midmorning, shortly after Captain Dennis and his force withdrew there from Queenston. His arrival and the steps he took next revealed one of the most striking differences between the British and American armies. Ironically, these forces had both lost their two most important commanding officers; Solomon Van Rensselaer wounded, Isaac Brock killed. Whereas Solomon's loss left Stephen Van Rensselaer without the mastermind upon whom he depended, Brock's place was quickly filled by Sheaffe. As the command of the American army stumbled and lost control, the British command was resumed and Sheaffe cooly directed his force more than half of which was composed of experienced, highly trained officers and men.

Unlike his predecessor who charged headlong into the fray, Major General Sheaffe carefully determined the strength of his enemy's position before deciding on a course of action. Captains Derenzy and Holcroft arrived at Durham's soon after the general did and advanced into the village. Meanwhile Captain Dennis's men tended to the wounded and found water and food for themselves. The British regulars and militia had been on the alert for days and, as Lieutenant John Robinson of the 3rd York Regiment recalled, "great was the fatigue which our men underwent from want of rest and exposure to the inclement weather."[32] They had been spared, however, the long, soggy marches that their adversaries had suffered and here, in a brief respite from pressure under fire, they were able to reconstitute themselves, a luxury that the temporary victors on the Heights never enjoyed.

By the time Captain Crooks's detachment of militia arrived from Fort George, Durham's "house [was] filled with wounded men, both our own and of the enemy," as Crooks recounted, "and in a bed chamber my worthy friend the gallant Lieut-Colonel McDonell … [was] lying mortally wounded."[33] The militia had heard about Brock's death on the march from Niagara and twice along that route officers from the 3rd York who had not joined Captain Duncan Cameron's advance on Queenston told Crooks that he was "mad" to go any further, that the Americans were infiltrating the woods to the immediate west and that he and the others were bound to be captured. Undaunted, the captain ordered his men to load their muskets and quicken their pace. The detachment of the 41st Foot under Lieutenant Angus McIntyre had already arrived and the Durham farm had been transformed into a bivouac. While waiting for the general to decide on his deployments, Crooks sent his men, who had complained about being hungry, into one of Durham's fields to dig potatoes. "This was soon done," he wrote, "and every pot and kettle in the house was soon walloping on the fire in the kitchen."

During this interval the last of the detachments from Fort George arrived under the command of Ensign John Martin, 41st Foot.[34] The size of this force was approximately 100 and it included every regular soldier who was fit to walk; Lieutenant John Winslow, who had been suspended from duty for ungentlemanly conduct in the officers' mess is said to have taken up a musket and joined the march. In Martin's detachment there were also men from the various militia companies who had not gone with Crooks, and the Coloured Company, three dozen black rank and file, commanded by Captain Robert Runchey, lately of the 1st Lincoln Regiment. Lieutenant William Crowther also arrived with a pair of 3-pdr. field guns from Fort George transported by the car brigade, a group of militia under Captain Isaac Swayze, who acted as drivers for the artillery. Lieutenant Hamilton Merritt was there as well, having ridden up with his companion Captain Hamilton, ready to carry orders at the general's request; Hamilton suffered an injury, probably due to a tumble off his horse, and joined Holcroft's artillery for the rest of the day. Merritt was soon riding hard to Chippawa

**U.S. Artillery at Fort Niagara**
This romantic view depicts American artillery at Fort Niagara and an oven used to heat shot. While there is no evidence that women joined the gunners on 13 October, legend has it that Mrs. Fanny Doyle participated in an artillery exchange late in November 1812. Her husband, Private Andrew Doyle, First U.S. Artillery, was captured at Queenston and Fanny sought vengeance after the British refused her pleas for his release.[10] (T. Walker, National Archives of Canada, C-121163)

with orders for Captain Richard Bullock to bring up a detachment of regulars and militia; he may have been the militiaman who encountered Norton's people near Portage Road.

Still commanding at Fort George, Major Evans planned to head for Queenston right after he sent Martin up the road, but at this time the Americans renewed their cannonade from Fort Niagara and the Salt Battery. Evans rode into the fort and discovered a group of militia running away in a panic, crying out that a hot shot had landed in the roof of the magazine, which contained 800 barrels of powder. Evans hurried to the eastern end of the fort, where the magazine was situated in a hollow, and there witnessed the engineer Captain Henry Vigoreux on top of the building working with several men to pry the smouldering shot from where it had embedded itself in the tin roof and a supporting beam. The magazine was a heavily-built stone structure with a vaulted ceiling, but a burning roof was potentially lethal. Vigoreux and his colleagues gingerly extracted the shot and rolled it off the roof, preventing an explosion that would have killed them and destroyed the fort. About the same time at the other end of the river, British guns at Fort Erie that had spent a good part of the day engaged with the batteries at Black Rock scored a direct hit on an American magazine, which exploded in a eruption of flame, smoke and debris, severely damaging a nearby barracks and putting an end to that part of the day's contest.

At Fort George, the challenge of silencing the American guns for a second time was greater than it had been in the morning. Ensign John Smith, 41st Foot, who had remained in the fort, wrote that "there were only 7 of our regiment and 2 of the 49th and a few Militia and most of them were sent out of the hospital that day – Yet we play'd on the Opposite Garrison to the best of our Judgement."[35] In time, Smith, Evans, Vigoreux and the others managed to stop the opposing guns, but, much to Evans's frustration, the delay kept him from riding to the battle at Queenston.

Sometime around 1:00 p.m. Major General Sheaffe concluded that he had gathered as strong a force at Durham's as was possible – this including some of Derenzy's light infantry – and that it was time to confront the enemy. After considering his options, Sheaffe decided to take a roundabout route as Norton's people had done and approach the American line from the south, down Portage Road. To this end, he ordered the regulars and militia formed up in column, amounting to about 650 men, and began a cross-country march to the southwest. The call for assembly sounded before Captain Crooks's men could enjoy their lunch so "the poor hungry fellows were obliged to leave their potatoes behind them."[36] The column advanced across the cultivated fields between Durham's and York Road, taking down the fences as it went. James Dennis rode up with a group of stragglers and Crooks, who had heard that Dennis was wounded, remembered that "although the blood had ceased to flow, he appeared much exhausted yet he would not leave the field till all was over."

Sheaffe's column arrived at York Road near the spot, one mile west of Queenston, where the Iroquois had ascended the escarpment, and followed this path up the hill and across the upper plain until it reached Portage Road. Sheaffe turned to the northeast and advanced along the road past Daniel Rose's fields, coming to a halt on the Phelps property. There he decided to wait until the reinforcements he had ordered down from Chippawa arrived, which he expected imminently.

In the meantime Sheaffe had to arrange his line for attack and this proved to be a problem. For some unexplained reason, the general, or whoever directed the formation of the column at Durham's, had the men line up with their backs to the American stronghold on the escarpment. When the order to march sounded, the column advanced with the left flank at the head and the right flank trailing so that when it stopped at Elijah Phelps's field, the left flank still led and was closest to the military reserve. Had the column been ordered to face the enemy and wheel around in a line parallel to the military preserve, preparatory to a charge, the left flank would have been where all the training manuals required the right flank to be. A single company of experienced soldiers would have been able to adjust to this reversal of the norm. But it was impossible to suddenly improvise a new series of orders to 650 men who had been trained under the exact opposite circumstances, and included militia who barely understood the basics of company movements let alone battlefield evolutions.

As a result of the mistake in the order of marching, Sheaffe was forced to reorganize his column by reversing everyone's position. This resulted in a chaotic scene that excited the comment of more than a few officers. As Ensign Smith somewhat facetiously described it later to Henry Procter,

> Right Wing was ordered to the Front (much the Militia knew about this).... the direction of the Column was Changed so as to face toward Queenston then ordered to Deploy *so as to extend to the Right* ... (*Much the Militia who were intermixed knew about this*) ... [after which] many of the Right division were in the Field of the opposite side of the road ... scarcely able to move being up to their knees in mud and water. The Line was then faced to the Left and marched till the Left was brought in rear of the old camp ground [in the military reserve] again – and the right in the Field to the S.W. of the Chippawa road – where they were ordered to lay down to conceal them from the Enemy [guns in Fort Gray].[37]

This incident revealed that even the relentlessly trained British could get fouled up at a critical point in a battle. Roger Sheaffe had never led a brigade into action before and, despite his reputation for being a parade ground martinet, his management of the brigade on Phelps's fields does not speak well for his practical skill and forethought. Ironically, it was upon Sergeant Gordon Lyons, one of that class of non-commissioned officers who had been the object of Sheaffe's wrath in the past, that the general now depended. As Smith noted, "Sergt Lyons was very fortunately present and by some means or other got them form'd so."[38]

Smith also made another astute observation by suggesting that "had they [the Americans] attacked them [the British] in the *Field* (while Changing Front Deploying) they certainly would have defeated them."[39] This would have been a perfect time for the Americans to go on the offensive and, had they been reinforced properly, might have led to a very different result on Queenston Heights.

While the British straightened out their order, the senior American officers held another council of war. Their situation was getting worse by the minute: the Grand River people had maintained their sniping at the western flank, appearing and disappearing like phantoms, killing and wounding, and leaving the exhausted troops on edge; the British were massing for an attack; and the numbers of men in the American lines continued to dwindle. Lieutenant Colonel Scott later claimed that there were only 139 regulars and 250 militia remaining to fight while estimates by others ranged from 250 to less than 500.[40] Aligned as they were in their two positions, one fronting the village with the redan battery as its right flank and the second along the military reserve fence, facing south and west, they did not present much opposition to the British. So it is no wonder that the idea of retreating while there was still time became the prime topic of discussion.

Major General Van Rensselaer fuelled the talk of retreat by sending a note to Brigadier General Wadsworth in which he admitted the best that could be done at Lewiston was to send over some more ammunition. He and others had implored the reluctant militia to cross but without success, so he was leaving "the course to be pursued much to his [Wadsworth's] own judgment." Van Rensselaer plainly told Wadsworth that "if he thought

**Battle of Queenston Heights**

A print of the Battle of Queenston Heights, showing all stages, first appeared in *Martial Achievements of Great Britain* by Thomas Sutherland shortly after the War of 1812 with the notation that it had been based upon a drawing by "Major Dennis." That print and others like it vary in detail from this depiction of the battle, which has long been credited to James Dennis, 49th Foot. (Major James Dennis, courtesy of RiverBrink, Home of the Weir Collection, Queenston, Ontario)

1 The Americans land in force about 4:30 a.m. 500 yards south of Queenston.

2. Artillery at Fort Gray covers the American landing.

3 The first exchange of fire, about 5:00 a.m. The British fire from the landing at Queenston to stop the advance of the Thirteenth U.S. Infantry at the base of the escarpment below the redan battery.

4 Americans land at Hamilton Cove, about 6:30 a.m. Dennis may have intended to represent the sharp fight that took place when Lieutenant Colonel Fenwick landed with four boatloads of men at the northern end of Queenston.

5 The first British counterattack on the redan battery, about 7:30 a.m. The British marching up the hill in formation, beyond a figure lying on the ground and attended by officers, are most likely the first attempt to sweep the Americans out of the redan battery, during which Brock was killed.

6 Just after 3:00 p.m. the British advance against the American position on the Heights.

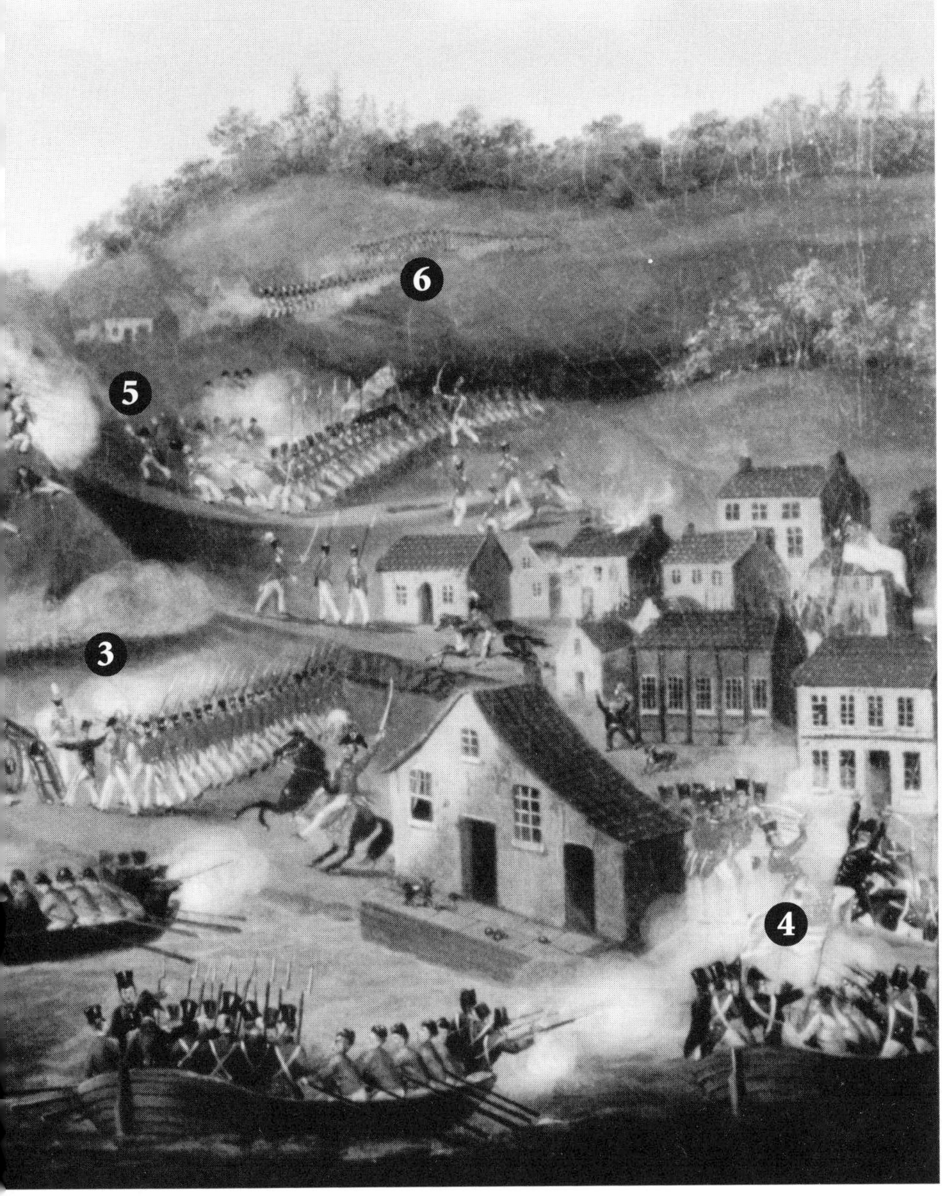

best to retreat, I would endeavour to send as many boats as I could command, and cover his retreat by every fire I could safely make."[41] Wadsworth, who from the beginning of the campaign had admitted his military incompetence but never shunned his duties, now showed the note around the huddle of officers to seek their opinions. As Lieutenant Colonel Chrystie later told the story, he had recommended a retreat around noon to Lieutenant Colonel Scott, who rejected the idea, but now, near 3:00 p.m., Chrystie stated that retreat was out of the question as it was too late to organize a coherent withdrawal. Having read Van Rensselaer's note, Captains Totten and Gibson, Major Mullany and Lieutenant Colonel Stranahan (as Chrystie recalled) all agreed to retreat immediately. Others spoke forcibly against such action, with Lieutenant Colonel Mead insisting that they should stand and "maintain the ground for which so many of our brave men had bled."[42] The council ended with a decision to stay and fight and the officers hurried to their units to get the men ready.

Roger Sheaffe had placed the main body of his regular troops from the 41st Foot and 49th Foot directly in front of the American line at about 400 yards distance. On the western flank he deployed the light infantry of both regiments and, beside them, Runchey's Coloured Company. In the area of the larger woods in the western extreme of the military reserve he positioned Norton's men (lately joined by about twenty more warriors from Niagara), their activity now coordinated by Lieutenant Walter Kerr of the Glengarry Light Infantry Fencible Regiment, the only member of his regiment on the Niagara. Joseph Willcocks, who had helped Brock gain the support of the Grand River people, also appeared on the battlefield at this time and joined Norton's party.

It appears that the militia were intended to form in a line behind and to the left of the main body of regulars, but some confusion persisted as to their place, although Lieutenant Colonels Johnson Butler and Thomas Clarke of the Lincoln Regiments had conferred with Sheaffe. Just before Sheaffe gave the order to advance Captain Richard Bullock arrived from Chippawa with about 150 men of the 41st, the majority being from that regiment's grenadier company. With Bullock came parts of the flank companies of the 2nd Lincoln Regiment under Captain Robert Hamilton and John Rowe, numbering perhaps 100 rank and file; the whole of the

Chippawa force was sent to the right flank of the line. Sheaffe now commanded more than 900 men on the Heights, with Holcroft's guns distracting the enemy from the village.[43]

The weather had improved during the day, the northerly wind having lost most of its early-morning force. The cloud cover had broken and Captain Crooks could see the American "bayonets glistening in the sun."[44] On the other side of the field John Chrystie perceived the British to be "about 1500 strong. They are principally fresh troops, in perfect order, amply provided with artillery, and well prepared in every respect."[45]

Finally, just after 3:00 p.m., Sheaffe gave the order to advance, and the main part of the British line moved forward to within 100 yards of the Americans. At this point the Americans officers suddenly decided to organize a retreat. Quickly, they formed a plan for the line fronting the village and the militia who composed the eastern flank of the main body to proceed down the escarpment to the landing, covered by the rest, who would peel away from the fence in order east to west and follow the others to the river. Before they could begin the manoeuvre, Sheaffe gave the order for the engagement to commence.

The 3-pdrs. barked their greetings, Norton's party gave a war whoop, and the regulars fired their first volley. Traditionally this was considered the most effective volley in a battle since the men had had time to load carefully and the officers could keep them in tight coordination. The American 6-pdr. roared back and the infantry let loose its own mass volley. Lovett's battery fired also and the major, the general's aide, the dependable clerk and bon vivant, witnessed another reality of war that he would never forget; "the mountains seemed to shake beneath the stride of death," he wrote.[46]

Descriptions of how the British approached the American line are unclear, but it seems likely that they advanced, stopped and fired by company or platoon and then marched on until the order came to quicken the step and storm the enemy position. Evidence shows that the light companies and the Grand River nations closed their range on the Americans quickly, firing independently. A blanket of thick white smoke soon covered Samuel Street's field and engulfed the British as they moved forward. Men recalled not being able to see where they were going nor hear when orders were given.

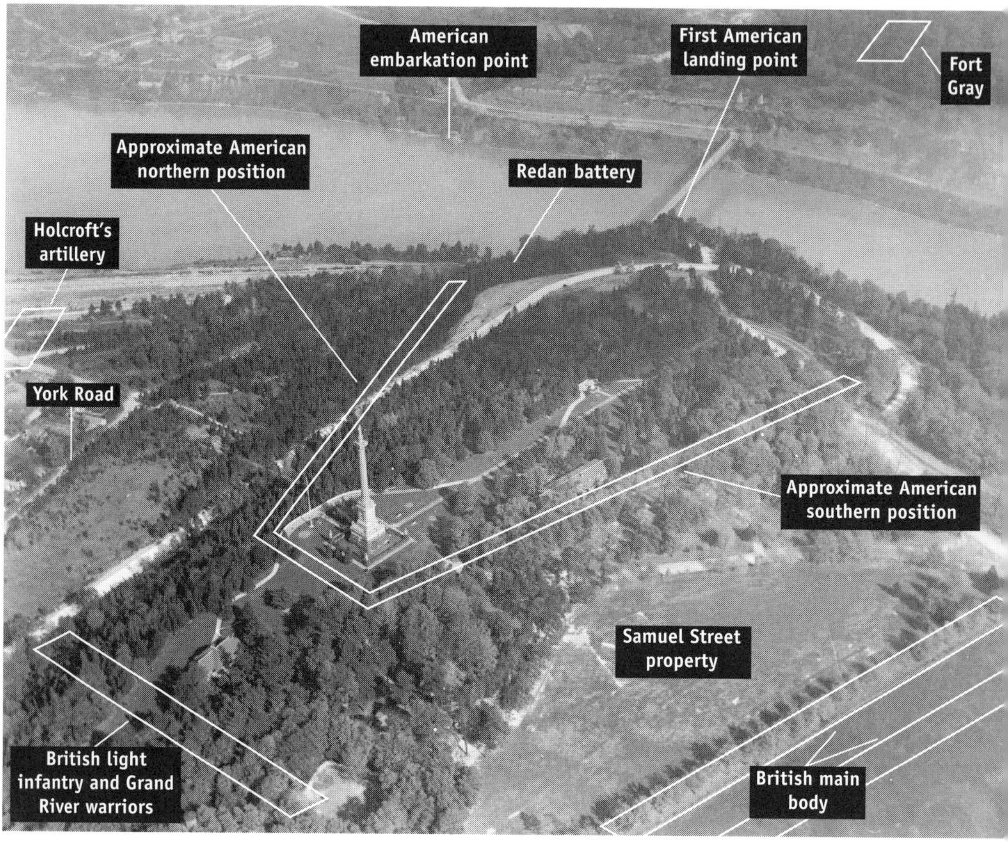


**Queenston Heights, aerial view, 1924**
This aerial photograph shows the main portion of Queenston Heights Park with Brock's monument near the centre of the frame. The approximate British and American positions in the final phase of the battle are shown. The area on the Heights between the monument and the river was covered by oak trees in 1812. It was later cleared and replanted. Note one of the early bridges that spanned the Niagara River between 1898 and 1962. (Based on photo courtesy of the Niagara Parks Collection)

Among the militia the confusion as to their deployment persisted, much to the disgust of Captain Crooks. Sheaffe sent them in a file to the west across the field behind the regulars when the advance began and then seemed to forget them. "Seeing a company in front fall into confusion upon hearing the booming of the two 3 pounders," remembered Crooks, "... I no longer hesitated to face to the front, and at double quick we soon encountered the enemy."[47]

After firing their first mass volley, the Americans started to retreat, with the militia on the east flank marching under control down Portage Road toward the village. For some of the militia, however, the measured steps soon quickened and then became frantic leaps down the hill. Though a tremble seemed to go through the entire American formation, the officers were able to keep most of the regulars and militia under control, returning the British fire as well as they could, before making "an orderly retreat" as more than one officer described it.[49] Chrystie claimed to be the last regular officer in the cantonment and that the remains of his Thirteenth Infantry "*brought up the rear* [and] was *the last that broke*."[48]

When Crooks's militia emerged from the smoke, the British regulars had crossed over the snake fence and entered the oak copse and were exchanging fire at nearly point blank range with the retreating Americans. Crooks and his men found themselves staring down the barrel of Gibson's 6-pdr., sitting unattended. All around them the fighting raged in pell-mell fashion. "I have been in many hail storms," recollected Crooks, "but never in one when the stones few so thick as the bullets on this occasion."[50] Lieutenant George Ridout of the 3rd York could barely find words for the scene when he wrote to his father the next day: "the discharge of small arms, the whizzing of the balls and yells that issued from all quarters, exceed description."[51]

Norton's warriors had burst into the former British cantonment and were wreaking havoc. Their reputation for merciless treatment of their enemies was proven as they shot and hatcheted anyone who was not clearly an ally. James Crooks and others reacted too slowly to save Private Thomas Smith of the 3rd York who, dressed in civilian clothes, too closely resembled an American militiaman. "While pressing forward into the thick of the battle," wrote Crooks, "I espied an Indian giving the coup de grace to a Militia man who he mistook for a Yankee.... The poor fellow put his hand to his head and it was all over with him."[52]

The threat of a similar fate induced some of the panicked Americans to leap over the edge of the cliff and fall to their deaths in the gorge below. Others threw down their weapons and ran for the landing, where the main body of troops collected, but there was not a single batteau left to retrieve any of the men, who made one last attempt to fight off the British. "We obstinately opposed them," recalled Rifleman Willson, "against a shower of Grape-Shot and musketry – but at length fatigued and over powered by numbers, we were forced to lay down our arms."[53]

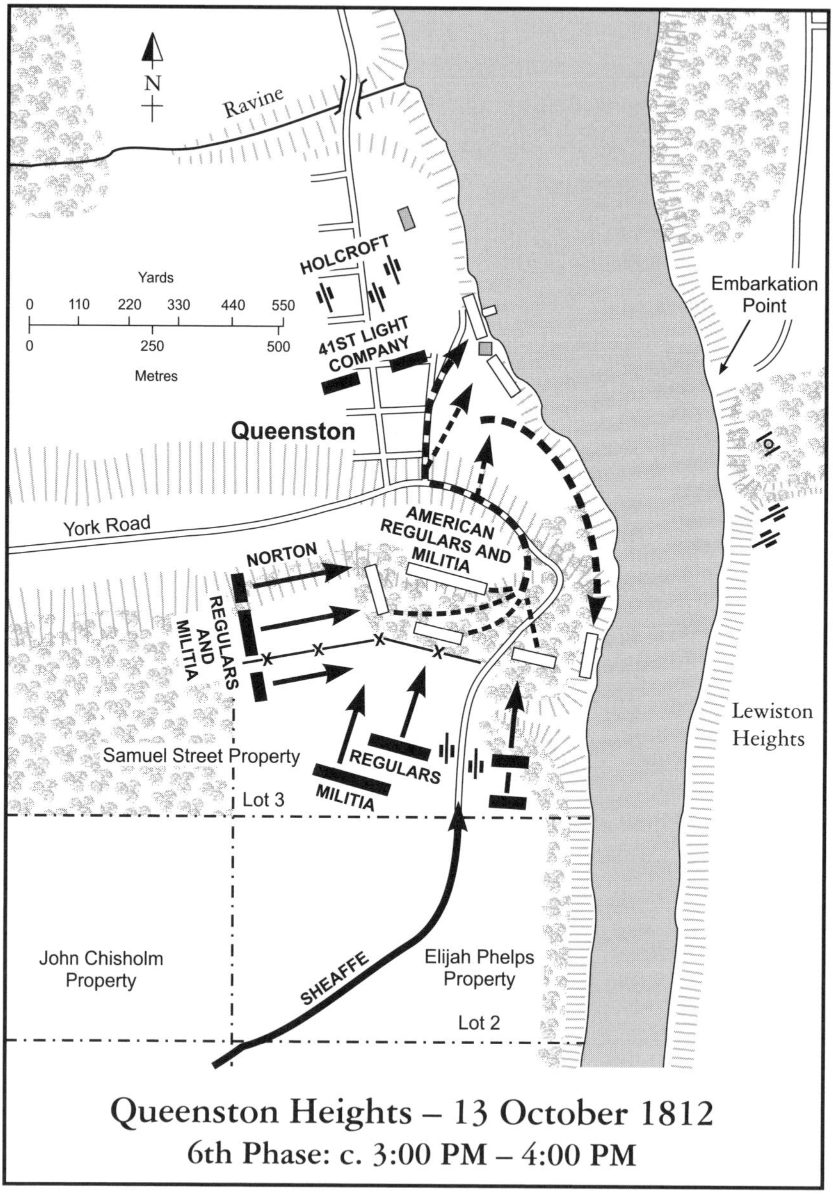


1. Holcroft's guns and Norton's attacks prevent the Americans from establishing a stronger position.
2. Few Americans cross the river. Many begin to abandon the battle line.
3. Sheaffe's column advances north on Portage Road, forming up, after some confusion, in Phelps's fields.
4. The British advance on two fronts, northward and eastward across Street's fields.
5. The Americans resist briefly and then retreat.
6. The fighting becomes close and severe, soon ending in surrender by the Americans.

Surrender was not as easy it sounded; Lieutenant Colonel Scott wrote that it took three attempts with a flag of truce to get the attention of someone in authority. As the British closed in on the Americans, the Iroquois got in among them, trying to separate out individuals. Many of the Americans fled their grasp southward along the narrow steep bank of the gorge, taking cover wherever they could find it. These men who had fought the final phase of the battle were no doubt surprised to find hundreds of their comrades who had taken shelter earlier among the trees in the gorge. Major James Mullany was one of the officers who found a safe refuge until rooted out of his hiding place by a British guard. Others, with all their escape routes cut off, dived into the river and attempted to swim to safety, a sight pathetic to the eyes of Lieutenant Robinson: "the river presented a horrid spectacle, filled with poor wretches who plunged into the stream from an impulse of fear, with scarcely the prospect of being saved."[54] With the blood of battle still boiling, British regulars, militia and natives tried to pick off the frantic swimmers.

Up on the shoulder of the Heights James Crooks watched the Americans struggling with the currents of the Niagara and decided to join the duck-shoot. He borrowed a musket from one of his men who had been wounded and had just begun to take shots at the hapless swimmers when he saw an officer making his way across in a small boat. Crooks directed the musket's dubious aim at this officer until someone told him it was Lieutenant Walter Kerr carrying a note from Sheaffe to Van Rensselaer.

About this time, 4:00 p.m., a repeated bugle-call finally stopped the musketry and order was established across the battlefield. Crooks led his men down the hill, where he met Roger Sheaffe and enthusiastically exchanged congratulations with him. As they stood talking, a party of redcoats and militia brought William Wadsworth to the general. Crooks recalled that Wadsworth "drew his sword and presented the handle to General Sheaffe who said, 'I understand General that your people have surrendered,' to which Wadsworth made no other answer than bowing his head in token that it was so."[55] Almost immediately Winfield Scott arrived in the care of Dr. James Muirhead, who with Lieutenants Robinson and Ridout had only just managed to save Scott from the scalping knife. Sheaffe guaranteed both men that they and their followers would be treated with respect and safe from lurking dangers; aside, he directed Crooks to help

Captain Derenzy round up prisoners and conduct them to Fort George as quickly as possible.

With the din of battle ended, the survivors had time to contemplate how close they had come to death as they began to feel injuries they had not noticed in the heat of combat and saw where their clothing had been nicked by passing shots. "I had been struck by two balls," wrote John Chrystie, "and had seven or eight bullet holes in my clothes."[56] The smoke and confusion lifted off the shore, the hillside and the Heights and revealed the waste of battle. "The view of dead bodies which strewed the ground," John Beverley Robinson explained, "and the mangled carcasses of poor suffering mortals, who filled every room in the village, filled us with compassion."[57] Queenston was now abuzz with a new urgency, the need to retrieve the wounded, tend to their needs, round up the captives, guard them against abuse and marshal them onto the road to confinement at Fort George. Daylight began to slip away as slowly as it had arrived twelve hours earlier. The sun set around 5:40 p.m. and night crept in.

Archie McLean had spent half the day at Durham's farm recovering from his wound after it had been dressed, but in the falling dark he felt well enough to seek a way back to his quarters at Brown's Point. He limped out to River Road and saw a wagon approaching, driven by Captain Swayze of the car brigade, and inquired if he might get a lift. The old militiaman gave the young lawyer from York a hand up to the seat beside him and it was then that McLean noticed that the wagon carried a third passenger. It was Brock, recalled McLean, "whom I had seen in the morning in full health and strength hastening to the scene of Action to meet the Enemies of his country."[58]

Down the muddy road Swayze's wagon creaked, following in the straggling column of victors and conquered, now veterans all. They tramped away from Queenston Heights and a day by which they would always mark the passage of their lives.

# 11

# *"The undaunted bravery of veterans"*

## THE RESULTS OF THE BATTLE

The dead lay out all night on Queenston Heights, some stripped of clothing and equipment, some with their skulls exposed by the ragged incisions of scalping knives. Shortly after dawn on Wednesday, 14 October 1812, soldiers of the 49th Foot were on the hillside and the plain above and tramping through the underbrush on the bank of the gorge, gathering the dead (and discovering the last of the skulkers and wounded). By the time Stephen Van Rensselaer's query about the retrieval of bodies arrived at Queenston, Captain Dennis's men had completed their burial chores and those who had stood and died for the United States were left in their unmarked graves.[1]

A precise accounting of the losses suffered by the Americans in the Battle of Queenston Heights has never been made; estimates ranged from 160 total casualties to 500 killed and drowned alone.[2] The closest that Stephen Van Rensselaer came to making an exact statement about the human cost of the battle was in a letter to Henry Dearborn in which he estimated that there were 60 known dead and 170 wounded.[3] Many of the American wounded ended up in British hands, most of them transported to Niagara, where the churches were turned into temporary hospitals. Van Rensselaer sent surgeons over to help tend them and Sheaffe immediately offered to return any who were strong enough to be moved.

Those wounded who had been evacuated back to Lewiston during the battle were treated in their tents or whatever accommodations could be found, but conditions were rough and no doubt contributed to a steady toll of deaths over the subsequent weeks. Concerned for Solomon Van Rensselaer's survival in the main camp ("he is badly shot to pieces"), John Lovett, who was rendered deaf by his service at Fort Gray, put the lieutenant colonel "on a cot, rigged with cross-bars and side poles and a Detachment of Major Moseley's Riflemen brought him by hand to Schlosser."[4] From there they went to Buffalo, and at Landon's Hotel Lovett secured "quiet quarters where [Solomon] has every attention." None of the rank and file received such treatment, and even the other officers had difficulty finding suitable shelter in which to nurse their wounds. An ensign from the Thirteenth Infantry who had taken ill and remained near Albany finally caught up to his regiment on 24 October and then searched for his trunk. He found it in the care of his captain, Richard Malcom, at a small log cabin a mile west of Lewiston. Captain Henry Armstrong, Lieutenant William Clarke and Ensign James Lent were there with him, convalescing, "crowded together in one room the same occupied by the family being in fact the only one in the house – their situation was deplorable."[5]

The British took two days to finalize the number of Americans captured, ending with 436 regulars and 489 militia for a total of 925.[6] They sent the walking wounded back across the river the day after the battle, soon followed by all the militia. Officially, they were on parole and were honour-bound not to take up arms until formally exchanged for British prisoners. Brigadier General William Wadsworth was also allowed to return because Major General Sheaffe hoped that "his going with the Militia will ... only tend to ensure a strict execution of the agreement."[7] At Wadsworth's request, Major James Mullany and Captain Peter Ogilvie were given permission to return, "there being particular circumstances in the state of their families." Other regular officers crossed over a few days later when Sheaffe and Colonel William Winder, who acted as the representative of the American general, finally worked out an exchange agreement. In return for officers taken during the fight for the *Caledonia* and *Detroit* on 9 October, Captains James Gibson, John Machesney and Joseph Totten and Lieutenant Thomas Randolph won their freedom and right to fight for their country again.

This quick, and seemingly liberal, return of the militia on parole and exchange of regulars provoked "the annoyance of the brave men who conquered them," observed Ensign Smith of the 41st Foot, "and I am sorry to say [has] much exasperated the Indians."[8] Sheaffe's decision to expedite these arrangements earned him a blunt rebuke from Prevost, who felt that he had been too lenient, especially in the case of letting someone of Wadsworth's rank avoid captivity. From those who benefitted by these arrangements, there were few complaints. Rifleman Jared Willson reflected the attitude of his paroled comrades in arms when he wrote, "I am no longer a resident of the 'tented field.' The savage War-Hoop will not again break my slumbers, hoarse clangor of the trumpets call me to the field of Battle. Thanks be to God, that my bones are not now bleaching on the awful Heights of Queenstown."[9]

The British gathered up a considerable bounty of American arms from the battlefield. There was the iron 6-pdr., all its accoutrements and its ammunition wagon containing sixteen rounds, mainly canister. Although one anecdote told of more than 1,200 abandoned muskets and another mentioned 1500, the authorized tally showed only 435 "French" muskets, half as many cartridge belts, 380 bayonets and 141 scabbards; the balance of the weapons must have been seized by stealthy hands before the army could get them. Nearly 5,000 musket cartridges were discovered, half with ball and buckshot and the rest with buckshot only. The single most-valued prize from Queenston Heights was a stand of colours from one of the New York Militia units. This was described as being "made of blue, or purple-coloured changeable silk, about a yard and a half square, with the arms of the United States on one side and those of New York on the other – both surrounded by a circle of stars."[10] The arms were said to show "The American Eagle perched upon the globe, above a shield showing the sun rising over water. Supporters at each side of the shield, one with a cap of liberty. Motto, 'Excelsior.'" The colours were conveyed to England for presentation to the king and subsequent display in the Chapel Royal at Whitehall and later the Royal Hospital at Chelsea.

During their short stay at Fort George and the town of Niagara, some of the Americans shocked the locals with their appearance and provoked this description from George Ridout: "The Americans taken Prisoners officers and men are the most savage looking fellows I ever saw. And to strike a greater terror on their enemies they allowed their beards on their upper lips to grow. This however had no other effect upon us except to raise emotions of disgust."[11]

The prisoners, in their turn, had a story or two to tell about their captivity, especially the regulars for whom there was little hope of a quick passage home. Winfield Scott recalled how the officers were housed at a Niagara inn to which two Iroquois gained entrance one evening. They argued with the unarmed Americans and drew knives on them and were only stopped from mischief when Sheaffe's aide-de-camp Lieutenant Colonel Nathaniel Coffin arrived to invite Scott and the others to dinner with the general. Similar acts of courtesy and respect were shown to Scott and his fellow officers as they sailed first to Kingston and then to Montreal. One exception was Prevost, who earned Scott's contempt when he "behaved like a renegade in causing the prisoners to be marched, on their arrival at Montreal along the front of its garrison, drawn up in line of battle."[12]

Detention at Quebec only lasted until the final week of November when exchanges were negotiated, and the Queenston prisoners, along with others captured at Detroit, embarked in several transports for Boston. Their ordeal was not over because a series of storms of such violence struck the convoy in the Gulf of St. Lawrence that some of the vessels had to put in to Cape Breton Island to save themselves. Other ships struggled until they reached Portland, where they anchored to give the suffering crews and prisoners some relief. In most of the detachments of prisoners – they had been organized into small groups under commissioned officers – one or two men died as a result of the tempestuous voyage. Relief came at last a few weeks later when the ships reached Boston and the men were at liberty to walk on home soil.

The butcher's bill was less expensive for the British: 20 were killed during the battle, the 49th Foot suffering the most with 8 dead. Eighty-five sustained wounds; the 49th led the list again (33), followed by the 41st with 3 dead and 16 wounded and the York militia who had 2 dead and 17 wounded. Twenty-two men were captured, but soon exchanged. Anecdotes suggest that the casualty count was slightly higher than described in despatches which failed to mention the 5 Grand River warriors killed or the uncounted wounded natives, including John Norton himself.[13]

This rate of casualties was considered to be "comparatively small" but its seeming insignificance was obscured by the fact that the toll included Isaac

Brock.[14] The dead general was universally mourned, his death seen as the most heroic of sacrifices, an unmitigated tragedy. "We have to deplore the loss of our gallant Commander, General Brock," wrote George Ridout, "who fell under a fire of musquetry, that can be compared to nothing but the throwing of gravel."[15] "In the midst of his faithful troops ... whom he loved with the affection of a Father ... that great commander gloriously fell when preparing for victory," reported the *Kingston Gazette.*[16] "That General who led our army to victory, whose soul was wrapped up in our prosperity, is now shrouded in death," grieved John Beverley Robinson.[17] John Macdonell succumbed to his wounds on Wednesday morning, 14 October, and was sorrowfully missed as well: "one of the most enterprising men ... has appeared and passed away from us like a brilliant meteor in the firmament," lamented the *Niagara Bee.*[18]

Brock and Macdonell lay in state at Government House until their burial service on 16 October. This evolved into one of the grandest events ever to have taken place in Upper Canada as thousands flocked to the town of Niagara to witness the procession. Graves were opened in the northernmost bastion at Fort George and a cordon was formed between there and Government House by regulars, militia and Iroquois. At 10:00 a.m. the procession got underway with the band of the 41st Foot playing funeral dirges, Brock's horse draped in black led by four grooms, Macdonell's casket passing first followed by Brock's, both strapped to ammunition wagons. Nine pall bearers escorted the general, among them Evans, Glegg, Dennis and Holcroft, all wearing black crepe on their sword knots and black arm bands. The Reverend Robert Addison read the graveside service, and as the caskets were lowered into the earth, guns roared out their salute; on the American side a similar salute was given, at the arrangement of Lieutenant Colonel Scott.[19]

While many in the Canadas were downcast and determined to outdo each other in eulogizing Brock, at least one person aired his thoughts, albeit privately, about the wisdom of Brock's decision to lead the charge on the redan battery. This was Major Thomas Evans, who wrote a brief description of the battle for Colonel Henry Procter's eyes, and after describing Brock's death, opined "here you will recognize that impetuosity of disposition, that fixed untempered by discretion which characterized our fallen ... general what a Pity a Mind so noble and generous had not

**The death of Brock**
This fanciful version of the death of the hero reflects the mythical aspects of Brock's sad fate as well as an inaccurate portrayal of British troops, their native allies and the field of battle. (Oil painting by John D. Kelly, National Archives of Canada, C-273)

possessed that prudence which might have easily saved his own valuable life."[20] Months later Evans alluded to another aspect of the general's character that no one else mentioned. In explaining deficiencies that were evident in the militia and commissariat, Evans revealed that the general had been told about them, but "Poor General Brock's high spirit would never descend to particulars, trifles I may say in the abstract, but ultimately essentials."[21]

Evans was virtually alone in his criticism. Even members of that segment of the population whom the general had doubted, the Grand River Six Nations, sought an opportunity to express "the sorrow and deep regret with which his loss has filled our hearts."[22] They held a special service in the council house at Fort George on 5 November, attended by senior military officers and prominent chiefs. John Norton and William Claus were present but during the presentation of eight strings of white wampum and a large white belt, it was a chief named Little Cayuga who memorialized Brock. He ended by speaking directly to Major General Sheaffe, referring to him as "the successor of our departed friend" whom the Grand River people wanted to assure that they would "support him to the last."

Roger Hale Sheaffe had now risen to the top as Brock's death made him the commander of the forces in Upper Canada and administrator of the provincial government. Proclamations of support and reverence such as he received from the Iroquois paled in comparison, however, to the encomiums heaped upon Brock. It was almost as if Queenston Heights had been Brock's victory rather than Sheaffe's. The Executive Council of the legislature of Upper Canada praised Sheaffe for "the happy effect of the coolness, intrepidity and Judgment which you displayed in that eminent situation."[23] When news of the victory reached England, the Prince of Wales, acting as Prince Regent during King George III's most recent bout of madness, expressed his "entire approbation of the distinguished Services of [Sheaffe] on this occasion" and conferred a baronetcy upon the general.[24] Locally, there were muted words of praise for Sheaffe's management of the latter stages of the battle, such as a mention in the *Kingston Gazette* that he "proved himself worthy to fill that important, tho' difficult and dangerous situation."[25] Evans referred to the outcome of the day as "this brilliant success" and to the general as "the distinguished officer who, with his gallant troops, achieved it," and John Beverley Robinson mentioned "the cool though determined and vigorous conduct of General Sheaffe."[26] But when others described what William Holcroft termed "a very brilliant affair," the day after the fighting, they offered no glowing adjectives for the new commander in Upper Canada.[27] Isaac Brock had left an imposing image in the minds of most of those who outlived him; he was still considered "the only man worthy of being at the head of affairs."[28]

Besides the parole of the American militia, there were other issues which occurred in the first days of Sheaffe's term as commander in Upper Canada that sparked indignation.[29] By early evening on 13 October there was a movement afoot among the militia at Niagara to immediately attack and destroy Fort Niagara, perhaps as revenge for the fire-damage suffered in the town. When Captain William Derenzy returned from Queenston with his men (and a party of Americans under guard) he offered to cross the river and effect the destruction, but Sheaffe forbade it, probably because he was unwilling to over-extend his exhausted troops. Instead, he and Van Rensselaer agreed on an armistice of three days to allow for the movement of wounded and the parole and exchange of prisoners. When this project was still incomplete on 16 October, the two generals agreed to extend it for three more days, whereupon another agreement was made to let the truce last indefinitely; it ultimately ended on 20 November. The lull allowed Sheaffe to attend to his new civil duties at York and for essential repairs and improvements to be made on both sides of the line, but it was unpopular in the communities of Niagara.

"This was the most ruinous policy that could be adopted by us," wrote Hamilton Merritt. "The Militia were kept out en masse, doing nothing, consequently most of them went home, as their property was suffering, and no appearance of their being wanted on the frontier."[30] Prevost was also displeased with the lengthy armistice, although he had always favoured a defensive posture. He implied his misgivings to Sheaffe, and months later openly criticized him in a despatch to the home government by asserting that "Sir R. H. Sheaffe lost a glorious opportunity of crossing the Niagara River during the confusion and dismay which then prevailed, for the purpose of destroying Fort Niagara, by which the command of the Niagara River would have been secured to us during the war."[31]

Sheaffe's report about the battle generally gave credit where it was deserved.[32] Routine in its businesslike description of the action at Queenston, the account expressed Sheaffe's grief at the loss of Brock, praised the "judicious" conduct of Holcroft, described the contributions of Dennis and Williams, and noted the "essential assistance" provided by Glegg, Fowler and Kerr and by Norton and his men. Sheaffe listed seventeen of the militia officers present, but his omission of Captain John Chisholm, 2nd York, Lieutenant John Ball of the Lincoln Artillery and his own aide-de-camp, and brother-in-law, Nathaniel Coffin was noticed. This error was corrected in time, but an eyebrow or two must have been raised to see these men overlooked when the general had made a point of noting that Lieutenant Colonel Myers missed the affair because he was at Fort Erie.

Eyebrows were also twitching at some of the orders Sheaffe issued through October and into November. From his arrival at Niagara, district general orders from Sheaffe tended to have a harder edge than Brock's, which was a pattern that continued after the battle. The flank companies of the 49th Foot, for instance, were quickly replaced at Queenston by two companies of the 41st and marched back to Fort George. Although the casualties they had suffered was reason enough for them to be withdrawn, the move was considered "very odd" by some of the officers.[33] It was in part explained by what Ensign Smith said were "the irregularities which took place with them" and by a district general order chastising the drunkenness of certain regulars and the sale of liquor by unlicensed vendors. Sheaffe was also concerned about the conduct of the militia and ordered the rounding up of absentees and the strict drill of each company. Sheaffe did make a point of praising those militiamen who had stuck to their posts and he recognized the efforts of some of the regular officers and their men, but, as his predecessor had suggested about the major general, there was something in Roger Sheaffe's manner that grated on people. Decades after the battle, James Crooks was still chewing over the confusion during the deployment of the troops on Queenston Heights and blamed it on Sheaffe. "The General must have seen all this [disorder]," wondered Crooks, "following the attack as he did with a stick in his hand."[34] For Crooks, this was a lasting image of Sheaffe as the remote commander, nearly the exact opposite of his predecessor.

Sheaffe's first weeks of command were loaded with military and civil duties and taken up with a steady concern for what the Americans were going to do next. In preparation, he shifted some of the forces from one point to another as he watched the activity on the far shore. The war was by no means over and the movements of the Americans led him to believe that an attack would come in the upper river.[35]

While the British buried Brock, and Roger Sheaffe took command in Upper Canada, the situation on the American side of the river changed drastically. Stephen Van Rensselaer wrote his despatch to William Eustis on 14 October in which he reviewed at length the events leading to the battle, his intentions, the early success and the failure of the militia to support the men on the Heights. He praised Solomon Van Rensselaer, John Fenwick, John Chrystie, James Mullany and a couple of the militia commanders but failed to mention John Wool, William Wadsworth and Winfield Scott, among others. Van Rensselaer concluded his report by stating that "*the victory was really won, but lost* for the want of a small reinforcement; *one-third of the idle men might have saved all.*"[36]

On 16 October Stephen Van Rensselaer handed command of the army along the Niagara to Alexander Smyth and went to Buffalo, where he took up accommodations in Landon's Hotel with Lovett and Solomon. He then wrote to Henry Dearborn, offering his resignation.[37] While Stephen waited for a response, Daniel Tompkins arrived on 23 October and stayed at Landon's where he had a long consultation with his defeated general; the governor pointedly avoided visiting the convalescing Solomon, a decision that elicited wide comment. Of the governor's sudden appearance, John Lovett painted a particularly sardonic image: "Governor Tompkins, by exceeding hard driving has so managed, and economized his time as to be able to be in season to get here too late.... He has been closeted almost the whole day with the General but I cannot learn that he has any plan, or plan of a plan, or copy of a plan's plan's plan."[38] The outcome of the meeting was that Tompkins accepted Stephen Van Rensselaer's resignation.

Rather than a storm of criticism, Stephen Van Rensselaer was surprised and gratified to be welcomed home with tributes almost befitting a conquering hero; "we are proud in acknowledging the meed of praise which is due the veteran Van Rensselaer," declared one sympathetic editor.[39] There was no inquiry convened to examine his command of the army, but his days in the field were over. And so were his hopes of attaining the governorship, which he pursued through the winter but lost to Daniel Tompkins in the elections of 1813.

Solomon had recovered well enough by the second week of November to hobble home on crutches with the ever-attentive Lovett at his side, where he too was warmly greeted. He rejoiced to be once more with his children and Arriet, but the glory of war still lured him and he expected to be given command of a regiment in the regular army. Although his supporters lobbied for that appointment, it was not to be, and Solomon resumed his role as adjutant general of the New York militia and never again went on active service.[40]

Brigadier General Alexander Smyth was quick to reorganize the army on the Niagara.[41] He sent Colonel Winder to command at Fort Niagara, leaving Fort Gray in the hands of the militia artillery, broke up the camp at Lewiston and withdrew the remaining militia to Fort Schlosser. Of the more than 2,200 men in the five regiments of detached militia present at or near Lewiston just before the battle, all but about 450 men had deserted or been paroled or killed, and these were concentrated into one regiment under Lieutenant Colonel Hugh Dobbin, who was hard pressed to keep them in line. The Thirteenth Infantry had been so depleted that the remaining men from Chrystie's battalion were distributed among available officers of that unit to form three companies and then united with the sparsely-manned Fifth Infantry, the whole commanded by Colonel Peter Schuyler while Colonel Homer Milton of the Fifth received permission to take a furlough.

Confident that he could form his brigade into an effective force and supported by a large detachment of Pennsylvania militia which arrived midway through October, Smyth made plans to achieve what Van Rensselaer had failed to do. Dearborn was in full agreement with this initiative and made recommendations about how "to pass into Canada and secure good winter quarters."[42] Secretary of War Eustis also hoped for a victory on the Niagara and informed Smyth about military reinforcements sent to Commodore Chauncey at Sackets in expectation that the two commanders would coordinate their operations. Smyth began his offensive with a series of bombastic proclamations in which he vowed: "Where I command, the vanquished and the peaceful man, the child, the maid, and the matron shall be secure from wrong. If we conquer, we will 'conquer but to save.'"[43] His first attempt to conquer came on 28 November with simultaneous attacks near Fort Erie and Chippawa, but after some initial success, the troops were forced back into their boats. A second attempt two days later got no further than the embarkation before it was cancelled, after which Smyth's command dissolved into disorder. Worn out from a late-season campaign, never equipped or trained with any consistent degree of thoroughness, the American army on the Niagara was finished for the year. Its latest commander sought a leave from active duty and never served in the field again.

By the time Alexander Smyth rode away from the Niagara River, controversies were already flaring up over the way the attack on Queenston had been handled and the finger-pointing had begun. Captain Peter Ogilvie, Thirteenth Infantry, travelled home to New York on parole and there gave details of the fight, leaving the impression, unwittingly, that he had led the party which captured the redan battery. When published in a number of newspapers, the account was noticed immediately by officers, including John Wool, who took offence at Ogilvie's comments. Ogilvie was quick to write the editor of the *New York Evening Post* to assure the public that he had not intended to create "a misconception."[44] How strongly this taint attached itself to Ogilvie is difficult to assess, but it might have proven to be a factor in his decision to resign his commission in June 1813.

John Chrystie was one of the officers who came to Wool's support after he reached New York in December following his exchange, by which time Chrystie felt himself very much hard done by. Ordered to take post at Canandaigua, which he saw as a "a penance for Queenstown," Chrystie became incensed when he learned that Major James Mullany was being toasted and pushed forward in the service. Chrystie explained to his patron, Secretary of the Treasury Albert Gallatin, that, while they were prisoners, he, Winfield Scott and the engineer Captain Joseph Totten had ridiculed what they perceived to be Mullany's avoidance of hard fighting during the battle. "When he told me at New York," wrote Chrystie, "he was going to Washington, I advised him from sheer charity not to, thinking it might induce some officer to attack and drive him out of the service!"[45] Such did not happen, and, as Chrystie alleged, Mullany's "*party* connection" earned him a promotion to lieutenant colonel of the Twenty-Third Infantry.

Chrystie's accusations did not end with Mullany. He placed the blame for the defeat at Queenston "in the character of the men who held the reins of that army, and in their military and political relations." "The statements promulgated from Albany are designed to deceive," he believed and his own discomfiture at Canandaigua was no surprise, given "the animals I have had to deal with." Chrystie was soon promoted to the colonelcy of the Twenty-Third but it seems likely his resentment continued until his untimely death from one of the contagious fevers at Fort George in September 1813. After briefly serving as Chrystie's subordinate, James Mullany rose to colonel and quartermaster general before his honourable discharge from the U.S. Army in 1818.

Death saved John Chrystie from Solomon Van Rensselaer's wrath. In a lengthy diatribe to James Wilkinson (no stranger to controversy himself) about how the battle had been reported, Van Rensselaer charged that, when the first wave crossed, Chrystie "did shamefully retreat at a most critical moment, … and ordered the two boats next to him … to follow."[46] He quoted the observations of Captain William Lawrence, who was in one of the other boats, to support his claim and even to reveal that the lieutenant colonel's wound to his hand had actually been a cut he received while scrambling over rocks along the bank of the river. "He had disobeyed orders and retreated in the face of the enemy," wrote Van Rensselaer. "I had only to make the charge and nothing could have saved him."

In 1836, after John Armstrong published *Notices of the War of 1812,* which included Chrystie's 1813 version of the battle, Solomon produced *A Narrative of the Affair of Queenstown* as a rebuttal and stated that had Chrystie reached the proper landing, as he should have, "no delay need have been occasioned at the important crisis when I became disabled. ... To his failure may mainly be attributed all our disasters."[47]

Solomon's publication motivated an indirect rebuttal from John Wool, who had kept private his wounded sense of honour over the years. In 1838 William L. Stone published his *Life of Joseph Brant,* which featured a section on Queenston Heights, in which Brant's son John had been involved. Wool read the book and then wrote to Stone to advise him that his account relied too much on Solomon's distorted view of the affair. Van Rensselaer "failed to do justice to those who accompanied him on that memorable morning," Wool insisted after describing in detail the activity of the Thirteenth Infantry during the initial landing, the officers involved and the casualties suffered, which were "not even mentioned in the official despatch."[48] Wool was correct; Stephen Van Rensselaer had made no reference to the role the Thirteenth had played early in the fighting and Solomon's account was surprisingly thin in its depiction of the first phase of the battle. Solomon claimed credit, Wool pointed out, "for conduct that belongs to another, and which as a brave and gallant soldier he should never have appropriated to himself."

Another officer who had been in the thick of things but never went back to war had a similarly critical view of Stephen and Solomon Van Rensselaer. "The whole business of that day," wrote rifleman Jared Willson, "and the untimely attack were authorized by the commander, at the instigation of his Aid – Solomon Van Rensselaer.... [t]he ambition of one man [Solomon] and the folly of another brought disgrace upon our country. This you will find to be a fact."[49]

Henry Dearborn's finger pointed in the same direction as Jared Willson's. Terming the attack on Queenston "mortifying" and "extraordinary," he suggested to Secretary of War Eustis that "If 6000 men had been sent over instead of 1000, complete success would undoubtedly have been the result."[50] Dearborn stated inaccurately that Smyth had not been informed of the attack and concluded that "Brig. Gen. Wadsworth, ... I presume with one or two others, was the projector of this extraordinary measure." Forgetting that he had offered Van Rensselaer an operational plan very similar to the one actually followed, Dearborn absolved himself of responsibility by claiming that he had given the general "explicit" directions on how to proceed but "for some unaccountable fatality" Van Rensselaer went ahead with an attack of which he himself would have disapproved. Dearborn expressed his hope that the "past misfortune this season" would be retrieved, but Alexander Smyth's campaign soon failed and Dearborn's own desultory effort on the border of Lower Canada midway through November was yet another calamity.

The deeper reasons underlying the ultimate failure of the Niagara campaign were known, and the editors of such newspapers as the *Northern Whig*, of Hudson, New York, which was sympathetic to the Federalist party, used the facts to berate the Republican administration. Here, the resistance of the majority of the militia to cross was seen as justifiable. "Nothing could be constitutionally demanded of these men, but to defend the country against invasion," it argued.[51] The editor blamed the administrations (in Washington and Albany), "the projector of the enterprize," for not ensuring that "the regular troops with such of the militia as volunteered" were prepared and strong enough in numbers to accomplish the aim of the operation at Queenston. "Not one single department of the war system has been able to perform its duty," pointed out the editor, in part because the administration had hesitated to invoke a taxation system to support it properly, for fear of making an unpopular war look even less appetizing.

Although obviously political in its slant, this editorial came close to covering all the reasons behind the inability of James Madison's government to punish Britain by achieving its objective for 1812 – conquering a large portion of the Canadian provinces. Unwilling to admit these flaws publicly, the president briefly described the Queenston affair in his annual address to Congress in November with the regret that "Our loss has been considerable, and is deeply to be lamented."[52] He did feel optimistic, however, that it had been fought by "Inexperienced soldiers, who must daily improve in the duties of the field." Governor Tompkins's public statement was similarly tempered and when he addressed the state legislature early in November he said, "Although the attack on Queenstown did not eventuate propitiously, yet it cannot for a moment be doubted that the issue of the contest will be glorious for our country."[53] Such reverses were to be expected with a new army, the governor explained, but they were not due to a want of bravery or resources. He insisted that the "army and the militia have invariably exhibited the deliberate and undaunted bravery of veterans," and he proposed that the legislature make provisions for the families of militiamen who had been disabled or killed.

President Madison was nearly felled in the polls by the disastrous campaign. Backed by Federalists and a strong faction of the Republican party, De Witt Clinton was his opponent in the presidential election that took place in October and November. In New York State, where Clinton's support ran high, a committee met publicly to produce the "Address to the People of the United States," which essentially became Clinton's election platform. "The nomination of De Witt Clinton," the address read, "... proposes to the Union ... a relief from the evils of an inefficient administration, and of an inadequately conducted war."[54] Clinton offered an enticing alternative to Madison and, though he eventually lost, the election was the closest since 1800 with the president receiving 128 electoral votes to Clinton's 89. The sharp divide in regional voting showed how unpopular the war was in the northern states; only two (Pennsylvania and Vermont) of the nine states north of Maryland and Kentucky supported Madison. Such a division along regional lines would not be seen again until 1860.

The battle at Queenston solved few problems for the British. They were able to repel Smyth's invasion in November and Major General Sheaffe proudly noted a continuation of the "strong proof of the valor which has uniformly distinguished the militia of this country when called into action."[55] But the attacks in the upper river led to bitter criticism of Sheaffe by local officers who openly doubted his commitment to the defence of the populace between Chippawa and Fort Erie. The resultant gossip and calumny undermined Sheaffe's authority and set a tone that pervaded his entire term as commander in Upper Canada until it ended shortly after his defeat at York in April 1813. In the larger context, however, Sheaffe, and Prevost, continued to earn the praise of the British government for their defence of the provinces and Earl Bathurst, the minister for war and the colonies, wrote that the monarch and the government gave their "entire approbation of the Conduct of Troops employed in Upper Canada."[56]

As the first snow fell in December 1812 the British could congratulate themselves on having withstood what many had believed would be a cakewalk by the Americans. But there were plenty of problems on the horizon. In December the stalwart militia on the Niagara frontier deserted in large numbers mainly because of "the want of assistance in various ways either for providing for their comfort or their subsistence during the winter," as Sheaffe explained to Prevost.[57] The quick and effective manner in which Commodore Chauncey gained control of Lake Ontario before the navigation season ended was also cause for concern, and Sheaffe and others advised Prevost about improvements needed in the Provincial Marine, asking that a Royal Navy detachment be sent to take control on the lakes. The fighting on the Niagara and Detroit Rivers had reduced the strength of the regular forces with little hope of their substantial reinforcement until transports could arrive at Quebec from across the Atlantic in the spring. With winter about to descend, Sheaffe found himself scrambling to ensure that his troops were fed, clothed and paid and that work moved ahead to improve the province's defences, especially in the naval department.

In light of the difficult situation in Upper Canada during the winter of 1812/13, the victory at Queenston Heights proved to have little in the way of strategic importance. At the end of the day, the British held onto their territory, but their defences were weakened, not just in numbers but due to the loss of the seemingly irreplaceable Isaac Brock. The outcome on the Heights provided only a temporary reprieve from attack. Even if Sheaffe had crossed the river following the battle and destroyed the fortifications and camps along the American shore of the river, little of lasting effect would have been accomplished. The American government did not lose its determination to seize the Canadian provinces. The next spring an invasion force that included only a few elements of Van Rensselaer's army launched operations from Sackets Harbor before moving to re-establish a presence on the Niagara River.

Although the battle failed to solve much strategically, it was a pertinent lesson in warfare, providing numerous examples of how not to launch a river crossing. [58] At the basic level of logistical preparations, the Americans had serious lapses: insufficient batteaux, lack of ammunition and entrenching tools on site and ready for use, inadequate control in the staging area where the troops concentrated and at the embarkation point, and no apparent provision for control of the return of batteaux from Queenston.

Tactically, the operation had some soundness in that it was intended to send several organized waves of troops, with artillery support, to capture the high ground above Queenston, but focusing the assault on only one landing place was a mistake. Why Van Rensselaer's council of war did not decide to enter Canada on a wider front, with several points of landing at, above and below Queenston is difficult to explain; after all, such a plan had been put on paper earlier in the campaign.[59] Van Rensselaer and his staff and the regulars and militia who had been on the river all summer were familiar with the British positions in and around Queenston. They must have known that the flank companies of the 49th Foot were concentrated in the village while militia sub-units held the batteries downriver. Nevertheless, Solomon Van Rensselaer made his landing at the enemy's strongest point and placed the troops at the foot of the escarpment, where they were caught between British fire in the village and on the Heights.

Although the attack was supposed to occur in a series of waves, the Thirteenth Infantry was put in the vanguard, despite having no practical knowledge of the area under assault. Lieutenant Colonel Chrystie might have made a brief observation of the terrain and batteries at Queenston when he visited Van Rensselaer on 11 October but none of his officers or men had ever seen the foreign shore they were expected to attack in the black of night. A better choice for leadership in the first wave would have been Lieutenant Colonel Fenwick, who had been on the frontier since September and was also senior to Chrystie, and with whom Solomon Van Rensselaer already had a working relationship. Exhausted though they were from the first attempt to cross, Fenwick and his detachments of artillery and infantry (with Major Mullany) at least knew the ground they would attempt to seize. Perhaps Fenwick would have been less impetuous than Chrystie who ignored the instructions he had received about sharing the first wave with the militia.

**Monument on the grave of Solomon Van Rensselaer**
Solomon died in April 1852 and was buried beside Arriet (who had died in 1840) at the North Dutch Church Cemetery in Albany. When such old cemeteries were closed, the Van Rennselaers were re-interred at the Albany Rural Cemetery in Menands, New York. (Photo by the author)

The generalship of Stephen Van Rensselaer and the advice he obtained from Solomon and the other senior officers led to the logistic and tactical errors of the attack on Queenston. Van Rensselaer's inexperience also revealed itself in other ways. In preparation for the invasion of Canada, he failed to balance the distribution of his troops in the manner followed by Brock. His regulars were concentrated at the ends of his line, at Fort Niagara and Black Rock, with the militia mainly in his centre, at Manchester and Lewiston. He knew that regiments of regulars were due to arrive early in October and he might have ordered them to encamp at Manchester while he sent the units of detached militia to Black Rock. The regulars would then have been nearby on 12 October and, trained properly or not, they would not have had the option of refusing to cross the river as the militia did. Stephen Van Rensselaer lacked the military skill to make such arrangements, and his advisors, in particular the much-lauded Solomon, did not counsel him adequately.

When the chorus of critics began to harp loudly on Monday, 12 October, about the need to take decisive action, the general seems to have panicked. He ordered his worn-out troops into action again, allowed a newcomer to the scene, John Chrystie, to assume a leadership role, and then refused to let Winfield Scott cross with his artillerymen although they had lately clashed, successfully, with the British at Fort Erie. Furthermore, Stephen Van Rensselaer clearly did not prepare himself for leading his army in the field, relying almost completely on the skill of his second cousin. Once Solomon was removed from the fight, the general was lost and so was any hope of victory. From that point no one seemed to have the kind of control that is a requisite for battlefield success.

It can be argued that any gains the Americans might have made by capturing Queenston would have been transient. Midway through September Brock realized that he lacked sufficient men and resources to launch an effective attack into New York State and so he conceded to Sir George Prevost's defensive policy. [60] Van Rensselaer, despite his numbers, was in a similar situation. His army, weakened by the long and uncomfortable weeks in camp, was still suffering from lack of supplies in the second week of October and there was little indication that either of these problems would be quickly remedied. Commodore Chauncey could not have provided much assistance since it was not until November that he hounded the Provincial Marine off Lake Ontario and the severe weather limited his operations to the eastern extremes of the lake. If Van Rensselaer had conquered Queenston, he would still have had to deal with the British regulars and militia posted on the upper river. Smyth would certainly have crossed in October to challenge this force, but as the events of November revealed, his brigade was hardly ready for battle. In all likelihood, the attack on

**Monument on the grave of Stephen Van Rensselaer**
After his death in January 1839, Stephen was buried in a private family cemetery. He was later re-interred with his wife at the Albany Rural Cemetery. (Photo by the author)

Queenston would have amounted to little more than a single, brief victory, followed by a return to the *status quo*. Van Rensselaer's decision to cross was essentially a desperate effort to retrieve a difficult and disappointing campaign.

When it is considered in the broadest perspective, the campaign on the Niagara frontier was doomed to fail long before Stephen Van Rensselaer took command. His defeat was a product of the many inadequacies of the American army, the discord in Congress that produced unwieldy legislation and the administration's inability to comprehend the realities of a divided campaign in the northern wilderness. Daniel Tompkins expended all his resources to prosecute war along the Niagara River, although his political biases made circumstances difficult at times. His main liaison with the administration, Henry Dearborn, handicapped the campaign with his lethargy and myopia more than any other individual and should have been relieved of his command. William Eustis might have thought about removing Dearborn, but he was experienced enough to know who would pay for the disastrous outcome of the summer and autumn, as he explained to Dearborn, "Fortunately for you, the want of success which has attended the campaign will be attributed to the Secretary of War."[61] And so it was; Eustis, whom many had come to consider unfit for his job, resigned his office on 3 December. Secretary of State James Monroe replaced him briefly until the president convinced Brigadier General John Armstrong to take on the portfolio. In the months that followed, some improvements were made in the administration of the army, but Madison, Armstrong and the rest of the cabinet decided to continue waging war in 1813 with a strategy based on multiple thrusts into Canada, and Dearborn lingered on in command. It was as if the administration had learned little from its harsh experiences in 1812.

The best outcome for the Americans at Queenston Heights, as Madison pointed out, was that it served as the first proving ground for a new generation of officers and men. The experiences of managing a military camp in the field, running an effective training program in drill and tactical manoeuvres, leading troops into position and withstanding the horrors of a battlefield helped to foster the development of an efficient army. Out of the disaster at Queenston emerged young officers like Winfield Scott, who would return to Niagara and eventually prove his worth as a brigade commander in 1814; he died a distinguished lieutenant general in 1866. John Wool was promoted to major in the Twenty-Ninth Infantry in April 1813 and the next year, for commendable conduct at Plattsburgh, he was breveted a lieutenant colonel. He retired as a major general in 1863 and died six years later. Lieutenant Stephen Kearney, Thirteenth Infantry, Engineer Captain Joseph Totten and Captain Nathan Towson, Second Artillery, also rose to the rank of major general during lengthy and active careers.[62] It was around officers such as these that the U.S. Army developed during the first half of the 19th century.

On the British side, Isaac Brock's defence of the Niagara frontier was undeniably effective. He balanced the strengths of the four key posts on the river between regulars and militia and only the absence of a large body of reinforcements (which he would have posted in Pelham, a central location) kept his plan from being a classic example of how a river front should be defended.[63] Brock's men suffered for want of provisions, clothing, shelter and arms (though not as severely as the Americans did), yet he and his staff were able to maintain their health and readiness for action. The general issued clear and detailed orders (concerning an invasion of the upper river, at least) and patrolled the entire length of his command on a regular basis. It was only in the final hours of his life that Brock's impetuosity prompted him to race off to Queenston without leaving orders at Fort George and to make his three critical errors on the battlefield. He was killed shortly after Solomon Van Rensselaer was injured, but Sheaffe took his place and soon controlled the concentration and deployment of the British force. Although Sheaffe's final preparations for battle were done with less than textbook efficiency, he managed to send his regulars, militia and native fighters across Samuel Street's fields, where they easily overawed their enemy.

For the British army, Queenston was another in a long string of victories and not an especially significant one in the context of its many and mighty accomplishments. Still, for the units and men involved in it, the battle was important.[64] The regulars of the 41st Foot and the 49th had not been in action for more than a decade, yet their conduct at Queenston added another achievement to their regiments' proud histories. The regiments were both granted battle honours for the affair and allowed to add "Queenstown" to their colours. Sheaffe received a baronetcy, while Captains James Dennis, John Williams, William Holcroft and William Derenzy were promoted by brevet to major; Major Thomas Evans was made a lieutenant colonel by brevet.

The battle also served to tighten the bond between the Grand River Six Nations and the British army, establishing an alliance that would last until the making of peace. Sheaffe chose to honour John Norton for his contribution at Queenston by giving him the title of "Captain of the Confederate Indians." This was a title Norton's mentor Joseph Brant had received and it demonstrated to all the close link between the Grand River peoples and the army. Its relevance was further supported when some of the native leaders were given appointments, as Brock had suggested would be necessary, and the warriors received gifts in the form of supplies to make up for the crops that had gone to ruin during their absence.

There were no similar rewards for the officers and men of the Lincoln and York militia who had ably supported the regulars. Following the battle some promotions were made to fill vacancies, but the only militia officer singled out for special notice was Lieutenant John Beverley Robinson of the Second Flank company of the 3rd York. Although only twenty-one years old, Robinson was Sheaffe's selection to take the place of John Macdonell as attorney general.

The militia were left, however, with a pride in having fought in a victorious major battle, an accomplishment that must have grown even more impressive when word reached the Canadian side of the river that most of the New York militia had refused to fight. Of course, the officers and men from the Niagara and York had been fighting to defend their families and homes, which gave them a determination their opponents lacked, but this did not diminish the clear proof of their bravery and loyalty. It has been argued that the contribution made by the Canadian militia during the War of 1812 has been overstated and glorified and that too many men dodged service by any means possible.[65] This was true in numerous instances, but not at Queenston Heights. For the farmers and millers, shop owners and lawyers who answered the call, the battle was a defining moment. They would forever be veterans of that battle and, like veterans everywhere, they would strive to keep the remembrance of their accomplishment alive – and rightly so.

EPILOGUE

# *"May its effects not be lost upon the rising generation."*

Within a year of the Battle of Queenston Heights, efforts were underway to honour the memory of Isaac Brock and those who had fought with him. They began in Britain in July 1813 when Parliament sponsored a "military monument" for the fallen general. It eventually found a home on one of the columns in the south transept of St. Paul's Cathedral in London, where Nelson and Wellington are laid to rest.

In Upper Canada the legislature followed suit the next spring when it voted £500 "for the express purpose of erecting a monument on the heights of Queenstown near the spot where he fell."[1] A committee made inquiries about suitable monuments the next year and wrote to Brock's brothers for their opinions. In 1817 Savery Brock travelled to Canada to show the committee a design by Richard Westmacott, who had created the Brock memorial in St. Paul's. This proposal featured an eight-foot bronze statue of the general atop a granite pedestal and base around which were reliefs of his actions at Detroit and Queenston. The whole structure would stand eighteen and a half feet tall and cost about £2,500, but while the committee accepted Westmacott's scheme for further consideration, the design was not used.

After ten years of irregular consultations and the accumulation of only £2,200, the committee finally gained approval from the government to erect a monument designed by Francis Hall. A spot was chosen in the military reserve on the edge of Queenston Heights northeast of the blockhouses constructed in the old camp ground during the latter stages of the war. Early in 1824 Hall supervised the excavation and construction of the foundation and a tomb for the fallen hero and his aide. On 13 October that year the remains of Brock and Macdonell were removed from their graves in the bastion at Fort George and carried to Queenston in a procession that attracted dignitaries and thousands of citizens. Work then continued on the monument, which was finished sometime after 1827, but without, apparently, some of the ornate features intended in its original design. As it stood, however, Brock's first monument was 135 feet tall and comprised a Tuscan column on a lofty base with a winding wooden staircase in its core that allowed visitors to ascend to an observation platform just below the summit. Unprecedented in North America, the monument became a "must-see" for travelers.[2]

On Good Friday, 17 April 1840, a bomb exploded inside the base of the memorial, shattering the staircase, blowing off part of the top section of the tower and cracking the column. Benjamin Lett, an Irish-Canadian, is alleged to have planted the bomb to wreak vengeance for the death of a

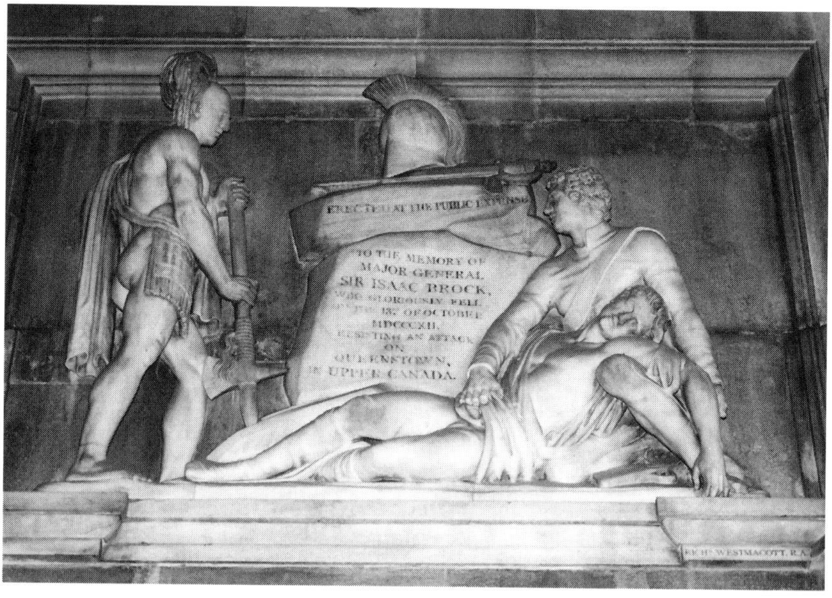


**Britain's monument to Brock**

This military monument, sponsored by the British parliament and designed by Richard Westmacott, is mounted on a column in the west ambulatory of the south transept of St. Paul's Cathedral, London. (Photo by the author)

relative killed by the British during the Rebellion of 1837, but he was never brought to justice over the incident.

The attack was viewed as a public outrage and resulted in Lieutenant Governor Sir George Arthur calling a public meeting on Queenston Heights the following July. About 8,000 people attended the day's festivities and listened to the province's leading men deplore the act of vandalism and make a series of proposals about how to honour Brock and the veterans of 1812. One of these resolutions concerned the building of a new monument but although patriotism ran high that day, it took thirteen years for sufficient funds to be acquired and a decision made to use the design of William Thomas, a prominent architect in the province.[3]

The old tower did not collapse, as had been predicted in 1840, and it took demolition crews several explosive charges to bring it down in July 1853. Workers then climbed into the tomb to remove the remains of Brock and Macdonell and, finding that the caskets had been crushed by either the 1840 incident or the demolition, "the clownish and ignorant workmen proceeded, without ceremony, to shovel up the bones, dust and dirt, all together."[4] This account appeared in a local newspaper and prompted an instant denial from William Thomas, who explained that he had carefully transferred the remains into two pine "shells" and interred them, with all due respect, in the family cemetery on the grounds of Willowbank, the mansion built in Queenston by the Hamilton family in the 1830s.

Thomas then laid out a site for the new monument, 200 or so yards west of the first tower. His crews went to work building a foundation, the tomb with its twin vaults and the base, finishing this part of the project in time for the reburial of the heroes.

The anniversary of the battle, 13 October 1853, was once more chosen as the date for the ceremony. As in the past it attracted crowds of thousands, including Colonel Donald Macdonell, brother of the late aide-de-camp. Before being carried in the elaborately decorated funeral car up the hill to the gathering at the tomb, the remains were transferred into fresh caskets. These the correspondent for the *Niagara Mail* considered inappropriate to the memory of the fallen. "They ought to have been of the full size of men whose ashes were laid in them," he wrote. "They were not over five feet in length we are told and a future generation examining them, might conclude that Brock was a mere pygmy in stature."[5]

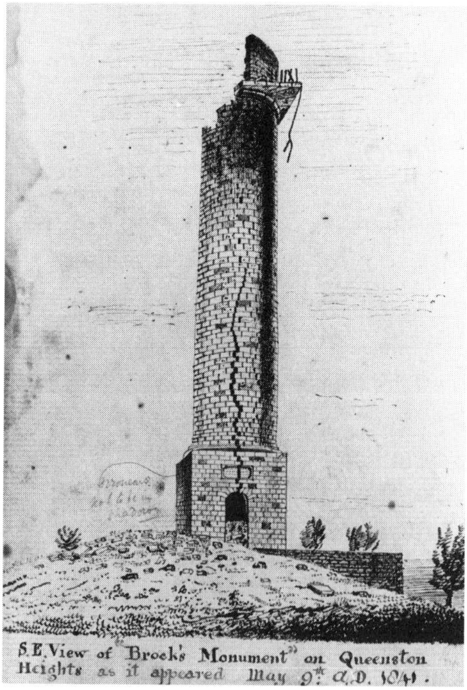

S.E. View of Brock's Monument on Queenston Heights as it appeared May 9th A.D. 1841.


**Two views of the first Brock monument, 1840-41**

The view above does not show the extent of the damage it suffered when a bomb exploded inside it on 17 April 1840. A note on the reverse observes that the cracks in the tower are due to "gunpowder by some officer." (Watercolour by Philip John Bainbrigge, National Archives of Canada, C-11799)

The view at left shows the damage more graphically. A newspaper article recorded that "The pedestal was cracked on one side, the shaft of the column was extensively cracked in several places, and that portion of the column, above the gallery, was dreadfully shattered. The wooden staircase, inside, was blown into a mass of ruins."[12] (Archives of Ontario, ACC 4579 S 12404)

The correspondent need not have worried. By this time Brock's place in Canadian history was well established, as shown by the attendance of between twelve and fifteen thousand people at this, the fourth burial of the general and his aide, on the forty-first anniversary of the battle. They surrounded the base of the monument where three lofty flag staffs stood flying the Union Jack and, as the procession came up the lane from Portage Road and stopped at the tombs, the crowd fell silent.

The pall bearers took the caskets down from the car, solemnly carried them to the vaults and slid them into their final resting places, Brock in the northern chamber, Macdonell to the south. Next Colonel Macdonell stepped forward to lay the corner stone, assisted by Colonel De Salaberry, deputy adjutant general for the province and son of the officer who had beaten the American army at the Battle of Chateauguay in 1813. A brief commemoration of the battle was read, following which a parcel of coins, newspapers and other mementoes was placed inside each vault and the vaults were sealed.

The artillery fired a salute. The Canadian Rifles gave three volleys.

William Hamilton Merritt, chairman of the monument committee, rose and approached the lectern at centre stage. The correspondent for *The Mail* observed that Merritt seemed nervous and uncomfortable speaking before such a large throng, but the depth of feeling in his words was not to be missed. "We have reason to be thankful, that so many, then Brock's compatriots, are still spared to witness this imposing ceremony. May its effects not be lost on the rising generation."[6] Merritt then recounted, at considerable length, the events of the war and paid homage to the veterans, their general and everything they had risked their lives to achieve so many years before. At the end of his speech Merritt emphasized the prize won by those who fell at Queenston and on other battlefields, and the importance of monuments like the one rising on the Heights.

"If Canada is worth preserving we owe it to them," he said. "If it is asked, why take this trouble, what object is to be gained – my reply is this – it will for the next generation at least keep up a feeling of patriotism, a love of country, which every right minded man should cherish."

Merritt and his friends would be pleased to see how Brock's memorial has served the purpose for which it was built. Each year thousand of visitors climb the monument, picnic in the lush grounds around it, follow the paths to read the tablets marking the battle's scenes and wonder about that day.

**Picnic at Brock's Monument in 1871**

Commemorations of the battle at Queenston Heights were often held through the 1800s, as the lines of veterans gradually diminished. (Courtesy of the Niagara Historical Society, 989.166)

# A Glossary of Terms

Military terms are precise and require a great deal of knowledge in the reader. This glossary has been compiled to provide relatively simple explanations for terms used in the text. Terms appearing in bold print within definitions have been defined separately in the glossary. The chief source for this glossary was Charles James, *A New and Enlarged Military Dictionary, or, Alphabetical Explanations of Technical Terms....* London: T. Egerton, 1802, which the reader who wishes a more comprehensive explanation of terms in the context of the War of 1812 should consult.

**aide-de-camp:** An officer assigned as an assistant to a commanding officer

**action:** A battle, a clash between opposing forces.

**armistice:** A temporary cessation of hostilities.

**artificer:** In the **artillery**, this was the soldier who prepared fuses for **bombs** or **shells**. The term also referred to a military blacksmith, cooper or other skilled craftsman.

**artillery:** Heavy weapons, "cannons," also known as ordnance, including **garrison guns**, **field guns**, **carronades**, **howitzers** and **mortars**.

**ball:** The lead projectile fired by a **musket**, .71 inch in diameter in British muskets and .65 inch in diameter in American muskets.

**baronet:** Any member of the lowest hereditary titled British order, below a baron but above a knight, and addressed as "Sir."

**bastion:** A four-sided defensive structure which projects from the main **rampart** of a fortification which permits the defenders to fire along the face of the main rampart.

**batman:** An individual hired to look after an officer's horse.

**battalion:** This is a force generally consisting of between 600 and 1000 men in ten **companies**. The term was used interchangeably with the terms "**regiment**" and "**unit**," although some regiments comprised more than one battalion. In 1812 the Americans on the Niagara frequently referred to battalions of **rifles**, which usually comprised only two weakly manned companies.

**battalion company:** One of eight **companies** out of ten companies in a **bat-**

**talion** or **regiment**, stationed in the centre of the battalion when it is in **formation**. The **grenadier** and **light companies** flanked the battalion companies in formation.

**batteau:** An open, flat-bottomed boat powered by oars and/or a simple rig, commonly used for transportation of **troops**, arms and provisions.

**battery:** Any position where **artillery** was mounted for action against an enemy.

**bayonet:** An edged weapon with a triangular cross section that could be fitted to the end of a **musket** for hand to hand fighting while still allowing the musket to be fired.

**blockhouse:** A military building, typically two stories high, used for storage, accommodation and defensive purposes.

**boarding party:** A group of seamen or marines delegated to capture another vessel by storming over its sides either from boats or from their own ship.

**bomb:** See **shell**.

**bombardier:** A soldier in the artillery who operated mortars and howitzers.

**bore:** The hollowed out cavity of a piece of **artillery**, **musket**, **rifle** or **pistol**.

**brevet:** Promotion by brevet meant that an officer's rank was raised one level, but his pay was kept at the former level.

**brigade:** A force usually under the command of a **brigadier general**. It consisted of a number of **regiments** of **infantry** (or parts thereof), but could also be **squadrons** of **dragoons** or a **battalion** of **artillery**.

**brigade major:** An officer appointed by the **brigadier general** to assist him in the management of the **brigade**.

**brigadier general:** The army rank above **colonel** for an officer who commanded a number of **regiments** operating as a force.

**buckshot:** Lead shot measuring .24 to .31 inches in diameter added to a **musket cartridge**.

**campaign:** The period of time (spring through autumn, for example) during which an army kept in the field during war time.

**canister:** A projectile fired by **artillery**, consisting of a tin can filled with small lead bullets, referred to by the Royal Artillery as **case shot**.

**cannon:** See **artillery**.

**captain:** The first officer in a **company** of **foot** or **artillery** or a **squadron** of **horse**.

**carriage:** The wooden framework upon which a piece of **artillery** was mounted so that it could be fired and moved.

**carronade:** A piece of **artillery** with a short barrel and a wide, smooth **bore**. It required a smaller gun crew and smaller charges than a long gun, though its effective range was limited to about 500 yards.

**cartridge:** The container of propellant used to fire a projectile, for a **musket** a paper tube holding about six or eight drams of black powder, for a long gun a paper or flannel bag holding about ⅓ the weight of the projectile in black powder, for a **carronade** the same package holding on average $^1/_{10}$ the weight of the projectile in black powder.

**cartridge box:** A box worn on the soldier's right hip and suspended by a belt over his left shoulder in which are kept **cartridges** for his **musket**.

**case shot:** See **canister.**

**cavalry:** Soldiers who served on horseback. See **dragoon.**

**change front:** To face in a different direction.

**colonel:** The commanding officer of a **regiment.**

**colours:** A large silk flag representing a **battalion** usually carried into battle by an **ensign.**

**column:** A long, deep **file** of **troops.**

**commander-in-chief:** The senior person in charge. Sir George Prevost and James Madison was the commanders-in-chief of their respective armies. Daniel Tompkins was the commander-in-chief of the New York State **militia.**

**commission:** The document issued to officers from the rank of **ensign** and above in the army which stated their specific assignments and was signed by the highest authority. Its date was important in resolving matters of seniority among officers of the same rank.

**commissioned officer:** An officer who had received a **commission.** In ascending order of seniority they were **ensign, lieutenant, captain, major, lieutenant colonel, colonel, brigadier general, major general,** lieutenant general and captain general (the Americans did not have the latter two ranks in 1812).

**commodore:** A temporary position of responsibility awarded to a naval captain, involving the overall command of more than one warship for a specific assignment.

**company:** This was a group of **infantry** or **artillery,** numbering usually between 50 and 120 men, and commanded by a **captain, lieutenant** and **ensign.** There were usually ten companies (**subunits**) in a **unit** (a **regiment** or **battalion**).

**cornet:** The third ranking **commissioned** officer in a **troop** of horse, about equivalent to an **ensign** in the **infantry.**

**corporal:** A **rank and file** soldier between the **private** soldiers and the **sergeants** who had charge of a portion of the **company.**

**cutting out expedition:** A surprise attack by a force of men in small boats upon a warship for the purpose of capturing the vessel at an anchorage and sailing away in it.

**detach:** To send out a number of men from the main body of the company, battalion or larger force.

**detached regiment:** In 1812 in New York State these were the **militia regiments** consisting of **companies** detached from their normal militia regiments for temporary service on the war fronts.

**detachment:** A body of men detached for a specific service.

**dragoon:** A horseman, also referred to as being part of the **cavalry.** Along the Niagara in 1812, dragoons generally acted as couriers or **express** riders.

**dress:** To realign the position of the individual soldiers so that they stood in an exact continuous line upon whatever **front,** or in whatever shape, the **battalion** was formed.

**elite:** See **light, grenadier** and **flank companies.**

**engagement:** A synonym for **action** or battle.

**ensign:** Next in rank to the **lieutenant** in a **company,** this was the lowest ranking **commissioned officer** in a **company**. It was usually an entry point for young men into the army. Ensigns were usually charged with carrying the **colours** into battle.

**evolutions:** The well-practiced steps to be taken when a force was required to change its position to meet the circumstances of a battle in the most effective manner possible.

**exchange:** Prisoners of opposing forces were sometimes exchanged on a one-for-one basis, or by some other arrangement, and could thereafter join their **battalions** for active service. It was common for a prisoner to be returned to his side before an exchange could be completed, with the agreement that he would not enter active service until one was arranged.

**express:** Any messenger sent with specific instructions, such as a **dragoon** ordered to deliver information to a commanding officer as quickly as possible.

**fencible regiment:** In the British army, a regiment raised for a limited service, such as the Royal Newfoundland Fencibles and Glengarry Light Infantry Fencibles who would only serve in British North America.

**field carriage:** A carriage of lighter construction than a **garrison carriage**, mounted on large wheels and made to be hauled by a team of horses into battle.

**field:** The ground of a battle. Also the **campaign** of an army, as in: "the army in the field."

**field gun:** A piece of **artillery** attached to a **field carriage** for being transported and used on the battlefield. Most field guns were 12-pounders or smaller and often made of brass which made them lighter than iron guns.

**file:** A line, of any length, of men drawn up one behind each other. To file was to move in a file forward or to the rear or to a **flank**.

**firelock:** See **musket.**

**flank company:** A company placed on the **flank** of a force. In the British army these were the **light** and **grenadier** companies, which because of their high level of skill, were also referred to as the **elite** companies.

**flanking movement:** An attack upon an enemy's flank without being exposed to the fire of his entire force.

**flanks:** In regards to the position of a force, the parts of the force that were placed on the right and left ends of the position. The flanks of a **battery** were the areas to its right and left.

**flintlock:** The **hammer** of a **musket**, **rifle or pistol** that gripped a piece of flint in a vise.

**flotilla:** A group of small boats, such as **batteaux**.

**foot:** See **infantry**.

**forage:** Hay, straw and oats for horses.

**formation:** The arrangement of any given number of men on foot according to prescribed rules and regulations.

**fort:** A small fortified place, surrounded on all sides with a ditch (or **fosse**), a **rampart** and a **parapet** and intended to control some high ground or the passage of a river.

**fosse:** The defensive ditch on the outside of a fortification.

**frizzen:** The curving aperture in the firing mechanism of a **musket**, **rifle** or **pistol** that was brought down to cover the powder in the **pan** and upon which the flint struck sparks (which fall into and ignited the powder in the pan) after the trigger was pulled.

**front:** When a battalion was in formation, it faced forward or toward the front. The order "front" meant to turn to this position.

**garrison:** A force housed in a fort for the purpose of defending it against an enemy or for controlling the location population or for taking up winter quarters.

**garrison carriage:** A heavily-built **carriage,** mounted on small iron wheels known as **trucks**, and used inside a fixed position such as a **battery** or **bastion.**

**garrison gun:** A piece of **artillery** mounted on a **garrison carriage**.

**general:** The commanding officer of an army. The different ranks of generals in the British army general were (in descending order): captain general, lieutenant general, **major general**, **brigadier general**. In the American army, the highest rank in 1812 was major general.

**governor:** The senior political leader of a state, such as Daniel Tompkins. Sir George Prevost was the governor-in-chief of British North America and superior to the **lieutenant governors** of each of the colonies or provinces.

**grapeshot:** A projectile fired from artillery consisting of a canvas shroud quilted over nine small round **shot** (resembling grapes of notably large proportion) positioned around a iron spindle fitted into a circular iron plate.

**grenadier company:** In the British army, the soldiers in one of two **elite** companies in a **battalion**. They were selected for their military prowess and intimidating size and stood on the right **flank** of the **battalion** and were generally the first forward in an attack.

**gun:** A piece of **artillery**.

**headquarters:** The place where the commanding officer of an army resided.

**horse:** When used in terms of a "**troop** of horse," this referred to a group of **cavalry**.

**Horse Guards:** The administrative headquarters of the British army, located in Parliament Street, Westminster, London.

**howitzer:** A short-barrelled piece of **artillery** with a wide bore, mounted on a field **carriage** used to fire explosive projectiles (see **shells**) on a higher trajectory than a **field gun**.

**impressment:** The practice of enlisting unwilling individuals for service in a warship.

**infantry:** The **foot** soldiers in an army, that is, the individually armed men who marched to battle.

**lieutenant:** The officer next in line to the **captain** within a **company** of **foot** or **artillery** or **squadron** of **horse**. Lieutenants within a company were usually numbered in order of seniority.

**lieutenant colonel:** The second officer of a **regiment**, below the **colonel** in rank.

**lieutenant governor:** See **governor**.

**light company:** One of the two **flank**, or **elite**, companies in a **battalion**, the light company took its position on the left flank of the battalion. It was composed of highly trained, intelligent recruits capable of acting independently in loose formation in front of the battalion or elsewhere as the commander ordered.

**light infantry:** **Troops** trained to act effectively as independent small groups in loose formation in front of a **battalion**, on the flanks, or elsewhere, and also known as **skirmishers.**

**limber:** A two-wheeled wagon, drawn by a team of horses, to which the rear end, or trail, of a **field gun** could be attached.

**line of battle:** The arrangement of an army in preparation for battle.

**long gun:** Commonly known improperly as a **"cannon,"** a piece of **artillery** with a long, smooth **bore** barrel.

**magazine:** A building or compartment in which black powder and "**fixed**" cartridges, which had been prepared for use, were stored.

**major:** This officer was below the **lieutenant colonel** in rank, his job being to ensure the **regiment** was well drilled, marched well and was ready for action. He carried messages for the **colonel** during an **action.**

**major general:** A major general had seniority over **brigadier generals.** See **general.**

**major of brigade:** See **brigade major.**

**marquee:** A large tent.

**match rope:** A piece of twisted rope, treated to maintain a smoldering ember with which to ignite a piece of **artillery.** Used as an alternative to a **port fire.**

**militia:** A force separate from the regular army called to service under arms within the boundaries of their state, province or country, although they could volunteer to cross those boundaries for military purposes.

**mortar:** A short, squat piece of **artillery** designed to fire explosive projectiles (see **shell**) in a high, curving trajectory.

**musket:** A **smooth-bore**, hand-held firearm composed of a firing mechanism, a **stock** and a barrel, that was relatively cheap to manufacture and easy to operate, although prone to inaccuracy and misfire. Also known as a **firelock.**

**muster roll:** A list of troops after they have been formally inspected to determine their condition, how many are present, the state of their weapons, dress, etc.

**muzzle:** The end of the barrel in a **musket, rifle** or piece of **artillery** where the powder and **ball** were inserted.

**national standard:** A nation's flag.

**noncommissioned officer:** An officer, such as a sergeant, who was appointed by the regimental commander.

**oblique:** A direction that was less than perpendicular to the original line of **formation.**

**operation:** The attempt to achieve predetermined goals, through movements involving, among other things, minor and major **actions.**

**ordnance:** See **artillery.**

**palisade:** A wooden wall on the perimeter of a fort constructed of upright sharpened posts or plain poles.

**pan:** The small bowl adjacent to the **vent** of a **musket, rifle** or **pistol** into which a small amount of powder was poured to later ignite the charge in the base of the barrel's **bore.**

**parapet:** A mound of earth, usually in a fort, raised to protect **troops** from the enemy's fire.

**parole:** A promise given by a prisoner of war that, if set at liberty to return home, he was not to fight until he had been formally **exchanged** with one of the enemy's captured men.

**pistol:** A small firearm, usually held in one hand to fire

**platoon:** A small body of **troops**.

**port fire:** A device for igniting artillery. It consisted of a combustible substance that would burn slowly in a rolled paper tube. See **match rope**.

**powder horn:** A container, often fashioned from a cow horn, worn by a gunner in which a supply of fine black powder is kept for priming the vent or touch hole of his piece of artillery.

**priming wire:** A copper wire inserted into the vent of a piece of **artillery** to perforate the **cartridge** bag so that the **wick** could be inserted.

**private:** The lowest ranking and most numerous class of soldiers in the army.

**purchase:** In the British army, officers could rise to a higher **rank** by purchasing a **commission** for that rank (up to **lieutenant colonel**), although by 1812 this method was limited by tight rules and was becoming less prevalent.

**quartermaster:** An officer tasked with looking after quarters for the soldiers, their clothing, bread, ammunition, firing, etc. There was a quartermaster in each **regiment** of **foot** or **artillery** and one in each **troop** of **horse**.

**quartermaster general:** This officer was responsible for identifying the route of march and encampments and with organizing the camps and quarters for the officers. In regards to the Niagara **campaign** in 1812, quartermaster generals seemed mostly involved with supplying the material needs of the forces.

**rampart:** Usually, a mound of earth raised to cover the insides of a defensive position.

**rank:** A straight line of men drawn up beside each other.

**rank and file:** The soldiers who carried **muskets** and stood in the **ranks**, that is, the **privates** and **corporals**.

**ration:** The amount of food given to a soldier.

**redan battery:** A fortification in the field, constructed in a wide V-shape. When joined together, a series of redans looked like the teeth of a saw.

**regiment:** This was a force, commanded by a **colonel**, consisting of one or more **battalions** of **infantry** and was often used synonymously with the term "battalion." It could also mean a force consisting of one or more **squadrons** of **cavalry**.

**regular:** **Troops** of the national army who could be put under arms in any place, unlike **fencible regiments** or the **militia**.

**rifle:** A **musket-like** weapon, with a **bore** scored with a series of fine, spiralling grooves (known as rifles, threads or rays). The **ball** was tightly rammed into the barrel and when fired took on a spin that increased its accuracy over that of the smooth-bore **musket**.

**rifleman:** A soldier carrying a **rifle**, often employed on **light infantry** assignments.

**round:** One unit of projectile and powder.

**round hat:** Worn by officers and gentlemen, this hat resembled the modern top hat, and varied in design.

**round shot:** A solid, spherical, iron projectile, its weight determined the strength of the piece of **artillery** used to fire it. A 9-pdr. **gun** fired a shot weighing 9 pounds, and measured 4 inches in diameter. A typical 24-pdr. shot measured 5.33 inches in diameter.

**scabbard:** A sheathe for a **bayonet** or sword.

**sentinel:** A private soldier posted to watch for the enemy to prevent surprises and to challenge passers-by.

**sentry:** See **sentinel.**

**sergeant:** A **non-commissioned officer** appointed by the **regimental** commander to train and discipline the **rank and file.**

**shell:** A hollow, iron projectile filled with powder and ignited by a fuse so that it would explode near the enemy. Also referred to as a "**bomb.**"

**shot:** See **round shot.**

**skirmish:** A brief, less controlled **action** between small forces.

**skirmishers: Troops** sent ahead of the formation to act as **light infantry** were referred to as skirmishers.

**slide:** A flat platform with a centre-slot in which the piece of **artillery**, usually a **carronade**, recoiled after firing.

**slow match:** See **match rope.**

**spherical case:** A British projectile for artillery. A hollow iron sphere containing powder and balls that scattered when the powder exploded. Used in much the same way as **shells**, although also fired by **field guns** up to 12-pdrs.

**spike:** To choke the **vent** of a piece of **artillery** with a soft iron rod (the spike) bent inside the **bore** by a strong thrust of a ram rod to incapacitate the gun. **Bayonets** were said to have been used to spike guns on occasion by being broken off in the vents.

**squad:** Any small number of men on foot or on horse.

**squadron:** A group of **cavalry**, roughly equivalent in size to a **company** of **infantry**, composed of two **troops.** In naval terms, a small group of warships.

**stand of colours:** A regiment's **colours.**

**stand of grape:** A single round of **grapeshot.**

**stock:** The wooden part of a **musket** or **rifle.** Also a neck piece worn by soldiers. Officers' stocks were black silk or velvet while the rank and file wore stiff leather stocks.

**subaltern:** An officer below the actual level of command; that is, when an **infantry company** was in service under the command of its **captain**, the **lieutenants** and **ensigns** were subalterns.

**sub-unit:** See **company.**

**tactics:** The steps taken by a commander to secure the objective of an **engagement** with an enemy from the first order through subsequent orders which were given to suit the flow of the **action** as it developed.

**touch hole:** See **vent.**

**tour of duty:** The period of time during which an individual or **regiment** was assigned to a specific place.

**transport:** The carrying of the army's baggage, etc.

**troop of horse:** A group of **cavalry.** There were usually two **troops** in a **squadron.**

**troop:** Any group of soldiers, often used as "troops."

**trucks:** The heavy, small-diameter "wheels" on a **garrison gun carriage.**

**unit:** A term usually used synonymously with **regiment** or **battalion.**

**vent:** The narrow hole in the rear of a piece artillery through which a priming tool was inserted to pierce the **cartridge** so that a priming tube, containing a train of fine powder, could be inserted for igniting the weapon. Also a similar hole adjacent to the firing mechanism of a **musket**, **rifle** or **pistol** and at the base of the weapon's **barrel**. Also known as the **touch hole.**

**volunteer:** Someone who entered into military service of his own accord.

**wheel:** A type of **evolution** in which a force, or portion thereof, changed its position by moving in a circular manner around a pivot point.

**wick:** A wooden tube which was filled with slow burning combustibles and cut to a length that caused the **shell** or **spherical case** to explode at the desired location in relation to the enemy.

**The "Châteauguay Musket"**
This U.S. Model 1795 musket was discovered in the Châteauguay River and is believed to have been discarded by an American soldier during the battle there in October 1813. Shown here after conservation are the musket, its bayonet and a cartridge with which it was loaded. (Courtesy of Parks Canada)

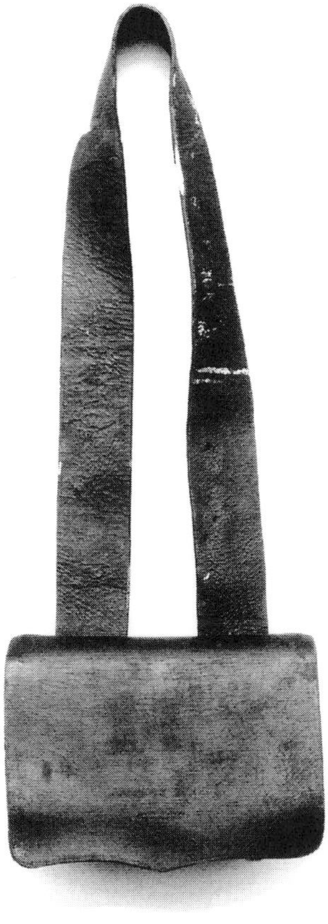

**Model 1808 U.S. Army cartridge box**
Made of glazed, stout, black leather, this box, worn on the soldier's right hip, contained a pine block with holes bored in it to receive twenty-six cartridges. There was also a small compartment for additional cartridges, flints and oil rags. (Courtesy of Parks Canada)

# Appendices

## APPENDIX A

## *The Last Words of Isaac Brock*

As with the untimely demise of any hero, the death of Isaac Brock has been described with varying degrees of melodrama. This except from a biography of the general published in Guernsey in 1919 exemplifies the more fanciful treatments.

> He was turning to shout to the messenger, 'Push on the York Volunteers,' when he was struck by a ball in the right breast, which passed completely through his body. He rolled off his horse, had just breath enough left to bid the officer nearest him to keep his fall concealed, and was dead within the minute. His corpse was carried downhill to Queenston, and hidden under a pile of blankets, in obedience to his orders.[1]

Accounts of Brock's death began appearing immediately after the battle and in them his reputed call for the advance of the York militia was central. Lieutenant George Ridout, 3rd York Militia, wrote to his father on 14 October, "while rallying the men at the hill, … he was shot through the breast, and immediately fell and expired, saying at the same time "*Push on the Brave York Volunteers.*"[2] The next day Lieutenant Archibald McLean, also of the 3rd York, proudly noted "The York Volunteers, to whom he was particularly partial, have the honor of claiming his last words. Immediately before he received his death-wound, he cried out to some persons near him to push on the York Volunteers."[3] Lieutenant John Beverley Robinson, another of the young officers from York, shared the day's experiences with Ridout and McLean but had a different remembrance. When he wrote to the Reverend John Strachan on the day after the battle his only comment was that Brock "was proceeding up the right of the mountain to attack them in flank when he received a ball in his breast. Several of the 49th assembled around him. One poor fellow was severely wounded by a cannon ball and fell across the general."[4] Robinson was not on the hillside with Brock when he was killed and neither were Ridout and McLean since the 3rd York was on the grounds of the Hamilton house at the time and only approached the hill as part of the second counter attack on the redan battery. It appears that their source for the story of Brock's death was word-of-mouth. Nevertheless, Ridout and McLean's letters soon gained publication in newspapers, which helped to popularize their version of events.

Another individual who reported Brock's last words but remained at Fort George throughout 13 October was Ensign John Smith, 41st Foot. Writing to Lieutenant Colonel Henry Procter at Fort Malden several days after the battle, he explained that Brock "received a Musket ball below his Breast that lodged near his back bone, which put an end to his existence – he died like a hero for as he fell he said 'never mind me My boys push on.'"[5] On 24 October *The Niagara Bee* published an account of Brock's fall in which he was supposed to have said, "push on, *never mind me*."[6] William Hamilton Merritt, 1st Troop Lincoln Cavalry, who was not present when the general was killed, recorded in his journal that "He fell in the act of Cheering his Men. His last words, were: 'Push on my Brave fellows."[7]

Despite the common mention of "Push on" in the oral histories of the battle, few of Brock's biographers have included it as part of their narratives of his death. Instead, they have frequently chosen to feature the general's reported request that his fall be concealed from his men.[8] The origin of this statement is found in a letter Captain John Glegg wrote to William Brock on 14 October:

> The ball entered his right breast and passed through on his left side. His sufferings, I am happy to add, were of very short duration, and were terminated in a few minutes, when he uttered in a feeble voice: "My fall must not be noticed or impede my brave companions from advancing to victory." His lifeless corpse was immediately conveyed into a house at Queenston … upon victory declaring in our favour I hastened to the spot, and finding my lamented friend in the same concealed place where we had left him in the morning, the body was immediately conveyed to Fort George.[9]

Glegg was in Queenston when Brock was killed, close enough to the general to direct his removal from the battlefield, and this proximity to the incident might be the reason why his version of Brock's last words has been popular among biographers. Others have chosen to question or ignore Glegg's remembrance, however; one writer discussed the different accounts of Brock's last moments and wrote, with a tinge of reverse idolatry, "It is not likely, however, that a plain man like Brock would have struck an attitude so dramatic."[10]

The most popular view held by historians and biographers is that the general died without a word.[11] From all accounts, the bullet that killed Isaac Brock entered his chest just above his breastbone and to one side. Whether it struck him on his right or left side or passed through his body is not clear from the various contemporary accounts of the wound and even a modern analysis of the coat Isaac Brock wore at the time did not resolve these questions irrefutably.[12] What is clear from all the available evidence, is that Brock was shot at relatively close range and that his wound was so devastating that death came quickly. When trying to describe this scene, most of Brock's biographers have pictured him dying wordlessly, apparently basing their versions on the most compelling account of the general's demise. This was written by fifteen-year old George Stephen Benjamin Jarvis, a gentleman volunteer with the 49th Foot who followed closely behind Brock when he made his final charge:

> On arriving at the foot of the mountain, where the road diverges to St. Davids, General Brock dismounted and waving his sword climbed over a high stone wall, followed by the troops: placing himself at the head of the light company of the 49th, he led the way up the mountain at double quick time in the very teeth of a sharp fire from the enemy's riflemen, and ere long he was singled out by one of them, who, coming forward, took deliberate aim and fired; several of the men noticed the action and fired – but too late – our gallant General fell on his left side, within a few feet of where I stood. Running up to him I enquired, "Are you much hurt, Sir?" He placed his hand on his breast and made no reply, and slowly sunk down. The 49th now raised a shout, "Revenge the General!" and regulars and militia, led by Colonel Macdonell pressed forward.[13]

Whether Brock, moments before he was shot, ordered someone to have the York militia hurry to the attack or called on his comrades to continue their assault on the redan battery is a moot point that may never be resolved. What seems most likely is that the general was as shocked as any of his men to be suddenly felled by an American bullet and expired before he had the time to reflect on his plight. Into that gap stepped those who could not allow such a well-loved individual to pass without crediting him with a few heroic last words.

APPENDIX B

# *Brock's Monuments and Queenston Heights Today*

After the burial of Brock and Macdonell in the new monument on Queenston Heights in October 1853, work continued for four years until the project was completed. An article in an 1852 issue of the *Canadian Journal* described William Thomas's original plan for the work, some aspects of which were altered during construction.[1]

The foundation is 40 feet square and 10 feet deep and, like the rest of the structure, made of Queenston limestone. The base is composed of the sub-basement and plinth and measures 38 feet square and 27 feet high, enclosing the vaults, the base of the stairwell and a gallery that surrounds them. Light is transmitted to the interior by a series of portals, decorated with wreaths, and a door, originally intended to face south, but later relocated to the east side. A sculpted lion stands on each of the upper corners of the base, proudly holding a shield bearing Brock's coat of arms.

Upon the plinth rests a pedestal 16 feet 9 inches square and 38 feet high, the sides of which have bas reliefs depicting Brock's achievements and his coat of arms. Next is the cap, or die, from which rises the fluted Roman column, 10 feet in diameter and 95 feet high.

On the summit of the column sits the capital, with a sculpture of winged Victory on each face. Thomas had planned for the construction of an observation deck on the 15-foot square abacus above the capital, but this feature was not included. Instead, the 235 stone steps (originally there were to be 250) of the stairwell end in the cramped cippus, a stone-clad, cast-iron cylinder 6 feet in diameter with a series of small wreathed portals and a hatchway through which visitors may enjoy the view. The 16-foot statue of Brock stands on the cippus, rising to a height of 185 feet. At the time of its construction, the monument was the second tallest structure of its kind in the world. Only Sir Christopher Wren's column erected to commemorate the great fire of London in 1666, at 202 feet, was taller.

The finishing touches to the work included the construction of a 77-foot square dwarf wall around the sub-basement, the corners of which hold sculpted military trophies 20 feet tall. The provincial legislature provided an additional grant to landscape the surrounding area, turning the old military reserve into a parkland. In 1857 and 1858 forty acres of property were cleared and fenced, additional trees were planted, a large and impressive gateway was erected adjacent to Portage Road, and an avenue for carriages was constructed leading up to and around the

**Brock's Monument**

At the peak of the second monument built to honour his memory, Major General Sir Isaac Brock points northward over the province he died defending. (Photos by the author)

tower in a circle. A stone lodge was also built at the eastern end of the grounds.

The monument was formally commemorated on 13 October 1859 and, as with previous events, drew dozens of dignitaries and thousands of spectators. For a shilling the visitors could walk around the tombs and climb the stairway to the viewing post. It was a celebration of British-Canadian loyalty and homage to the past. The correspondent for the *Daily Globe* noted that "old comrades, severed from each other for years met, and 'fought their battles o'er again,' with vivacity increased by the presence of those who had assisted in their conflicts; many a heartfelt shake of the hand was given ... that after so long a period they should once more meet upon so auspicious an occasion."[2]

William Thomas was responsible for another memorial to Brock, an obelisk intended to mark the spot on which he fell and to be the centrepiece for a ceremony involving the Prince of Wales (the future King Edward VII). This commission appears to have arisen abruptly in the summer of 1860 and left Thomas with insufficient time to verify the exact location where Brock died. He had the stone manufactured and put in place for the prince's visit on 19 September, but the spot he chose, directly below the second monument at the very bottom of the hill, is at least 200 yards west of where the general was killed.

In 1885 parklands were created on both sides of the Niagara River and so Brock's Monument and the old military reserve fell under the jurisdiction of the Queen Victoria Niagara Falls Park Commission, which eventually evolved into the Niagara Parks Commission. Today, the parkland around the monument amounts to 175 acres of picnic grounds, playing fields, gardens and woodland paths and is visited by many thousands of people annually. The monument is open from mid-spring until mid-autumn, its well-worn limestone steps proof to the fact that it still poses an irresistible attraction to young and old.

The battlefield at Queenston is easily accessible by vehicles. The village and the Heights are situated just north of the Queenston-Lewiston Bridge, one of the major border crossings along the Niagara River and the junction between Highway 405 in Ontario and Highway 190 in New York State. From Toronto, travel to Niagara via the Queen Elizabeth Highway (QEW) to Highway 405 (one mile east of the St. Catharines Skyway); exit at Stanley Avenue (turn left to pass over the 405) or at the final exit before the border (turn left on the Niagara Boulevard to pass under a portion of the Queenston-Lewiston Bridge). Either way will bring you to Queenston Heights, unmistakable at a distance due to the sight of Brock's Monument standing above the trees. From Buffalo take Highway 190 nearly twenty miles north to the bridge. This route is also accessible from Interstate 90 via Highway 290.

At the monument you can find directions for the self-guiding tour of the battlefield. This covers key locations in the battle, such as the redan battery and the approximate place where the Americans scaled the gorge. Interested visitors should diverge from the tour's beaten path and take time to follow the streets of the village down to the river's edge at the docks, formerly the ferry landing. At the base of the escarpment and adjacent to the Mackenzie House Museum is a small park with several memorials of the battle: the 1860 obelisk, a simple boulder bearing a plaque honoring John Norton's Grand River peoples, and a small sculpture of the legendary Alfred.

To properly retrace Brock's last charge, climb from the obelisk diagonally up the hill toward the redan battery, trying to envision the slope with a scattered covering of trees, bracken, weeds and wild flowers, heavily cloaked in a fog of white smoke.

## APPENDIX C

# *United States Army Personnel Involved at Queenston Heights*

Shown here are companies from the various U.S. Army regiments that participated in the Battle of Queenston Heights. The lists have been compiled from pay and muster rolls completed during 1812 and early 1813 and include names of officers and men who appear to have been with the companies when the rolls were compiled. Some individuals had deserted or died, been transferred or removed from the rolls prior to October 1812, so their names are not listed. For instance, portions of Captain Malcom and Wool's companies (Thirteenth Infantry) are not included here because they were transferred into the Twenty-Third Infantry in August, presumably at Greenbush, which accounts for the relative smaller size of their companies. Where a name was illegible, it has been marked and when spelling is uncertain, a question mark has been inserted. Since no definitive rolls were taken immediately before and after the battle, the exact composition of each company on 13 October 1812 cannot be verified here.

Few of the rolls indicate casualties suffered or prisoners taken at Queenston; for some of the companies, there are several short rolls listing detachments in captivity. There appears to be no roll in existence for the whole of Captain John Machesney's Sixth Infantry company during this period; the information shown for that company, incomplete as it is, is based on four separate prisoner of war detachment rolls and is supplemented by reference to a return done at Fort Niagara. Deaths noted within weeks of the battle might have been attributed to the battle, but they have not been noted as such here.

The information for the Twenty-Third Infantry Regiment also requires separate explanation. Sources show that there were difficulties in the enlistment for this regiment and for desertions while on the Niagara frontier. Only one captain, David Scott, appears to have been at that post and returns indicate that the men were placed into detachments under Lieutenants Clarke and Wendel. The available musters do not clearly delineate which men were under which officer and so all the officers and men have been listed under Scott's overall command.

The sources for this information are the pay and muster rolls of the individual regiments held by the United States National Archives in Washington, D.C., specifically, RG94, Records of the Adjutant General's Office, Muster Rolls of the Regular Army, 1780-1917. Pay and muster roll dates and box numbers have been provided for each individual company.

**Legend**
KIA = killed in action WIA = wounded in action POW = prisoner of war

## Sixth Regiment of Infantry

**Capt. George Nelson KIA**
**1st Lieut. Londus L. Buck**
**2nd Lieut. Henry Wendell WIA**

*Sergeants*
Goodman, Noah
Medicott, Henry
Pawley, Francis POW

*Corporals*
Allen, Curtis
Barlow, John
Burgess, Seth
James, Thomas POW

*Privates*
Allan, William
Baldwin, Alexander
Bartely, Darcy
Bennett, William
Benthouse, Ephrain
Bettes, John
Brown, James POW
Burnett, William
Cahoon, John
Carriff, John
Clark, James POW
Diamond, Thomas
Edmonds, Mathew
Fink, Jacob
Ford, Simon
Griffith, John G. POW
Hangan, David
Hannon, William
Hawkins, Alfred
Hoyt, John
Hughes, Elias POW
Johnson, George
Johnson, Ben
Joy, Jesse
Kinter, Solomon POW
Lake, Enoch
Langdon, David POW
Loveland, Horace
Lusher, George
Lyman, Hill
McCarty, William
McCoy, John
McIntosh, Garnet
Mirise, Israel POW
Misner, Owen POW
Muir, William
Newman, Robert
Notingham, James
Olsaver, Thomas
Osburn, Phineas
Ostrander, Tunis
Patterson, John POW
Peck, Peter
Prontyn, Levi
Rennick, Samuel
Ruderkirk, Isaac POW
Rutherford, John
Severin, Gideon
Skiff, Jacob
Southard, Jinard
Stanton, Daniel
Thornton, Reuben POW
Truax, Isaac
Van Derhule, Samuel
Van Yeveren, Alyndert
Van Kleke, James
Van DeBorgart, Daniel
Van DeBorgart, Jeremiah POW
Vosburgh, Isaac
Walderon. Mans
Westland, Dewitt POW
White, John
Williams, Thomas
Williamson, William
Wood, John

**Total =74 officers and men**

Source: Sixth Regiment of Infantry, Box 262, Muster Rolls: July–December 1812

**Capt. John Machesney POW**
**Lieut. Henry Shell**
**En. Isaac L. Dubois**

*Sergeants*
High, Joel POW
Schenk, Henry P. POW
Wynn, Hiram POW

*Corporals*
Simpson, John POW

*Privates*
Barns, John POW
Burrell, James POW
Clark, Olney POW
Davis, William POW
Doty, Joseph W. POW
Ennis, James POW
Fuller, John POW
Green, William POW
Hawkins, John POW
Haslet, John POW

| | |
|---|---|
| Little, Carr | POW |
| Morrel, Mathew | POW |
| Morris, Jacob | POW |
| Newell, Alpheas | POW |
| Partridge, Liba | POW |
| Rood, Amasa | POW |
| Reynolds, William | POW |
| Sanford, Solomon | POW |
| Swartout, Henry | POW |
| Zeleman, Gabriel | POW |

**Total = 27 officers and men**

Source: Sixth Regiment of Infantry, Box 262C. Muster Rolls: September–December 1812

The Morning Report of the Garrison of Fort Niagara . . ., 30 September 1812 showed that Machesney's company included 1 lieutenant, 1 ensign, 4 sergeants, 4 corporals and 65 privates for a total of 76, Cherry Hill, SVRMP, Box 12, F10.

## Thirteenth Regiment of Infantry

**Lieut. Col. John Chrystie WIA, POW**

| | |
|---|---|
| **Capt. Myndert Dox** | |
| **1st Lieut. Israel Turner** | **POW** |
| **En. George Reabe, Jr.** | **POW** |
| *Sergeants* | |
| Kemble, Moses | POW |
| Parker, James W. | POW |
| Wooster, William D. | POW |
| *Corporals* | |
| Bergen, William | POW |
| Davis, James L. | POW |
| Hughes, Joseph | POW |
| *Privates* | |
| Ackley, Benjamin | POW |
| Adams, Oliver | |
| Andrew, William | |
| Austin, Asa | |
| Bartely, Joseph | |
| Bell, Thomas | |
| Bellamy, John | |
| Blakely, Abel | POW |
| Blanchard, Benjamin A. | |
| Bonker, James | |
| Brewster, Plato | |
| Buckingham, Jaud | POW |
| Bundy, William | |
| Corlis, Ira C. | POW |
| Darling, Sylvester | |
| Dean, Leonard | |
| Demarest, John | |
| Elsworth, Peter | |
| Fisk, John L. | POW |
| Freelove, Barney | POW |
| Goodwin, Joseph | |
| Griggs, William | POW |
| Hagerman, Joseph A. | POW |
| Hall, Samuel | POW |
| Hardy, Nathan | POW |
| Hathaway, Henry | |
| Hews, Joseph | |
| Hibbert, Joseph W. | POW |
| Howell, Jonathan | POW |
| Huntley, Nathan | |
| James, John | |
| James, Lammie | POW |
| Johnson, David | POW |
| Knapp, James | POW |
| Kugell, Andrew F. | |
| Lewis, Isaac | POW |
| Masters, William | POW |
| Mewman, Thomas | |
| Miller, Gordan | POW |
| Moody, John | POW |
| Moore, Patrick | |
| Moulton, Elisha | POW |
| Mudrock, Isaac | |
| Mumm, Charles | |
| Muster, William | |
| Nicholes, James | |
| Norris, James | POW |
| Parkhurst, Elisha | |
| Pray, Horace | |
| Reed, Alexander | POW |
| Robinson, Simon | |
| Rose, Abraham | |
| Rowland, William | |
| Rumsville, Asahel B. | POW |
| Scott, William | POW |
| Scuyler, Reuben | |
| Simmons, Elias | |
| Smith, Alexander | POW |
| Smith, Justus | |
| Smith, William J. | |
| Snow, Daniel | POW |
| Southworth, Sylvenus | POW |
| Stewart, William | POW |
| Thomas, Alexander | POW |
| Thursten, George | POW |
| Victor, John | |
| Wheeler, Uriah | POW |
| Whitmore, Stephen | POW |
| Wood, Thomas F. | POW |
| Wymas, David | POW |

**Total = 79 officers and men**

Source: Thirteenth Infantry, ca 1812-1815, Box 340. Muster Rolls of Recruits and Detachments: April, June, October–December 1812.

| | |
|---|---|
| **Capt. Henry B. Armstrong** | **WIA** |
| **1st Lieut. Wessel Gansevoort** | |
| **2nd Lieut. Richard H. Root** | |
| **En. John Williams** | |
| *Sergeants* | |
| Abbe, Samuel | |
| Lawrence, Isaac | |
| Truax. John B. | POW |
| Worden, Joseph W. | POW |
| *Corporals* | |
| Glazier, Samuel | |
| Harry, Francis | |
| Kinney, Elijah | |
| Kinney, Jesse | |
| Warner, Zelotus | POW |
| *Musicians* | |
| Holdredge, Elisha | |
| Stephens, John L. | |
| *Privates* | |
| Avery, Ichabod | |
| Berry(?), Patrick | |
| Bristol, Abraham | POW |
| Brown, William | |
| Bump, Jacob | |
| Burns, C. | |
| Caldwell, Daniel B. | |
| Carey, Benejah | |
| Clark, John | |
| Coby, Henry I. | |
| Cowden, David | POW |
| Cutler, Jonas | |
| Darby, Eleazer | |
| Davey, Henry | |
| Demmon, Joseph | |
| Donnelly, Andrew | |
| Dunham, samuel | |
| Elderkin, David H. | |
| Fleming, Jacob | POW |
| Foreman, Robert F. | |
| Foster, George | |
| Francis, Seth A. | POW |
| Gillesprie, Francis | |
| Green, Caleb | POW |
| Greenleaf, Samuel | POW |
| Harrison, Joseph B. | |
| Hawver, Peter | |
| Haynes, Nicholas | |

Hendrickson, Henry Jr.
Hendrickson, William
Henstreet, John
Herring, Robert
Hodges, Ephraim
Houghton, Iasiah
Hoyt, Lyman
Jewell, Moses
Jones, Henry POW
Leonard, Bartlett
Mannah, John
McClanaking, John
McGee, Patrick
Moody, George
Munduffy, Joseph
Oldfield, Eli
Platt, Robert
Pool, Alanson
Reace, Anthony
Remough, John
Reynolds, James M. POW
Shepherd, Conrad POW
Simond, Bejamin
Smith, Job
Smith, Joshua
Stanton, Charles C.
Streeter, John
Sullivan, Isaac
Tompson, Robert D. POW
Towsley, Reuben
Turner, Abner POW
Van Vleet, Garet
Vedder, Albert
Walker, David POW
Webber, Olver
Wilcox, John
Winecoop, Elisha

**Total = 80 officers and men**

Source: Thirteenth Infantry, ca 1812-1815, Boxes 338 and 340B. Pay and Muster Rolls: August, September–December 1812.

**Capt. William D. Lawrence WIA**
**1st Lieut. John Campbell**
**2nd Lieut. Jacob Sammons POW**
**En. Robert Morris KIA**

*Sergeants*
Boyle, Michael
McKittrick, Joseph
[illegible]
Shall, Edward

*Corporals*
Barr, Peter
Campbell, John W.
Dempsey, James
Ludlow, Samuel
Manly, Joseph
Morris, Morris

*Musicians*
Bryan, William
Hall, Samuel

*Privates*
Armstrong, Joel
Bannon, Michael
Barnes, Gilbert
Barrett, Edmund
Beams, Peter
Blakeny, Robert
Boyce, Peter
Brower, Abraham POW
Bryan, Thomas
Burns, Peter
Carey, Warren
Carl, Samuel
Carman, Isaac
Carr, Dale POW
Cern, Samuel POW
Classen, Daniel
Coles, John
Covill, Peter POW
Cowen, David
Crissey, Andrew
Cronks, George
Crum, Peter R.
Dalton, John
Davis, David POW
Donelly, Felix
Doxey, Jonathan POW
Eastburn, John
Eldredge, Adonirum
Ellis, John
Elms, John H.
Ennis, William POW
Goodheart, George
Goodnow, Ezekiel POW
Goslin, Richard
Haggerty, Daniel
Hamillton, Andrew
Harley, James
Hart, Joseph
Hassan, Joseph
Hayman, James
Hendricks, John
Hogland, William POW
Howard, Benjamin
Howell, Benjamin B.
[illegible]
Jackson, William
Johnson, Nicholas
Kelly, Henry
Lambertson, Robert
Lee, Daniel D.
Logan, Timothy
Loveborough, William
McBraherty, Patrick
McCammon, Joseph
McCormick, John POW
McCullagh, Robert
McGowan, Michael
McLaughlin, William
Mooney, Matthew
Moores, William
Morrison, Robert POW
Oakley, Isaac POW
Paine, Ezekiel
Parecells, Paul POW
Peel, Daniel
Petty, John
Pooler, John
Price, Nehemiah
Price, Obadiah POW
Rareshire, Augustus
Requar, Gilbert
Richardson, Thomas
Rumsey, Peter POW
Ryde, Michael
Ryer, George
Sabin, Benjamin F. B.
Saunderson, John
Searles, Lott
Sperry, Henry
Sweet, Noah D.
Thorp, Richard
Tillotson, William POW
Van Tassell, Isaac
Vreedenburgh, John
Wakeman, Seth
Warren, William W.
Weddell, Isaac
Wilson, James
Wilson, Benjamin POW
Yager, Philip POW

**Total = 105 officers and men**

Source: Thirteenth Infantry, ca 1812-1815, Boxes 339B and 340B. Pay Role: August, September–December 1812.

**Capt. Richard Malcom WIA**
**1st Lieut. John Valleau KIA**
**2nd Lieut. William W. Carr POW**
**En. Joseph W. Dwight**

*Sergeants*
Corben, David E. W.
Ormsbee, Benjamin F.
Slyter, Sylvester POW

| | |
|---|---|
| Thomas, Jeremiah | |

*Corporals*

| | |
|---|---|
| Ferguson, John | |
| Lasher, Peter D. | |
| Ranny, William | POW |
| Royce, Joseph | |
| Sillaway, Hezekiah | POW |

*Musicians*

| | |
|---|---|
| Hurlbet, William H. | |
| Shepherd, Lemuel | |

*Privates*

| | |
|---|---|
| Adams, William | POW |
| Allen, Alonzo | |
| Amberman, Daniel | |
| Ames, Amos | |
| Baker, Ammon F. | |
| Ball, Charles, Booth, | |
| Bartlett, Henry | |
| Booth, Benjamin | POW |
| Bradner, Isaac B. | |
| Burrows, Elisha | |
| Canfield, Ludewich | |
| Canfield, Reuben | |
| Carter, Daniel | POW |
| Close, Abel | |
| Coffer, Anthony | |
| Coney, Luke | |
| Crushaw, Joseph | |
| Curray, Joyhn | |
| Dana, Chester | |
| Dawes, John | POW |
| Dugat, Amos | POW |
| Dunham, Philemon | |
| Frasher, Alexander | |
| Gill, James | |
| Gower, John W. | |
| Green, Ira | |
| Greenwalt, John | |
| Guiness, John | |
| Hamilton, Robert | |
| Handy, Prince | POW |
| Heartendorf, Abraham | |
| Hendricks, David | |
| Higby, Ira | POW |
| House, Frederick | |
| Laker, Henry | |
| Looker, John | |
| Martin, Henry | |
| McGee, Ebernezer | POW |
| Middleton, Lewis | |
| Milks, John | |
| Mudd, Levi | |
| Munsel, Thomas L. | |
| Olds, Alvan | |
| Parrott, William | |
| Proper, George | |
| Rand, Israel | |
| Reed, Daniel | |
| Ruddy, Christian | |
| Scott, Lemuel | |
| Shaw, Daniel | |
| Shepherd, Zerros | POW |
| Silaway, Hezekiah | POW |
| Van Alstine, Thomas | |
| Watson, John | |
| Weeks, James | POW |
| Wells, Henry | |
| Westley, Benjamin F. | POW |
| Wooley, Henry | |
| Wright, John | |

**Total = 74 officers and men**

Source: Thirteenth Infantry, ca 1812-1815, Boxes 339B and 340B. Pay and Muster Rolls: August, September–December 1812.

| | |
|---|---|
| **Capt. Peter Ogilvie, Jr.** | **POW** |
| **1st Lieut. John Fink** | **POW** |
| **2nd Lieut. John Brown Jr.** | |
| **En. Thomas W. Denton** | |

*Sergeants*

| | |
|---|---|
| Butterfield, Benjamin | |
| Delano, Benjamin | |
| Risley, William | POW |
| Smith, Frederick? | |

*Corporals*

| | |
|---|---|
| Andrews, Samuel | POW |
| Bramble, John | |
| Depew, John | POW |
| Fash, George | |

*Musicians*

| | |
|---|---|
| Laumit, Dennis | POW |
| Moore, Samuel | |

*Privates*

| | |
|---|---|
| Aimes, Matthias | |
| Alexander, James | POW |
| Bailey, Moses | |
| Baker, Joseph | POW |
| Balmon? Albert A. | |
| Blaney, Henry | |
| Bradlow, Andrew | |
| Brown, Charles | |
| Brown, John | |
| Buchanan, Peter | |
| Budd, Peter E. | |
| Burbeck, Josiah | |
| Campbell, Daniel | |
| Canfield, Stephen | |
| Chase, Daniel | |
| Clark, Enoch N. | |
| Clougheton, Jacob | |
| Cochran, James | |
| Collins, Patrick | |
| Conden, Michael | |
| Crane, Ichabod | |
| Croman. Anthony | POW |
| Cummings, Samuel | |
| Denning, John | |
| Deny, John | |
| Dodger, Stephen | |
| Downey, James | |
| Duboise, John | |
| Fair, John | |
| Fisher, Elijah | |
| Fitzgerald, John | |
| Flowers, John | |
| Gerake, William | |
| Goodrich, Allen | |
| Grimmon, Ebenezor | |
| Hadley, William | |
| Halsey, Hezekiah | |
| Hammond, Daniel | |
| Harrington, Daniel | POW |
| Hubbard, Allen | |
| [illegible] | |
| Kelly, John G. | |
| Khale, Conrad | |
| Kimball, Benjamin | |
| Lamplin, Jacob | |
| Lee, John D. | |
| Leonard, Chauncey | POW |
| Light, Lewis | |
| Lockyer, Benjamin | POW |
| Loomis, David | |
| Mann, John P. | |
| Mannell, John | POW |
| Mason, John | POW |
| McBride, James | POW |
| McElroy, Charles | POW |
| McIntire, Robert B. | |
| Mulliker, Robert | |
| Nowler, Jonathan | |
| Owen, John | |
| Palmer, Josiah | |
| Philips, Joseph | POW |
| Picket, William | |
| Poilloon, Richard | |
| Rand, Ephraim | |
| Riker, Abraham T. | |
| Robert, George | |
| Savary, Solomon | POW |
| Sherwood, Henry | |
| Smith, James | |
| Spooner, Nathan | |
| Squire, Isaac | |
| Terwillager, Moses | |
| Thomas, Permit | POW |
| Tyler, Thomas | |

| | |
|---|---|
| Valentine, John | |
| Van Selder, Abraham | POW |
| Van Zile, John | POW |
| Vandenmark, Cornelius | POW |
| Venus, Richard | |
| Venus, Philip | POW |
| Walker, John | |
| Warner, Elisha | POW |
| Watts, Jason | |
| Webb, Jacob | POW |
| West, Jonathan | |
| Wiley, John | |
| Wilklow, William | POW |
| Wilson, William | POW |
| Wood, Ezkiel | |
| Yost, Jacob | |

**Total = 104 officers and men**

Source: Thirteenth Infantry, ca 1812-1815, Boxes 339B and 340B. Pay and Muster Rolls: August , September–December 1812.

**Capt. John E. Wool WIA**
**1st Lieut. Stephen Kearney POW**
**2nd Lieut. Daniel Hugunin POW***
**En. John Gates, Jr.**

*Sergeants*

| | |
|---|---|
| Blanchen, Seth | |
| Egleston, Lina P. | |
| Young, Thomas L. | POW |

*Corporals*

| | |
|---|---|
| Clasler, Abraham | POW |
| Dillon, James | |
| Groesbeck, William | |
| Hill, Artemis | POW |
| Strate, Henry | |
| Williams, Daniel W. | |

*Musicians*

Stoner, John
McGee, Thomas

*Privates*

| | |
|---|---|
| Ambler, Henry | |
| Andrews, Oliver | POW |
| Blancher, David | |
| Bounds, James | |
| Bowen, Solomon | |
| Bois, Joseph | |
| Boyd, James | |
| Brown, James | |
| Carpenter, John Jr. | |
| Casler, Joseph T. | POW |
| Casler, Thomas | |
| Day, John | |
| Dean, Jedediah | |
| Delong, Peter | |
| Dennis, Job | |
| Duel, Joseph | |
| Ferris, Daniel | |
| Friesler, Anthony | |
| Garlick, Elias | |
| Gates, Robert Jr. | |
| Golden, Benjamin | POW |
| Greene, Joseph V | |
| Hammond, Thomas | POW |
| Harrown, John | |
| Hatch, Sampson | |
| Hill, Jonathan | |
| Hull, Warner | POW |
| Huffman, James | |
| Jones, Henry | |
| Lambert, John F. | |
| Lane, Asa | |
| Livingstone, Peter T. | |
| Mattoon, Levi | |
| McKee, John | POW |
| McKee, William | |
| McNelly, Hugh | |
| Miles, Reuben | |
| Miller, James | |
| Peterson, Hezekiah | |
| Rice, William | POW |
| Robbins, Conrad | POW |
| Roe, John R. | |
| Russell, Asa | |
| Smith, James G | POW |
| Smith. Nelson | |
| Sparks, Joseph | POW |
| Steel, Harvey | |
| Swett, James | |
| Swine, William | POW |
| Turk, Benjamin | |
| Turner, James | |
| Turner, John | POW |
| Walker, John Jr. | POW |
| Walters, William | |
| Wells, William | |
| Wilson, Alexander | |
| Young, Jacob L. | |

**Total = 70 officers and men**

* Second Lieutenant Daniel Hugunin does not appear on the rolls of Wool's company, but a second lieutenancy was vacant in the August roll and Hugunin, who was identified as a prisoner, may have filled that vacancy.

Source: Thirteenth Infantry, ca 1812-1815, Boxes 339B and 340B. Pay and Muster Rolls: July–December 1812.

**Capt. Hugh R. Martin***
**2nd Lieut. Alfred Phelps* WIA/POW**
**En. James Lent* POW**

*Sergeant*

| | |
|---|---|
| Wilson, James | POW |

*Privates*

| | |
|---|---|
| Boyle, Dennis | POW |
| Conner, Thomas | POW |
| Fonda, Jacob | POW |
| Fort, Abraham | POW |
| Jackson, Robert | POW |
| Roach, James | POW |
| Roach, William | POW |
| Van Slyck, Nicholas | POW |

The main body of Martin's company remained at Black Rock where it had arrived just before the battle. It appears that Martin was sent to Lewiston to command Myndert Dox's company. The rank and file noted here were from his company and were identified as prisoners.

*Phelps and Lent were also identified as prisoners, but their names do not appear on any of the relevant musters. It is speculated that they were sent as supernumeraries to assist Martin.

## Twenty-Third Regiment of Infantry

**Maj. James Mullany POW**

**Capt. David Scott**
**1st Lieut. William Clarke WIA/POW**
**1st Lieut. John McCartey POW**
**2nd Lieut. Henry Whiting**
**2nd Lieut. Peter L. Hogeboom**

*Sergeants*

| | |
|---|---|
| Box, Benjamin | |
| Case Aaron | |
| Comstock, John | |
| Crosby, Benjamin | |
| Lewis, M. | |
| Little, William W. | |
| Pierson, William | POW |
| Van Allen, Peter | |
| Wooster, William D. | |

*Corporals*

Bartholemew, John
Coltvin, John

| | |
|---|---|
| Furman, Jeremiah | POW |
| Hull, Horace | |
| King, Nathaniel | KIA |
| Lawrence, Joseph | WIA |
| Lewis, Ira | POW |
| Little, William W. | |
| McDonald, Botsan | |
| Manger, Clark | |
| Hull, Thomas | |
| Young, Harvey | |
| *Musicians* | |
| Atwood, Hezekiah | |
| Cooby, Elias | |
| Heely, Horace | |
| McDowel, John | |
| Pathout, Richard | |
| *Privates* | |
| Allen, Arthur | |
| Allen, Samuel | POW |
| Annis, Jacob | |
| Armstrong, Amos | |
| Avery, Ira | |
| Avery, Charles | |
| Bacon, Nathan | |
| Barr, Phineas | |
| Bartholemew, John | |
| Bartlett, Solomon | |
| Bates, Eli | |
| Beebe, Roswell | |
| Bellow, John | |
| Bennet, Ezekiel | |
| Bennett, Gabriel | POW |
| Bennett, Larry | |
| Bills, Chester | POW |
| Blanchard, Benjamin | |
| Blanden, John | |
| Blodget, Eli | |
| Blodgett, Benjamin | |
| Brooks, Roswell | POW |
| Brown, Nathaniel | |
| Brown, Matthias | |
| Brown, William | |
| Brown, John | POW |
| Brumaige, Daniel | |
| Bryan, Augustine | |
| Budd, Solomon | |
| Budd, Edward | |
| Burgan, Willaim | |
| Burgess, David | |
| Burnet, Zadock | |
| Burnet, Daniel | |
| Butler, Ira | |
| Caldwell, William | |
| Canfield, Stephen | |
| Carpenter, Thomas W. | |
| Carpenter, Aldridge | |
| Carter, Julius D. | |
| Case, Aron | |
| Chambers, William | |
| Chappell, Joshua | POW |
| Crocker, Elizur | |
| Collins, Burnage | |
| Coleman, Samuel | |
| Converse, Laurence | |
| Cornell, Benjamin | |
| Cory, David | POW |
| Courstock, John | |
| Crane, Joseph M. | |
| Crane, Jabez | |
| Crosett, John | |
| Curtis, Daniel | POW |
| Daniel, Joseph | |
| Davis, John | |
| Dawson, Frederick A | |
| Dean, Randal | POW |
| Dibble, Nathaniel | POW |
| Dibble Ira | POW |
| Doyle, Charles C | |
| Engles, William H. | |
| Fairfield, Solomon | |
| Fanchiti, George A. | |
| Forsyth, William | |
| Fox, Timothy | |
| Fox, Benjamin S. | |
| Frisbee, Manlius | KIA |
| Fuller, Chester | |
| Fuller, Henry | |
| Gee, Jonathan | |
| Gibbs, Reuben M. | POW |
| Godfrey, Phineas | |
| Gould, Solomon | |
| Green, Elisha | |
| Green, Josiah | KIA |
| Hall, Ferington | POW |
| Hall, William | |
| Harris, Edward | |
| Hartwell, William | POW |
| Hatch, George | |
| Hawkins Robert | POW |
| Hewitt, Valentine | |
| Hibbard, Samuel | |
| Higley, Ebenezer | POW |
| Hill, Valentine | |
| Hinman, Joseph | |
| Hood, Thomas | |
| Hooker, Rufus | |
| Hoste, Thomas | |
| Howard, Barnabus | POW |
| Hudson, Sylvenius | |
| Huggins, Thomas | |
| Humes, Daniel | |
| Jay, Joseph | |
| Jennings, Darius | |
| Johnson, Jacob | |
| Johnson, Joel | |
| King, Nathaniel | POW |
| Kirkpatrick, Hugh | |
| Knight, John | |
| Lake, Nicholas | |
| Lamy, James | |
| Lee, Allen | POW |
| Lenzley, Anson | |
| Lewis, Daniel | |
| Lewis, Isaac | |
| Lewis, Otis | |
| Lewis, Thomas W. | |
| Long, Joseph | POW |
| Lowercoot, William | |
| Lundy, Jesse | |
| Marshall, John | |
| Martin, John | |
| Masson, Jesse | |
| McCandra, John | |
| McCans, Michael | |
| McDowel, John | |
| McGraw, Joseph | |
| McMullin, Andrew | |
| McQueen, John | |
| McIntyre, Royal | |
| Mead, Alfred | |
| Mead, Seth | |
| Mills, Joseph | POW |
| Mills, Levi H. | |
| Mobbs, Samuel | POW |
| Monroe, Lawrence | |
| Neering, Simon W. | |
| Newton, Asa | POW |
| Nichols, Elijah | POW |
| Norris, James | |
| Northrup, Ebenezer | |
| Olas, Oron | |
| Osburn, Major | POW |
| Parish, Gilbert V. | |
| Parker, Thomas | |
| Parks, Rufus | |
| Pelltyer Stepehen | |
| Quigly, Robert | |
| Ramsay, Nathaniel | |
| Reynolds, James | POW |
| Robards, William | |
| Roberts, Nathan | |
| Robins, Richard | |
| Rogers, Able | |
| Rose, Peter | |
| Rosebeck, Seth | |
| Rouse, Asariah | POW |
| Sarlt, David | |
| Savercoot, Abraham | |
| Shannon, Baxter | |
| Shield, Solomon R. | |

Simon, Phineas
Skinner, Daniel
Sloan, Sylvanus POW
Smith, Benjamin POW
Smith, David
Smith, Junius
Smith, Thomas
Smith, Wheeler B.
Spicer, Sylvester
Spring, Levi
Sprout, James
Stephens, Roswell
Thomson?, Peter
[illegible], Levi
Van Allen, Peter
Ware, Michael
Water, Paschal P.
Weed, Alexander
West, David POW
Wheeler, Philip
Wheeler, Seth
White, Jacob
White, Daniel
White, Valentine W.
Wilkinson, David
Witt, Ira POW
Woods, James
Woods, Asa
Wooster, William
Wright, Samuel
Young, Richard

**Total = 215 officers and men**

Source: Twenty-Third Infantry, ca 1812-1815, Box 360D, Box 361A, Box 361C. Muster Rolls: July 1812, February 1813.

The Morning Report of the Garrison of Fort Niagara . . . , 30 September 1812 showed 116 officers and men under Captain Scott, 39 under Lieutenant Wendell (of the Sixth Infantry) and 63 under Lieutenant Clarke for a total of 218, Cherry Hill, SVRMP, Box 12, F10.

## First Regiment of Artillery

**Capt. Nathan Leonard**
**1st Lieut. John Gansevoort**
**2nd Lieut. Samuel B. Rathbone KIA**
**2nd Lieut. Christopher Van De Venter**

*Sergeants*
Jones, Ferdinand
Rockhead, Andrew
Rodgers, Dean
Soriggs, Levin

*Corporals*
Andries Samuel
Brown, Joseph
Higgins, John
[illegible], Abraham W.

*Musicians*
Carrole John
Cole James
Lush, Sylvester
Shepherd, Elias

*Artificers*
Haswell, Elijah
Hubbard, Elijah
Hubbard, Jasper
Jones, Vincent
Lawton, James
Lewis, Silas
McLaughlin, Jonathan
McLaughlin, James

*Privates*
Allen, Tideman POW
Barber, Jemez
Beck, Christian
Billings Jonathan
Brainbridge, Charles
Brown, John
Brugg, John
Burkirk, Garret
Bush, Abraham
Campbell, Fred
Carley, William
Chamberlain, Rufus POW
Culver, Peter
Davis, William POW
Davis, Thomas
Dougherty? Dan
Doyle, Andrew POW
Dunbar, Silas
F[illegible], John H. POW
F[illegible], Manuel
G[illegible], Richard
H[illegible], Henry
Hollister, Jesse
Holmes Asu
Holmes, Joseph
Howard, David
Howe, William
Hughs, James
[illegible], W-[illegible]
[illegible], S-[illegible]
[illegible], Barnaby
[illegible], John POW
[illegible], Henry
Jadwia, Charles
Jones, Phineas
Joyce, Alonson
Kennedy, Thomas
Kimvol, John
Knapp, John POW
Lazarino, George
LeForge, Stephen POW
Lesso, John
Lonas, John
Lush, George W.
Mahoney, Jeremiah
McElroy, John
McManus John
McMaster, James
McWade, Edward
McWilliam, William
Miller, Joseph
Moore, Thomas POW
Morrison, William
Nunn, Jonathan
O'Bryan, Thomas
P[illegible], William POW
Powers, John
Queen, John
Sager, James
Schumerhone, Abraham
Seaver Luther
Shaft, Jacob
Shaw, Lewis KIA
Sheffield, Joseph
Shelton, Elias
Smith, Benjamin
Smith, Abner
Smith, Joseph T.
Southard, William
Stickney, Abijah
Stone, John F. W.
Thomas, William WIA
Todd, John
Todd, Elmer KIA
Turner, Isaac
Valentine, Elijah WIA
Van Valkenburg, John POW
VanDeBogart, Nicholas
Ven De Water, Benjamin
Ward, Graves
Warrell, James
Welsh, Nicholas WIA
West, Joseph
Wiers, Seth KIA
Williams, John
Williams Samuel
Wilson, Sam

**Total = 111 officers and men**

Source: First Regiment of Artillery, Box 38A. Muster and Pay Rolls: September–December 1812.

## Second Regiment of Artillery

**Lieut. Col. Winfield Scott POW**

**Capt. Nathan Towson**
**1st Lieut. Isaac Roach WIA**
**2nd Lieut. Joseph Hook**

*Sergeants*
Baker, Theophilus
Pindle, Thomas
Schmucke, Jacob
Steeds, John

*Corporals*
Book, John
Elroy, William
Patterson, Adam

*Musician*
Switzer, John

*Artificers*
Gorsuch, Stephen
Whealer, Willison
Wire, Zachariah

*Privates*
Barrackman, William
Bowen, Thomas
Bowermaster, Henry
Caley, James
Clinton, James
Conrad, Aquilla
Corbitt, John
Dougherty, Edward
Duncan, James
Fisher, William
Goodwin, Moses
Greenwood, Henry
Hannah, William
Harrison, John
Hedrick, George
Herrick, Thomas
Holland, Daniel
Howrigan, Thomas
Irwin, John
Jones, Enoch
Kearney, John
Kelly, Michael
Lishway, Lewis
Lowderman, John
Lutz, Joseph
Maloney, Edward
Montooth, William
Pedroe. Peter
Reamy, William
Roberts, Zachariah
Rorpaugh, Cornelius
Rowe, Michael
Runicker, Frederick
Stansbury, Samuel
Stewart, Joseph
Traynor, James
Wallace, Thomas
Walleger, Thomas
West, Hugh
Whitely, David
Williams, Richard
Wineman, Matthias
Wood, Moses

**Total = 56 officers and men**

Source: Second Regiment of Artillery, Box 46A. Muster and Pay Rolls: September–December 1812.

**Capt. James N. Barker**
**1st Lieut. Patrick McDonogh**
**2nd Lieut. Isaac Davis**

*Sergeants*
Biglow, Stephen
Chase, Ezra
Cook, Martin
Rigden, James

*Corporals*
Hathaway, Daniel
Hillis, Hensen M.

*Artificers*
Leech, Joseph
West, Samuel

*Privates*
Anderson, Thomas
Auner, Peter G.
Beard, John
Bolton, Joseph
Boyle, William
Butcher, John
Duffield, James
McCrosson, James
Peters, William
Read, Hugh
Ridlin, Henry
Roy, James
Ruark, Thomas
Shell, Jacob
Shippen, William
Shriver, Jacob
Snyder, Peter
Swartz, Peter
Thomas, Benjamin
Thompson, James
Wilkins, Samuel
Williams, John
*Sixteen present were missing due to damage to the roll.*

*Surgeon's Mate*
Near, Louis L.

**Total: 50 officers and men**

Source: Second Regiment of Artillery, Box 43 Muster Roll: August–October 1812

## Third Regiment of Artillery

**Capt. James McKeon**
**1st Lieut. Robert M. Bayly POW**
**2nd Lieut. Joseph H. Rees**

*Sergeants*
Bangs, Oliver
Converse, Augustus H.
Murphy, Richard F.
Salisbury, Samuel
Simons, Amos

*Corporals*
Carter, Isaac F. POW
Coon, John POW
Guile, David POW
McFarlin, John

*Musicians*
Lowe, Samuel
Phelps, Ambrose, M
Robinson, Elijah E.
Stewart, John

*Artificers*
Howard, Caleb
Randall, Andrew

*Privates*
Adams, Sam
Adams, William
Adsit, Benjamin
Auger, John
Badgrow, John POW
Baker, Daniel
Baston, Enoch
Bates, Cyrus
Bennett, Daniel
Bless, David D
Blodgett, Henry
Buman, James
Burnham, William

Burnham, Benjamin
Cassada, John
Chadwick, James
Chamberlin, Russell
Chestner, Joseph C
Church, Jonathan
Clark. Reuben
Clarke, Levi L.
Cole, Edward
Conkling, Samuel
Curtiss, Abel
Curtiss, David B.
Darling, Lyman
Darling, Daniel
Debsen, William
Dickinson, Ira POW
Dutcher, James POW
Emmons, John
Ennis, Jacob
Fargo, William C.
Force, Isaac
Foster, Alanson POW
Fowler, Justus
Francishus, Jacob
Goodell, Andrew P.
Hancock, Thomas POW
Harrington, Adams POW
Harvey, Asa
Hight, Isaac KIA
Hill, William
Howard, Thomas H.
Hyatt, Lewis
Isinhour, Philip
Jacobs, John
Johnson, Thomas
Kenyon, Bradford
Ketchum, Aaron
Lacy, Israel
Learned, Lyman
Lee, John L.
Little, Stephen WIA
Mason, Royal
McFarlin, John
McNair, Arnold
McNair, Robert
Moore, Thomas
Murry, Ichabod G.
Myers, William
Ormsby, Jesse
Potter, Charles H.
Pottle, Loring
Preston, David S. POW
Provost, John
Rawson, Luther
Roberts, Benjamin
Rodney, Michael
Rose, Elijah
Roy, Charles
Sabins, Olvier POW
Sleight, Peter
Smith, Henry
Stevenson, James POW
Storrs, Thomas
Thomas, Allen B. POW
Thomas, Lewis B.
Torry, Abner POW
Wardon, Lippett
Weaver, EbenezerKIA
Welch, Walter,
Wells, John
Wheadon, Allan
White, Joseph
Wilkinson, Samuel.

**Total = 104 officers and men**

Source: Third Regiment of Artillery, Box 49A. Muster Rolls: August–September 1812 and July–August 1813.

## Regiment of Light Artillery

**Lieut. Col. John Fenwick WIA/POW**

**Capt. James Gibson POW**
**1st Lieut. Benjamin Branch**
**2nd Lieut. John R. Bell**
**2nd Lieut. Thomas B. Randolph POW**

*Sergeants*
Gayer, Casper
Hilliard, David POW
Naughton, William

*Corporals*
Case, Daniel
Kelley, Samuel
Mullon, James
Shane, Arthur

*Musicians*
Dunn, Thomas P.
Rodney, Henry

*Artificers*
Joyce, William
Lincoln, William POW
Lloyd, Richard
Lockard, Thomas
McGuire, James
Rock, John

*Privates*
Boyle, Robert POW
Breen, Edward
Brooks, Luther
Bower, Jacob W.
Brice, James
Barrow, Patrick
Bell, Samuel
Bishop, William
Beckwith, Harvey
Clever, Anthony
Cobson, James
Deny, Thomas
Duggs, Jesse
Fox, Joseph
Guice, Adam
Gosner, Peter
Guest, Joseph
Gardner, James
Gamble, James
Hotten, James POW
Hogart, William POW
Haines, Daniel POW
Hopkins, John POW
Hoke, Henry POW
Hulsboom, Garrett POW
Jones, Thomas
Ilgenfritz, Daniel POW
Kemans, Patrick POW
Lesley. James
Meanan, John
McClaim, Archibald
Miller, Jacob POW
McMahon, William
McLane, William POW
Martin, Nathan C.
Mullin, John
Maginley, John
McCullo, James
Nixon, Aaron
Pickett, John
Piper, Joseph
Rhineart, John F.
Slip, James
Simon, Frederick A.
Smiley, Samuel
Shields, Neill POW
Summerfield, Thomas
Sutton, William
Thompson, George
Talbert, David, POW
Taylor, William
Wooddend, John POW

**Total = 70 officers and men**

Source: Regiment of Light Artillery, Box 101. Muster Roll: August–October, 1812.

APPENDIX D

# *New York State Militia and Volunteer Personnel in the American Army on the Niagara River, 1812*

In all, approximately 7,480 officers and men, regulars and militia, appeared in camps on the Niagara River between the spring and fall of 1812.[1] Presented here are the names of militia and volunteer officers and the units and sub-units to which they belonged along with an indication of those who were killed, wounded or captured at the battle, according to the available records. For want of space, the complete rolls of the many different companies have been omitted. As with the other military records in this work, an attempt has been made here to overcome the problems caused by variant spellings and illegible handwriting typically seen in period documents.

The most detailed sources for information about the militia are the seventeen boxes of returns found in the records of the Adjutant General's Office, Transcriptions of War of 1812 Payrolls for New York State Militia Units, 1812-1815, reference number BO811-85, in the New York Archives at Albany. Four boxes of similar material are held by the United States National Archives in Washington: Record Group 94, Office of the Adjutant General, Volunteer Organizations and State Militia. Names, affiliations, records and company type (battalion, rifles, light infantry, cavalry or artillery) and organizational material can be found in Hugh Hastings, ed., *Military Minutes of the Council of Appointment of the State of New York, 1783-1821*, and in Hastings's *The Public Papers of Daniel D. Tompkins, Governor of New York.* Some informative papers are also contained in Ernest A. Cruikshank, ed. *Documentary History of the Campaigns upon the Niagara Frontier in 1812-1814.*

New York State militia forces involved in the battle at Queenston fell into four categories: detached, independent, volunteer and un-detached militia.

## A. Organization of the "Detached" Militia

In the spring of 1812, the militia of New York State, numbering about 105,000 officers and men, comprised 164 regiments of infantry, 12 regiments each of cavalry and artillery and 14 battalions of specialized infantry, made up of rifle and light infantry companies. The regiments and battalions were grouped into brigades, which were combined into divisions. Major General Stephen Van Rensselaer, for instance, commanded the First (and only) Division of Cavalry, which consisted of twelve regiments formed into three brigades. Lieutenant

Colonel Peter Allen (of the village of Bloomfield, Ontario County) commanded the Twenty-Second Regiment of Infantry in the Thirty-Ninth Brigade commanded by Brigadier General William Wadsworth, which was in the Seventh Division of Infantry commanded by Major General Amos Hall.[2]

The "Act to authorize a detachment from the Militia of the United States" became law on 10 April 1812 and gave permission to the president to require state officials "to organize, arm and equip ... and hold in readiness to march at a moment's warning, their respective proportions of one hundred thousand militia."[3] The president called for a detachment of the militia to be mobilized late in April, and when the Department of War issued its schedule of militia quotas for the states on 28 May 1812, New York's requisite portion was 13,500 officers and men.

On 18 June 1812 Governor Daniel Tompkins's office released a general order stating that the state's detachment of militia would consist of eight brigades formed into two divisions.[4] Major General Van Rensselaer was appointed to command the First Division, consisting of Brigades Four through Eight, and Major General Benjamin Mooers commanded the Second Division, consisting of Brigades One, Two and Three. Within each brigade there were "new" regiments, each of which was a hybrid, formed from local companies of infantry, squadrons of cavalry, and companies of artillery, rifles and light infantry. It seems that many of the best militia companies available were placed into these new units and in this way Governor Tompkins and his staff organized the detachments along lines very similar to Major General Isaac Brock's formation of strong flank companies of militia in Upper Canada.

By way of example of how the detached units were organized, Lieutenant Colonel Peter Allen was appointed to command the Twentieth Regiment of Detached Militia, which was drawn from the various companies in Ontario County rather than only from his Twenty-Second Regiment of Infantry.[5] The Twentieth Detached, along with the Eighteenth Detached (Lieutenant Colonel Hugh Dobbin, Seneca County) and the Nineteenth Detached (Lieutenant Colonel Henry Bloom, Cayuga County), formed the Seventh Brigade of Detached New York Militia commanded by Brigadier General William Wadsworth. The Seventh Brigade was one of the five under the command of Major General Stephen Van Rensselaer.

Twenty-two detached regiments were formed across the state in this manner to complete the state's quota, which excluded about 92,000 officers and men, such as Major General Amos Hall, from active service in June 1812.

The following are the detached units that were mustered on the Niagara River during the campaign of 1812 around the time of the attack on Queenston.

**Legend**
KIA = killed in action    WIA = wounded in action    POW = prisoner of war

# FIRST DIVISION OF DETACHED MILITIA

**Major General Stephen Van Rensselaer, commanding**
**Lieutenant Colonel Solomon Van Rensselaer, aide-de-camp (WIA)**
**Major John Lovett, Secretary**
**Major Stephen Lush, aide-de-camp to Lt. Col. Van Rensselaer**

## Sixth Brigade of Detached Militia

**Brigadier General Daniel Miller, commanding**
**Major of Brigade and Inspector Thomas Greeley**
**Quartermaster Nathaniel R. Packard**

### Sixteenth Regiment of Detached Militia

**Lieutenant Colonel Farrand Stranahan, commanding (POW)**

*Staff*
First Major Cyrus Steer
Second Major Joseph Sprague
Adjutant George Morell
Quartermaster Anson Higby
Chaplain John Smith

| *Captains* | *Lieutenants* | *Ensigns* |
|---|---|---|
| Jacob Badgeley | Jacob Cady | |
| Ephraim Beach | Elijah Norton | Edward Gaylor |
| | John Schuyler | John Denton (POW) |
| | Henry Hanson | |
| Stephen Clarke (KIA) | Simeon Houghton (POW) | |
| Jehiel Felt (POW) | Taylor Rosel | |
| Peter Magher | David Woodburn | William Allen |
| Lemuel Pettengill (POW) | William Smith (POW) | Peter Peck (POW) |
| Elisha Saunders (KIA) | Richard D. Shepherd (POW) | |
| Esek Steere | Benjamin Elwood | Isaac Burch |
| Joseph Westcoat | James Culley (POW) | |

### Seventeenth Regiment of Detached Militia

**Lieutenant Colonel Thompson Mead, commanding (POW)**

*Staff*
First Major J. Randall
Second Major Walter Clark
Paymaster Charles Pompelly
Quartermaster Asa Norton
Quartermaster Sergeant Henry Green
Surgeon's Mate Richard Brown
Sergeant Major Washington Winsor
Chaplain Elisha Ransom

| *Captains* | *Lieutenants* | *Ensigns* |
|---|---|---|
| Eli Bacon (POW) | John Field (POW) | Jesse White (POW) |
| Reuben Gray | Charles Randall (POW) | John Haight (POW) |
| Daniel Root (POW) | David Chase | Jabez Robinson |
| David Seymour | John R Wildman | Eli Culver |
| Solomon Smith | Bruce Agariah | John T. Smith (POW) |
| Nathan Taylor | Price French | |
| Thornton Wasson | Jedathan Gray (POW) | Rufus Weatherbee |
| David Williams | Jesse McQuigg | Hooker Bishop |

## Seventh Brigade of Detached Militia

**Brigadier General William Wadsworth, commanding (POW)**
**Major William H. Spencer, aide-de-camp (POW)**
**Major of Brigade and Inspector Julius Keyes**
**Quartermaster Henry Wells**

### Eighteenth Regiment of Detached Militia

**Lieutenant Colonel Hugh W. Dobbin, commanding**

*Staff*
First Major John Morrison
Second Major David Burbach
Adjutant Gerrit L. Dox
Quartermaster Timothy Shead
Pay Master Thomas Rosewell
Surgeon Joshua Lee
Surgeon's Mate William Cornet
Quartermaster Sergeant Samuel Sexton
Sergeant Major John S. Sabin
Chaplain Reverend John Stewart

*Captains*
Daniel Buel
Jonas Cleland
James Dike
Seth Gates
James Gronk (POW)
Joel S. Hart
Seymour Kellogg
Joseph McClure (POW)
Jehiel Moore

*Lieutenants*
Woody Freeman
Samuel D. Wells
Phineas Stanton
Dan Adams (KIA)
G Hibbard
Jacob Gillett
Chester Burrows
Frederick Richmond (POW)
David Eaton

*Ensigns*
Thomas Alcott Jr.
John Kennedy (POW)
Rufus Carey
Elias Piersons
Nathaniel White
Hebediah Morse
Phineas Stanton
Reubin Newton
Charles Burritt

### Nineteenth Regiment of Detached Militia

**Lieutenant Colonel Henry Bloom, commanding (POW)**

*Staff*
First Major Hoah Olmstead
First Major Aranthus Evarts
Adjutant Archer Green
Quartermaster James Collier
Pay Master Arad Joy
Surgeon Ben P. Bailey
Surgeon's Mate Alex Comstock
Quartermaster Sergeant Martin Kellog
Sergeant Major Joseph Babbot

*Captains*
Martin Barber (POW)
Abraham Bloom
Henry R Brinkeroff (POW)
Asa Burch
Daniel Eldridge (POW)
Peley Ellis (POW)
John Phelps
William Sutton

*Lieutenants*
Liberty Brown
Comfort Butler
Elishawa Holcomb (POW)
John Daniels (POW)
Alexander Price (POW)
Caleb Fichenor
Frederick Kisher (POW)
James De Mott

*Ensigns*
William Cobb (POW)
William Pew
Philo Sperry (POW)
Lewis Love
Martin Davis
Derrick Deatts
George Walldroft (POW)
Samuel Seton

### Twentieth Regiment of Detached Militia

**Lieutenant Colonel Peter Allen (POW)**

*Staff*
First Major George Smith
Second Major Thomas Lee
Adjutant Benjamin Ganson
Quartermaster James Henderson
Pay M Joshia Robinson (POW)
Surgeon George Holloway
Surgeon's Mate Daniel Brainard
Quartermaster Sergeant Augustus Bennett
Sergeant Major John M. Low

| *Captains* | *Lieutenants* | *Ensigns* |
|---|---|---|
| James Bogert | Asa Cole | Azariah Finch |
| John Brown (POW) | Sam Soverhill | Joseph Luse |
| Elijah Clarke (POW) | Joshua Phillips (POW) | Joseph Clarke |
| Abraham Dox | John Sweney (WIA) | Justus Dobbin |
| Caleb Harrington | Nathaniel Case | Levi Treadwell |
| Joel S. Hart | Noah Gillett | Zebediah Morse |
| Josiah Morehouse | Enoch Wilcox | Zelotis Sheldon |
| Salma Stanley (POW) | John van Ankin | Jacob Cast (POW) |

## B. Mobilization of Independent Companies and the One Hundred Sixty-Third Infantry Regiment

When it appeared in September 1812 that the regiments of detached militia would not be strong enough to support an invasion of Upper Canada on the Niagara River, Governor Tompkins gave Major General Van Rensselaer permission to order up "independent"companies of riflemen, light infantry, artillery and cavalry. They were detached from their normal regimental affiliations and ordered to the front to supplement the militia force there. Many, but not all, responded to the call and mustered their forces in the Niagara camps. These were all specialized companies, being identified as riflemen, light infantry, cavalry and artillery.

Other similar sub-units had apparently arrived already on the front or did so later. Major General Amos Hall remarked to Governor Tompkins on 13 August "should it be thought advisable to make a descent into Upper Canada, many of the militia in the western part of the State would volunteer. There has been several tenders of the services of companies and battalions since I have been on the line."[6] This voluntary service appears to have been informal, rather than under the conditions of the "Act authorizing the President of the United States to accept and organize certain Volunteer Military Corps" of 6 February 1812.[7] On 9 September Governor Tompkins informed Stephen Van Rensselaer that some of the companies recently identified for mobilization "are not Volunteers according to law, but just volunteers to accompany me personally."[8] Although Tompkins had no fixed plan to travel to the Niagara River at that time, these companies, having not been part of the original detachment, volunteered their services to the state in the governor's name.

The One Hundred Sixty-Third Regiment of Infantry, commanded by Lieutenant Colonel Silas Hopkins, appears to fit into this informal voluntary category. Centred in the village of Cambria in Niagara County, the unit first appeared on the Niagara River early in July as part of the emergency call up. Unlike the other units and companies that also joined this call up, listed in section D, elements of Hopkins's Regiment remained at their posts until December.

The following are independent companies, troops of horse and Hopkins's Regiment mustered on the Niagara River during the campaign of 1812 around the time of the attack on Queenston.

## Independent Companies of Riflemen

| *Captains* | *Lieutenants* | *Ensigns* |
|---|---|---|
| **Major Elihu Granger's Battalion** | | |
| Nathan Parke | Jared Willson (POW) | George H. Boughton (POW) |
| Jacob Westfall | Herman Granger | Peter Westfall |
| **Other Independent Companies** | | |
| William Bacon | Joel Fordham | James Coles |
| William Higgins | Henry Davis | Ezekiel Rogers |
| William Ireland (POW) | John Alexander (POW) | William Ireland Jr. (POW) |
| | James H. Johnson | Zephaniah Silcox |
| Witter Steward | Uriah James | Wm Worden |

## Independent Companies of Light Infantry

| *Captains* | *Lieutenants* | *Ensigns* |
|---|---|---|
| Elizur Hills | | David Doolittle |
| William McKinistry | Jacob Bryan | |
| Russell Nobels | Absalom Greene | John Seymor |
| William Sutton | James De Mott | Samuel Seton |
| David White | | |

## Independent Companies of Artillery

| *Captains* | *Lieutenants* | *Ensigns* |
|---|---|---|
| John H. Compston[9] | | |
| Andrew A. Ellicott | Henry Wilder | |
| | Chauncey Keys | |
| Reuben Hart | John A Stevens | |
| | Joshua McKenzie | |
| Samuel Ingersoll | John Larawa | |
| | John Ingersoll | |
| Sam Jacks | John Harris | |
| | William Hooper | |
| John Pierce | Henry Skinner | |
| | George W. Jones | |

## Independent Troops of Cavalry

| *Captains* | *Lieutenants* | *Cornets* |
|---|---|---|
| Nathaniel Allen | Ephraim Cleveland | Joseph W. Marsh |
| | Isa Wilder | |
| William Peters | | |
| Isaac W. Stone | Nathan Nye | Herman Norton |
| | Elisha Beach | |

## One Hundred Sixty-Third Regiment of Infantry

**Lieutenant Colonel Silas Hopkins, commanding**

| *Captains* | *Lieutenants* | *Ensigns* |
|---|---|---|
| Benjamin Clough | | |
| Ezekiel Cook | | |
| Asap Harris | Ezekiel Sheldon | George Keith |
| Ezekiel Smith | | |
| Rufus Spalding | John Simms | |
| Parkhurst Whiting | | |

## C. Volunteer Units

Some commanding officers volunteered their units to serve under the conditions of the Act of 6 February 1812. The most prominent of these was Lieutenant Colonel Philetus Swift's Regiment, although the completion of formal paper work needed to confirm this arrangement appears to have taken months.[10] He had commanded the Seventy-First Regiment of Infantry, centred in the village of Phelps, Ontario County, but when his offer to form a regiment of volunteers was tentatively accepted, most of the officers Swift selected appear not to have been in his militia regiment, as was the case with the formation of detached units mentioned above. The rifle battalions listed here had existed prior to the war and appear to have been among the state's elite, "uniformed" organizations.[11]

Three companies of militia, referred to as "volunteers," from Pennsylvania arrived in the first week of October and were posted to Buffalo.[12]

### Lieutenant Colonel Philetus Swift's Volunteer Regiment

| *Captains* | *Lieutenants* | *Ensigns* |
|---|---|---|
| Daniel Curtis | Phipps W. Hewett | Isaiah Golding |
| Thomas Dougherty | Levi Moore | Isaac Gradit |
| Elias Hull | David Perine | William Guest |
| William Hull | Israel Wilcox | Philip Peckham |
| Samuel Jennings | Joel B. Clarke | Truman Phelps |
| Abraham Mattison | Lewis Palmer | Charles Chaffey |
| James McNair | | |
| Samuel Terry | John Reynolds | Lodowick Dobbin |
| Joseph Wells | Asahel Adkius | Samuel Edsall |

### Rifle Companies[13]

| | | |
|---|---|---|
| **Major Asa Gaylord's Battalion** | | |
| Abraham Brundage | William White | Stephen White |
| James Sanford | Asa Tolbert | Henry Switzer |
| **Major Francis McClure's Battalion** | | |
| Lawrence Powers | John Gaynor | Mathew Byrnes |
| John Richardson | Silas Chatfield | Seth Burgess |
| **Major Charles Moseley's Battalion** | | |
| Charles B Bristol | Samuel Smith (POW) | George M Grosvenor |
| Leonard Kellogg | William Gardiner | Hezekiah Ketchum |

### Troop of Cavalary

| | |
|---|---|
| Herman Camp[14] | Jesse Owen |

## D. Units Serving Temporarily, Early Summer 1812

After the declaration of war became public knowledge, an alarm spread through the American settlements along the Niagara River that a full-fledge attack by the British Army or raids by their native allies were imminent. At that time only Lieutenant Colonel Philetus Swift's regiment was camped near the river and the call went out to local regimental commanders to reinforce the defences during this emergency. When he arrived at the front in the first week of July, Brigadier General William Wadsworth reported to Governor Tompkins that "Two regiments of militia, one from Genesee, commanded by Lieut-Colonel Daniel Davis, and one from Niagara County, when notified of the importance of having additional strength on the line, very promptly appeared with haste to the field. Lieut.-Colonel Daniel Davis's regiment appeared fuller than at any former call."[15] Davis's regiment was the Seventy-Seventh Infantry, centred in Caledonia, Genesee County, while the regiment from Niagara was that of Lieutenant Colonel Silas Hopkins, the One Hundred Sixty-Third Infantry, from the village of Cambria. The records show, however, that parts of other units were mustered briefly along the Niagara River between late June and early August; they are listed here. None of these units was included among the list of regiments officially detached for service during this period and they all left the front before mid-August. Elements of Hopkins's 163rd remained until December and for that reason his regiment has been listed above among the independent organizations (see section B above).

### Seventy-Seventh Regiment of Infantry[16]

**Lieutenant Colonel Daniel Davis, commanding**

| *Captains* | *Lieutenants* | *Ensigns* |
|---|---|---|
| Samuel Church | Benajah Holbrook | Jesse Church |
| Shubal Dunham | Elisha Kellogg | Samuel Hall |
| | Norton S. Davis | Oliver Platt |
| Ephraim Judd | Oliver Stanford | |
| Daniel Kelsey | Samuel Gleason | |
| Rufus McCady | Daw Hale | Levi Lacey |
| Robert McKay | Thomas Deever | |
| Isaac Marsh | | |
| William Pennock | John Russ | |
| Elias Streeter | Noble Douglas | Cornelius Faulkner |

### One Hundred Sixty-Fourth Regiment of Militia[17]

**Lieutenant Colonel Worthy L. Churchill, commanding**

| *Captains* | *Lieutenants* | *Ensigns* |
|---|---|---|
| Rufus Hart | Herman Holden | |
| George Lathrop | Richard Peck | Rufus Munger |

### Independent Companies[18]

| *Captains* | *Lieutenants* | *Ensigns* |
|---|---|---|
| Joseph Bancroft | Samuel Felt | Josiah T. Kellogg |
| George Culver | Pardon Durfee | James Stoddard |
| Nathan Marvin | Simcoe Cummings | Cornet William Bush |
| Benjamin Pearson | | |
| James Rees | Ralph Wood | George Sondry |
| Robert Spencer | Harvey Steele | |

APPENDIX E

# Van Rensselaer's Army on the Niagara River, October 1812

No one in the American army on the Niagara River in October 1812 stated its exact strength at the time of the battle of Queenston Heights. Several officers recommended in July that it would take 5,000 men to successfully invade the Canadian side of the river.[1] Henry Dearborn estimated midway through September that when the 2,400 Pennsylvania militia and all the other units and sub-units sent forward reached the river the army would consist of "upwards of three thousand regular troops and four thousand militia."[2] But the only tabulation of the army's actual strength that appears to have done by a contemporary officer was the one that Solomon Van Rensselaer published in *The Affair of Queenstown* in 1836 and which is reproduced here in Table One.

Recent general treatments of the war have stated that Van Rensselaer's army stood 6,000-strong or more, although no clear accounting for this figure has been given.[3] The information shown in Appendices C and D shows how muster and pay rolls have been examined to determine which regular and militia units and sub-units were on the Niagara River at the time of the battle and what their strengths were. Several returns of elements of the force found among the Van Rensselaer Papers at Cherry Hill in Albany were also examined. This led to the discovery of about two dozen companies and troops of horse that had not been previously identified as part of the army. Although many of their rolls show no casualties or prisoners taken at the battle, the rolls were dated before and after the battle as having been taken in one of the camps along the river just as those of the better-known five detached regiments of militia were. There is little doubt that all the units and sub-units shown here were present and part of the army. This evidence has been produced here in Table Two.

The synthesis of the various primary sources reveals that the strength of Stephen Van Rensselaer's Army on the Niagara River at the time of the Battle of Queenston Heights was about 6,710 officers and men, consisting of about 2,480 regulars and 4,070 New York State militia and about 160 militia from Pennsylvania. The available returns showed that the average "effective" strength of the various units and sub-units was about 80 per cent of their nominal strengths, due to illness, detention, absence, etc. With this rate in mind, Van Rensselaer's effective strength was about 5,400.

Excluding the units and sub-units camped at Black Rock and Buffalo, Van

Rensselaer had about 1,280 regulars and 3,350 militia between Manchester and Fort Niagara at the time of the battle. Units marched from both places to cross the river into Canada and, therefore, the total force immediately available to him for employment in the attack at Queenston was approximately 4,600, excluding the number posted at Fort Niagara.

## Table One

According to Solomon Van Rensselaer, the strength of Major General Van Rensselaer's army was 2,656 militia and 2,550 regulars for a total of 5,206 officers and men.[4] Solomon used the term "brigade" to categorize the six groups, although only Miller, Wadsworth and Smyth were general officers.

| *Brigades* | *Where Stationed* | *Total Present for Duty* | *Remarks* |
|---|---|---|---|
| D. Miller | Lewiston | 588 | militia |
| J. Fenwick | Lewiston | 550 | regulars |
| P. Swift | Black Rock | | |
| and S. Hopkins | Buffalo | 386 | militia |
| W. Wadsworth | Lewiston | 1682 | militia |
| A. Smyth | Black Rock | 1650 | regulars |
| J. Chrystie | Lewiston | 350 | regulars |
| | **Total** | **5206** | |

## Table Two

The examination of returns and musters reveals that Van Rensselaer's army numbered 2,484 regulars, 4,070 New York militia and 160 Pennsylvania militia for a grand total of 6,714 officers and men.[5]

### Regular Army, Total = 2484

| | |
|---|---|
| **From Fort Niagara to Manchester** | **Total = 1284** |
| Lieutenant Colonel John R. Fenwick, commanding[6] | |
| Artillery Detachment | Total = 257 |
| First Regiment, N. Leonard | 115 |
| Third Regiment, J. McKeon | 103 |
| Light Regiment, B. Branch | 39 |
| Infantry Detachment[7] | Total = 512 |
| Major James Mullany | |
| Fourth Regiment | 3 |
| Sixth Regiment | |
| J. Machesney | 75 |
| G. Nelson | 77 |
| Thirteenth Regiment | |
| M. Dox | 129 |
| Twenty-third Regiment | |
| D. Scott | 116 |
| W. Clarke | 63 |
| H. Wendell | 49 |

| | | |
|---|---|---|
| Four Mile Creek | | |
| Thirteenth Regiment [8] | | |
| J. Chrystie | 380 | |
| Lewiston | Total = 135 | |
| Light Artillery, J. Gibson[9], | 30 | |
| Second Artillery, W. Scott[10] | | |
| N. Towson | 56 | |
| J. Barker | 49 | |
| **Black Rock and Buffalo[11]** | **Total = 1200** | |
| Smyth's Brigade of Infantry | | |
| Fifth Regiment, H. Milton | | |
| Twelfth Regiment, T. Parker | | |
| Thirteenth Regiment, P. Schuyler | | |
| Fourteenth Regiment, W. Winder | | |

## New York State Militia, Total = 4070

| | | |
|---|---|---|
| **Fort Niagara to Manchester** | **Total = 3366** | |
| Miller's Sixth Detached Brigade[12] | Total = 914 | |
| Sixteenth Regiment, F. Stranahan | 486 | Manchester |
| Seventeenth Regiment, T. Mead | 428 | Manchester |
| Wadsworth's Seventh Detached Brigade[13] | Total = 1300 | |
| Eighteenth Regiment, H. Dobbin | 448 | Lewiston |
| Nineteenth Regiment, H. Bloom | 409 | Lewiston |
| Twentieth Regiment, P. Allen | 443 | Lewiston |
| Independent Companies, Troops of Horse and Hopkins's Regiment | | |
| S. Hopkins's Regiment | Total = 84 | |
| B. Clough | 12 | Manchester |
| R. Spalding[14] | 62 | Lewiston |
| P. Whiting[15] | 10 | Manchester |
| Riflemen[16] | Total = 260 | |
| *Granger's Battalion* | | |
| N. Parke | 21 | Lewiston |
| J. Westfall | 47 | Lewiston |
| *Other Independent Companies* | | |
| W. Bacon | 36 | Manchester |
| W. Ireland | 59 | Lewiston |
| W. Higgins | 25 | not stated |
| J. Johnson | 14 | Manchester |
| W. Steward | 58 | Lewiston |
| Volunteer Riflemen | Total = 208 | |
| *Gaylord's Battalion* | | |
| A. Brundage | 49 | Lewiston |
| J. Sanford | 62 | Lewiston |
| *Moseley's Battalion* | | |
| C.Bristol | 46 | Fort Niagara |
| L. Kellogg | 51 | Lewiston |

| | | |
|---|---|---|
| Light Infantry[17] | Total = 203 | |
| E. Hills | 29 | Manchester |
| W. McKinistry | 35 | Mancester |
| R. Nobels | 32 | not stated |
| W. Sutton | 75 | Manchester |
| D. White | 32 | not stated |
| Artillery[18] | Total = 211 | |
| J. Compston | 20 | not stated |
| A. Ellicott | 43 | Lewiston |
| R. Hart | 48 | Manchester |
| S. Ingersoll | 42 | not stated |
| S. Jacks | 30 | Fort Niagara |
| J. Pierce | 28 | Lewiston |
| Cavalry[19] | Total = 186 | |
| N. Allen | 40 | Fort Schlosser |
| W. Peters | 31 | Lewiston |
| I. Stone | 51 | Lewiston |
| Volunteer Cavalry | | |
| H. Camp | 64 | Lewiston |
| **Black Rock and Buffalo** | **Total = 704** | |
| Hopkins's Regiment, S. Hopkins[20] | Total = 185 | |
| E. Cook | 57 | Buffalo |
| A. Harris | 66 | Buffalo |
| E. Smith | 62 | Buffalo |
| Volunteer Riflemen | Total = 18 | |
| *McClure's Battalion*[21] | | |
| L. Powers | 18 | Buffalo |
| P. Swift's Volunteer Regiment[22] | Total = 501 | |
| D. Curtis | 63 | Black Rock |
| T. Dougherty | 71 | Black Rock |
| E. Hull | 72 | Black Rock |
| W. Hull | 60 | Black Rock |
| J. McNair | 66 | Black Rock |
| A. Mattison | 66 | Black Rock |
| S. Terry | 65 | Black Rock |
| J. Wells | 38 | Black Rock |
| **Pennsylvania State Militia**[23] | **Total = 157** | |
| Allison | 50 | Buffalo |
| Collins | 62 | Buffalo |
| Philips | 45 | Buffalo |

# American Order of Battle, 13 October 1812

Organizing the American order of battle is problematical due primarily to uncertainties about the involvement of the New York militia and volunteers. A preamble is needed, therefore, to explain this particular depiction of the American force.

The size of the American force which crossed to Queenston is here estimated to have totalled 1,353. This number combines 613 regulars with 740 militia and does not include the majority of the Second Regiment of U. S. Artillery (103) left at Lewiston and two companies of New York State Militia artillery (71). With those figures added, the total involved is 1,527. These numbers are presented as well-founded probabilities in the hope of clarifying the strength of the American attack.

An exact count of the Americans who attacked Queenston was not calculated at the time and Major General Sheaffe's observation that the those who "effected a landing, probably amounted to thirteen or fourteen hundred men" is as good an estimate as is available.[1] Similarly, the casualty count was never verified; the best Stephen Van Rensselaer could do was suggest that there were 60 killed and 170 wounded, some of whom were among the 436 regulars and 489 militia (925) taken prisoner.[2]

With this information in mind, the number of regulars presented here (716) is based upon anecdotal comments and muster and pay roll information.

A calculation of the militia involvement is more difficult because little relevant anecdotal information is available. Companies are listed here because there is evidence they suffered casualties, and/or had prisoners taken, at Queenston. The company commander is listed with this tally in brackets. Companies marked with an asterisk (*) had a notation on their rolls stating "This company was involved in the Battle of Queenston Heights," although no specifics may have appeared otherwise.

Some of the militia rolls were incomplete and uninformative in regards to the battle. Undoubtedly, many more militiamen were involved than were identified as such. Some of the militia rolls showed large numbers of men being discharged at periods later in October, suggesting that they were among the prisoners returned on parole, although no reasons for their discharge are mentioned. Their numbers have not been added to the totals for each company here nor has the number of men shown to have died later in October, even though some of them certainly died of wounds suffered at the battle.

The number of militia known to have crossed (371), then, is a bare-bones figure which excludes many of the wounded, killed, captured and missing. It is not unreasonable to suppose that twice this number of men actually crossed into Canada and that other companies mentioned in Appendices D and E were involved in the fighting.

### Staff Officers

| | |
|---|---|
| Major General Stephen Van Rensselaer | Commander of Forces on the Niagara River |
| Lieutenant Colonel Solomon Van Rensselaer | Aide-de-camp to Stephen Van Rensselaer |
| Lieutenant Colonel Peter Porter | Quartermaster General, Niagara |
| Brigadier General William Wadsworth | Commander, Seventh Brigade N. Y. Militia |
| Brigadier General Daniel Miller | Commander, Sixth Brigade N. Y. Militia |
| Brigadier General Alexander Smyth | Commander, Brigade of regulars, Black Rock |
| Lieutenant Colonel James Fenwick | Commander, Detachment of regulars, Fort Niagara |
| Major John Lovett | Aide-de-camp to Stephen Van Rensselaer |
| Major Stephen Lush | Aide-de-camp to Solomon Van Rensselaer |
| Major W. H. Spencer | Aide-de-camp to William Wadsworth |
| Captain Joseph G. Totten | Engineer |

### U.S. Army Regulars

Number reported to have crossed = 613[3]
Second Artillery at Lewiston = 103[4]
Total regulars involved = 716

| | |
|---|---|
| Thirteenth Infantry[5] | |
| J. Chrystie | 260 |
| Infantry Detachment[6] | |
| Sixth Regt. | |
| Thirteenth Regt. | |
| Twenty-third Regt. | |
| J. Mullany | 240 |
| Second Artillery[7] | |
| W. Scott | 105 |
| Artillery Detachment | |
| First Regt. | |
| Third Regt. | |
| Light Infantry | |
| J. Fenwick[8] | 110 |
| Engineer Corps | |
| J. Totten | 1 |

## New York Militia and Volunteers

Number known to have crossed = 371[9]
Speculated total who crossed = 740
Number in two artillery companies = 71
Total militia involved = 811

Sixteenth Regiment (104)[10]
Lieutenant Colonel F. Stranahan
Major A. Stafford
E. Beach (23)
S. Clarke (16)
J. Felt (3)
P. Magher (9)
S. Pettengill (27)
E. Saunders (18)
J. Westcoat (6)

Seventeenth Regiment (67)[11]
Lieutenant Colonel T. Mead
Major J. Randall
E. Bacon (13)
R. Gray (13)
D. Root (13)
D. Seymour (4)
S. Smith (3)
N. Taylor (3)
T. Wasson (10)
D. Williams (6)

Eighteenth Regiment (103)[12]
D. Buel (11)
S. Gates (5)
J. Cleland (15)
J. Gronk (30)
J. Hart (3)
S. Kellogg (4)
J. McClure (9)
J. Moore (26)

Nineteenth Regiment (12)[13]
Lieutenant Colonel H. Bloom
M. Barber (2)
A. Brinkeroff (3)*
A Burch
D. Eldridge (2)
P. Ellis
J. Phelps (2)

Twentieth Regiment (51)[14]
Lieutenant Colonel P. Allen
Major G. Smith
J. Robinson
J. Bogert (6)
J. Brown (5)
E. Clarke (10)
A. Dox (5)
C. Harrington (1)
J. Morehouse (7)
S. Stanley (14)*

Silas Hopkins's Regiment[15]
R. Spalding (5)

Rifle Companies (23)[16]
C. Bristol (1)
W. Ireland (14)
L. Kellogg (1)
N. Parke (6)
J. Westfall *

Artillery Companies (71)[17]
Major John Lovett
A. Endicott (43)
J. Pierce (28)

## Artillery in Action [18]

| | |
|---|---|
| Fort Gray | 2 x 18-pdr. |
| Near Fort Gray | 1 mortar |
| Second U. S. Artillery | 2 x 6-pdrs. |
| U. S. Light Artillery | 1 x 6pdr. |

APPENDIX G

# British Army Personnel Involved at Queenston Heights

About 600 officers and men of the British army participated in the fighting at Queenston Heights. Their names and the units to which they were attached are listed below, with casualties indicated as the available documentation allows.

This information was obtained from pay and muster lists and casualty returns held by the Public Record Office in Kew, England. As with any set of such rolls, legibility, remarks and overall organization present problems to interpretation. This was especially true with the material dealing with the 41st Foot, which showed that most of the ten companies were split up and posted on the Niagara River and the Detroit River. The companies were divided again into platoons and posted at Fort George or Chippawa so that there were about 280 men at the former and about 200 at the latter on 30 September 1812.[1] No captain's individual company was specifically identified in this material, nor was any subaltern named. As well the number of sergeants in the companies seemed unusually small. A list was compiled here for each post, made up of platoons which took casualties at the battle. Captain Bullock led 150 of the 41st Foot to the battle from Chippawa, but that exact number could not be identified from the lists, so 200 names are shown here for that post, most of whom likely marched with Bullock. Identification of the officers is based on the various reports of their involvement and Sutherland's *His Majesty's Gentlemen.* Captain Peter Chambers has not previously been credited with involvement with the battle, although Major Thomas Evans mentioned that he carried news of the outcome to Fort George after the battle.

The pay lists for the 49th Foot were more informative and led to straight forward identification of the men involved. Only ten of the forty casualties suffered by the 49th and one of the six men captured could be identified. The service of Ensign Edward Danford, which has not previously been credited, was mentioned in a note by Major General Sheaffe.[2]

The list for the Royal Artillery was also easy to assess although it shows the full strength of Holcroft's company which was detached to posts along the Niagara River, at Fort Malden and elsewhere in Upper Canada. His detachment at the battle numbered about 40 and it is presumed their names are among those shown here.[3]

**Legend**

KIA = killed in action   WIA = wounded in action   WIAd = died of wounds   POW = prisoner of war

**Staff Officers**

Major General Isaac Brock, KIA
Major General Roger Hale Sheaffe
Captain John Glegg, 49th Foot
Lieutenant Walter Kerr, Glengarry Light Infantry Fencibles

## 41st Regiment of Foot – Fort George

**Lieuts. William L. Crowther, William Derenzy, Angus McIntyre, John F. Winslow**
**En. Thomas Martin**

*Sergeants*

Lyon, Gordon
Merryweather, George KIA

*Corporals*

Bignall, John
Emmerson, George
Gillepsie, Michael
Hinnagan, Patrick
McCarty, Florence
McKenna, James
McPherson,John
Meany, Laurence
Mitchell, Thomas
Morrow, Francis
Murray, Andrew
O'Brien, William
Oliver, James
Osborne, Sampson
Page, Charles
Plunket, Peter
Preston, John
Quinn, Francis
Russell, James
Sweeney, Daniel
Terue, John
Wade, Francis

*Privates*

Adams, James
Addison, Thomas
Albert, John
Allen, Henry
Allison, Peter
Andal. John
Armstrong, Thomas
Aylward, Martin
Barry, James
Barry, Thomas
Bennett, Andrew
Bennoy, William
Braithwaite, George
Brasol, William
Brenan, Thomas
Brett, Charles
Brinker, James
Broadhead, William
Brown, John
Brown, Joseph
Brown, Julius
Brown, Mathew
Buckley, John
Buckmaster, William
Bulger, James
Burke, Michael
Burns, Patrick
Burton, Philip
Callahan, John
Carroll, James
Carty, James
Caruthers, Charles
Cash, William
Cassidy, John
Chitley, Robert
Cleary, James
Clement, Robert
Collier, Thomas
Collins, James
Company, Richard
Conlan, Richard
Connelly, John
Connelly, Mathew
Conroy, John
Cooney, John
Cooney, Michael
Coulston, Thomas
Cox, Thomas
Crafton, Archibald
Crievy, Daniel
Crookes, Samuel
Cuddy, Thomas
Daley, John
Dandy, William
Daniels, William
Davey, Melchinock
Davis, Christopher
Davis, John
Davis, Robert
Day, Richard
Denny, William
Desmond, Andrew
Dillon, Frederick
Dixon, Henry
Doe, John
Doher, John
Driskell, Timothy
Duffey, Pearce
Duffey, Thomas
Dunn, Peter
Dwyne, Michael
Dymoke, Elias
Eagan, Daniel
Eagan, John
Ellis, Nathaniel
Evans, Timothy
Evans, William
Evans, David
Fahey, Daniel
Falkner, John
Fallon, Patrick
Finletter, Thomas
Ford, Hugh
Foy, Michael
Francis, John
Frickleton, Richard WIAd
Gallon, John
Game, James
Gaynor, Samuel
Geeves, Thomas
Gibson, Gideon
Gildea, Patrick
Gill, William
Gilliland, Richard
Gilmore, Alexander
Gilstain, Arthur
Green, Thomas
Greenwood, Michael
Gregory, John
Grey, James
Grey, John
Groves, Richard
Hall, Martin
Halton, John
Hane, Patrick
Harley, Patrick
Henderson, James
Herbert, Thomas
Hinchey, Paul
Holden, Richard
Holmes, William WIA
Horidell, John
Hudell, George
Hughes, John WIA
Hughes, Thomas

Hughes, William
Hume, John
Hyde, Walter WIA
Jameson. Andrew
Jones, David WIAd
Jones, Thomas
Keeling, Barnard
Keeling, Patrick
Kelly, John
Kelly, Thomas
Kennedy, Andrew
Keough, James
Kinney, Peter
Langan, Arthur
Lawless, John
Leahy, Daniel
Leary, Joseph
Leaver, James
Lennon, Patrick
Levins, Thomas
Lewis, Willam
Lilly, John
Lloyd, Hugh
Lucky, Charles
Lyford, Charles
Lynch, Michael
Lynn, Michael
Lyons, Edmund
Maddigan, Michael
Maloney, Jeremiah
Maloney, Michael
Mangan. John
Mangan, Patrick
Mardell, Robert
Marra, Edward
Marran, Michael
Martin, Patrick
Mason, Jonathan
Matthews, Patrick
McCabe Michael
McCabe, William
McCann, John
McClosky, Michael
McCoy, Frederick
McCreat, Joseph
McGinnis, Barnard
McGrath, Thomas
McGuine, Nicholas
McGuine, Patrick
McKenney, James
McKiever, Hugh
McLeod, Edward
McMahon, Michael
McNamara, Daniel
McNamee, Patrick
McQueade, Henry
Merrick, John WIAd
Middleton, Samuel
Miller, Arthur
Millett, Abraham
Montgomery, Thomas
Moran, John
Morgan, Edward
Mullen, Patrick
Murdock, William
Murphy, George
Murphy, John
Murphy, Patrick
Murray, Thomas
Neal, John
Neanon, Timothy
Nesbitt, Thomas
Newington, Abraham
Newman, William KIA
Nixon, James
Nottman, James
O'Byrne, James
O'Miara, john
O'Neil, Thomas
Owens, William
Padden, Luke
Pallas, Christopher
Pead, Alexander
Petreham, Jeremiah
Porter, Thomas
Porter, William
Powell, John
Reardon, John
Reed, Andrew
Reed, Edward
Reed, Thomas
Regan, John
Ricks, John
Riley, James
Robertson, Zachariah
Robinson, James
Roughan, John
Rudden, John
Schofield, John
Scotchmore, John
Seymour, Edward
Sharp, James
Sheppard, John
Shields, James
Sibbald, James
Slaynes, Denis
Smith, James
Smith, Hugh
Smith, John KIA
Smith, Ralph
Soley, William
Spooner, Joseph
Stanger, James
Stevens, Robert
Stevens, William
Sweeney, Patrick
Terve, John
Thompson, Robert
Thompson, Thomas
Wales, Alexander
Walker, John
Walker, Joseph
Wallace, Joseph
Warner, John
Warren, John
Watts, James
Webb, Thomas
Wells, Thomas
Wells, William
Wheatley, William
Whelan, Patrick
Whitaker, John
Whitebread, Thomas
Wilkinson, Thomas
Williams. William
Wilson, Francis
Wilson, James
Wilson, Thomas
Woodward, Robert
Wright, John

**Total = 285 officers and men**

Source: WO 12, 5416 and 6044. Pay list for the 41st Regiment of Foot June–December 1812.

## 41st Regiment of Foot – Chippawa

**Capts. Richard Bullock, Peter L. Chambers and William C. Saunders**
**Lieuts. Richard Bullock, William G. Gardiner, Benjamin Geale, George Taylor**
**En. Dennis Fitzgerald**

*Sergeants*
Clarke, Henry
Keely, Davis WIA
Kelly, Thomas
Kerby, Richard
Williams, Robert

*Corporals*
Baxter, John
Jeffcott, William WIA
Summer, Nicholas

*Volunteer*
Wilkinson, Alexander

*Privates*

Adams, John
Alforth, John
Aspden, John
Baker, Joseph
Ball, Richard
Baxter, William
Bellows, George
Bendix, John WIA
Bent, William
Birchill, George
Bishop, John
Blake, William
Bone, Robert
Bostock, James
Bow, James
Boyle, Patrick
Breach, John
Brewer, George
Brierly, John
Browne, William
Browne, Edward
Brunker, John
Buckley, Cornelius
Bullock, John
Burge, Thomas
Burgess, Thomas
Burgess, Thomas
Burke, John
Buxton, John
Caroley, James
Carry, Luke
Chester, Benjamin
Clapton, Samuel
Clarke, Abram
Cleary, Thomas
Cokely, Cornelius
Collier, Thomas
Collier, William
Collins, Robert
Collins, Thomas
Cooper, Edward
Cortrell, William
Cottrell, Bejamin
Currant, James
Dane, John
Daniels, Samuel
Deane, William WIA d
Dinor, John
Draper, William
Dukes, Richard
Dunford, David
Dunford, James
Dunford, Isaac
Durham, Thomas
Ellis, William
Elsmore, Thomas
Evenall, William
Farmer, William
Faulkner, John
Field, Francis
Flynn, Michael
Ford, John
Ford, Thomas
Foster, James
Frith, Samuel
Fry, Luke
Garlic, Benjamin
Gibbs, Thomas
Gilerist, Robert
Glanville, James
Gooding, Thomas
Green, David
Green, William
Grist, Thomas
Hall, John
Hall, Henry
Hall, Joseph
Hamm, Thomas
Hampton, Robert
Harding, James
Hardy, Jacob
Harriby, Robert
Hastings, James
Hawkins, Edward
Hawley, William
Haynes, Thomas WIAd
Head, William
Heather, JamesHerd, William
Hodkinson, Thomas
Holmes, Asa
Holt, James
Holt, Cornelius
Hurtley, John
Ingram, Philip
Isabel, Richard
Jeffry, Henry
Jeptha, William
Jones, David WIAd
Keating, Cornelius
Kellow, Nicholas
Kettlewell, Joseph
Kirk, Thomas
Knight, Richard
Knowles, Samuel
Laferty, William
Lennard, John
Longshaw, William
Lovis, William
Maddock, William
Magee, Thomas
Mathews, Richard
McCall, Edward
McCoy, Michael
McGuire, John
Middleton, Abner
Molineaux, Thomas
Monro, James
Moulton, Richard
Mountain, Mathew
Newman, William
Nightingale, Thomas
Norris, William
Oliver, Thomas
Osmond, John
Ottes, James
Pagenton, Thomas
Paid, Mathew
Pandice, Joseph
Pate, John
Payne, Joseph
Pike, William
Plummer, William
Pollard, James
Pomroy, Thomas WIA
Poole, William
Prescott, John
Quin, James
Raynes, Henry
Reburn, Thomas WIAd
Regan, Edward
Robinson, John
Rosewell, Thomas
Rummel. William
Sainesburg, John
Sanders, James
Sanders, Richard
Scott, John
Sharp, Jarvis
Silcox, James
Simkins. George
Sims, John
Smith, Edward
Smith, John
Smith, William
Snow, William
Standburg, John
Symes, William
Talyor, James
Thomas, John
Thorley, George
Toole, Michael
Topham, John
Tracey, Peter
Trump, John
Tucker, William
Turner, Daniel
Tyson, Robert
Vickers, Richard
Wadsworth, George
Ward, Charles

Ware William
Warlaw, William
Watkins, Thomas
Watts, Samuel
Watts, William
Weaver, John
Webb, Robert
Webber, James
Webber, Thomas
Wells, Nathaniel
Westcote, William
White, James WIA
White, Mathew
Whitehead, John
Wickham, Thomas
Williams, William
Wilmot, Robert WIA
Wilsoncroft, Joseph
Windsor, William
Wood, Daniel
Woods, Henry

**Total = 209 officers and men**

Source: WO 12, 5416 and 6044. Pay list for the 41st Regiment of Foot June–December 1812

## 49th Regiment of Foot – Queenston

**Capt. James Dennis WIA**
**Lieut. John Shaw**

*Sergeants*
Boyd, John
McCarty, Florence
Osborne, Sampson
Wade, Frances

*Corporals*
Gillespie, Michael
Flinagan, Patrick
Mitchell, Thomas
Russell, James

*Musicians*
Bowen, John
Jones, Thomas
Schroder, John

*Volunteers*
Augustine, Thompson
Shaw, Richard

*Privates*
Aitcheson, James
Albert, John
Anclue, John
Barry, James
Braithwaite, George
Brown, Joseph
Brown, Julius
Buckley, John
Bunker, James
Burton, Philip
Cash, William
Chitley, Robert
Cooney, John
Cooney, Michael
Cox, Thomas
Crafton, Archibald
Cuddy, Frances
Dandy, Williams
Daniels, William
Darby, Mathew
Denny, William
Edgar, John
Fahey, Daniel
Falkner, John
Foy, Michael
Frickleton, Richard WIAd
Galvin, Christopher
Game, James
Gildea, Patrick
Greenwood, Michael
Gregory, John
Grey, John
Hall, Martin KIA
Harley, Patrick
Hatton, John
Hughes, William
Hume, John
Kelly, John
Langan, Arthur
Levin, Thomas KIA
Lewis, William
Lynn, Richard
Matthews, Patrick
McCabe, Michael
McCabe, William
McGuire, Nicholas
McKeaver, Hugh
McMahon, Michael
Merrick, John WIAd
Mullen, Patrick
Muliney, Jeremiah
Muliney, Michael
Murdell, Robert
Murphy, John
Murphy, Patrick
Nottman, James
Neanon, Timothy
Newington, Abraham
Newman, William KIA
O'Byrne, James
Paddon, Luke
Pallas, Christopher
Petreham, Jeremiah
Porter, Thomas
Robinson, James
Rodden, John
Rereghan, John
Scofield, John
Smith, John KIA
Smith, Ralph
Sobey, William
Stanger, James
Warner, John
Williams, William
Wilson, James
Wilson, Thomas
Wright, John

**Total = 92 officers and men**

Source: WO12, 6044. Pay list for the 49th Regiment of Foot June–December 1812

**Capt. John Williams WIA**
**En. Edward Danford**

*Sergeants*
Bradley, Thomas
Brew, Francis
Jenery, Zachariah
Little, Edward
Riley, Mathew

*Corporals*
Brickley, Thomas
McGurigh, John
Montgomery, Robert
Pogson, Jonathan
Sullivan, John

*Musicians*
Bell, Æneas
Burns, Edward
Connolly, John

*Volunteer*
Jarvis, George POW

*Privates*
Acres, Frances
Adams, George
Armstrong, Andrew
Armstrong, William
Austin, John
Ballantine, John
Brown, Mathew
Burns, John
Burns, Joseph
Buller, John

Byrne, Thomas
Byron, Patrick
Campbell, James
Carty, Laurence
Carty, Miles
Collins, Thomas
Copeland, Patrick
Cunningham, Edward
Davis, Evan
Denny, Patrick
Desmond, Jeremiah
Dillon, John
Dooley, John
Doran, Francis
Edgar, Michael
Edgar, William
Farmer, William
Flaherty, Patrick
Fraser, Daniel
Gee, Thomas KIA
Gillespie, Hugh
Gorman, John
Gorman, Timothy
Hanlon, John
Hardingham, Josias
Hassett, Mathew
Highland, John
Hinty, John
Hughes, Henry
Hughes, James
Kennedy, Thomas
Kilden, Thomas
Liston, Edward
Mauwrue, William
Martin, George
McClair, Owen
McDonald, William
McGurigh, John
McGurigh, Patrick
McLughlin, John
McLughlin, Patrick
Moore, James
Morgan, Thomas
Nawton, John
O'Brien, Patrick
Oliver, William
O'Neil, Francis
Owens, Peter
Phillips, John
Rennicks, John
Richmond, William
Roberts, Henry
Rort, James
Rossitter, Thomas
Scott, John
Sullivan, John
Thomas, John
Tucker, Thomas
Wade, Richard KIA
Walford, Alexander
White, James
Williams, David
Williams, William
Wright, John
Wright, Richard

**Total = 92 officers and men**

Source: WO12, 6044. Pay list for the 49th Regiment of Foot June–December 1812

## Royal Artillery Regiment, 4th Battalion

### Capt. William Holcroft

*Sergeants*
Mills, William
Pilmour, William
Richards, John
Watson, John

*Corporals*
Gibb, John
Ellerton, Thomas
Marr, Thomas
Patterson, John

*Drummers*
Brown, James
Telford, T. A.

*Bombardiers*
Haywood, William
Jackson, James
Johnston, John
Kitson, James
Malcom Benton
Mitchell, David
Needham, William
Nisbet, George
Robertson, Robert

*Gunners*
Allen, Anthony
Amos, John
Anderson, James
Anderson, Joseph
Anderson, Gilbert
Ball, William
Barbar, George
Bartles, John
Beattie, John
Beattie, Martin
Berrie, Andrew
Berrie, John
Bickley, Edward
Birch, William KIA
Blackie, James
Bradberry, Joseph
Brownhill, John
Cartwright, John
Clark, Thomas
Claxton, William
Clegg, Isaac
Clough, Thomas
Cooper, Thomas
Couley, Joseph
Coulter, David
Crossley, John
Dawson, John
Dochard, George
Dochard, John
Duncan, John
Dutson, William
Elder, Robert
Finister, James
Fraser, Hugh
Gaging, John
Gerrard, John
Gerrard, Robert
Gladwin, George
Goldsmith, John
Gover, James
Granger, Robert WIA
Grant, Richard
Green, John
Greenwood, James
Hagu, Stephen
Hargraves, Isaac
Hargraves, David
Harrison, Thomas
Henderson, Thomas
Holding, Adam
Hunt, Henry WIA
Irvin, Robert
Jackson, Abraham
Jackson, James
Jennings, James
Jones, Samuel
Kalroyd, Thomas
Kenney, John
Kershaw, John
King, Minter
Kinmouth, John
Knowles, Matthew
Lamb, James
Lang, James
Lawrence, John
Livingston, James
Lloyd, Thomas
Lock, John

Main, Donal
McLaughlin, John
Mitchell, William
Moriarty, Jerimiah
Morrison, Alexander
Nellum, Jacob
Nelson, Alexander
Nichol, James
Palmar, Joseph
Park, William
Parratt, Samuel
Ramage, Henry
Redfern, Ebenezer
Seath, William
Shaw, George
Shillito, George
Sloane, John
Smith, James
Stephens, John
Sterland, Joseph
Stott, Samuel
Straney, Edward
Sutherland, William
Thompson, George
Thompson, Robert
Tuxton, William
Urquhart, John
Walker, Alexander
Walker, Peter
Walters, Adam
Watson, George
Webster, George
Whithead, Benjamin
Williams, Hugh
Wilson, John
Wittles, John

**Total = 123 officers and men.**

Source: WO 10, 912. Muster Roll: October 1812.

## APPENDIX H

# *Upper Canada Militia Personnel Involved at Queenston Heights*

Early in 1812 there were about 13,300 officers and men in the militia of Upper Canada, divided into thirty regiments of infantry among the province's seven districts. Major General Isaac Brock did not believe he could effectively outfit and train such a large force to deal with the pending hostilities and so, as head administrator of the government, he introduced a bill into the legislature which would revise the Militia Act of 1808. Among its several provisions, the supplementary act required that two "flank" companies be immediately formed within each regiment. These were new sub-units within the regiments and were to be filled up to 100 officers and men, taken from the battalion companies, who would drill six times per month. It was an opportunity for service which caught the eye of some patriotic young Canadians as the comment made by George Ridout at York in June indicates: "I have the honor to be an Ensign in a Battalion company. Col. Chewett has given me to understand that in a short time I am to be promoted to a Lieutenancy in the Grenadier compy. which is a Flank compy composed of picked men nearly of a size, and who are tolerably well disciplined. D. Cameron is the Captn."[1]

At the time of the declaration of war companies of cavalry and artillery were also formed. Documentation for the militia during this period is incomplete, the best guide for the organization of the Upper Canada militia being William Gray's *Soldiers of the King*.[2] A partial list of militia casualties is included here separately from the regiments and companies.

## Provincial Staff

Major General Æneas Shaw, Adjutant General
Lieutenant Colonel Cecil Bisshopp, Inspecting Field Officer
Lieutenant Colonel Robert Nichol, Quarter Master General
Lieutenant John Johnston, Assistant Adjutant General, Home District
Lieutenant James Cummings, Assistant Quarter Master General, Niagara District

## Niagara District

### 1st Lincoln Militia Regiment

Colonel William Claus, commanding
Lieutenant John Clark, Assistant Adjutant General
Captain John Powell, aide-de-camp

| *Captains* | *Lieutenants* | *Ensign* |
|---|---|---|
| James Crooks | Martin McClellan | Van Courtland Secord |
| | William Powers | |
| | Anslem Foster | |
| John McEwan | William Servos | |
| | George Adams | |
| *Coloured Company* | | |
| Robert Runchey | George Runchey | |
| | James Robertson | |

### 2nd Lincoln Militia Regiment

Lieutenant Colonel Thomas Clarke, commanding

| *Captains* | *Lieutenants* | *Ensigns* |
|---|---|---|
| Robert Hamilton | James Cooper | Christopher Boughner |
| | John Burch | |
| John Rowe | Anthony Upper | James Thompson |
| | Thadeus Davis | |

### 3rd Lincoln Militia Regiment

Major John Warren, commanding

| *Captains* | *Lieutenants* | *Ensigns* |
|---|---|---|
| William Powell | Shubal Park | William Duff Miller |
| | Benjamin Hardison | |
| | John Putman | |

### 4th Lincoln Militia Regiment

Lieutenant Colonel Johnson Butler, commanding

| *Captains* | *Lieutenants* | *Ensigns* |
|---|---|---|
| Abraham Nelles | Thomas Butler | |
| | James Dedrick | |
| Jon Moore (until 24.08.12) | Henry Hixon (until 24.08.12) | |
| | John Henry (until 24.08.12) | |
| William Crooks (from 24.08.12) | Henry Nelles (from 24.08.12) | |
| | William Servos (from 24.08.12) | |

### 5th Lincoln Militia Regiment

Lieutenant Colonel Andrew Bradt, commanding

| *Captains* | *Lieutenants* | *Ensigns* |
|---|---|---|
| Samuel Hatt | Robert Land | Daniel Showers |
| James Durand | William Davie | John Birnie |

### Niagara Troops of Horse

Major Thomas Merritt, commanding

| *Captains* | *Lieutenants* | *Cornet* |
|---|---|---|
| *1st Troop of Lincoln Niagara Light Dragoons* | | |
| Alexander Hamilton | William Hamilton Merritt | |
| *2nd Troop of Niagara Light Dragoons* (21 June to 12 July) | | |
| George Hamilton | James Cummings | John Pell |

### 1st Lincoln Artillery

| *Captains* | *1st Lieutenants* | *2nd Lieutenant* |
|---|---|---|
| John Powell | William Servos | Alexander McKee |
| Alexander Cameron | John C. Ball | Alexander Bryson |

### 2nd Lincoln Artillery

| *Captain* | *1st Lieutenants* | *2nd Lieutenants* |
|---|---|---|
| James Kerby | Lewis Clement | Jacob A. Ball |
| | John McClellan | |

### Car Brigade

*Captain*
Isaac Swayze

## Home District

### 1st York Militia Regiment

Colonel William Graham, commanding
Major William Allan
Adjutant John Johnson

| *Captain* | *Lieutenants* | *Ensigns* |
|---|---|---|
| John Selby | Reuben Richardson | |
| | Barnet Vanderburgh | |

### 2nd York Militia Regiment

Colonel Richard Beasley, commanding

| *Captain* | *Lieutenants* | *Ensigns* |
|---|---|---|
| John Chisholm | George King | George Chisholm |
| | William Heyburn | |
| William Applegarth | Joseph Atkinson | William Chisholm |

## 3rd York Militia Regiment

Lieutenant Colonel William Chewett, commanding

| *Captain* | *Lieutenants* | *Ensigns* |
|---|---|---|
| Duncan Cameron | William Jarvie | |
| | Archibald McLean, WIA | |
| | George Ridout | |
| Stephen Heward | Edward McMahon | |
| | John B. Robinson | |
| | Robert Stanton | |
| | Samuel P. Jarvis | |

## Militia Casualties at Queenston Heights[3]

**Niagara District**

| *Name* | *Rank* | *Regiment* | *Company* | *Condition* |
|---|---|---|---|---|
| James Secord | Sergeant | 1st Lincoln | | WIA |
| William Brown | Private | | Crooks | KIA |
| Daniel Stewart | Private | | Crooks | WIA |
| Morris Derrick | Private | 2nd Lincoln | | WIA |
| Stephen Peer | Private | | | WIA |
| Adam Book | Private | 5th Lincoln | Hatt | WIA |
| John Gordon | Private | | Hatt | WIAd |
| John Green | Private | | Durand | WIA |
| William Hannan | Private | | Durand | WIAd |
| John Kelly | Private | | Hatt | WIA |
| Robert S. Kerr | Private | | Hatt | WIA |
| John McIntyre | Adjutant | | Hatt | WIA |
| Lewis Reveaux | Private | | Hatt | WIA |
| David Treanor | Private | | Durand | WIA |
| Timothy Street | | Light Dragoons | | WIAd |
| **Home District** | | | | |
| Henry Cope | Private | 2nd York | Applegarth | KIA |
| Joseph Crawford | Private | 3rd York | Cameron | WIAd |
| Simon Devins | Private | | Cameron | WIAd |
| Andrew Kennedy | Private | | Cameron | WIA |
| Francis Lee | Private | | Cameron | WIA |
| Thomas Major | Private | | Cameron | WIA |
| Thomas Smith | Private | | Cameron | KIA |

APPENDIX I

# *Brock's Army on the Niagara Frontier, October 1812*

In early October 1812 Major General Isaac Brock's army was composed of approximately 2,340 officers and men, including about 1,230 regulars, 810 militia and 300 native allies. Sufficient sources exist to establish, with reasonable certainty, the strength of the regular units, but less reliable sources are available for determining the exact size of each militia company. As a result, their numbers are based upon a few random returns and anecdotal records and are referenced as completely as possible.

Soon after news of the declaration of war reached Upper Canada, Brock formally organized his defence of the Niagara River into four divisions, an arrangement which he maintained throughout his term as commander.[1] None of the divisions of troops were completely concentrated around their central posts, since portions of each division were deployed at remote batteries and camps. For instance, the main body of regulars in the Fourth Division was housed in Fort George, but some of the men, along with the militia, were on duty at the batteries west of the fort and up the river at Two Mile Point, Brown's Point and Vrooman's Point. The following shows the organization of the army along the Niagara River prior to the battle at Queenston.

## Upper Canada

**Major General Isaac Brock, commanding**
Captain John Glegg, aide-de-camp
Lieutenant Colonel John Macdonell, provincial aide-de-camp

### Niagara District

**Major General Roger Hale Sheaffe, commanding**
Lieutenant Colonel Nathaniel Coffin, aide-de-camp

### Queenston to Fort Erie

Major General Æneas Shaw, commanding[2]

| **First, or Right Division – Fort Erie and dependencies** | | **Total = 476** |
|---|---|---|
| Major Adam Ormsby, 49th Foot, commanding | | |
| 49th Regiment of Foot | 252 | |
| Royal Newfoundland Fencible Regiment | 118 | |
| Royal Artillery | 6 | |
| Total Regulars[3] | 376 | |
| 3rd Lincoln Militia[4] | 100 | |

| **Second Divison – Chippawa and dependencies** | | **Total = 436** |
|---|---|---|
| Captain Richard Bullock, commanding | | |
| 41st Regiment of Foot | 323 | |
| Royal Artillery | 13 | |
| Total Regulars[5] | 336 | |
| 2nd Lincoln Militia[6] | 100 | |

## Fort George to Queenston

Colonel William Claus, commanding

| **Third Division – Queenston** | | **Total = 420** |
|---|---|---|
| Captain James Dennis, commanding | | |
| 41st Regiment of Foot | 10 | |
| 49th Regiment of Foot | 184 | |
| Royal Artillery | 6 | |
| Total Regulars[7] | 200 | |
| 5th Lincoln Militia | 100 | |
| Lincoln Artillery | 40 | |
| 2nd York Militia | 80 | |
| Total Militia[8] | 220 | |

| **Fourth, or Left Division – Fort George and dependencies** | | **Total = 1005** |
|---|---|---|
| Major Thomas Evans, commanding | | |
| 41st Regiment Foot | 277 | |
| Royal Artillery | 33 | |
| Royal Engineers | 1 | |
| Glengarry Light Infantry Fencibles | 1 | |
| Total Regulars[9] | 312 | |
| Car Brigade | 10 | |
| 1st Lincoln Militia | 100 | |
| 4th Lincoln Militia | 100 | |
| 1st York Militia | 40 | |
| 3rd York Militia | 80 | |
| Coloured Company | 38 | |
| Niagara Dragoons | 25 | |
| Total Militia[10] | 393 | |
| Grand River Peoples[11] | 300 | |

APPENDIX J

# British Order of Battle, 13 October 1812

The total number of British regulars and militia, and the native allies, involved in the fighting at Queenston is 1366.

## Staff Officers

| | |
|---|---|
| Major General Isaac Brock | Commander of Forces in Upper Canada |
| Major General Roger Hale Sheaffe | District Commander, Niagara |
| Colonel William Claus | Division Commander, Fort George and Queenston |
| Major General Æneas Shaw | Division Commander, Fort Erie and Chippawa |
| Lieutenant Colonel Christopher Myers | Deputy Quartermaster General, Canadian Command |
| Lieutenant Colonel Thomas Nichol | Quartermaster General, Upper Canada Militia |
| Major Thomas Evans | Major of Brigade, Niagara |
| Lieutenant Colonel John Macdonell | Aide-de-camp to Brock |
| Captain John B. Glegg | Aide-de-camp to Brock |
| Lieutenant Colonel Nathaniel Coffin | Aide-de-camp to Sheaffe |

## Force at Queenston Total = 450

| Regulars | Total = 200 |
|---|---|
| 49th Foot[1] | |
| J. Dennis | 92 |
| J. Williams | 92 |
| 41st Foot[2] | 10 |
| Royal Artillery[3] | 6 |

| Militia | Total = 250 |
|---|---|
| 5th Lincoln[4] | |
| S. Hatt | 50 |
| J. Durand | 50 |
| 1st Lincoln Artillery[5] | |
| John Ball | 40 |
| 2nd York[6] | |
| J. Chisholm | 40 |
| W. Applegarth | 40 |
| From Brown's Point and Vrooman's Point | |
| 3rd York[7] | |
| D. Cameron | 15 |
| S. Heward | 15 |

## Force from Fort George Total = 666

| Regulars | Total = 263 |
|---|---|
| Royal Artillery | |
| W. Holcroft | 33 |
| 41st Foot | |
| W. Derenzy[8] | 90 |
| A. McIntyre[9] | 140 |

| Militia and Others | Total = 403 |
|---|---|
| 1st and 4th Lincoln and 1st York | |
| J. Crooks[10] | 130 |
| Niagara Dragoons | 25 |
| Regulars and Militia | |
| T. Martin | 100 |
| R. Runchey[11] | 38 |
| Car Brigade | |
| W. Crowther[12] | 10 |
| Grand River Nations | |
| J. Norton[13] | 100 |

## Force from Chippawa Total = 250

| | |
|---|---|
| 41st Foot | |
| R. Bullock[14] | 150 |
| Militia | |
| T. Clarke[15] | 100 |

## Artillery in Action[16]

| | |
|---|---|
| Redan Battery | 1 x 18-pdr. |
| | 1 x 8-in. mortar |
| Queenston Battery | 1 x 9-pdr. |
| Vrooman's Point | 1 x 12pdr. |
| | 1 x 18-pdr. carronade |
| Holcroft's Guns | 2 x 6-pdrs. |
| | 1 x 5.5-in. howitzer |
| Crowther's Guns | 2 x 3-pdrs. |

# *Endnotes*

**Abbreviations**

| | |
|---|---|
| *AC* | U.S. Congress, *Annals of The Congress of the United States.* Washington: Gales and Seaton, 1853, 12th Congress. |
| AGO | Adjutant General's Office |
| *ASP:MA* | U.S. Congress, *American State Papers: Military Affairs.* Washington, D. C.: Gales and Seaton, 1832, Volume 1. |
| BECHS | Buffalo and Erie County Historical Society |
| CO | Colonial Office, Britain |
| *DAB* | *Dictionary of American Biography.* New York: Scribner, 1958-1964. 22 vols. |
| *DCB* | *Dictionary of Canadian Biography.* Volumes V-IX. Toronto: University of Toronto, 1976-1988. |
| *DDT* | Hastings, Hugh, ed. *The Public Papers of Daniel D. Tompkins, Governor of New York.* Albany: J. B. Lyon Company, 1898, 1902, 3 vols. |
| *DHC* | Cruikshank, Ernest A., ed. *Documentary History of the Campaigns upon the Niagara Frontier in 1812-1814* (titles vary slightly). Welland: Tribune Press, 1896-1908, 9 vols. |
| NYSA | New York State Archives |
| SVRP | Solomon Van Rensselaer Papers, Historic Cherry Hill, Albany |
| SVRMP | Stephen Van Rensselaer Military Papers, Historic Cherry Hill, Albany |
| MG | manuscript group |
| OA | Archives of Ontario |
| NAC | National Archives of Canada |
| RG | record group |
| USNA | United States National Archives |
| WO | War Office, Britain |

*Notes for picture captions are at the end of the Endnotes.*

**Preface**

1. Dearborn to Eustis, 21 October 1812, USNA, RG 107, Letters Received by the Secretary of War, Registered Series, Sept. 1811 – Dec. 1812, (C, D).
2. Willson, "A Rifleman of Queenston," 375.
3. Holcroft's account, *Quebec Mercury*, 27 October 1812, *DHC*, 4:117. Robinson, "Account of the Battle of Queenston Heights," 14 October 1812, OA, F44, John Beverley Robinson Papers. General Order by Baynes, 21 October 1812, NAC, RG 8, I, 1168:320. Evans to Procter, 22 October 1812, USNA, RG 59, M588, 7:123. Ensign John Smith, 41st Foot, also referred to "this Brilliant affair," Smith to Procter, 18 October 1812, USNA, RG 59, M588, 7:115. Solomon Van Rensselaer, *The Affair of Queenstown*, vii. Brigadier General James Wilkinson, termed the capture of Queenston Heights by American troops in the morning "this brilliant affair," Wilkinson, *Memoirs of My Own Times*, 1:578; while Major John Lovett considered this feat among "The advantages they had so brilliantly gained," Lovett to Alexander, 14 October 1812, SVRMP, Box 18, F5.

**Prologue: "Do justice to the occasion."**

1. All quotes in the prologue are taken from *The* [Niagara] *Mail*, 20 October 1853. The correspondent referred to King Street, meaning, apparently, the present Queenston Street. During the early 1800s this avenue was named Queen Street, the name used here.

**Part 1 Title Page**

1. "Journal of Major Isaac Roach, 1812-1824," 132.

**Chapter 1: "In the midst of the labors of man"**

1. Sutherland, *Merritt Journal*, 1. Merritt biography, *DCB*, 9:544. Merritt's nineteenth birthday was on 3 July 1812. The captain of the 1st Troop, Niagara Light Dragoons was Captain Alexander Hamilton, son of the late Robert Hamilton of Queenston. Captain George Hamilton, another of Robert's sons, formed the 2nd Troop late in June, but it was disbanded and merged with the 1st Troop on 12 July, Sutherland, *Merritt Journal*, 1.
2. Sutherland, *Merritt Journal*, 1.
3. Jackson, *St. Catharines, Ontario: Its Early Years*, 29, 24-31. Scott, *An Archeological Survey of Artpark*, 3-5.
4. Scott, *An Archeological Survey of Artpark*, 3-148.
5. Nafus, *Navy Island*, 13-15. Dunnigan and Scott, *Old Fort Niagara in Four Centuries*, 5-10.
6. Cited in Wilson, *The Enterprises of Robert Hamilton*, 264.
7. Ormsby, "Building a Town: Plans, Surveys and the

Early Years of Niagara-on-the-Lake," Merritt, Butler and Power, eds., *The Capital Years*, 15-44.

8. Cited in Jackson, *St. Catharines, Ontario: Its Early Years*, 99. Merritt, Butler and Power, eds., *The Capital Years*, 7.
9. Cited in Palmer, "James Fenimore Cooper and the Navy Brig *Oneida*," 96.
10. Minutes of the Town Meeting, 2 March 1812, OA, Municipal Records of the Township of Newark/ Niagara, 1793-1899, item 20.
11. Report on the State of the Fortified Military Posts in Both the Canadas, by Bruyeres, 24 August 1811, *DHC*, 3:19. Desloges, *Structural History of Fort George*.
12. Cited in Jackson, *St. Catharines, Ontario: Its Early Years*, 86. Burghardt, "The Origin and Development of the Road Network of the Niagara Peninsula."
13. Campbell, *Life of DeWitt Clinton*, 125-6.
14. Cited in Wilson, *The Enterprises of Robert Hamilton*, 264.
15. Cited in Seibel, *The Niagara Portage Road*, 136. Wilson, *The Enterprises of Robert Hamilton*. Hamilton biography, *DCB*, 5:402. Green, "The Niagara Portage Road." Dimitroff, "The Portage Era of the Niagara River Region."
16. J. C. Ogden, cited in Green, "The Niagara Portage Road," 277. Wilson, *The Enterprises of Robert Hamilton*, 60-5, 73-4, 86-7.
17. Cited in Green, "The Niagara Portage Road," 282. Elizabeth Simcoe mentioned in her diary on 23 June 1793, "The Queens Rangers have left the Huts at Queenston and encamped on the Mountain above. It is a fine dry healthy spot and the Tents look extremely pretty among the large Oaks which grow on the Mountain," Innis, *Mrs. Simcoe's Diary*, 96. The "worm fence," also known as a "snake fence," is mentioned in Crook to Maclear, 17 March 1853, OA, Miscellaneous Collection, MU2144, 1853, #14; also "Recollections of the War of 1812," *Niagara Historical Society*, No. 28 (1916) [hereafter: Crooks Account]. The description of the military reserve and lots derives from maps made by William Hawkins in 1838 and 1854. Of the gap cut into the trees along the edge of the escarpment, John Norton wrote: "The Space between the Field and the Brink of the Mountain was clear of wood, & about twenty paces in breadth, until within sixty Paces of the Sheds or Cabins, where a Copse of Oak Wood expanded so much as to render it impractical to press the Enemy," Klinck and Talman, *Norton Journal*, 308.
18. Campbell, *Life of DeWitt Clinton*, 132.
19. Report on the State of the Fortified Military Posts in Both the Canadas, by Bruyeres, 24 August 1811, *DHC*, 3:19.
20. Chazanof, *Joseph Ellicott*, 9-28, 94-99, 209. Populations of individual settlements are taken from Moffat, *Population History of Eastern U.S. Cities and Towns, 1970-1870*, 101-145.
21. Cited in Scott, *An Archeological Survey of Artpark*, 135. Spafford, *A Gazetteer of the State of New York*, 228. See also pages 127-146 in Scott for a description of surveying and settlement and population of Lewiston being sixty individuals, 135. The population of Youngstown is given as forty individuals in 1820 while Lewiston had about sixty individuals in 1812 in Moffat, *Population History of Eastern U.S. Cities and Towns, 1970-1870*, 145.
22. Spafford, *A Gazetteer of the State of New York*, 334.
23. Campbell, *Life of DeWitt Clinton*, 128. Chazanof, *Joseph Ellicott*, 100.
24. Swift and Barton to Tompkins, 24 June 1812, *DHC*, 3:71. Lovett to Alexander, 14 August 1812, Bonney, *Gleanings*, 205. Dunnigan and Scott, *Old Fort Niagara*. Leonard's company was part of the U.S. Regiment of Artillery, which became known as the First Regiment of Artillery after the army was expanded early in 1812.
25. Population data taken from: Provost, *Recensement de la Ville de Québec*, 279; Lankevich and Furer, *Brief History of New York*, 74; Moffat, *Population History of Eastern U.S. Cities and Towns, 1970-1870*, 101-145; Potter, "Growth of Population in America [USA]," 664; and, Riley, *Population History of U.S. Cities and Towns, 1790-1870*, 100. Available statistics for years closest to 1812 for the provinces are: Lower Canada, 1790 – 161,311; 1822 – 427,465; Upper Canada, 1811 – 77,000; Nova Scotia, 1817 – 81,351; New Brunswick, 1824 – 74,176. The first comprehensive census was taken in 1851; see Kalbach and McVey, *The Demographic Bases of Canadian Society*, 17.
26. Errington, *The Lion, the Eagle and Upper Canada*, 46. This discussion of relations with the United States is based upon Errington, 35-75. See also, Cruikshank, "A Study of the Disaffection in Upper Canada in 1812-15."
27. Sutherland, *Merritt Journal*, 1.

**Chapter 2: "An armor and an attitude"**

1. Stagg, *Mr. Madison's War*, 48-119. Brant, *James Madison*, 13-31. Hickey, *The War of 1812: A Forgotten Conflict*, 5-28. Hitsman, *The Incredible War of 1812*, 3-24. Haythornthwaite, *The Napoleonic Source Book*, 11-37. Nettels, *The Emergence of a National Economy*, 396. North, *The Economic Growth of the United States*, 220-1. Perkins, *Prologue to War*. Horsman, *The Causes of the War of 1812*.
2. Hamilton to Rodgers, 28 May 1811, Dudley, *Naval War of 1812*, 1:49. One of the deserters from the *Chesapeake* was hung, one died of natural causes and two survived who were returned to Boston. The British provided a cash grant to the men, and their families, involved and publicly endorsed the immediate recall of Vice Admiral George C. Berkeley after the original incident, Mahan, *Sea Power in its Relations to the War of 1812*, 1:255.
3. John Randolph, the dissident Republican representative from Virginia, described the proposed hostilities as "a war not of defence, but of conquest, of aggrandizement, of ambition; a war foreign to the interest of

this country, to the interests of humanity itself." Speech by Randolph, 11 December 1812, *AC*, 12, 1:441. The voting patterns within the two parties are presented in Hatzenbuehler, "The War Hawks." See also: Stagg, *Mr. Madison's War*, 120–76; Hickey, *The War of 1812*, 32-40; Risford, "Election of 1812."

4. A message from President Madison, 5 November 1811, *Journal of the House of Representatives* ..., First Session, Twelfth Congress, 8:7.
5. John Calhoun, a representative from South Carolina, answered John Randolph of Virginia who he quoted as suggesting "why not declare war immediately." Calhoun responded with: "The answer is obvious; because we are not yet prepared," 12 December 1811, *AC*, 12-1, 476. Calhoun biography, *DAB*, 8:364. A description of the U.S. Army and the manner in which the officer corps changed from being Federalist-supporting to largely Republican-supporting during the Jefferson administration is shown in Crackel, *Mr Jefferson's Army*. Crackel argues that the army was improved during this period and that Secretary of War "Eustis – with the apparent support of Madison – undid much of what Jefferson and Dearborn had created," 182. Additional criticisms of Eustis and the effect of the unhealthy climate on the army in the vicinity of New Orleans where more than 2000 men were stationed in 1809 had is pointed out in Coffman, *The Old Army*, 27-40. For a history of the organization of the army and the various units in this study, see Rodenburgh and Haskin, *The Army of the United States: Historical Sketches of Staff and Line with Portraits of Generals-in-Chief.*
6. An Act for completing the existing Military Establishment, 24 December 1811, Twelfth Congress, Session 1, Chapter 10. An Act to raise an additional Military Force, 11 January 1812, *ibid.*, 14. An Act authorizing the President of the United States to accept and organize Volunteer Military Corps, *ibid.*, 26. An Act supplementary to the act entitled "An act authorizing the President of the United States to accept and organize certain volunteer military corps," 6 July 1812, *ibid.*, 138.
7. John Calhoun heard directly from Eustis and passed it on to Macbride, 16 March 1812, Meriwether, *Papers of John C. Calhoun*, 1:93. See also Calhoun to Noble, 22 March 1812, *ibid.*, 95. Smyth to Eustis, 5 June 1812, *ASP:MA*, 1:319. Return of Troops ..., by Nicoll, 6 June 1812, *ibid.*, 320. Eustis to Anderson, 8 June 1812, *ibid.* Eustis to Anderson, 9 June 1812, *ibid.*
8. Stagg, "Enlisted Men in the United States Army," 620-1.
9. Return of the Militia of the United States, by William Eustis, 15 February 1811, *ASP:MA*, 1:291. An Act to provide for calling forth the Militia to execute the laws of the Union, suppress insurrection and repel invasions, 28 February 1795, Third Congress, Session 2, Chapter 36. An Act to authorize a detachment from the Militia of the United States, 10 April 1812, Twelfth Congress, Session 1 Chapter 55. An Act to organize the Militia of this State, 29 March 1809, *Laws of the State of New York*, 6:530. An Act to amend the Act, entitled An Act to organize ..., 2 April 1810, *ibid.*, 7:42. The three governors who refused to follow the militia call up, on constitutional grounds, were Caleb Strong of Massachusetts, Roger Griswold of Connecticut and William Jones (not to be confused with the later secretary of the navy) of Rhode Island, Hickey, *The War of 1812*, 259-60. Skeen, *Citizen Soldiers in the War of 1812.*
10. An Act to authorize a detachment from the Militia of the United States, 10 April 1812, Twelfth Congress, Session 1, Chapter 55. See Cress, "Citizens in Arms," 165-177.
11. An Act authorizing the President of the United States to accept and organize certain Volunteer Military Corps, 6 February 1812, Twelfth Congress, Session 1, Chapter 21. A supplement gave the president power to award commissions which was given to the governors in the first act and resulted in complications. An Act supplementary to the act entitled "An act authorizing the President of the United States to accept and organize certain volunteer military corps," 6 July 1812, Twelfth Congress, Session 1, Chapter 138.
12. Governor Tompkins's office at Albany received frequent requests from companies that offered "to uniform and equip themselves" and he made special notice of how they "distinguished themselves by their appearance and behavior" during public parades, General Order by Paulding, 18 April 1809, *DDT*, 1:217; General Order by Paulding, 18 September 1811, *ibid.*, 224. Also see, General Order by Lamb, 6 April 1811, *ibid.*, 277 and General Order by Paulding, 19 September 1809, *ibid.*, 229.
13. An Act authorizing the President of the United States to accept and organize certain Volunteer Military Corps, 6 February 1812,Twelfth Congress, Session 1, Chapter 21. The tally of volunteer tenders is mentioned in Stagg, *Mr. Madison's War*, 163.
14. Campbell to Worthington, 17 June 1812, cited in Stagg, *Mr. Madison's War*, 163. See the other comments during the debate of Volunteer Corps Act in *AC*, 12:1:723-801.
15. An Act to establish a Quartermaster's Department, and for other purposes, 28 March 1812, Twelfth Congress, Session 1, Chapter 46. An Act to amend an act entitled An act to establish a Quartermaster's ..., 22 May 1812, *ibid.*, 92. Eustis had been trying to get a bill passed to form a proper quartermaster general's department from the time he took office in 1809 in part to get rid of inefficiency and over spending. Tench Coxe held the office of Purveyor during this time and his strong involvement in politics had earned him numerous enemies in Congress who used the opportunity of the bills in 1812 to remove him from office. Risch, *Quartermaster Support of the Army*, 135-172. Cooke. *Tench Coxe and the Early Republic*, 475-87. Stagg, *Mr. Madison's War*, 155-161.

16. Smyth to Eustis, 5 June 1812, *ASP:MA*, 1:319. Smyth was the colonel of the U.S. Regiment of Rifles, from 1808, and was not commissioned a brigadier general until 6 July 1812, Heitman, *Historical Register of the U.S. Army*, 1:905. Chartrand, *Uniforms and Equipment of the United States Forces*, 24-34, 84-86. Gero and Maples, "Notes on the Dress of the 13th Regiment." McBaron and Kochan, "22nd U.S. Infantry Regiment." An Act authorizing the purchase of ordnance and ordnance stores ..., 14 January 1812, *Public Statutes At Large*, 2:674. Graves, "American Ordnance of the War of 1812." Reports on the state of the Twelfth and Fourteenth U.S. Infantry Regiments at Buffalo in October 1812 showed that they lacked proper uniforms, tents, camp equipment and medical supplies. Their muskets were generally good, but lacked slings, worms, picks and brushes, etc. Reports by King, 4 October 1812, *ASP:MA*, 1:491. The U.S. Arsenal at Harper's Ferry, Virginia was producing 850 muskets per month in 1812, Report of Arms Manufactured at Harper's Ferry, 1 October 1812, USNA, RG 107, Letters to the Secretary of War, Unregistered Series.
17. An Act concerning the Naval Establishment, 30 March 1812, Twelfth Congress, Session 1, Chapter 47. An Act making further provision for the Corps of Engineers, 29 April 1812, *ibid.*, 72. An Act making appropriations for the support of the Military Establishment ..., 21 February 1812, *ibid.*, 26, 27. An Act making appropriations for the support of the Government ..., 26 February 1812, *ibid.*, 33.
18. An Act to raise an additional Military Force, 11 January 1812, Twelfth Congress, Session 1 Chapter 14. An Act making further provision for the Army of the United States and for other purposes, 6 July 1812, *ibid.*, 137. The longest serving brigadier generals were James Wilkinson (from 1792), Wade Hampton (1809) and Peter Gansevoort (from 1809, he was known to be dying by June 1812 and passed away on 2 July 1812). The three new brigadier generals were Joseph Bloomfield (27 March), James Winchester (27 March) and William Hull (8 April ). The brigadiers generals created during the summer were Thomas Flournoy (18 June), T. H. Cushing (2 July), John Armstrong (6 July), Alexander Smyth (6 July), John Chandler (8 July), William H. Harrison (22 August) and John P. Boyd (26 August), Heitman, *Historical Register of the U.S. Army*, 1:21.
19. Scott, *Memoirs*, 1:35-6. Scotts's comments are widely quoted: Hickey, *The War of 1812*, 8. A similar opinion was held by Mordecai Myers, a contemporary to Scott, who remembered being advised upon entering the army "that I would find very many above me who would be more fit to obey than to command," Myers, *Reminiscences*, 13. See Skelton, "High Army Leadership in the Era of the War of 1812," for an analysis of the officer corps which generally substantiates Scott's claim about amateurism within the corps, but argues that the men "represented a cross-section of America's political and social leaderships," (p. 274) and were not as destitute of competence as Scott averred. Two of the West Point graduates who served on the Niagara frontier in 1812 were Lieutenant Samuel Rathbone, First Artillery, who was mortally wounded at the Battle of Queenston Heights and Engineer Captain Joseph G. Totten, Aimone, "West Point's Contribution to the War of 1812."
20. Tompkins to Eustis, 17 January 1812, *DDT*, 2:434. Tompkins wrote similar letters for other men of the Thirteenth, such as Captain Myndert M. Dox (*ibid.*, 2:442). Letters of acknowledgment from the officers may be found in volumes of the USNA, RG 94, Letters received by the Office of the Adjutant General, 1805-1821, such as Richard M. Malcom's letter of 1 May 1812 in which he refers to his militia experience, (micro reel 13). Data and officers' career information is taken from Heitman, *Historical Register of the U.S. Army*, such as for Peter Philip Schuyler, 1:867, James Robert Mullany, 1:735, Myndert M. Dox, 1:382, Richard M. Malcom, 1:685. Other captains who fought at Queenston were: Henry Armstrong, Heitman, 1:170; William Lawrence, 1:619; Peter Ogilvie, 1:757; and John Wool, 1:1059. All these officers, except Lawrence (Rhode Island) were natives of New York State. As noted in Hastings, *Military Minutes of the Council of Appointment*, Mullany had been a New York militia captain of infantry (2:1351), Wool an ensign in a rifle battalion (1:1268) and Malcom a captain in an artillery regiment (1:815). See Appendix C for unit data. Alexander, *History of the Thirteenth Regiment United States Infantry*. The speculation that this regiment was dressed in the "drab" uniforms issued during this period because of a shortage of properly prepared wool is made in Gero and Maples, "Notes on the Dress of the 13th Regiment." The scene of the battle, as painted by Captain James Dennis, 49th Foot, depicts all American troops in their traditional blue uniforms. Dennis seems to have devoted considerable attention to the uniform details and so his image serves as the best available information about the uniforms of the American forces at Lewiston. Information regarding the collection of the regiment at Greenbush and its deployment are mentioned in Ensign Joseph Dwight's "Journal of an Ensign in the War of 1812" and Captain Mordecai Myers, *Reminiscences 1780 to 1814.*
21. Calhoun to Macbride, 18 April 1812, Meriwether, *Papers of John C. Calhoun*, 1:99.
22. Armstrong to Eustis, 2 January 1812, *DHC*, 3:29. Armstrong biography, *DAB*, 1:355. Hull biography, *DAB*, 5:363.
23. Crackel, *Mr. Jefferson's Army*, 76, 78.
24. Foster to Castlereagh, 21 April 1812, OHC, 3:53. Dearborn biography, *DAB*, 3:174. Eustis to Dearborn, 9 April 1812, USNA, RG 107, Letters Sent by the Secretary of War, 5:335.
25. Madison to Jefferson, 17 August 1812, Hunt, *Writing of James Madison*, 8:210. Dearborn's strategic plan is described in: Brant, *Madison*, 6:45; and Stagg, *Mr. Madison's War*, 193.

26. Eustis to Dearborn, 9 and 10 April 1812, USNA, RG 107, Letters Sent by the Secretary of War, 5:335 and 363. Eustis's instructions for Dearborn to expedite the military movements in New York are seen in Eustis to Dearborn, 4 and 26 June 1812, USNA, RG 107, 5:424 and 458 and 9, 15 and 20 July 1812, USNA, RG 107, 6:15, 26 and 35. Eustis sent copies of his correspondence to Hull and Dearborn to help coordinate their activities: Eustis to Dearborn, 26 July 1812, USNA, RG 107, 6:199; Eustis to Hull, 20 August 1812, USNA, RG 107, Letters Received by the Secretary of War, Unregistered Series. Hull's thoughts about the 1812 campaign are found in his *Memoirs of the Campaign of the Northwest Army*, 18-24. Another example of support for a multi-front campaign may be seen in Major A. Stoddard's plan for an attack on Canada, 20 August 1812, USNA, RG 107, Letters Received by the Secretary of War, Unregistered Series. For Peter Porter's views on the conquest of Upper Canada, see Stagg, "Between Black Rock and a Hard Place."
27. Clay to Monroe, 15 March 1812, Hopkins, *Papers of Henry Clay*, 1:637. An Act laying an embargo on all ships and vessels …, 4 April 1812, Twelfth Congress, Session 1, Chapter 49.
28. Prideaux Selby, April 1812, cited in Sheppard, *Plunder, Profit and Paroles*, 40. Brock to Prevost, 2 December 1811, NAC, RG 8, I, 673:171. Playter Diary, 27 June 1812, Firth, *The Town of York*, 279.
29. Prevost to Brock, 24 December 1811, Tupper, *Life of Brock*, 133.
30. Prevost biographies, *DCB*, 5:693; *DNB*, 16:320. [Brenton,] *Public Life of Sir George Prevost.* [Richardson], *The letters of Veritas.* office. Hitsman, "Sir George Prevost's Conduct." Turner, *British Generals in the War of 1812*, 24-57. Sutherland, *His Majesty's Gentlemen*, 25-6. Because of the size of Prevost's command, and the distance between Quebec and Halifax, the Atlantic centre, Lieutenant General Sir John Coape Sherbrooke oversaw activity in the Atlantic colonies, although he was subordinate to Prevost and passed official correspondence with London through Prevost's office.
31. Selected Brock biographies, *DCB*, 5:109; Tupper, *Life of Brock*; Nursey, *The Story of Isaac Brock*; Read, *The Life and Times of Major-General Sir Isaac Brock*; Turner, *British Generals in the War of 1812*, 58-83; Whitfield, "The Battle of Queenston Heights."
32. Nelson to Parker, late March 1801, cited in Pope, *The Great Gamble*, 283. See also Bennett, *Nelson the Commander*, 181-208.
33. Twenty-seven commissioned officers, 35 sergeants, 19 drummers,623 rank and file, as well as 95 women and 69 children, showed on the returns prepared after the transports *Tartar*, *Peggy*, *Richard* and *Norfolk* docked at Quebec; returns for the 49th Foot enclosed with Hunter to Browrigg, 24 August and 13 September 1802, OA, Miscellaneous Collection, 1797-1802, MU 2100, 1802, #2.
34. Merritt Journal, Wood, *Select British Documents*, 3:545.
35. Attributed to Stanley Hatch and cited in Kosche, "Contemporary Portraits of Isaac Brock: An Analysis," 23. The Brock portraits are discussed in this article, while a forensic examination of his uniforms is the topic of Kosche, "Relics of Brock: An Investigation."
36. Attributed to George Sanderson and cited in Kosche, "Contemporary Portraits of Isaac Brock: An Analysis," 23.
37. Brock to Irving Brock, 10 January 1811, Tupper, *Life of Brock*, 87. Brock to Irving Brock, 19 February 1811, *ibid.*, 92. Baynes to Brock, 11 October 1810, *ibid.*, 85. William Brock's bankruptcy and its effects on Isaac, Irving and John Savery Brock are detailed in a Brock family history, NAC, C0 42, MG 11, 353:218.
38. Brock to Savery Brock, 7 October 1811, Tupper, *Life of Brock*, 111. Brock to Irving Brock, 30 October 1811, *ibid.*, 112. William Brock to Brock, 31 October 1811, *ibid.*, 114. Torrens to Brock, 17 October 1811, *ibid.*, 116. Prevost to Brock, 22 January 1812, *ibid.*, 140. Baynes to Brock, 23 January 1812, *ibid.*, 140. Brock to Prevost, 12 February 1812, *ibid.*, 151,
39. Troop strengths from 1808 based upon Monthly Returns for Officers, Non-Coms, Rank and File: January 1808, NAC, MG 13, WO 17, 1514:13; December 1808, *ibid.*, 73; December 1809, *ibid.*, 163, 166; December 1810, *ibid.*, 1515:142, 144, 146; December 1811, *ibid.*, 281, 283, 284; January 1812, *ibid.*, 1516:4, 5, 6.
40. Brock to Prevost, 2 December 1811, NAC, RG 8, I, 673:171.
41. Brock to Prevost, 2 December 1811, NAC, RG 8, I, 673:171.
42. Brock to Prevost, 3 July 1812, NAC, RG 8, I, 676:115.
43. Brock to Prevost, 2 December 1811, NAC, RG 8, I, 673:171.
44. Brock to Gordon, 6 September 1807, Tupper, *Life of Brock*, 64.
45. Prevost to Brock, 24 December 1811, *DHC*, 3:26. Baynes to Brock, 19 March 1812, *ibid.*, 45.
46. Brock to Gordon, 6 September 1807, Tupper, *Life of Brock*, 64.
47. Brock to Baynes, 12 February 1812, Tupper, *Life of Brock*, 147. Brock to Prevost, 2 December 1811, NAC, RG 8, I, 673:171.
48. Prevost to Brock. 24 December 1811, Tupper, *Life of Brock*, 133. Mahon, "British Command Decisions," 221.
49. Prevost to Brock, 30 April 1812, Tupper, *Life of Brock*, 171.
50. Brock to Prevost, 16 May 1812, Tupper, *Life of Brock*, 173.
51. Brock to Prevost, 22 April 1812, Tupper, *Life of Brock*, 167. Prevost to Brock, 27 May 1812, *ibid.*, 177.
52. Baynes to Brock, 21 November and 12 December 1811, Tupper *Life of Brock*, 122 and 132. Brock to Baynes, 26 January 1812, *ibid.*, 143. Baynes to Brock,

20 February and 14 May 1812, *ibid.*, 152 and 172. Summer and Chartrand, *Military Uniforms*, 71-2.

53. Baynes to Brock, 10 March 1812, Tupper *Life of Brock*, 159. Baynes to Brock, 21 November 1811, *ibid.*, 122. Brock to Baynes, 12 February 1812, *ibid.*, 147.
54. Prevost to Liverpool, 25 June 1812, *DHC*, 3:73.
55. Baynes to Brock, 25 June 1812, *DHC*, 3:74. John Jacob Astor of the South West Company was suspected of passing news of the declaration into Canada, Haeger, *John Jacob Astor*, 146.

**Chapter 3: "We shall have our hands full."**

1. Cited in Irwin, *Daniel D. Tompkins*, 59. Tompkins biography, *DAB*, 9:583; *ANB*, 21:738
2. Tompkins to Eustis, 18 November 1809, *DDT*, 2:217. Eustis to Tompkins, 29 April 1809, cited in Irwin, *Daniel D. Tompkins*, 134. See also, *ibid.*, 61-75. Casey, "North Country Nemesis." Strum, "A Gross and Unprovoked Outrage." Sears, *Jefferson and the Embargo.*
3. Tompkins to the Assembly, 27 January 1812, *DDT*, 2:443. Tompkins to Van Vechten, 4 February 1812, *ibid.*, 459. For evidence of organization of military resources, see: Tompkins to the Assembly, 11 March 1811, *ibid.*, 257; Clinton to Tompkins, 26 February 1811, *ibid.*, 261; Report of ... Warlike Stores, 27 February 1811, *ibid.*, 263.
4. Eustis wrote to Tompkins in advance of the passage of An Act to authorize a detachment from the Militia of the United States, 10 April 1812, Twelfth Congress Session 1, Chapter 55. Eustis to Tompkins, 24 March 1812, cited in Irwin, *Daniel D. Tompkins*, 142. Tompkins to Eustis, 31 March 1812, *DDT*, 2:520. Tompkins to Porter, 13 May 1812, Peter Porter Papers, BECHS, Roll 2, A25. General Order by Lamb, 2 April 1812, *DHC*, 3:47. Tompkins to Swift, 2 April 1812, *ibid.*, 48. Tompkins to Paulding, 1 April 1812, *DDT*, 2:522. Tompkins to Hall, 2 April 1812, *ibid.*, 528. Tompkins to Porter, 18 April 1812, *ibid.*, 555. See Appendix D for unit data.
5. Tompkins to Eustis, 30 April 1812, *DDT*, 2:574. Tompkins to Eustis, 13 May 1812, *ibid.*, 602. Tompkins to Porter, 13 May 1812, *ibid.*, 605. Tompkins to Bellinger, 11 May 1812, *ibid.*, 592. Eustis to Tompkins, 8 May 1812, Peter Porter Papers, BECHS, Roll 2, A22. Tompkins to Porter, 11 May 1812, *ibid.*, A24.
6. Tompkins to Eustis, 19 April 1812, USNA, RG 107, Letters Received by the Secretary of War, Main Series. Porter biography, *DAB*, 8:99. Hatzenbuehler, "The War Hawks and the Question of Congressional Leadership in 1812." Porter was made quartermaster general on 1 February 1811, Hastings, *Military Minutes of the Council of Appointment*, 2:1238. Before that he had commanded a regiment of infantry as lieutenant colonel. For Peter Porter's views on the conquest of Upper Canada, see Stagg, J.C.A., "Between Black Rock and a Hard Place."
7. Porter, Stanard, Selay and Field to Tompkins, 15 April 1812, Peter Porter Papers, BECHS, Roll 2, A13. The two regiments that had turned out late in June were under Lieutenant Colonel Daniel Davis of Genesee and a second from Niagara, Wadsworth to Tompkins, 6 July 1812, *DHC*, 3:101.
8. Tompkins to Swift, 29 April 1812, *DDT*, 2:569. Tompkins to Hall, 1 May 1812, *ibid.*, 580. Tompkins to Eustis, 30 April 1812, *ibid.*, 574. Tompkins to Simmons, 13 May 1812, *ibid.*, 606. Tompkins to Canandaigua Arsenal Superintendent, 20 June 1812, *ibid.*, 629. Tompkins to Lewis, 26 June 1812, *ibid.*, 643. Tompkins to Porter, 21 April 1812, Peter Porter Papers, BECHS, Roll 2, A16. Tompkins to Porter, 20 June 1812, *ibid.*, A37. Tompkins to Eustis, 15 April 1812, *DDT*, 2:552. Tompkins to Wildrig, 17 April 1812, *ibid.*, 553. Tompkins to Williams, 21 April 1812, *ibid.*, 557. Tompkins to the Commissioners of Fortifications, 25 April 1812, *ibid.*, 563. Tompkins to McClure, 20 June 1812, *ibid.*, 628.
9. Tompkins to Porter, 8 July 1812, *DDT*, 3:19.
10. Dearborn to Eustis, 21 May 1812, USNA, RG 107, Letters Received by the Secretary of War, Main Series. Eustis to Dearborn, 9 and 10 April 1812, USNA, RG 107, Letters Sent by the Secretary of War, 5:335 and 363. Gansevoort biography, *DAB*, 4:127. The three governors who refused to follow the militia call up, on constitutional grounds, were Caleb Strong of Massachusetts, Roger Griswold of Connecticut and William Jones (not to be confused with the later secretary of the navy) of Rhode Island, Hickey, *The War of 1812*, 259-60.
11. Eustis to Dearborn, 26 June and 4 June 1812, USNA, RG 107, Letters Sent by the Secretary of War, 5:458 and 424.
12. General Order by Paulding to Wadsworth, 23 June 1812, *DHC*, 3:71. General order by Paulding to Ellis, Hall and Porter, 23 June 1812, *ibid.*, 69-71. Division Orders by Hosmer, 26 June 1812, *ibid.*, 74. Wadsworth's birth date is given as 1732 (making him eighty-years old in 1812), in *Harper's Encylcopedia*, 4:106, and Wadsworth's obituary shows he was seventy-three at the time of his death. A private note from David Parish, historian for Geneseo, NY, shows his life dates as 1761-1833, based on the tombstone record. *Livingston Register*, 13 March 1833. See Appendix D for a description of the New York State militia.
13. Tompkins to Hagner, 9 October 1816, *DDT*, 2:669.
14. Tompkins to Dearborn, 28 June 1812, *DHC*, 3:83. Tompkins to Eustis, 27 June 1812, *DHC*, 3:80.
15. Hall to Tompkins, 1 July 1812, *DHC*, 3:88. Swift and Barton to Tompkins, 24 June 1812, *ibid.*, 71. Hall to Tompkins, 28 and 29 June, 1812, *ibid.*, 78, 79. A. Porter to P. Porter, 2 July 1812, *ibid.*, 90. See also Kutolowski, "Commission and Canvases: The Militia and Politics in Western New York, 1800-1845." See Appendix D for a description of this element of the New York State militia.
16. Wadsworth to Tompkins, 28 June 1812, *DHC*, 3:77.
17. Tompkins to Hall, 8 July 1812, *DDT*, 3:21. For Hall's

militia status see New York Military Index, 4 July 1812, Hastings, *Military Minutes of the Council of Appointment*, 1:1400.

18. Tompkins to Porter, 8 July 1812, *DDT*, 3:19. Tompkins also wrote letters about Gray to Wadsworth, 6 July 1812, *ibid.*, 12 and to Hall, 8 July 1812, *ibid.*, 21.
19. Tompkins to Swift, 8 July 1812, *DDT*, 3:17.
20. Tompkins to Hall, 8 July 1812, *DDT*, 3:21. A portion of the Canadian Voltigeurs defied their orders at Montreal on 16 June, de Salaberry to Freer, 18 June 1812, NAC, RG 8, I, 796:118.
21. Paulding to Hall, 2 July 1812, *DHC*, 3:93.
22. Brock to Prevost, 22 April 1812, Tupper, *Life of Brock*, 167. Brock to Baynes, 12 February 1812, *ibid.*, 147. Brock to Prevost, 25 February 1812, *ibid.*, 153. Brock to Nichol, 8 April 1812, *ibid.*, 163. Brock to Prevost, 16 May 1812, *ibid.*, 173. Gray, *Soldiers of the King*, 1-35. See Appendix H for more on the Upper Canada militia.
23. Brock also made reference to "a Mr. Willcocks and his vile coadjutors" in this letter to Prevost, 9 March 1812, Tupper, *Life of Brock*, 156. Soon after the winter session of the legislature Brock met with Willcocks at Government House at York and used his skills of diplomacy to earn his allegiance. Willcocks subsequently softened his anti-government stance; see Graves, *Joseph Willcocks and the Canadian Volunteers*, 23-4.
24. 12 May 1812, *Kingston Gazette*. Similar letters were submitted to this newspaper by "Falkland" (Richard Cartwright), 4 February, 3 March and 7 April 1812.
25. Brock to Prevost, 16 May 1812, Tupper, *Life of Brock*, 173.
26. Brock to Prevost, 24 December 1811, Tupper, *Life of Brock*, 133. Brock to Freer, 26 January 1812, *ibid.*, 141. Brock to Prevost, 25 February 1812, *ibid.*, 153. Brock to Freer, 24 March and 16 May 1812, *ibid.*, 161, 175. Allen, *His Majesty's Indian Allies*, 111-122. Dickason, *Canada's First Nations*, 193-200.
27. Benn, *The Iroquois in the War of 1812*, 10-66. Weaver, "Six Nations of the Grand River, Ontario." Population of the Grand River grant based upon An Indian Census, 1810, 1811, Johnston, *Six Nations*, 281.
28. William Baldwin, 6 April 1813, cited in Murray, *John Norton*. Norton biography, *DCB*, 6:550. Norton was born on 16 December 1770, according to a private note received by the author from Carl Benn.
29. Klinck and Talman, *Norton Journal*, 286.
30. Brock to Prevost, 3 July 1812, Tupper, *Life of Brock*, 194.
31. Klinck and Talman, *Norton Journal*, 293.
32. Brock to Prevost, 3 July 1812, NAC, RG 8, I, 676:115.
33. Klinck and Talman, *Norton Journal*, 293. Swift and Barton to Tompkins, 24 June 1812, *DHC*, 3:71.
34. The history of the 41st is found in Chichester and Burges-Short, *Records and Badges of the British Army*, 535-44 and Koke, "The Britons who Fought on the Canadian Frontier." See also Carter-Edwards, "At Work and Play." Service records of Richard Bullock and William Derenzy, Sutherland, *His Majesty's Gentlemen*, 81, 123. New recruits, Baynes to Brock, 21 November 1811 and 19 March 1812, Tupper, *Life of Brock*, 122, 161. 41st ordered home, Baynes to Brock, 21 May 1812, *ibid.*,176. See Appendices G and I for unit data.
35. Brock to his brothers, 3 September 1812, Tupper, *Life of Brock*, 284. The poor quality of some officers in the 41st is mentioned in, Baynes to Brock, 21 May 1812, *ibid.*, 176, and described in Carter-Edwards, *At Work and Play*, 16-20, 87-92. Brock's impatience with Lieutenant Colonel Thomas St. George and Procter is shown in Brock to Prevost, 28 July 1812, *DHC*, 3:148. He later disagreed with them concerning tactics at Detroit in August, and referred to an element of "envy" over his success against General William Hull's army, Brock to his brothers, 3 September 1812, Tupper, *Life of Brock*, 284. St. George entered military life as an ensign in 1771 and so must have been close to sixty years old when the war began. Service records of William Crowther, Angus McIntyre, Thomas Martin, Henry Procter, Thomas B. St. George, Sutherland, *His Majesty's Gentlemen*, 112, 243, 257, 305, 323. Memorial of Richard Bullock, 2 June 1815, NAC, RG 8, I, 914:60. The publication of Brock's comments about the 41st Foot in Tupper's *Life of Brock*, provoked a letter of rebuttal to the editor of the *New York Albion*, 28 March 1846 and published in Higginson, *Major Richardson's Major-General Sir Isaac Brock and the 41st Regiment*; the author of the letter is thought have been John Richardson of the 41st Foot. See also Lomax, *A History of the Services of the 41st (Welch) Regiment, from its Formation in 1719 to 1895*, *passim*. See Appendices G and I for unit data.
36. Brock to Prevost, 12 July 1812, *DHC*, 3:122. The history of the Royal Artillery is found in Chichester and Burges-Short, *Records and Badges of the British Army*, 143-147 and Koke, "The Britons who Fought on the Canadian Frontier." See also Laws, *Battery Records of the Royal Artillery*, *passim*. Service record of William Holcroft, Sutherland, *His Majesty's Gentlemen*, 194. See Appendices G and I for unit data..
37. Brock to Prevost, 7 September 1812, NAC, RG 8, I, 677:64. Burdened with the additional responsibilities of training and supervising two companies of militia artillery, Holcroft sought Brock's support when he petitioned Major General George Glasgow, commanding the Royal Artillery in Canada, for an additional "command" allowance, Holcroft to Brock, 13 September 1812, NAC, MG 13, WO 44, 245:387, 388. Duncan, *History of the Royal Regiment of Artillery*, 2:88-9, 159.
38. Malcomson, "'Not Very Much Celebrated.'" Douglas, W. A. B. "The Anatomy of Naval Incompetence."
39. General Orders by Robinson, 18 and 22 April 1812, NAC, RG 8, I, 11:105, 107. General Order by Baynes, 24 April 1812, *ibid.*, 1168:129. Malcomson, "Management of Batteaux by the British in the War of 1812."

40. The deployment of the regulars and militia is described in District General Order by Evans, 2 July 1812, "District General Orders of Maj.-Gen. Sir Isaac Brock from June 27th, 1812–Oct. 16th 1812," *Transactions of the Women's Canadian Historical Society*. No. 19 (1920), 6.
41. Wadsworth to Tompkins, 6 July 1812, *DHC*, 3:101. Brock to Prevost, 12 July 1812, NAC, RG 8, I, 676:150. See also Snow, "Salvage Archaeology of the Redan Battery."
42. District General Order by Evans, 27 June 1812, "District General Orders of Maj.-Gen. Sir Isaac Brock," 5. Biographies for Clark, Claus and Nichol, *DCB*, 6:147, 151 and 539.
43. Glegg to William Brock, 30 December 1813, Kosche, "Relics of Brock," 79. Service records for Henry Procter, Thomas Evans and John Baskerville Glegg, Sutherland, *His Majesty's Gentlemen*, 305, 138, 163. Evans biography, *DCB*, 9:245
44. Macdonell biography, *DCB*, 5:521. Also see Whitfield, "The Battle of Queenston Heights." Macdonell met William Warren Baldwin on 3 April 1812 to resolve Baldwin's insult at remarks Macdonell made in court. Macdonell refused to return Baldwin's fire and the matter ended, although their enmity continued. Halliday, *Murder Among Gentlemen*, 50-3.
45. Brock to Prevost, 3 July 1812, NAC, RG 8, I, 676:115.

**Part 2 Title Page**

1. Lovett to Alexander, 16 August 1812, SVRMP, Box 18, F4.

**Chapter 4: "A strictly amateur militia general"**

1. Troop movements are described in Hall to Porter, 1 July 1812, *DHC*, 3:88; O'Connor to Porter, 1 July 1812, *ibid.*, 89; Hall to Tompkins, 29 June 1812, *ibid*:79. Tompkins's patronage is seen in Tompkins to Eustis, 17 and 25 January 1812, *DDT*, 2:434, 436. Clarke to the Adjutant General, 25 March 1812, USNA, RG 94, Roll 8. M. Dox to Adjutant General, 26 March 1812, *ibid.*, Roll 9. McKeon to Adjutant General, 20 March 1812, *ibid*, Roll 12. See Appendix C for unit data.
2. Adams to Porter, 3 July 1812, *DHC*, 3:97. Reports in the various documents conflict as to the size of Wadsworth's brigade in July, ranging from 1700 to 2500: Wadsworth to Tompkins, 6 July 1812, *ibid.*, 101; Porter to Tompkins, 9 July 1812, *ibid.*, 117; Gray to Tompkins, 22 July 1812, *ibid.*, 139. The total used here is based upon the above reports and the items in the *Aurora* in Philadelphia, 11 and 18 July 1812, *ibid.*, 89, 104. The captains and approximate company sizes of these units in the Twentieth Detached were: Abraham Dox, 40; Selma Stanley, 30; James Bogert, 60; Joel Hart, 55. Elements of three regiments turned out late in June and in July under Lieutenant Colonels Davis and Churchill from Genesee County and Hopkins from Niagara County, as well as a number of independent companies, Wadsworth to Tompkins, 6 July 1812, *DHC*, 3:101. See Appendices D and E for unit data.
3. Benn in *The Iroquois in The War of 1812*, p. 30, remarks that "at the same time as [Granger] asked them to remain quiet, he threatened the already insecure tribespeople: if they took up arms against the United States, then the Americans would take away their land, and the British, sure to lose Canada in the coming months, would have no alternative territory to give as they had in 1784. See also 42-3. A transcription from Granger's meeting with the Six Nations is in *DHC*, 3:105-13.
4. Wadsworth to Tompkins, 6 and 8 July 1812, *DHC*, 3:101, 116. Peter Porter echoed Wadsworth's pleas about deficiencies. "This force, raw as it is ... is in my opinion barely sufficient for protection of this river," Porter to Tompkins, 9 July 1812, *ibid.*, 117.
5. Gray to Tompkins, 22 July 1813, *DHC*, 3:139. Gray referred here to the light company captained by Abraham Dox of Lieutenant Colonel Stephen Colt's Forty-Second New York Infantry of the village of Geneva, Ontario County, which Allen had taken into the Twentieth Detached, Hastings, *Military Minutes of the Council of Appointment*, 2:1241, 1408 Tompkins's shipment of materiel is mentioned in Tompkins to Hall, 8 July 1812, *DDT*, 3:19. More was sent later in the month: Order to Vernor, 21 July 1812, *ibid.*, 49.
6. Tompkins to Hall, 8 July 1812, *DDT*, 3:21. *Buffalo Gazette*, 28 July 1812, *DHC*, 3:150.
7. Elting, *Amateurs, to Arms*, 38. See also: Hitsman, *Incredible War of 1812*, ("his only qualification for promotion to that rank in the militia had been his status as a successful politician"), 57; Coles, *The War of 1812*, ("a leading Federalist ... wholly without military experience"), 59; Hickey, *The War of 1812*, ("with no previous military experience... . A rich and powerful Federalist"), 86.
8. Stephen Van Rensselaer biography, *DAB*, 10:211; *ANB*, 5:244. Barnard, *A Discourse ... Stephen Van Rensselaer*. F. Van Rensselaer, *The Van Rensselaers in Holland and America*. Redway, "General Van Rensselaer and the Niagara Frontier." K. Van Rensselaer, "The Van Rensselaers of Rensselaerwyck." Fink, "Stephen Van Rensselaer: The Last Patroon." Whitfield, "The Battle of Queenston Heights."
9. Hammond, *The History of Political Parties in the State of New York*, 162.
10. Barnard, *A Discourse ... Stephen Van Rensselaer*, 46, 44
11. Redway, "General Van Rensselaer and the Niagara Frontier," 15. Barnard stated that Van Rensselaer, in 1787, pledged "himself to a life of temperance, simplicity, truth and purity", ( *A Discourse*, 37), so the general seems to have eschewed spirits during the tavern visits Redway speculated he made. His commission as major general of cavalry in 1800 was listed in Hastings, *Military Minutes of the Council of Appointment*, 1:514.
12. Tompkins to Eustis, 27 June 1812, *DHC*, 3:80. Gen-

eral Order by Paulding, 18 June 1812, *DDT*, 1:336. Eustis to Tompkins, 3 July 1812, USNA, RG 107, Letters Sent by the Secretary of War, 6:8. Tompkins to Van Rensselaer, 13 July 1812, *DDT*, 3:27.

13. Barnard, *A Discourse ... Stephen Van Rensselaer*, 54-6.
14. Barnard, *A Discourse ... Stephen Van Rensselaer*, 55. Fox, *The Decline of Aristocracy in the Politics of New York*,172-3. The idea that Tompkins picked Van Rensselaer to win the favour of the Federalists or to injure his opponent's popularity was proposed soon after the campaign ended, Wilkinson, *Memoirs*, 564. It has been repeated in modern treatments of the topic: Mahon, *The War of 1812*, 75; Hickey, *The War of 1812*, 86; Redway, "General Van Rensselaer and the Niagara Frontier," 20; Whitfield, "The Battle of Queenston Heights," 44. Of the Van Rensselaer appointment, Tompkins's biographer said nothing regarding political intrigue, Irwin, *Daniel D. Tompkins*, 136-7, 155.
15. Tompkins had clashed with the Council of Appointment on occasion, Memo by Tompkins, July 1810 (?), *DDT*, 2:344. Tompkins to Paulding, 24 February 1812, *ibid.*, 497. The council had nothing to do with appointments for the militia detached for service in 1812, including the appointments of Stephen Van Rensselaer, Solomon Van Rensselaer and John Lovett none of which appear in Hastings, *Military Minutes of the Council of Appointment*. All the appointments appear to have been the sole responsibility of the governor's office with Stephen Van Rensselaer's appointment being approved by Secretary of War William Eustis.
16. Fox, *The Decline of Aristocracy in the Politics of New York*, 160-174. Irwin, *Daniel D. Tompkins*, 117-24. Stagg, *Mr. Madison's War*, 240-2. Hosack, *Memoir of De Witt Clinton*, 52. Bobbé, *De Witt Clinton*, 181-2. Clinton biography, *DAB*, 2:221; *ANB*, 5:77. Clinton's appointment as the "major general of the militia of the state," was made on 20 June 1812, Hastings, *Military Minutes of the Council of Appointment*, 2:1409. Strum, "New York and the War of 1812."
17. Tompkins to Hall, 8 July 1812, *DDT*, 3:21.
18. Tompkins to Dearborn, 14 August 1812, *DDT*, 3:81.
19. Eustis to Tompkins, 3 July 1812, USNA, RG 107, 6:8.
20. Madison to Dearborn, 9 August 1812, Hunt, *Writings of James Madison*, 8:205. Stagg, *Mr. Madison's War*, 241-2. Dearborn to Eustis, 28 and 30 July 1812, USNA, M221, September 1811–December 1812 (C, D).
21. Tompkins to Van Rensselaer, 13 July 1812, *DDT*, 3:27.
22. Tompkins knew that Van Rensselaer would soon become the commander and announced to Peter Porter on 8 July (*DDT*, 3:19) that "Van Rensselaer shall arrive ... in about a fortnight."
23. In a letter to his wife on 27 September 1812, Solomon revealed that he had never been close to Stephen, "The Patroon is in perfect health and more than fond of me and he is Really an amiable man, I never knew him before," SVRP, Correspondence, Box 9, F3. Solomon Van Rensselaer biography: *ANB*, 5:243. Stephen Van Rensselaer's uncle was the father of Solomon Van Rensselaer's father, making Solomon a second cousin to Stephen, as per the genealogical tables in Blackburn, *Cherry Hill: The History and Collections of a Van Rensselaer Family*. La Croix, "Solomon Van Rensselaer: His Career as Political Spoilsman." McLean, "A Survey of Some ... Activities in the Life of Solomon Van Rensselaer." Whitfield, "The Battle of Queenston Heights."
24. Bonney, *Gleanings*, 167; the affair with Jenkins is described in detail herein, 159-83.
25. Tompkins to Smith, 22 February 1812, *DDT*, 2:491.
26. Bonney, *Gleanings*, 194. Bonney's name is given as Catharina on the title page of her book, but the spelling used follows from Blackburn, *Cherry Hill*.
27. Solomon to Arriet, 18 May 1797, Blackburn, *Cherry Hill*. Solomon's wife's name is variously spelled as Arriet, Harriot and Harriet and Harriot, but Blackburn gives the name as Arriet, which also appears on Solomon's grave marker and so Arriet is used here. Van Vechten was not the first of their children to die; their third son, Rufus King, born in 1809, died at three months of age. Solomon's correspondence and military papers are found among the Van Rensselaer Papers at Historic Cherry Hill, Albany.
28. Bonney, *Gleanings*, 196.
29. Lovett to Alexander, 20 July 1812, Bonney, *Gleanings*. 196.
30. Lovett to Alexander, 20 July 1812, Bonney, *Gleanings*. 196.
31. Lovett to Alexander, 20 July 1812, Bonney, *Gleanings*, 196. Lovett wrote in this letter regarding the alarm at Utica: "Our General, therefore, thought it his duty to abandon the route to Niagara and visit Sacketts Harbour." On 8 July Governor Tompkins had written that he expected Van Rensselaer to be in Niagara within two weeks, implying that the general would take a direct route Tompkins to Porter, 8 July 1812, *DDT*, 3:19.
32. Lovett to Alexander, 23 July 1812, Bonney, *Gleanings*, 199. Stephen Van Rensselaer to Tompkins, 23 July 1812, *ibid.*, 199. Solomon Van Rensselaer to his wife, 22 July 1812, *ibid.*, 198. The Provincial Marine vessels had delivered 9-pdrs. and other materiel to Prescott where it was believed the Americans were about to attack from Ogdensburg, Fraser to Lethbridge, 28 July 1812, NAC, RG 8, I, 676:215.
33. Lovett to Alexander, 29 July 1812, Bonney, *Gleanings*, 201

**Chapter 5: "A cool calculation of the *pours* and *contres*"**

1. Brock to Irving Brock, 10 January 1811, Tupper, *Life of Brock*, 87. The Americans invaded Upper Canada at Sandwich on 12 July. Brock received notice of it on 20 July and complained to Prevost about Lieutenant Colonel St. George's slowness in reporting in Brock to Prevost, 20 July 1812, NAC, RG 8, I, 676:203.

2. Brock to Prevost, 3 July 1812, NAC, RG 8, I, 676:115.
3. General Order by Shaw, 4 July 1812, *DHC*, 3:97.
4. General Order by Macdonell, 10 July 1812, *DHC*, 3:119. Returns for the militia at Queenston show that company strengths dropped by seven or eight men each between 3 and 7 July, *DHC*, 4:18.
5. District General Order by Brock, 27 June 1812, *DHC*, 3:76. Brock to Prevost, 3 July 1812, *ibid.*, 93. Cummings to Clark, 3 July 1812, *ibid.*, 95. District General Order by Evans, 9 July 1812, "District General Orders of Maj.-Gen. Sir Isaac Brock from June 27th, 1812–Oct. 16th 1812," *Transactions of the Women's Canadian Historical Society*, No. 19 (1920), 9. Captain James Crooks, 1st Lincoln Militia, wrote that through "A number of Gentlemen of credit who formed themselves into what was called the 'Niagara and Queenston Association' ... several thousand pounds were issued in the shape of Bank Notes" to help pay the militia, Crooks to Maclear, 17 March 1853, OA, Miscellaneous Collection, MU 2144, 1853, #14 [hereafter Crooks Account]. This letter, written to Thomas Maclear who wanted to write a book about the battle and petitioned James Crooks for his version, was published as "Recollections of the War of 1812," *Niagara Historical Society*, No. 28, (1916), 31. Commissary General William H. Robinson reported having to fund the militia in Robinson to Prevost, 30 July 1812, NAC, RG 8, I, 1218:345 and Robinson to Herries, 30 July 1812, NAC, MG 13, WO 57, 14:52.
6. Brock to Prevost, 12 July 1812, NAC, RG 8, I, 676:150.
7. Brock to Prevost, 12 July 1812, NAC, RG 8, I, 676:150.
8. Brock to Irving Brock, 10 January 1811, Tupper, *Life of Brock*, 87. The Americans invaded Upper Canada at Sandwich on 12 July. Brock received notice of it on 20 July and complained to Prevost about Lieutenant Colonel St. George's slowness in reporting in Brock to Prevost, 20 July 1812, NAC, RG 8, I, 676:203.
9. Brock to Prevost, 26 July 1812, NAC, RG 8, I, 676:208. Militia General Order by Macdonell, 22 July 1812, *DHC*, 3:138.
10. Brock to Prevost, 26 July 1812, NAC, RG 8, I, 676:208.
11. Brock to Baynes, 29 July 1812, NAC, RG 8, I, 676:329. Brock to Prevost, 28 July 1812, *ibid.*, 386. Middleton and Landon, *The Province of Ontario: A History, 1615-1927*, 164-9.
12. Brock to Prevost, 29 July 1812, NAC, RG 8, I, 676:236. Dunnigan, *The British Army at Mackinac, 1812-1815*. For a discussion of the subsequent importance of the possession of Mackinac, see Malcomson, *Lords of the Lake*, 81-83, 284-5.
13. Roberts explained the reasons for his actions by referring to orders he had received from Brock in Roberts to Baynes, 17 July 1812, NAC, RG 8, I, 676:183. He referred to the receipt of orders sent on 26 and 27 June in Roberts to Brock, 12 July 1812, *ibid.*, 156. Brock's instructions from 4 July are mentioned in Roberts to Brock, 17 July 1812, *ibid.*, 232. Prevost's response was in Prevost to Brock, 12 August 1812, *DHC*, 3:167.
14. Proceedings of a Council at the Government Building at York, 3 August 1812, *DHC*, 3:162. Garrison Order by Heward at York, 29 July 1812, Wood, *SBD*, 1:399. Unit identification and data taken from Prize Pay List for the Surrender of Fort Detroit, *ibid.*, 1:474. District General Orders by Macdonell and Glegg, 11, 12, 14 and 15 August 1812, *ibid.*, 457-62. General Order by Glegg, 16 August 1812, *ibid.*, 468. At Thomas Evans's suggestion, the militia (including some from the 5th Lincoln and 2nd York) who went with Brock to Detroit were issued worn out uniforms from the 41st Foot, as Brock stated, "Your thought of clothing the militia in the 41st cast off clothing proved a most happy one, it having more than doubled our own regular force in the enemy's eye," Brock to Evans, 17 August 1812, *DHC*, 3:186. District General Order by Evans, 1 August 1812, "District General Orders," 15. Service record for Christopher Myers, Sutherland, *His Majesty's Gentlemen*, 276. This description of the Detroit campaign based upon Hitsman, *The Incredible War of 1812*, 65-82; Mahon, *The War of 1812*, 45-51; Hickey, *The War of 1812*, 80-6.
15. Brock to his brothers, 3 September 1812, Tupper, *Life of Brock*, 284. Of the victory, John Strachan wrote, "The brilliant victory obtained by our distinguished General has been of infinite service in confirming the wavering and adding spirit to the loyal," in a letter to Prevost, October 1812, Spragge, *Strachan Letter Book*, 12. In a letter to Brock published in the *Kingston Gazette* on 29 August 1812, "Falkland" (Richard Cartwright) wrote, "Permit me Sir, to offer my most cordial congratulations on the glorious result of your Expedition to the Westward."
16. Brock to his brothers, 3 September 1812, Tupper, *Life of Brock*, 284.
17. Brock to Prevost, 17 August 1812, NAC, MG 11, CO 42, 147:175.
18. Strachan to McGill, November 1812, Spragge, *Strachan Letter Book*, 25. Prevost to Bathurst, 26 August 1812, 26 August 1812, NAC, MG 11, CO 42, 147:159.
19. Frederick to Prevost, 7 October 1812, NAC, RG 8, I, 677:116. W. Brock to S. Brock, 13 October 1812, Tupper, *Life of Brock*, 281.
20. Van Rensselaer to Tompkins, 11 August 1812, Bonney, *Gleanings*, 204.
21. Tompkins to Hall, 8 July 1812, *DDT*, 3:21.
22. Hall to Tompkins, 13 August 1812, *DHC*, 3:173.
23. General Order by Solomon Van Rensselaer, 13 August 1812, SVRP, General Orders, Box 12, F7.
24. Lovett to Alexander, 16 August 1812, SVRMP, Box 18, F4.
25. Lovett to Alexander, 16 August 1812, SVRMP, Box 18, F4.
26. General Orders by Solomon Van Rensselaer, 16 and 17 August 1812, SVRP, General Orders, Box 12, F7.

Mullany's transfer, 26 August 1812, is shown in his career record, Heitman, *Historical Register of the U.S. Army*, 1:735.

27. General Orders by Solomon Van Rensselaer, 15 and 16 August 1812, SVRP, General Orders, Box 12, F7. Stephen Van Rensselaer to Tompkins, 19 August 1812, *DHC*, 3:191. Governor Tompkins ordered the Nineteenth Regiment of Detached Militia to Niagara on 13 August 1812, *DHC*, 3:177. Moseley had tendered his services to Tompkins who explained the advantages of the Volunteer Act of 6 February, Tompkins to Moseley, 27 April 1812, *DDT*, 2:563. Moseley's "battalion" existed within Lieutenant Colonel George Flemming's Militia Regiment, part of Brigadier General Jacob Brown's brigade of detached militia in Van Rensselaer's division. The two companies of rifles were commanded by Captains Charles B. Bristol and Leonard Kellogg. Their strengths were nominally forty-eight men each, though they did not appear to muster this many men consistently. Moseley's company had begun as a single "uniform" company in 1809 with Charles Moseley as the captain, Leonard Kellogg as the lieutenant and Charles Bristol as the ensign, General Order by Paulding, 19 September 1809, *DDT*, 1:229. The arrival of Captain Herman Camp's troop on 1 September is mentioned in Van Rensselaer to Tompkins, 1 September 1812, *DHC*, 3:228. The troop's volunteer status was mentioned in General Orders by Solomon Van Rensselaer, 15 September 1812, SVRP, General Orders, Box 12, F7 and in Tompkins to Camp, 2 July 1812, *DDT*, 1:659. See Appendices D and E for unit data.
28. General Orders by Solomon Van Rensselaer, 19 August 1812, SVRP, General Orders, Box 12, F7.
29. General Orders by Solomon Van Rensselaer, 19 August 1812, SVRP, General Orders, Box 12, F7.
30. Lovett to Alexander, 16 August 1812, SVRMP, Box 18, F4. General Orders by Solomon Van Rensselaer, 22 August 1812, SVRP, General Orders, Box 12, F7.
31. The sniping between the opposing sentries went on all through the campaign as mentioned in Lovett to Alexander, 16 August 1812, SVRMP, Box 18, F4 and District General Order by Evans, 12 July and 18 September 1812, "District General Orders of Maj.-Gen. Sir Isaac Brock," 11 and 37.
32. Comments of an old soldier, Bonney, *Gleanings*, 216. Lovett to Alexander, 16 August 1812, SVRMP, Box 18, F4. Lovett to Van Vechten, 28 August 1812, SVRMP, Box 18, F4.
33. Lovett to Alexander, 19 or 20 August 1812, Bonney, *Gleanings*, 209.
34. Solomon to Arriet, 21 August 1812, SVRP, Correspondence, Box 9, F3.
35. Prevost to Brock, 31 July and 2 August 1812, NAC, RG 8, I, 1218:349, 368. Baynes to Brock, 1 August 1812, *ibid.*, 157. Sheaffe to Prevost, 22 August 1812, NAC, RG 8, I, 677:55. Brock to Van Rensselaer, 25 August 1812, NAC, RG 8, I, 688A:238.
36. Bonney, *Gleanings*, 210-1. General Order, 18 August 1812, SVRP, General Orders, Box 12, F7. Dearborn to Prevost, 8 August 1812, NAC, RG 8, I, 677:14. Dearborn to Baynes, 8 August 1812, *ibid.*, 16. Baynes to Prevost, 12 August 1812, *ibid.*, 22. Terms of Agreement for the Armistice by Van Rensselaer and Sheaffe, 21 August 1812, *ibid.*, 51. Sheaffe wrote that there had been several issues to resolve during these meetings in Sheaffe to Prevost, 22 August 1812, *ibid.*, 55. Evans's Report on a Conference with Solomon Van Rensselaer, 19 August 1812, *ibid.*, 688a:212. Sheaffe's arrival was announced in District General Order by Evans, 19 August 1812, "District General Orders," 20.
37. Brock to his brothers, 3 September 1812, Tupper, *Life of Brock*, 284. Prevost wrote to Bathurst on 24 August 1812 (NAC, CO 42, MG 11, 147:147), "A suspension of hostilities therefore on a considerable portion of the extremely extensive line of Frontier which I have to defend has enabled me rapidly to strengthen the Flank [Detroit] attacked." As revealed elsewhere in his correspondence, this is an overstatement of what Prevost had actually been able to accomplish, though it does indicate a motive for the truce.
38. Brock to his brothers, 3 September 1812, Tupper, *Life of Brock*, 284.
39. Solomon to Arriet, 21 August 1812, SVRP, Correspondence, Box 9, F3.
40. Lovett to Alexander, 6 September 1812, SVRMP, Box 18, F5.
41. Gray to Tompkins, 19 August 1812, *DHC* , 3:193. The plan is also mentioned in Swift to Tompkins, 23 August 1812, *ibid.*, 202. Among the SVRP, General Orders, Box 12, F7, are two detailed plans: the first, describing a crossing "tomorrow" at Black Rock, Lewiston and Five Mile Meadow with diversions at Grand Island and Fort Niagara; the second, a general order describing the orders of march, encampment and battle. Both documents are undated and unsigned. The plan for crossing bears no similarity to the plan of attack that eventually took place in October nor to other aborted attempts.
42. Comments of an "old soldier" in Bonney, *Gleanings*, 216. Lovett described the state of Hull's army to Van Vechten, 28 August 1812, SVRMP, Box 18, F4.
43. Stephen Van Rensselaer to Dearborn, 26 August 1812, *DHC*, 3:216. Lovett to probably Alexander, probably 20 August 1812, Bonney, *Gleanings*, 209

**Chapter 6: "Redouble our exertions"**

1. Madison to Dearborn, 9 August 1812, Hunt, *Writings of James Madison*, 8:205. Eustis to Dearborn, 26 June 1812, USNA, RG 107, Letters Sent by the Secretary of War, 1800-1889, 5:458. Eustis to Dearborn, 9 and 15 July 1812, *ibid.*, 6:15 and 26.
2. Dearborn to Eustis, 28 July 1812, USNA, RG 107, Letters Received by the Secretary of War, Registered Series, Sept. 1811–Dec. 1812, (C, D). Eustis to Dearborn, 9 and 10 April 1812, USNA, RG 107, Let-

ters Sent by the Secretary of War, 5:335 and 363. Eustis's instructions for Dearborn to expedite the military movements in New York are seen in Eustis to Dearborn, 4 and 26 June 1812, USNA, RG 107, 5:424 and 458 and 9 and 15 July 1812, USNA, RG 107, 6:15 and 26.

3. Eustis to Dearborn, 1 August 1812, USNA, RG 107, Letters Sent by the Secretary of War, 1800-1889, 6:199. Dearborn wrote to Van Rensselaer to tell him to be ready to make diversionary motions even if he lacked the manpower for a full attack and then to be prepared to work in cooperation with Hull, Dearborn to Van Rensselaer, 3 August 1812, *DHC*, 3:161.
4. Eustis to Dearborn, 15 August 1812, USNA, RG 107, Letters Sent by the Secretary of War, 1800-1889, 6:200. Eustis wrote to Hull that "Orders have been given to General Dearborn to attack the enemies forts at Niagara and Kingston, as soon as may be practicable," Eustis to Hull, 20 August 1812, USNA, RG 107, Letters Received by the Secretary of War, Unregistered Series, 1789-1861, 1812 (A-K). News of Dearborn having command over the militia on the frontier was in Tompkins to Van Rensselaer, 14 August 1812, *DDT*, 3:78.
5. Dearborn to Eustis, 8 August 1812, USNA, RG 107, Letters Received by the Secretary of War, Registered Series, Sept. 1811–Dec. 1812, (C, D). Further evidence of Dearborn's poor understanding of the summer campaign is seen in this correspondence: "If I had early considered my command as extending into Upper Canada and had been directed to prepare an offensive operation in that quarter a force could have been assembled sufficient to have commenced operations as soon as Gen. Hull was ready at Detroit," Dearborn to Eustis, 15 August 1812, *ibid.*; "The moment I received your directions to make a diversion in favor of Gen. Hull, I adopted the measure," Dearborn to Eustis, 29 August 1812, *ibid.*; "My information in relation to Gen. Hull's operations and the extension of my command to Niagara was too late to give due effect to my measures," Dearborn to Eustis, 22 August 1812, USNA, RG 107, Letters received by the Secretary of War, Main Series, Sept. 1811–Dec. 1812, (C, D).
6. Dearborn to Stephen Van Rensselaer, 29 July 1812, *DHC*, 3:156.
7. Dearborn to Eustis, 2 September 1812, USNA, M221, Letters Received by the Secretary of War, Registered Series, Sept. 1811–Dec. 1812, (C, D). Dearborn notified Prevost of the termination of the armistice on 26 August 1812, NAC, RG 8, I, 677:58.
8. McDonogh to his parents, 13 September 1812, Reilly, "A Hero of Fort Erie," 71.
9. Dearborn to Eustis, 31 July 1812, USNA, RG 107, Letters Received by the Secretary of War, Registered Series, Sept. 1811–Dec. 1812, (C, D). Dearborn to Eustis, 8 and 29 August, 2, 14 September 1812, *ibid.*
10. General Order by Snyder, 25 August 1812, *DHC*, 3:206. Boileau to Irvine, 25 August 1812, *ibid.*, 207. Return of detached volunteer corps, 25 August 1812, *ibid.*, 208. Snyder to Dearborn, 26 August 1812, *ibid.*, 210. Eustis had written to Snyder on 13 August as mentioned in Snyder to Eustis, 26 August 1812, *ibid.*, 211. Re: New York regiments, General Order by Macomb, 27 August 1812, *ibid.*, 217. Re: "Independent Corps," Tompkins to Maher, 11 September 1812, *DDT*, 3:118.
11. Dearborn to Eustis, 2 September 1812, USNA, RG 107, Letters Received by the Secretary of War, Registered Series, Sept. 1811–Dec. 1812, (C, D). Tompkins to Dearborn, 14 August 1812, *DDT*, 3:83.
12. Tompkins to Porter, 9 September 1812, *DDT*, 3:195.
13. In this instance, Dearborn had neglected to tell militia Major General Benjamin Mooers that he would be superseded at Plattsburgh by regular army Brigadier General Bloomfield. Tompkins sent the necessary despatches: Tompkins to Bloomfield, 14 September 1812, *DDT*, 3:126; Tompkins to Mooers, 14 September 1812, *ibid.* Tompkins also had to put pressure on Morgan Lewis, the quartermaster general, for the U.S. Army to supply activated militia: Tompkins to Lewis, 18 and 26 August 1812, *ibid.*, 87, 93; Tompkins to Stranahan and Mead, 7 September 1812, *ibid.*, 3:94.
14. Dearborn to Eustis, 14 September1812, USNA, RG 107, Letters Received by the Secretary of War, Registered Series, Sept. 1811–Dec. 1812, (C, D).
15. Brock mentioned, "The prodigious quantity of Pork and Flower which have been observed landing on the opposite shore, from a number of Vessels and large boats," Brock to Prevost, 7 September 1812, NAC, RG 8, I, 677:64. Fenwick's career, Heitman, *Historical Register of the U.S. Army*, 1:417. Re: Fenwick's preparations and movements: Eustis to Fenwick, 7 May and 19 June 1812, USNA, RG 107, Letters Sent by the Secretary of War, 5:376, 450; Eustis to Dearborn, 16 May and 1 July 1812, *ibid.*, 391; 6:4. Careers of James Gibson, Benjamin Branch, John Machesney, George Nelson, Heitman, 1:454; 240; 668; 743. See Babcock, *A War History of the Sixth U.S. Infantry from 1798 to 1903, ..., passim.* Gibson to Adjutant General, 19 June 1812, USNA, RG94, Letters Received by the Office of the Adjutant General, 1805-1821, 6:1199. Machesney to Adjutant General, 25 March 1812, *ibid.*, 1612. Lieutenant James Branch was made a captain in the Light Artillery on 24 August 1812, though he was referred to as Lieutenant Branch through October in Van Rensselaer to Tompkins, 1 September 1812, *DHC*, 3:228. Solomon Van Rensselaer to Van Vechten, 5 September 1812, SVRP, Correspondence, Box 10, F8. See Appendices C, E and F for unit and individual data. Johnson's Landing at Four Mile Creek is named in Chrystie to Gallatin, 11 March 1813, Albert Gallatin Papers, Roll 26, 84.
16. Fenwick to Stephen Van Rensselaer, 8 and 10 September 1812, Van Rensselaer, *The Affair of Queenstown*, 46, 47. Solomon Van Rensselaer to Fenwick, 2 and 3 September 1812, *ibid.*, 39, 40.

Fenwick to Stephen Van Rensselaer, 3 September 1812, *ibid.*, 40. Re: the Salt Battery, see Fenwick to Solomon Van Rensselaer, 15 September 1812, SVRP, Box 18, F1.

17. Solomon Van Rensselaer to Lewis, 11 September 1812, Bonney, *Gleanings*, 231. Stephen Van Rensselaer to Dearborn, 5 September 1812, *DHC*, 3:238. See Appendices D and E for unit data.
18. Stephen Van Rensselaer to Dearborn, 1, 5 and 17 September 1812, *DHC*, 3:228, 238 and 270.
19. Brock to Prevost, 7 September 1812, NAC, RG 8, I, 677:64.
20. General Monthly Returns ... of the several Corps Serving in Canada, 25 July, 25 August and 25 September 1812, NAC, MG 13, WO 17, 1516:81, 94 and 106. Distribution of Forces in Canada, 12 November 1812, NAC, RG 8, I, 1707:60. Service records for James Dennis and John Williams, Sutherland, *His Majesty's Gentlemen*, 122, 379. Report on the Battle of Copenhagen, Tupper, *Life of Brock*, 21. See Appendices G and I for unit data. The arrival of the 49th is based on the observation of five British vessels anchoring off Fort George on 2 September, Stephen Van Rensselaer to Tompkins, 2 September 1812, Van Rensselaer, *The Affair of Queenstown*, 39.
21. Cited in *DCB*, 8:792. Other biographical sources for Sheaffe include: Turner, *British Generals in the War of 1812*, 84-100; Whitfield, "The Battle of Queenston Heights;" *DNB*, 17:1393; obituary, *The Gentleman's Magazine*, 36 (1851), 318.
22. Upon his promotion to major general, according to *DCB*, 8:793, Sheaffe lost a large portion of his annual salary by giving up the colonelcy of the 49th Foot.. Nevertheless, after Brock's death, Sheaffe purchased more than £600-worth of items in Brock's estate, far exceeding the purchases of any other officer, "Inventory of furniture, etc. belonging to the estate of Major General Isaac Brock ...," OH, MU 2143, Miscellaneous Collection, 1812, No. 1. Malcomson, *Burying General Brock*, 6.
23. Brock to Green, 8 February 1804, NAC, RG 8, I, 923:12. Details of the mutiny-plot are contained in: Sheaffe to Green, 13 August 1803, *ibid.*, 922:86; testimony of a private in the 49th Foot, *ibid.*, 80; Return of Deserters, 7 August 1803, *ibid.*, 85. An indication that Sheaffe was aware of his unpopularity may be found in a letter he wrote following his defeat at York in April 1813 when he explained the many complaints made about him as "a popular outcry that has been raised against me – it is quite in the natural order of things," Sheaffe to Bishop Mountain, n.d., probably May 1813, Millman, "Roger Hale Sheaffe and the Defence of York, April 27, 1813."
24. Militia General Order by Macdonell, 26 August 1812, *DHC*, 3:212. Brock to his brothers, 3 September 1812, Tupper, *Life of Brock*, 284. Regimental Orders by Chewett, 5 September 1812, *DHC*, 3:240.
25. Brock to Prevost, 18 September and 9 October1812, NAC, RG 8, I, 677:90, 123.
26. Procter to Brock, 16 and 30 September 1812, NAC, RG 8, I, 677:83, 100. Brock to Prevost, 18 September and 9 October 1812, *ibid.*, 90, 123.
27. Brock to Prevost, 7 September 1812, NAC, RG 8, I, 677:64. Willcocks to Macdonell, 1 September 1812, NAC, RG 8, I, 688b:30. Klinck and Talman, *Norton Journal*, 302-4.
28. Brock to Prevost, 13 September 1812, NAC, RG 8, I, 677:81.
29. The 11 January 1812 legislation to raise an additional force for the U.S. Army required each of ten new regiments of infantry to have 72 commissioned officers, 144 non commissioned officers, thirty-six musicians and 1800 privates, organized into two battalions of nine companies each, Twelfth Congress, Session 1, Chapter 14. A subsequent act on 26 June 1812 changed this to twenty-five infantry units of a more conventional strength, *ibid.*, 108.
30. The American manual was *Regulations for the Field Exercise, Manoeuvres and Conduct of the Infantry* written by Colonel Alexander Smyth of the Rifle Regiment which was based upon the French *Réglement* of the 1790s. Among various British manuals the most commonly used was *Rules and Regulations for the Formation, Field-Exercise and Movements of His Majesty's Forces* of 1798. Graves states that the militia used the Blue Book, "'Dry Books of Tactics,'" 54, although late in August Tompkins informed one of his militia colonels that Smyth's system had been adopted for both the regular and militia forces, Tompkins to Dodge, 26 August 1812, *DDT*, 3:91. A statement by Smyth as the Inspector General and dated 11 July 1812, states the regulations were to be "adhered to by the infantry of the United States without deviation" which suggests that the printed copies did not reach the hands of commanding offices until the summer campaign was underway, *Regulations*, v. Graves (*Where Right and Glory Lead!*, 38-9), explains that through1813 American officers used a variety of manuals after Smyth's removal from the army led to Duane's *Handbook for the Infantry* being temporarily endorsed. For a description of the relevant manuals, see: Haythornthwaite, *The Napoleonic Source Book*, 92-102 Muir, *Tactics and the Experience of Battle*, 51-104; Holding, *Fit For Service*, 257-377, Holmes, *Redcoat*, 3-12. See also Armstrong, *Hints to Young Generals by an Old Soldier*, for a more informal guide to command.
31. This description of muskets, rifles and equipment is based upon the following: Haythornthwaite, *The Napoleonic Source Book*, 71-81; Haythornthwaite, *Weapons and Equipment of the Napoleonic Wars*, 13-27; Chartrand, *Uniforms and Equipment of the United States Forces*, 83-94, 103-110; Darling, *Red Coat and Brown Bess*, 27-54; Graves, *Where Right and Glory Lead!* 29; Glover, *Warfare in the Age of Bonaparte*, 11-16; Holmes, *Redcoat*, 194-209.
32. Colonel George Hanger, *To All Sportsmen* (1814), cited in Haythornthwaite, *Napoleonic Source Book*, 73.

33. Sniping between opposing sentries along the Niagara River continued all summer. On one occasion a ball carried across the 300 yards of water at Queenston with fatal effect. John Lovett wrote, "one of our lads returned the Compliment; and put a ball so quick thro' a lad's head on the other side that he fell dead without even winking," Lovett to Alexander, 22 September 1812, SVRMP, Box 18, F5.
34. Tompkins explained that the state was liable for 2000 muskets "of French manufactory" that were borrowed from the federal government for use by the army on the Niagara and apparently lost at the battle of Queenston Heights, Tompkins to Miller, 2 January 1813, *DDT*, 3:219. The state had ordered thousands of muskets from Eli Whitney, with requests to make a number of changes in their specifications, such as increasing the strength of their parts, A correct statement of all and singular Warlike Stores and Property ..., by McLean, 20 February 1809, *ibid.*, 197. There may have been some British Land Pattern muskets among Van Rensselaer's army as the U.S. Government had purchased some and kept them in store in Philadelphia and New York, Chartrand, *Uniforms and Equipment*, 84-5.
35. T. Ridout to his father, 3 July 1811, OA, Ridout Family Papers, 1764-1824.
36. Fenwick to Stephen Van Rensselaer, 8 and 10 September 1812, Van Rensselaer, *The Affair of Queenstown*, 46, 47.
37. *A Manual for Volunteer Corps of Infantry* (1803), cited in Haythornthwaite, *Napoleonic Source Book*, 98.
38. This description of artillery is based upon the following: Haythornthwaite, *The Napoleonic Source Book*, 81-92, 106-9; Haythornthwaite, *Weapons and Equipment of the Napoleonic Wars*, 55-98; McConnell, *British Smooth-bore Artillery*; Muir, *Tactics and The Experience of Battle*, 29-50; Gooding, *An Introduction to British Artillery* ; Graves, "American Ordnance in the War of 1812;" Holmes, *Redcoat*, 243-8; Glover, *Warfare in the Age of Bonaparte*, 16-9.
39. This account given by Solomon Van Rensselaer is related in Bonney, *Historic Gleanings*, 252. Solomon insisted that he saw the guns on 12 October, but other narratives show this was not possible and that he must have seen the guns on a previous visit. Only one 8-inch howitzer was captured at Detroit, whereas two 5.5-inch brass howitzers were seized at Mackinac. Captain Roberts remarked that the howitzers bore an inscription stating their original seizure from the British at Yorktown in 1781. Roberts to Glegg, 29 July 1812, NAC, RG 8, I, 688A:154. Return of ordnance: 160. Return of ordnance taken at Detroit, August 16 1812, *ibid.*, 179.

**Chapter 7: "We have but one object."**

1. Lovett to Alexander, 6 September 1812, SVRMP, Box 18, F5. Stephen Van Rensselaer to Governor Tompkins, 31 August 1812, Bonney, *Gleanings*, 223. Solomon Van Rensselaer to Van Vechten, 5 September 1812, SVRP, Correspondence, Box 10, F8.
2. One series of courts martial, starting on 19 September 1812, is found in SVRP, Box 12, F8. Two other series, beginning on 31 August and 9 and 12 September 1812, are reported as General Orders by Solomon Van Rensselaer, *ibid.*, F7.
3. Sentence of Reuben Schuyler, Reuben Robbins and Thomas Moore, General Order by Stephen Van Rensselaer, 9 September 1812. The general's commutation of the sentence was encouraged by a petition of several regular officers, enclosed with General Order by Solomon Van Rensselaer, 17 September 1812, 19 September 1812, SVRP, Box 12, F7.
4. Solomon Van Rensselaer to Bloom, 17 September 1812, SVRP, Box 12, F8.
5. Solomon Van Rensselaer to Lewis, 11 September 1812, SVRP, Correspondence, Box 10, F8. He also claimed, "Peter B. Porter has been only twice in Camp since we have been here, and instead of getting the feast ready, is attending to his own private affairs; he is an abominable scoundrel and I have made no Secret in telling his friends so," Solomon Van Rensselaer to Van Vechten, 5 September 1812, *ibid.* See also Bonney, *Gleanings*, 287-92.
6. Solomon Van Rensselaer to Porter, 14 September 1812, in the *United States Gazette*, 30 January 1813, *DHC*, 3:262. This publication was delayed "for prudential reasons," according to John Lovett who was to have acted as Solomon's second in the proposed duel, Lovett to Alexander, 8 October 1812, SVRMP, Box 18, F5. Porter's brother wrote to him after seeing the letter in the *Albany Gazette* and urged him not to oblige Van Rensselaer with a duel, but to "abuse him back in the papers, and if you come across him personally kick and cuff him," A. Porter to P. Porter, 3 February 1813, *DHC*, 5:55.
7. Solomon to Arriet, 17 September 1812, SVRP, Correspondence, Box 9, F3; Matilda was eight years old, Margaretta was two. Van Vechten to Solomon, 10 September 1812, *ibid.*, Box 11, F2.
8. Lovett to Alexander, 6 October 1812, SVRMP, Box 18, F5.
9. Solomon to Arriet, 27 September 1812, SVRP, Correspondence, Box 9, F3.
10. Dearborn to Stephen Van Rensselaer, 17 September 1812, *DHC*, 3:276. On 17 September Dearborn revealed his concern that the army at Niagara might be attacked by the British at any time and gave Van Rensselaer advice on how to conduct a cautious retreat. The general had already considered this possibility and rejected it, writing to Daniel Tompkins, also on that Thursday, "A retrograde movement of this army ... would stamp a stigma upon the national character which time could not wipe away," Stephen Van Rensselaer to Tompkins, 17 September 1812, *DHC*, 3:275.
11. Dearborn to Eustis, 14 September1812, USNA, RG 107, Letters Received by the Secretary of War, Registered Series, Sept. 1811–Dec. 1812, (C, D).
12. Dearborn to Van Rensselaer, 29 September 1812,

USNA, RG 107, Letters Received by the Secretary of War, Registered Series, Sept. 1811–Dec. 1812, (C, D). Dearborn to Van Rensselaer, 21 August 1812, *DHC*, 3:198.

13. Dearborn to Stephen Van Rensselaer, 26 September 1812, *DHC*, 3:295. He repeated his scheme to Eustis, 26 September 1812, USNA, RG 107, Letters Received by the Secretary of War, Registered Series, Sept. 1811–Dec. 1812, (C, D). Dearborn complained about the length of time lost in carriage of the mail, despite his efforts to establish a series of express riders who would travel between Albany and Niagara in three days, Dearborn to Van Rensselaer, 29 September 1812, *ibid.* Van Rensselaer reported the same slow delivery of mail, Stephen Van Rensselaer to Dearborn, 27 September 1812, *DHC*, 3:297.
14. Dearborn to Van Rensselaer, 4 October 1812, USNA, RG 107, Letters Received by the Secretary of War, Registered Series, Sept. 1811–Dec. 1812, (C, D).
15. Smyth to Stephen Van Rensselaer, 2 October 1812, Van Rensselaer, *The Affair of Queenstown*, 69. Smyth announced his arrival in Smyth to Stephen Van Rensselaer, 29 September 1812, *ibid.*, 67.
16. This comment was made by William Duane whose own long-developed system of tactics was rejected in favour of Smyth's, Fredriksen, "Green Coats and Glory," 3. Smyth biography, *DAB*, 9:373. Of his abilities as an officer, John R. Elting wrote: "If Smyth showed any occasional competence in any of these military assignments, it remains to be discovered," Elting, *Amateurs to Arms*, 40. See Appendix E for unit data.
17. Smyth to Stephen Van Rensselaer, 29 September 1812, Van Rensselaer, *The Affair of Queenstown*, 67. Smyth's concept was not as outlandish as it may have seemed to Van Rensselaer, as it was exactly the kind of attack Isaac Brock was then expecting, Instructions Sent to Officers commanding Forts by Brock, probably late September 1812, "District General Orders of Maj.-Gen. Sir Isaac Brock," 34-41, 46. A plan for simultaneous crossings at various points, including the upper river, had been considered in August as seen in Swift to Tompkins, 23 August 1812, *ibid.*, 202. Among the SVRP, General Orders, Box 12, F7, are two detailed plans: the first, describing a crossing "tomorrow" at Black Rock, Lewiston and Five Mile Meadow with diversions at Grand Island and Fort Niagara; the second, a general order describing the orders of march, encampment and battle. Both documents are undated and unsigned.
18. Stephen Van Rensselaer to Smyth, 30 September 1812, Van Rensselaer, *The Affair of Queenstown*, 68.
19. Lovett to Alexander, 22 October 1812, SVRMP, Box 18, F5. Van Rensselaer to Dearborn, 17 September 1812, *DHC*, 3:270.
20. Lovett to Alexander, 6 October 1812, SVRMP, Box 18, F5.
21. Brock to Prevost, 13 September 1812, NAC, RG 8, I, 677:81.
22. Prevost to Brock, 14 September 1812, *DHC*, 3:260.
23. Brock to Prevost, 18 September 1812, NAC, RG 8, I, 677:90. Prevost to Brock, 25 September 1812, *DHC*, 3:295. Brock to Prevost, 28 September 1812, NAC, RG 8, I, 677:94.
24. Brock to Savery Brock, 18 September, Tupper, *Life of Brock*, 315.
25. Brock to Savery Brock, 18 September, Tupper, *Life of Brock*, 315.
26. Sheaffe to Procter, 24 September 1812, USNA, RG 59, M588, 7:115.
27. Sutherland, *Merritt Journal*, 2.
28. Various General Orders, 11 September to 2 October 1812; Instructions Sent to Officers commanding Forts by Brock, probably late September 1812, "District General Orders of Maj.-Gen. Sir Isaac Brock," 34-41, 46.
29. Stephen Van Rensselaer to Dearborn, 8 October 1812, *DHC*, 4:40.
30. Elliott to Hamilton, 9 October 1812, USNA, RG 45, Letters from Officers of Rank Below that of Commanders Received by the Secretary of the Navy, 1812, 3:95.
31. Lieutenant Jacob Miller of the Pennsylvania Militia recorded Scott's arrival at Buffalo in his diary (Pennsylvania State Archives, MG 6): " 7 October ... about 12 oclock arrived here a detachment of Artillery from Philadelphia commanded by Colonel Scott – about 100 in number with 4 field pieces mounted, 4 Ammunition Wagons and 4 Baggage Wagons – in uniform with Muskets, marched immediately to black rock or 1 mile below it."
32. Scott biography, *DAB*, 8:505. Careers of Winfield Scott, Nathan Towson and James Barker, Isaac Roach and Patrick McDonogh, Heitman, 1:870, 968, 190, 834, 663. Barker to Adjutant General, 1 June 1812, USNA, RG94, Letters Received by the Office of the Adjutant General, 1805-1821, 6:705. McDonogh to Adjutant General, 17 March 1812, *ibid.*, 1579. See also: Scott, *Memoirs of General Scott, Written by Himself*; O'Reilly, "A Hero of Fort Erie: Letters relating to the Military Service, Chiefly on the Niagara Frontier, of Lieutenant Patrick McDonogh;" and Roach, "Journal of Major Isaac Roach, 1812-1824." See Appendix C for unit data.
33. "Journal of Major Isaac Roach, 1812-1824,"133.
34. "Journal of Major Isaac Roach, 1812-1824,"136. This incident provoked a minor controversy when Lieutenant Elliott's report failed to mention the large part the Second Artillery played in the expedition and years later Nathan Towson explained his views on the matter, Towson to Elliott, 6 July 1843, *DHC*, 4:50. See also: Inquiry Respecting the loss of the *Detroit*, 27 October 1812, *ibid.*, 54.
35. Brock to Prevost, 11 October 1812, NAC, RG 8, I, 677:127.
36. General Order by Stephen Van Rensselaer, 18 September 1812, SVRP, General Orders, Box 12, F7. See Appendices D, E and I for unit data. Service record

of Joseph G. Totten, *Heitman*, 1:966. Totten to Stephen Van Rensselaer, 5 October 1812, *The Affair of Queenstown*, 60. See also, Boylen, "Strategy of Brock Saved Canada: Candid Comments of a U.S. Officer Who Crossed at Queenston" for a brief observation by Totten.

37. Hall to Stephen Van Rensselaer, 10 October 1812, Bonney, *Gleamings*, 246. The plan for the 6 October raid is mentioned in Van Rensselaer to Dearborn, 14 October 1812, *The Affair of Queenstown*, 62 and Lovett to Alexander, 8 October 1812, SVRMP, Box 18, F5.
38. Stephen Van Rensselaer to Eustis, 14 October 1812, *The Affair of Queenstown*, 62. In the text, this document is shown to be addressed to Dearborn and Eustis. It is presumed that the former received a copy of the original sent to the secretary of war. Bonney, *Gleanings*, 256, shows Eustis as the recipient, as *DHC*, 4:79 does.
39. Stephen Van Rensselaer to Eustis, 14 October 1812, *The Affair of Queenstown*, 62.
40. Dearborn to Van Rensselaer, 13 October 1812, USNA, RG 107, Letters Received by the Secretary of War, Registered Series, Sept. 1811–Dec. 1812, (C, D).
41. Dearborn to Stephen Van Rensselaer, 26 September 1812, *DHC*, 3:295. He repeated his scheme to Eustis, 26 September 1812, USNA, RG 107, Letters Received by the Secretary of War, Registered Series, Sept. 1811–Dec. 1812, (C, D). Dearborn complained about the length of time lost in carriage of the mail, having tried to establish a series of express riders who would travel between Albany and Niagara in three days, Dearborn to Van Rensselaer, 29 September 1812, *ibid.* Van Rensselaer reported the same slow delivery of mail, Stephen Van Rensselaer to Dearborn, 27 September 1812, *DHC*, 3:297.
42. Stephen Van Rensselaer to Smyth, 10 October 1812, *The Affair of Queenstown*, 71.
43. Stephen Van Rensselaer to Eustis, 14 October 1812, *The Affair of Queenstown*, 62. Bonney, *Gleanings*, 249.
44. Mullany to Stephen Van Rensselaer, 10 October 1812, Bonney, *Gleanings*, 250. Stephen Van Rensselaer to Mullany, 10 October 1812, *ibid.*
45. Journal of James Mullany.
46. Fenwick to Stephen Van Rennselaer, 10 October 1812, *ibid.*, 61. Stephen Van Rensselaer to Fenwick, 10 October 1812, *ibid.*, 62.
47. Journal of James Mullany.
48. The story of mishandled batteaux is mentioned in *The Affair of Queenstown*, 21-22; Stephen Van Rensselaer to Eustis, 14 October 1812, ibid., 62; Bonney, *Gleanings*, 249; Journal of James Mullany; and Chrystie to Gallatin, 11 March 1813, Albert Gallatin Papers. Simms's Christian name is not mentioned in these sources, but a Lieutenant John Simms appears on Captain Rufus Spalding's muster (part of Silas Hopkins's One Hundred Sixty-Third Militia Regiment) at Lewiston between September and December 1812, New York State Archives, Militia Records, Box 5, F15, Roll 915. Hopkins's regiment was centred in the village of Cambria in Niagara County and it is speculated here that John Simms would have been familiar with the river. How he managed to conduct his batteau and all the others up the river while his contained the majority of the necessary oars for the thirteen boats is difficult to imagine.
49. "Journal of Major Isaac Roach, 1812-1824,"137. Stephen Van Rensselaer to Smyth, 11 October 1812, *ibid.*, 72. Smyth's march and counter march are mentioned in Chrystie to Gallatin, 11 March 1813, Albert Gallatin Papers; Mcdonogh to his sister, 16 October 1812, O'Reilly, "A Hero of Fort Erie," 75.
50. Smyth to Stephen Van Rensselaer, 12 October 1812, *The Affair of Queenstown*, 72.
51. Smyth to Stephen Van Rensselaer, 12 October 1812, *The Affair of Queenstown*, 72

**Part 3 Title Page**

1. G. R. to his father, 14 October 1812, newspaper account, NAC, MG 13, WO 44:245.

**Chapter 8: "One incessant blaze from Musketry"**

1. Brock to Prevost, 11 October 1812, NAC, RG 8, I, 677:127. Concerned that he needed more militia, Brock summoned the flank companies of Norfolk, Oxford and Middlesex to Niagara, Macdonell to Talbot, 12 October 1812, *DHC*, 4:67. They did not arrive in time to participate in the fighting at Queenston.
2. Extract from the Diary of General T. Evans while serving as an officer on the staff of General Brock at Queenston, War of 1812 – 1814, Government House, Fort George, 15 October 1812, NAC, MG 24, Hellmuth Papers, [hereafter Evans Diary].
3. Evans Diary.
4. Evans Diary. Brock formally requested an exchange in Brock to Stephen Van Rensselaer, 11 October 1812, Bonney, *Gleanings*, 250. There were no militia men from Kentucky, Ohio or Tennessee present. Evans must have seen the riflemen from one of the New York militia companies, such as that of Major Charles Moseley. Evans later helped compile the list of American captives and knew which units were present and why he did not correct this error in his account is hard to explain.
5. Evans Diary.
6. Merritt mentions this gathering: "On the night before, my father, Major Merritt and a number of Officers were with him [Brock]. He expected an Attack, giving orders for a strict look out," Sutherland, *Merritt Journal*, 3.
7. Stephen Van Rensselaer to Eustis, 14 October 1812, *The Affair of Queenstown*, 62. The general apparently decided to make the attack before he received Smyth's note of 12 October 1812 (*ibid.*, 72) as revealed in Stephen Van Rensselaer to Smyth, 12 October 1812, *ibid.*, 73.
8. Dearborn to Van Rensselaer, 4 October 1812, USNA, RG 107, Letters Received by the Secretary of War,

Registered Series, Sept. 1811–Dec. 1812, (C, D). Dearborn to Van Rensselaer, 13 October 1812, *ibid.*

9. *The Affair of Queenstown*, 34.

10. Journal of James Mullany. Chrystie to Gallatin, 11 March 1813, Albert Gallatin Papers, Roll 26, 84.

11. Chrystie to Cushing, 22 February 1813, Armstrong, *Notices of the War*, 1:207. Chrystie received his commission on 12 March 1812, whereas Solomon's commission appears to have dated from 13 July 1812, the day he formally joined his general's suite. Fenwick was the most senior of the regular lieutenant colonels present (commissioned 2 December 1811). Scott mentions Fenwick's agreement to waive his rank in *Memoirs*, 1:57.

12. Alexander, *History of the Thirteenth Regiment United States Infantry*. Careers of Henry B. Armstrong, John Chrystie, William D. Lawrence, Richard Malcom, Peter Ogilvie, Peter P. Schulyer and John E. Wool, Heitman, 1:170; 300; 619; 685; 757; 867; 1059. Letters of acknowledgment from the officers may be found in volumes of the USNA, RG 94, Letters received by the Office of the Adjutant General, 1805-1821: Richard M. Malcom, 1 May 1812 ; William D. Lawrence, 19 March 1812. Information regarding the collection of the regiment at Greenbush and its deployment are mentioned in Ensign Joseph Dwight's "Journal of an Ensign in the War of 1812" and Captain Mordecai Myers, *Reminiscences 1780 to 1814*. Dwight was an ensign in Malcom's company, but fell ill and ended up marching with Schuyler to Black Rock early in October. Captain Myers also made that march and did not have his own company until after the battle. Alexander's regimental history states that the regiments was a Sackets Harbor at this time, but the primary sources refute this. See Appendix C for unit data.

13. Wilkinson to Gallatin, 27 January 1812, Albert Gallatin Papers. Gallatin to Madison, (month not noted) 1812, Adams, *The Writings of Albert Gallatin*, 1:500. In the latter, Gallatin implies that Chrystie was "obnoxious to Mr. Eustis" because he was "a great favourite of General Wilkinson." (Wilkinson's relations with the War Department had been strained, to say the least. *DAB*, 10:222). Gallatin also mentioned that Chrystie's nomination was fully supported by Vice President George Clinton and leaders in New York City. Chrystie was apparently related to Gallatin's second wife, Hannah Nicholson. See a memorial to Chrystie in *The Oracle of Dauphin* (Harrisburg, PA) 23 October 1813.

14. Alexander, *History of the Thirteenth Regiment United States Infantry*, 197-9. The speculation that this regiment was dressed in the "drab" uniforms issued during this period because of a shortage of properly prepared wool is made in Gero and Maples, "Notes on the Dress of the 13th Regiment." The scene of the battle, as painted by Captain James Dennis, 49th Foot, depicts all American troops in their traditional blue uniforms. Dennis seems to have devoted considerable attention to the uniform details and so his image serves as the best available information about the uniforms of the American forces at Lewiston.

15. Chrystie to Gallatin, 11 March 1813, Albert Gallatin Papers, Roll 26, 84.

16. Mullany provides the size and description of his detachment in Journal of James Mullany. Careers of William Clarke, John McCartey, Robert H. Morris and Henry Whiting, Heitman 1:308; 654, 728; 1030. Clarke was the first lieutenant in the company of Captain David Scott who does not appear to have been present at the time, perhaps due to illness, which was rampant. The Twenty-Third appears to have had difficulty recruiting so there were only portions of a second company at Niagara. At Greenbush men had been transferred from the Thirteenth companies of John Wool and Henry Armstrong into the Twenty-Third. Mullany listed Captain Martin among the officers present to attack Queenston, but this is the only mention of that individual in the relevant documents. He may have arrived with Schuyler's battalion and was sent to fill in for Dox who had done frequent duty carrying despatches. Lieutenant Israel Turner (Heitman, 1:974) of Dox's company is more likely the commander of this unit as his name does figure elsewhere. See Appendix C for unit data.

17. Of the three regular lieutenant colonels involved in the Queenston expedition, Fenwick was the most senior because his commission dated to 2 December 1811, followed by John Chrystie, 12 March 1812 and Winfield Scott, 6 July 1812. Scott mentions Fenwick's agreement to waive his rank in *Memoirs*, 1:57. Scott and Chrystie (Chrystie to Gallatin, 23 March 1813, Albert Gallatin Papers, Roll 26, 122) both stated that the former was senior in rank to the latter, but data in Heitman contradicts this. The Heitman date of Chrystie's commission is supported by his letter of acceptance, Chrystie to Eustis, 16 March 1812, USNA, RG 94, Letters received by the Office of the Adjutant General, 1805-1821. Scott states that he received his lieutenant colonelcy in July 1812 (supporting the Heitman date), *Memoirs*, 1:50. Both men joined the service on 3 May 1808, but Chrystie resigned for a brief period and perhaps this is why they concurred that Scott was the senior officer.

18. See Appendix F for artillery strength. Careers of Robert Mountjoy Bayly and John Gansevoort, Heitman, 1:201; 444.

19. "Journal of Major Isaac Roach, 1812-1824,"136-7. McDonogh to his sister, 16 October 1812, O'Reilly, "A Hero of Fort Erie, 75. Scott, *Memoirs*, 1:56-8.

20. According to a return of 2 October there were 440 officers and men in Swift's regiment and 121 in Lieutenant Colonel Silas Hopkins's regiment at Black Rock, SVRP, Box 12, F10, F11. Returns from other companies suggest there were up to 80 other militia at Black Rock in the second week of October. See Appendices D, E and F for unit data.

21. Mead's Statement, *DHC*, 4:90.

22. Solomon to Arriet, 10 October 1812, SVRP, Correspondence, Box 9, F3
23. Arriet to Solomon, 6 September 1812, SVRP, Correspondence, Box 9, F3
24. Solomon to Arriet, 5 October 1812, SVRP, Correspondence, Box 9, F3.
25. Philip Van Rensselaer to Solomon, 13 October 1812, SVRP, Correspondence, Box 9, F10.
26. The order of embarkation and how it went awry is described in *The Affair of Queenstown*, 24-5. See also, Chrystie to Cushing, 22 February 1813, Armstrong, *Notices of the War*, 207.
27. Crooks to Maclear, 17 March 1853, OA, Miscellaneous Collection, MU 2144, 1853, #14 [hereafter Crooks Account]. This letter, written to Thomas Maclear who wanted to write a book about the battle and petitioned James Crooks for his version, was published as "Recollections of the War of 1812," *Niagara Historical Society*, No. 28, (1916). The sun rises at 7:30 a. m. (Eastern Daylight Savings Time) on 13 October, or at 6:30 a. m. if the clock is left unadjusted. The sky lightens for at least ninety minutes in advance of dawn. The hour between 4:00 and 5:00 is therefore dark and for that reason the American time of departure of 4:00, noted by a number of the participants, has been chosen as the standard for this narrative. The British usually gave 3:00 as the time when the first wave struck out, but this would result in two hours of fighting in the dark which is not supported by the facts. British time as mentioned in most reports and anecdotes tended to be one hour behind the American time.
28. Wool to Stone, 13 September 1838. "Major-General John Ellis Wool to W. L. Stone on the Battle of Queenston Heights in October, 1812," *New York Public Library Bulletin*, 9 (1905), 120 [hereafter: Wool to Stone, 13 September 1838]. Wool wrote this letter to advise Stone about changes that he should make in his treatment of the battle in future editions of *Life of Joseph Brant* (1838).
29. These casualties are mentioned in Wool to his wife Sally Wool, 17 October 1812, BECHS, War of 1812 Letters.
30. Wool to Stone, 13 September 1838. This represents the most detailed description of the American landing available. With it, Wool intended to refute the description by Solomon Van Rensselaer in his *The Affair of Queenstown* (1836) in which he failed to mention the details of the landing other than to write: "The troops were formed and charged up the bank, where they met the enemy," 25.
31. The District General Order by Evans, 6 October 1812, "District General Orders of Maj.-Gen. Sir Isaac Brock," 42, stipulated that all regular and militia troops were "to be under arms in their quarters at the first break of day.... [and] one-third of the men in quarters to be clothed and accoutered during the night with their arms at hand, in readiness to turn out in a moment's notice."
32. At Thomas Evans's suggestion, the militia (including some from the 5th Lincoln and 2nd York) who went with Brock to Detroit were issued worn out uniforms from the 41st Foot, as Brock stated, "Your thought of clothing the militia in the 41st cast off clothing proved a most happy one, it having more than doubled our own regular force in the enemy's eye," Brock to Evans, 17 August 1812, *DHC*, 3:186. Lieutenant John Ball commanded the Lincoln Artillery in the absence of Captain John Powell who was at Fort George.
33. Ensign John Smith, adjutant, 41st Foot, referred to the presence of the small party of the 41st Foot in Smith to Procter, 18 October 1812, USNA, RG 59, M588, 7:115. His terminology may have derived from the fact that Captain Henry M. G. Vigoreux, of the Royal Engineers, had charge of various fatigue parties as per the District General Order by Evans, 4 September 1812, "District General Orders of Maj.-Gen. Sir Isaac Brock," 29. The one-third absent system in the militia is mentioned in Crooks Account. See Appendices H, I and J for unit data.
34. Lovett to Alexander, 14 October 1812, SVRMP, Box 18, F5.
35. Wool to Stone, 13 September 1838. Years later, in rebuttal to Winfield Scott's version of the battle (*Memoirs*), Wool named all the officers involved and mentioned that John Chisholm's militia (2nd York) was camped with Williams's light company and that Dennis's men operated a 3-pdr. field gun. Confirmation of this information is lacking. Wool to the editor of the *Herald*, 30 November 1865, *Historical Magazine*, 2 (1867), 283-5.
36. Wool to his wife Sally Wool, 17 October 1812, John Ellis Wool Papers. Wool biography, *DAB*, 10:513. According to Lovett, Wool was "shot thro' the buttocks," Lovett to Alexander, 14 October 1812, SVRMP, Box 18, F5. American artilleryman Robert Walcot reported seeing the blood trickling out of Wool's shoes, *The Philadelphia Times*, 22 November 1880, in Kosche, "Relics of Brock," 100. Career data for James Lent, Robert Morris, Samuel B. Rathbone, *Heitman*, 1:628; 728; 817. Rathbone died on 8 December 1812. Wool, Armstrong and Malcom and, presumably their subalterns (nine men in all) crossed with Van Rensselaer. Rathbone and Gansevoort were the other two regular officers. Of these men three died and four were wounded in the initial skirmish. Casualties for the First Artillery are shown in Muster and Pay Rolls, September to December 1812, USNA, RG94, Records of the Adjutant General's Office, Muster Rolls of the Regular Army, 1780-1917, First Regiment of Artillery, Box 38A.
37. Casualty Returns for the 41st Foot and 49th Foot, PRO, WO25, 1768 and 1829.
38. *The Affair of Queenstown*, 25.
39. Wool to Stone, 13 September 1838

**Chapter 9: "Are you much hurt, Sir?"**

1. Chrystie to Cushing, 22 February 1813, Armstrong, *Notices of the War*, 207. Solomon Van Rensselaer noted that three boats missed the landing point and were ordered back by Chrystie, citing the testimony of Captain William Lawrence as further proof, *The Affair of Queenstown*, 25.
2. Chrystie to Cushing, 22 February 1813, Armstrong, *Notices of the War*, 207.
3. Chrystie to Cushing, 22 February 1813, Armstrong, *Notices of the War*, 207. Journal of James Mullany.
4. Lovett to Alexander, 14 October 1812, SVRMP, Box 18, F5. Holcroft mentioned two mortars. "Their mortars and six pounders were silenced three different times, but the 18 pounder battery on the summit of the mountain was out of range," Holcroft's account, *Quebec Mercury*, 27 October 1812, *DHC*, 4:117. This account also details the British injuries.
5. Wool to Stone, 13 September 1838.
6. *The Affair of Queenstown*, 26.
7. Klinck and Talman, *Norton Journal*, 304. Evans Diary.
8. Crooks Account. Sutherland, *Merritt Journal*, 3.
9. Evans Diary.
10. Baynes to Brock, 4 March 1811, Tupper, *Life of Brock*, 98. About Craig's horse, Baynes explained to Brock, "Sir James will give him up to [Major Frederick G.] Heriot [Canadian Voltigeurs], whenever you fix the mode of his being forwarded to you." There are no other references to Alfred in the Brock correspondence. Whereas other generals have been described by their contemporaries as favouring a certain horse, such as Wellington's "Copenhagen" and Lee's "Traveller," not a single one of the men who were with Brock mentioned a preferred steed. The "Alfred" story appears to have originated shortly after Tupper's *Life of Brock* (2nd ed., 1847) was published, featuring Baynes's letter. Symons *The Battle of Queenston Heights* (1859) was one of the first books to have Brock riding Alfred. Subsequently, the tale was repeated: Read, *Life and Times of Major-General Sir Isaac Brock, K. B.* (1894); Marquis, *Sir Isaac Brock*, (1929); Goodspeed, *The Good Soldier*, (1964). The Alfred story has been just as frequently omitted: Carnochan, "Sir Isaac Brock," (1913); Edgar, *General Brock*, 1928; Berton, *The Death of Isaac Brock*,1991.
11. Nursey, *The Story of Isaac Brock: Hero, Defender and Saviour of Upper Canada*, (4th ed., 1923), 221. John Powell's daughter, Mrs. Mary Sophia Coxwell, was Walter Nursey's mother-in-law and he attributes the story to her, quoting her insistence that "These facts were well known to other members of the Coxwell-Powell family," 212. The present author agrees with the wisdom of listening to one's mother-in-law, but also in the discretion of not always putting her words in print. This story is more popular by word-of-mouth; while revising this chapter the author listened to a local raconteur and re-enactor claim that Brock remained in Canada to pursue his relationship with Sophie. Such romantic renditions are popular but few of Brock's biographers have used the story, especially individuals like Carnochan, "Sir Isaac Brock," (1913) whose article relates other personal information about Brock. McKenna, *A Life of Propriety*, though featuring intricate details of the society in which the larger Powell family lived, made no reference to the Sophie and Isaac engagement.
12. Glegg to William Brock, 30 December 1813, Kosche, "Relics of Brock,"79.
13. Robinson, "Account of the Battle of Queenston Heights," 14 October 1812, OA, F44, John Beverley Robinson Papers. This account appeared in *DHC*, 4:103 and in Robinson, *Life of Sir John Beverley Robinson*, 33. In this latter item, the author concluded that Robinson wrote the letter to John Strachan, Robinson biography, *DCB*, 9:668.
14. Robinson, "Account of Queenston Heights."
15. See Appendix A for a discussion of Brock's final words.
16. McLean to McNab, 22 July 1860, Carnochan, "Col. Daniel McDougal and Valuable Documents." [Hereafter: McLean Narrative, 1860.] This letter was written in response to McNab's inquiry about whether McLean knew the location of the exact spot where Brock fell; McLean did not know. McLean biography, *DCB*, 9:512.
17. Archibald McLean wrote "The 49th light company ... were called down by the bugle to oppose the landing of the boats," in McLean to unknown, 15 October 1812, *Quebec Mercury*, 27 October 1812. [Hereafter: McLean Narrative, 1812. This version conforms well with the one McLean wrote forty-eight years later.] Robinson also noted the order to call down the light company to fend off the landing of four boats, Robinson, "Account of Queenston Heights."
18. Journal of James Mullany.
19. Robinson, "Account of Queenston Heights." Chrystie to Cushing, 22 February 1813, Armstrong, *Notices of the War*, 207. Grosvenor's attempted rescue of Fenwick is mentioned in Lovett to Alexander, 14 October 1812, SVRMP, Box 18, F5.
20. Lovett to Alexander, 2 November 1812, SVRMP, Box 18, F5.
21. Journal of James Mullany. Career data for Robert Mountjoy Bayly, William Clarke, Alfred Phelps and Israel Turner, Heitman, *Historical Register of the U.S. Army*, 1:201, 308, 787, 974.
22. Robinson, "Account of Queenston Heights."
23. Crooks Account.
24. Smith to Procter, 18 October 1812, USNA, RG 59, M588, 7:115.
25. Chrystie to Cushing, 22 February 1813, Armstrong, *Notices of the War*, 207.
26. Brock's presence in the redan battery was mentioned by W. H. Merritt, (Sutherland, *Merritt Journal*, 3), and in Smith to Procter, 18 October 1812, USNA, RG 59, M588, 7:115, although neither man was at Queenston when Brock fell.
27. Later, a dispute arose as to whether Wool or Peter

Ogilive commanded the detachment at this point. Of those two officers, Wool was junior in rank but, at twenty-eight years of age, the oldest officer present. Wool to Sally, 17 October 1812, John Ellis Wool Papers. Wool to Solomon Van Rensselaer, 23 October 1812, *The Affair of Queenstown*, 14. Ogilvie was commissioned on 12 March 1812 while Wool's commission was dated 14 April, Heitman, 1:757, 1059. Wool's birthdate was 29 February 1784. Ogilvie to Wool, 21 December 1812, *DHC*, 4:156. Ogilvie to the Editor, *New York Evening Post*, 27 December 1812, *ibid.*, 157. Private George Jarvis, 49th Foot, described the locale as "At that time the top of the mountain and a great portion of its side was thickly covered with trees," Jarvis Narrative, *DHC*, 4:146.

28. Jarvis Narrative, *DHC*, 4:146. George Stephen Benjamin Jarvis biography, *DCB*, 10:379. Career data, Sutherland, *His Majesty's Gentlemen*, 205. Sutherland explains that gentlemen volunteers hoped to be recommended for commissions after proving their worth in active service, 4. Jarvis was commissioned an ensign in the 8th Foot on 3 August 1813. There were three other gentlemen volunteers at Queenston Heights, two with Dennis's grenadiers of the 49th Foot: Richard Shaw, commissioned an ensign in the 8th Foot on 24 February 1814; Augustus Thompson, commissioned an ensign in the 8th Foot on 5 August 1813; and one, Alexander Wilkinson, with the 41st which marched from Chippawa. Career data for Shaw, Thompson and Wilkinson, Sutherland, *His Majesty's Gentlemen*, 329 and 354, 378. Jarvis and Thompson's attachment to the 49th and Wilkinson's to the 41st were announced in a District General Order by Evans, 14 September and 8 October 1812, "District General Orders of Maj.-Gen. Sir Isaac Brock," 35. See also Glover, *A Gentleman Volunteer*, 1-2.
29. Jarvis Narrative, *DHC*, 4:146.
30. Robinson, "Account of Queenston Heights." Robinson was not on the hill when Brock died. See Appendix A for a discussion of Brock's final moments.
31. Several anecdotes remain of Americans who took credit for shooting General Brock, the one that most nearly matches conditions described by others being that of Robert Walcot, reputedly a private in the Thirteenth Infantry. Ordered to tend to the 18-pdr., Walcot told of leaving that post as soon as the general began his charge. He crept down toward the action line and borrowed a soldier's musket, into which he rammed a second ball. "I went to the edge of the line," recalled Walcot, "and, taking aim, fired at Brock. His face was partly turned to the troops as I fired. He fell almost instantly and I hurried back to my post." Several factors weigh against the legitimacy of Walcot's claim, such as the absence of his name from the musters of the Thirteenth, where he said he belonged to the company of Concordia Artillery under Captain Nathan Leonard in the Thirteenth Infantry, a clear misrepresentation of fact. His name does not appear on any of the rolls for the units involved at Queenston, see Appendix C for unit data. Perhaps the strongest argument against his claim is that he used the tale to prove the validity of his memory during a law suit in 1880. According to his own testimony, he would then have been 99 years old; his success with the law suit is not recorded. Memorial of Robert Walcot, *The Philadelphia Times*, 22 November 1880, in Kosche, "Relics of Brock," 100-2. Nursey featured the Walcot anecdote in *The Story of Isaac Brock*, 214.
32. Robinson, "Account of Queenston Heights." McLean Narratives, 1812 and 1860. Return of Casualties by Cameron, 5 January 1813, *DHC*, 4:124. Smith to Procter, 18 October 1812, USNA, RG 59, M588, 7:115. Smith only mentions "Private Thomas Haynes 41st Regt who was in the Engineers employed at Queenston was kill'd in the Battery." Sutherland notes that Lieutenant William Crowther, 41st Foot, served as an assistant engineer between July 1812 and May 1813, *His Majesty's Gentlemen*, 112.
33. Robinson, "Account of Queenston Heights."
34. Wool to Solomon Van Rensselaer, 23 October 1812, *The Affair of Queenstown*, 14.
35. McLean Narratives, 1812 and 1860. Robinson, "Account of Queenston Heights." Jarvis Narrative, *DHC*, 4:146. Smith to Procter, 18 October 1812, USNA, RG 59, M588, 7:115. Smith only mentions "Private Thomas Haynes 41st Regt who was in the Engineers employed at Queenston was kill'd in the Battery" without explanation about their task. After Captain Williams was wounded, command of the light company devolved to Ensign Edward Danford, Sheaffe to Prevost, 17 October 1812, "Letter Book of Gen. Sheaffe," 283.
36. Dennis entered the army on 2 September 1796 which made him senior to Glegg (1 June 1979) and Williams (11 May 1797) whose wound prevented him from participating any further that day, Sutherland, *His Majesty's Gentlemen*,122, 163, 379. Merritt mentioned that he met Dennis's force at Durham's (Lot 9, 1st Concession, River Road, Sutherland, *Merritt Journal*, 2, 20n) as did Crooks, Crooks Account, and others.
37. Willson, "A Rifleman of Queenston," 373. Wool to Solomon Van Rensselaer, 23 October 1812, *The Affair of Queenstown*, 14.
38. District General Order by Evans, 6 October 1812, "District General Orders of Maj.-Gen. Sir Isaac Brock," 42
39. Sutherland, *Merritt Journal*, 2.
40. Crooks to Maclear, 17 March 1853, OA, Miscellaneous Collection, MU 2144, 1853, #14. The alarm signal is mentioned in District General Order by Evans, 16 September 1812, "District General Orders of Maj.-Gen. Sir Isaac Brock," 36.
41. Evans Diary. See Appendix D for unit data.
42. Klinck and Talman, *Norton Journal*, 304-5. Only 160 of the 300 Iroquois at Niagara headed for Queenston under Norton, Benn, *The Iroquois in the War of 1812*, 91.

43. Evans Diary. Garrison Order by Leonard, 15 October 1812 and Anonymous Account, 16 October 1812, *Aurora of Philadelphia*, 4 November 1812, *DHC*, 4:127.
44. Evans Diary. Claus, "An Account of the Operations," 23-5. Crooks Account.
45. Anonymous Account, 16 October 1812, *Aurora of Philadelphia*, 4 November 1812, *DHC*, 4:127. Evans Diary. The data in the following ordnance returns is conflicting, but it is reasonable to assume that a dozen heavy guns were operational at Fort George in October: Return of the Brass and Iron Ordnance ...in Lower and Upper Canada, Quebec, 15 December 1812, By Glasgow, NAC, RG 8, I, 1707:82. Return of Brass and Iron Ordnance ... between York and Fort Erie in Upper Canada,19 December 1812, *ibid.*, 121.
46. Career data for George Fowler, Walter Kerr, Angus McIntyre, Sutherland, *His Majesty's Gentlemen*, 95, 216, 243. Sheaffe mentioned Kerr and Fowler in his report of the battle but neglected until 18 October to credit Coffin, Sheaffe to Prevost, 13 October 1812, NAC, MG 11, CO 42, 147:225; Sheaffe to Freer, 18 October 1812, NAC, RG 8, I, 677:140. Nathaniel Coffin was an ensign in the 40th Foot when he went on half pay in 1783 and was Sheaffe's brother-in-law; Sheaffe married Margaret Coffin of Quebec in 1808. Although Sheaffe refers to him as "Ensign Coffin," this officer was made a provincial aide-de-camp with the local rank of lieutenant colonel, Irving, *Officers of the British Forces*, 10. See Appendix D for unit data.
47. Crooks Account.

**Chapter 10: "Beneath the stride of death"**

1. Van Rensselaer to Eustis, 14 October 1812, *The Affair of Queenstown*, 62.
2. *Upper Canada Gazette*, 24 October 1812 in *Poulson's American Daily Advertiser* of Philadelphia, 24 November 1812, *DHC*, 4:126. Coombe, "The War of 1812 Losses Claims." Captain Wool referred briefly to "considerable property taken by the Soldiers," Wool to Sally Wool, 17 October 1812, John Ellis Wool Papers.
3. Samuel Jarvis to unknown, 15 October 1812, NAC, MG 23, K I 3, 1:2. Jarvis was a lieutenant in Stephen Heward's 2nd Flank company of the 3rd York Regiment.
4. Chrystie to Cushing, 22 February 1813, Armstrong, *Notices of the War*, 207. Journal of James Mullany.
5. *The Affair of Queenstown*, 29. John Lovett wrote: "I saw a Field Officer (Major Morrison) who had yelped his lungs sore, to go over, tied up his temples on the day of the battle, and at night told me he had '*hardly been able to keep off his bed the whole day*,'" Lovett to Alexander, 4 November 1812, SVRMP, Box 18, F5.
6. See Appendices D and E for a discussion of U.S. militia involvement in the attack.
7. Street owned Lot Three, Concession One of Niagara Township. Fronting on the Niagara gorge this lot, about 150 acres, had a wedge-like shape, its northern edge following the line of the military reserve along the escarpment. See survey maps done by William Hawkins in 1838 and 1854.
8. Chrystie to Cushing, 22 February 1813, Armstrong, *Notices of the War*, 207. Wool to Sally Wool, 17 October 1812, John Ellis Wool Papers. Thompson Mead account, 18 November 1812, *Albany Argus*, 30 March 1813, *DHC*, 4:90.
9. Chrystie to Cushing, 22 February 1812, Armstrong, *Notices of the War*, 207.
10. Scott's remembrance was that he "was permitted, at his repeated solicitation, to cross over and take command of our forces in conflict with the enemy," *Memoirs*, 58.
11. Chrystie to Cushing, 22 February 1813, Armstrong, *Notices of the War*, 207.
12. Journal of James Mullany.
13. Willson, "A Rifleman of Queenston," 374. Thompson Mead account, 18 November 1812, *Albany Argus*, 30 March 1813, *DHC*, 4:90.
14. Sutherland, *Merritt Journal*, 3. Evans Diary. Crooks Account. Smith to Procter, 18 October 1812, USNA, RG 59, M588, 7:115.
15. Holcroft's account, *Quebec Mercury*, 27 October 1812, *DHC*, 4:117. "Journal of Major Isaac Roach, 1812-1824,"137. Holcroft mentioned two American mortars, but Lovett claimed that there was only one.
16. Holcroft's account. Haythornthwaite, *Weapons and Equipment of the Napoleonic Wars*, 71.
17. Klinck and Talman, *Norton Journal*, 305. Present in the camp at Niagara were members of the Six Nations (Mohawk, Oneida, Onondaga, Cayuga, Seneca, Tuscarora), Delaware, Nanticoke, Tutelo, Creek, Cherokee, Munsey, Chippawa, Mississauga and Ojibway. How many of each nation followed Norton into action is uncertain. Benn, *The Iroquois in the War of 1812*, 88-97. Weaver, "Six Nations of the Grand River, Ontario," 525-7.
18. Klinck and Talman, *Norton Journal*, 305.
19. Klinck and Talman, *Norton Journal*, 306.
20. Willson, "A Rifleman of Queenston," 374.
21. Klinck and Talman, *Norton Journal*, 307.
22. "Journal of Major Isaac Roach, 1812-1824,"138. Scott's remembrance of how he took over command from Wadsworth was that when he "assumed command he did not know that there was a general officer on the ground. The latter, in plain clothes, modestly made his rank known, and insisted on supporting Scott, which he did, with zeal and valor, in every combat," *Memoirs*, 60.
23. Journal of James Mullany.
24. Klinck and Talman, *Norton Journal*, 307.
25. Thompson Mead account, 18 November 1812, *Albany Argus*, 30 March 1813, *DHC*, 4:90.
26. Thompson Mead account, 18 November 1812, *Albany Argus*, 30 March 1813, *DHC*, 4:90.
27. Chrystie to Cushing, 22 February 1813, Armstrong, *Notices of the War*, 207.
28. Klinck and Talman, *Norton Journal*, 308.

29. Lovett to Alexander, 14 October 1812, SVRMP, Box 18, F5.
30. Chrystie to Cushing, 22 February 1813, Armstrong, *Notices of the War*, 207
31. Chrystie to Cushing, 22 February 1813, Armstrong, *Notices of the War*, 207.
32. Robinson, "Account of the Battle of Queenston Heights," 14 October 1812, OA, F44, John Beverley Robinson Papers.
33. Crooks Account. It is difficult to identify these officers from the 3rd York, but those not mentioned as having gone to Queenston to participate in the morning's fighting are Lieutenants William Jarvie, George Ridout and Edward McMahon of Cameron's 1st Flank Company and Lieutenant Samuel Jarvis of Heward's 2nd Flank. Ridout and Jarvis were in the final phase of the battle, George Ridout to his father, 14 October 1812, newspaper account, NAC, MG 13, WO 44:245.
34. Evans Diary. Carter-Edwards, *At Work and Play*, 92. Evans mentions that William Martin led the final reinforcement from Fort George, but Sutherland, *His Majesty's Gentlemen*, 258, shows only Ensign William Neufville Martin, 104th Foot, while Ensign Thomas Martin was with the 41st from spring 1811. Evans is assumed, here, to have made an error. Robert Runchey (taken from McEwan's 2nd Flank Company of the 1st Lincoln) commanded the Coloured Company from 28 August 1812, District General Order by Evans, "District General Orders of Maj.-Gen. Sir Isaac Brock," 27. Sutherland, *Merritt Journal*, 3. See Appendices G, H, I and J for unit data.
35. Smith to Procter, 18 October 1812, USNA, RG 59, M588, 7:115. Evans Diary.
36. Crooks Account.
37. Smith to Procter, 18 October 1813, USNA, RG 59, M588, 7:115. Crooks also mentioned lying down to avoid the enemy shot, Crooks Account. Chrystie referred to "the enemy maneuvering with great caution if not with some hesitation … marches and countermarches" Chrystie to Cushing, 22 February 1812, Armstrong, *Notices of the War*, 207. Scott wrote, "The British general approached with an awful tediousness," Scott, *Memoirs of General Scott*, 60. "The attack on the heights appeared to be oddly managed," Crooks Account.
38. Smith to Procter, 18 October 1812, USNA, RG 59, M588, 7:115. Sergeant Gordon Lyon, 41st Foot, was one of the non commissioned officers selected to train the militia at Niagara, District General Order by Evans, 22 September 1812, "District General Orders of Maj.-Gen. Sir Isaac Brock," 39. Smith and Crooks mentioned lying down to avoid the enemy shot, Crooks Account.
39. Smith to Procter, 18 October 1812, USNA, RG 59, M588, 7:115.
40. Scott, *Memoirs of General Scott*, 61. Mullany claimed there were125 regulars and about 140 militia, Journal of James Mullany. Chrystie wrote that there were less than 300, Chrystie to Cushing, 22 February 1813, Armstrong, *Notices of the War*, 207. Mead said there were 500 men left in the final phase, Thompson Mead account, 18 November 1812, *Albany Argus*, 30 March 1813, *DHC*, 4:90.
41. Van Rensselaer to Eustis, 14 October 1812, *The Affair of Queenstown*, 62.
42. Thompson Mead account, 18 November 1812, *Albany Argus*, 30 March 1813, *DHC*, 4:90. Journal of James Mullany. Chrystie to Gallatin, 23 March 1813, Albert Gallatin Papers, Roll 26, 124.
43. Sheaffe to Prevost, 13 October 1812, NAC, MG 11, CO 42, 147:225. Butler was the lieutenant colonel of the 4th Lincoln Militia and Clarke was the lieutenant colonel of the 2nd.
44. Crooks Account. The order of the British battle line is based upon numerous descriptions, including that of Crooks Account; Smith to Procter, 18 October 1812, USNA, RG 59, M588, 7:115. A diagram of the deployment, signed by John Clark is in *DHC*, 5:6 and apparently from OA, Merritt Papers, MS 74.
45. Chrystie to Gallatin, 11 March 1813, Albert Gallatin Papers, Roll 26, 84.
46. Lovett to Alexander, 14 October 1812, SVRMP, Box 18, F5.
47. Crooks Account.
48. Chrystie to Cushing, 22 February 1813, Armstrong, *Notices of the War*, 207.
49. Mullany Journal. "The Battle of Queenston," (Particulars by Peter Ogilvie), *The War*, 31 October 1812, *DHC*, 4:118.
50. Crooks Account. "Without knowing or seeing (for the smoke was very dense) we, our company, came smack upon their field-piece," Private William Woodruff, 1st Lincoln, to Thorburn, 29 July 1840, *DHC*, 4:77.
51. G. R. to his father, 14 October 1812, newspaper account, NAC, MG 13, WO 44:245. By mention of his colleagues and participation, it seems obvious that George Ridout wrote this account, and that it is the one he referred to in a letter to a brother on 21 October 1812, *DHC*, 4:146.
52. Crooks Account.
53. Willson, "A Rifleman of Queenston," 374.
54. Robinson, "Account of Queenston Heights." The difficulty with the flags of truce is described in Scott, *Memoirs*, 61-2. Mullany's attempt to hide is mentioned in Mcdonogh to his sister, 16 October 1812, O'Reilly, "A Hero of Fort Erie, 75. The Americans attempting to swim to safety and being shot at by the British are mentioned in: Crooks Account; McLean Narrative, 1812; Smith to Procter, 18 October 1812, USNA, RG 59, M588, 7:115.
55. Crooks Account. Holcroft noted that Scott "an Officer with two epaulettes held up his pocket handkerchief. We received him just in time to save him from the Indians." Scott described his capture in *Memoirs*, 61-2. Robinson, "Account of Queenston Heights." McLean Narrative, 1860. The use of a bu-

gle to end the fighting is mentioned in Crooks and in George Ridout to his father, 14 October 1812, newspaper account, NAC, MG 13, WO 44:245.

56. Chrystie to Gallatin, 23 March 1813, Albert Gallatin Papers, Roll 26, 124. "Wadsworth had a ball pass through his coat," anonymous narrative, *Aurora*, 29 October 1812, *DHC*, 4:125. "[George] Grosvenor … had his Rifle cap shot through and all around, but he is unhurt," personal note cited in Lovett to Alexander, 14 October 1812, SVRMP, Box 18, F5.
57. Robinson, "Account of Queenston Heights."
58. McLean Narrative, 1860.

**Chapter 11: "The undaunted bravery of veterans"**

1. "Sam Jarvis and I … walked over the field of action, when the objects that met our eyes were truly horrible; most of the dead bodies were stripped entirely by the Indians, and several scalped," George Ridout to his father, 14 October 1812, newspaper account, NAC, MG 13, WO 44:245. Captain Ogilvie reported seeing "the lifeless body of Ensign [Robert] Morris [Thirteenth Infantry] stripped even of his shirt, and the skull of one that had been wounded was seen cloven," *The War*, New York, 31 October 1812, *DHC*, 4:118. Stephen Van Rensselaer to Sheaffe, 14 October 1812, Bonney, *Gleanings*, 264. Dennis to Stephen Van Rensselaer, 14 October 1812, *ibid.*, 265. Sheaffe to Van Rensselaer, 14 October 1812, *ibid.*
2. *Poulson's American Daily Advertiser*, 24 November 1812, *DHC*, 4:126. Holcroft's account, *Quebec Mercury*, 27 October 1812, *ibid.*, 117. "The Battle of Queenston Heights," *The War* (New York), 31 October 1812, an account based on particulars provided by Captain Peter Ogilvie, Thirteenth Infantry, ibid., 119 .
3. Stephen Van Rensselaer to Dearborn, 20 October 1812, *DHC*, 4:143. Stephen Van Rensselaer to Brock (thinking him still alive), 13 October 1812, *The Affair of Queenstown*, 76. Sheaffe to Van Rensselaer, 13 October 1812, *ibid.*
4. Lovett to Van Vechten 21 October 1812, Bonney, *Gleanings*, 271.
5. Ensign Joseph Dwight's "Journal of an Ensign in the War of 1812."
6. Return of killed, wounded and prisoners of war, by Evans, 15 October 1812, NAC, MG 11, CO 42, 147:19.
7. Sheaffe to Prevost, 17 October 1812, "Letter Book of Gen. Sheaffe," 283. Gibson, Machesney and Totten and Randolph were exchanged for Hamilton, Rolette, Kerr and Molloy, Sheaffe to Smyth, 18 October 1812, *ibid.*, 288; Smyth to Sheaffe, 19 October 1812, *ibid.*, 291.
8. Smith to Procter, 18 October 1812, USNA, RG 59, M588, 7:115. Sheaffe to Prevost, 8 November 1812, NAC, RG 8, I, 677:173. An article noted, "even the officers' side arms were returned to them… . such lenity is not to continue forever." Sheaffe is said to have allowed the paroled officers to carry their weapons as protection against native warriors, *The Niagara Bee*, 24 October 1812, OA, John Fisher Papers, MU 4198. Bathurst to Prevost, 9 December 1812, *DHC*, 4:295.
9. Willson, "A Rifleman of Queenston," 375.
10. Robinson, *Life of Sir John Beverley Robinson*, 43. Return of Ordnance, etc., Captured, by Holcroft, 13 October 1812, NAC, MG 11, CO 42, 148:21. Return of Ordnance, etc., Captured, by Smith, 1 December 1812, *DHC*, 4:74. George Ridout told his brother that there were "1200 stand of arms besides those seized by the Indians and militia, amounting to at least 400 more," George Ridout to Sam Ridout, 21 October 1812, OA, Ridout Family Papers. Crooks said there were 1500 muskets, Crooks Account. Tompkins explained that the state was liable for 2000 muskets borrowed from the federal government, apparently lost at the battle of Queenston Heights, Tompkins to Miller, 2 January 1813, *DDT*, 3:219.
11. George Ridout to Sam Ridout, 21 October 1812, OA, Ridout Family Papers. *Poulson's American Daily Advertiser*, 24 November 1812, *DHC*, 4:126.
12. Scott, *Memoirs*, 71. Scott also detailed (71-81) how twenty-three suspected British deserters were removed from the party of prisoners at Quebec, raising a diplomatic controversy between Washington and London. Scott described (81-85) the ferocity of the storm, horrid conditions on board the ships and the outbreak of scurvy. Among the rolls of the regulars involved at Queenston are records of small detachments of the various companies who were prisoners of war. Two examples are: Eighteen rank and file from John Wool's company, Thirteenth Infantry, were under the command of Ensign George Reab, Thirteenth Infantry, until December 1812 and beyond. One man died on the passage and one died at the hospital in Portland. A voucher for these prisoners was signed on 31 March 1813, USNA, RG94, Records of the Adjutant General's Office, 1780-1917, 13th Infantry, ca 1812-1815, Box 340B; Nine rank and file from James Gibson's company, Light Artillery, were under the command of Lieutenant R. M. Bayly, Third Artillery. One man died on passage from Quebec to Boston. The voucher was signed on 31 March 1813, *ibid.*, Regiment of Light Artillery, Box 101. Treaty for the release of Prisoners, by Dearborn and McDouall, 24 November 1812, NAC, RG 8, I, 690:32.The formal announcement of the exchange of most of the officers was in the General Order by Eustis, 18 January 1813, USNA, RG 98, 2:32.

| Unit | Killed | Wounded | Prisoner | Totals |
|---|---|---|---|---|
| Gen. Staff | 2 | 0 | 0 | 2 |
| 49th | 8 | 33 | 6 | 47 |
| 41st | 3 | 16 | 0 | 19 |
| RA | 1 | 2 | 0 | 3 |
| Linc. | 0 | 15 | 10 | 25 |
| York | 2 | 17 | 5 | 24 |
| Nat. | 5 | 2 | 1 | 8 |
| Totals | 20 | 85 | 22 | 128 |

Return of killed, wounded and prisoners … by Evans, 15 October 1812, NAC, MG 11, CO 42,

148:17. Returns sent by J. Smith to Procter, 18 October 1812, USNA, RG 59, M588, 7:115 shows thirty-two wounded and five captured in the 49th, one killed and fourteen wounded in the Lincolns while one of the ten wounded in the 41st died on 15 October. The 41st suffered three killed and sixteen wounded according to the Pay list for the 41st Regiment of Foot June–December 1812. PRO, WO 12, 5416 and 6044 and the return of NCOs, Dummers, Fifers and Privates of the 49th Foot died, transferred or missing, September to November 1812, PRO, WO 25, 1728. Holcroft reported that he had one man killed and two severely wounded, Holcroft's account, *Quebec Mercury*, 27 October 1812, *DHC*, 4:117. See Appendices G and H for names of some of the regular and militia casualties. Native casualties shown here are based on available evidence, but are presumed to have been greater. "On this occasion we lost two Cayuga Chiefs, one Onondaga warrior and two Oneidas killed besides several wounded," Claus, "An Account of the Operations," 23. John Norton was wounded (as were others: "two Chiefs and a Warrier killed and many wounded," Klinck and Talman, *Norton Journal*, 307) although this was not reported as part of the official casualties, Sheaffe to Prevost, 13 October 1812, NAC, MG 11, CO 42, 147:225. The capture of one of the native chiefs (the exchange of whom became a contentious issue) is mentioned in Sheaffe to Stephen Van Rensselaer, 17 October 1812 and Smyth to Sheaffe, 1 November 1812, "Letter Book of Gen. Sheaffe," 286, 298.

14. Sheaffe to Prevost, 13 October 1812, NAC, MG 11, CO 42, 147:225.
15. G. R. to his father, 14 October 1812, newspaper account, NAC, MG 13, WO 44:245.
16. *Kingston Gazette*, 24 October 1812.
17. Robinson, "Account of Queenston Heights."
18. *Niagara Bee*, 24 October 1812, OA, John Fisher Papers, MU 4198.
19. For details of the funeral see Malcomson, *Burying General Brock*, 3-8. Van Rensselaer to Sheaffe, 16 October 1812; Sheaffe to Van Rensselaer, 16 October 1812, "Letter Book of Gen. Sheaffe," 282-3. Scott, *Memoirs*, 67.
20. Evans to Procter, 22 October 1812, USNA, RG 59, M588, 7:123
21. Evans to Powell, 6 January 1813, *DHC*, 5:29.
22. Report of a council meeting, 6 November 1812, *DHC*, 4:198.
23. Executive council of Upper Canada to Sheaffe, no date, NAC, RG 8, I, 688A:6. Sheaffe undertook his civil duties immediately and went to York briefly on 20 October, probably to attend the Executive Council, 13 October 1812, "Letter Book of Gen. Sheaffe," 278. Sheaffe to Bathurst, 20 October 1812, *DHC*, 4:142. His appointment was formally announced in the General Order by Baynes, 21 October 1812, NAC, RG 8, I, 1168:320.
24. Bathurst to Prevost, 8 December 1812, NAC, RG 8, I, 677:237.
25. *Kingston Gazette*, 24 October 1812.
26. Evans Diary. Robinson, "Account of Queenston Heights."
27. "His Majesty's arms gained a complete victory over those of the United States yesterday in a very brilliant affair," Holcroft's account, *Quebec Mercury*, 27 October 1812, *DHC*, 4:117. "Thus ended this brilliant affair," Smith to Procter, 18 October 1812, USNA, RG 59, M588, 7:115. "We have a loss to deplore which the most brilliant success cannot atone for," Robinson, "Account of Queenston Heights." Prevost considered the events at Queenston as "the brilliant victory," General Order by Baynes, 21 October 1812, NAC, RG 8, I, 1168:320.
28. McLean Narrative, 1812.
29. Crooks Account. Smith to Procter, 18 October 1812, USNA, RG 59, M588, 7:115. Sheaffe to Van Rensselaer, 13 October 1812; Van Rensselaer to Sheaffe, 16 October 1812; Sheaffe to Van Rensselaer, 16 October 1812; Sheaffe to Prevost,19 October 1812; Smyth to Sheaffe, 19 November 1812; Sheaffe to Smyth, 19 November 1812, "Letter Book of Gen. Sheaffe," 277, 281, 282, 290, 310.
30. Sutherland, *Merritt Journal*, 3. "As to the Armistice, one can hardly approve of it, as had it not been made Fort Niagara must have fallen into our hands without a shot being fired. On the other hand our force was much exhausted," Crooks Account.
31. Prevost to Bathurst, 21 April 1813, NAC, MG 11, CO 42, 150:143. Sheaffe explained his reasons for extending the armistice in response to the criticism he saw in Prevost's letter of 27 October 1812, in his to Prevost, 8 November 1812, "Letter Book of Gen. Sheaffe," 305. Following Sheaffe's defeat at York on 27 April 1813, Prevost was very critical of him and recommended his removal from Canada, but left Sheaffe with quite a different opinion: "Sir George Prevost calls the popular clamour unjust, though he seems to think it necessary to yield to it – he says, too, that … his good opinion of me is not in the smaller degree impaired, Sheaffe to Bishop Mountain, n.d., probably May 1813, Millman, "Roger Hale Sheaffe and the Defence of York, April 27, 1813."
32. Sheaffe to Prevost, 13 October 1812, NAC, MG 11, CO 42, 147:225. Sheaffe to Prevost, 3 November 1812, NAC, RG 8, I, 677:166. General Order, 15 November 1812, by Baynes, *DHC*, 4:214. Officers not mentioned in Sheaffe's despatch regarding the battle were: Isaac Swayze, Nathaniel Coffin, John Chisholm, William Applegarth and John Ball.
33. Smith to Procter, 18 October 1812, USNA, RG 59, M588, 7:115. District General Orders by Evans, 18 and 20 October 1812, *DHC*, 4:136, 141. Militia Order, 28 October 1812, *DHC*, 4:169. One general order criticizing "the most shameful blasphemy on board the vessels" of the Provincial Marine was directly attributed to Sheaffe, 4 September 1812, "Dis-

trict General Orders of Maj.-Gen. Sir Isaac Brock," 30. Sheaffe's concern about close adherence to regulations is seen in these orders: District General Order by Evans, 22 October 1812, *DHC*, 4:154; Militia Order, 25 October 1812, *ibid.*, 165; General District Militia Order, by Glegg, 29 October 1812, *ibid.*, 171. Praise for the militia was seen in the Militia District Order by Evans, 1 November 1812, *ibid.*, 4:174.

34. Crooks Account.

35. Sheaffe to Prevost, 8 and 23 November 1812, NAC, RG 8, I, 677:173, 202. Examples of troop deployments are seen in various General Orders, 16, 18, 19 and 23 October 1812, *DHC*, 4:132, 136-7, 139 and 159.

36. Stephen Van Rensselaer to Eustis, 14 October 1812, *The Affair of Queenstown*, 62.

37. Smyth mentioned that he received command on both 15 and 16 October 1812, Smyth to Eustis, 20 October 1812, and Smyth to Dearborn, 24 October 1812, *DHC.*, 4:140, 159. Van Rensselaer to Dearborn, 20 October 1812, *ibid.*, 143.

38. Lovett to Alexander, 25 October 1812, SVRMP, Box 18, F5. *Buffalo Gazette*, 3 November 1812, Bonney, *Gleanings*, 277. Robert Macomb, who accompanied Tompkins to Buffalo explained that the governor awaited a formal invitation to visit Solomon as he did not think himself on good enough terms with Solomon to intrude upon his sick bed. When this explanation was published it sparked a quick, but polite rebuttal from Solomon himself, Macomb to Solomon Southwick, editor of the *Albany Register*, 22 March 1813, *ibid.*, 295. Solomon to Southwick, 24 March 1813, *ibid.*

39. *New York Evening Post*, 11 November 1812. "General Lewis is extravagant in his encomiums, he says you are to have a Regiment, and if no vancancy occur, one will be raised," Stephen Van Rensselaer to Solomon, 8 November 1812, Bonney, *Gleanings*, 280. Van Ness to Solomon Van Rensselaer, 23 November 1812, *ibid.*, 281. The Washington Benevolent Society, an organization opposed to the war, praised the "Services and Sufferings" of Solomon and Lovett early in December, *ibid.*, 281. Solomon to Arriet, 15 October 1812, SVRP, Correspondence, Box 9, F3.

40. Solomon detailed his unsuccessful attempts to gain a regular army commission in *The Affair of Queenstown*, 38-41.

41. Smyth to Eustis, 20, 24 October 1812, *DHC*, 4:140, 159. Incomplete companies under Captains Hugh Martin and Mordecai Myers were strengthened by the transfer of men from the five companies involved at Queenston, with John Sproul's company being the third sub-unit of the Thirteenth Infantry, USNA, RG94, Records of the Adjutant General's Office, 1780-1917, 13th Infantry, ca 1812-1815, Boxes, 339B and Dobbin's records of the reorganization of the militia are contained in the Dobbin Family Papers at the Geneva Historical Society which includes an article Dobbin provided to the *Geneva Gazette*, 29 July 1851.

42. Dearborn to Smyth, 21 October 1812, *DHC*, 4:151. Eustis to Smyth, 6 November 1812, *ibid.*, 184.

43. Address to the Men of New York by Smyth, 10 November 1812, *DHC*, 4:193. For a description of Smyth's November campaign, see Hitsman, *The Incredible War of 1812*, 103.

44. An account based on Ogilvie's comments appeared in *The War*, New York, 31 October 1812, (*DHC*, 4:118), the *Columbian*, New York, 27 October 1812, The *Western Star and Harp of Erin*, New York, 31 October 1812, among others. Ogilvie to the editor, *New York Evening Post*, 27 December 1812, *DHC*, 4:157. Randolph to Wool, 11 November 1812, *ibid.*, 156. Chrystie to Wool, 21 December 1812, *ibid.* Stephen Van Rensselaer to Wool, 24 December 1812, *ibid.*, 157. Heitman, 1:757.

45. Comments here taken from Chrystie to Gallatin, 11 and 23 March 1813, Albert Gallatin Papers, Roll 26, 84 and 122. Heitman, 1:300, 735.

46. Solomon Van Rensselaer to James Wilkinson, 7 January 1816, New York State Library, Solomon Van Rensselaer Papers, SC 7079, Box 83. Chrystie died of an illness at Fort George on 22 Septembert 1813, *The Oracle of Dauphin*, 23 October 1813.

47. *The Affair of Queenstown*, 28.

48. Wool to Stone, 13 September 1838. "Major-General John Ellis Wool to W. L. Stone on the Battle of Queenston Heights in October, 1812," *New York Public Library Bulletin*, 9 (1905), 120. Stephen Van Rensselaer's despatch (Stephen Van Rensselaer to Eustis, 14 October 1812, *The Affair of Queenstown*, 62) read: "Colonel Van Rensselaer with great presence of mind ordered his officers to proceed with rapidity and storm the fort. This service was gallantly performed and the enemy driven down the hill in every direction."

49. Willson, "A Rifleman of Queenston," 375.

50. Dearborn to Eustis, 21 October 1812, USNA, RG 107, Letters Received by the Secretary of War, Registered Series, Sept. 1811–Dec. 1812, (C, D). Dearborn to Eustis, 24 November 1812, *ibid.*

51. *Northern Whig*, 26 October 1812. A similar view was published in the *New York Evening Post*, 28 October 1812.

52. Madison to Congress, 4 November 1812, *Journal of the House of Representatives* ..., First Session, Twelfth Congress, 539.

53. Speech by Tompkins, 4 November 1812, *Northern Whig*, 9 November 1812.

54. "The Clinton Platform, 1812: 'Address to the People of the United States,' 17 August 1812," Schlesinger, *History of American Presidential Elections*, 1:282. Risjord, *Election of 1812*, *ibid.*, 1:249-72. Electoral vote, *ibid.*, 296.

55. Bisshopp to Sheaffe, 1 December 1812, NAC, RG 8, I, 677:229. Notes on the Conduct of Major General Roger Hale Sheaffe, November and December 1812, *DHC*, 5:35.

56. Bathurst to Prevost, 8 June 1813, *SBD*, 2:471.

57. Sheaffe to Prevost, 16 December 1812, NAC, RG 8 I, 677:260. Sheaffe to Prevost, 22 December 1812, *ibid.*, 288.
58. The critique of the battle's importance derives from discussions with Donald E. Graves, John Grodzinski, Gary Gibson and Donald Hickey, as well as from: Clausewitz, *On War*; Handel, Michael I., *Masters of War: Classic Strategic Thought;* British Army, "The Assault Crossing of Water Obstacles," Military Training Pamphlet no. 20, 1947; Kimball, "The Fog and Friction of Frontier War: The Role of Logistics in American Offensive Failure During the War of 1812;" Mahon, "British Command Decisions in the Northern Campaigns of the War of 1812."
59. A plan for simultaneous crossings at various points, including the upper river, had been considered in August as seen in Swift to Tompkins, 23 August 1812, *ibid.*, 202. Among the SVRP, General Orders, Box 12, F7, are two detailed plans: the first, describing a crossing "tomorrow" at Black Rock, Lewiston and Five Mile Meadow with diversions at Grand Island and Fort Niagara; the second, a general order describing the orders of march, encampment and battle. Both documents are undated and unsigned.
60. "I firmly believe I could at this moment sweep everything before me from Fort Niagara to Buffalo – but my success would be transient," Brock to Savery Brock, 18 September 1812, Tupper, *Life of Brock*, 315.
61. Eustis to Dearborn, 18 December 1812, USNA, RG 107, Letters Sent by the Secretary of War, 6:253.
62. For career data of Kearney, Scott, Totten, Towson and Wool, see Heitman, 1:586, 870, 964, 966 1059. See other biographical material for Scott and Wool in previous chapters and Boylen, "Strategy of Brock Saved Canada: Candid Comments of a U.S. Officer Who Crossed at Queenston" for a brief observation by Totten.
63. Brock employed the "direct defence" tactics described in Clausewitz, *On War*, 522-36, and would have established a large reinforcement within a day's march (Pelham) of any Niagara River crossing if such a force would have been available, Brock to Prevost, 7 September 1812, NAC, RG 8, I, 677:64. Captain Joseph Totten, later a brigadier, wrote in 1851 that the British "kept the strength of this country so attenuated, by stretching along a frontier of many hundred miles, that no great effort could be made anywhere; and upon the true point of attack reduced the efforts to means so feeble as to end only in discomfiture and disgrace," Boylen, "Strategy of Brock Saved Canada: Candid Comments of a U.S. Officer Who Crossed at Queenston."
64. Career Data for Dennis, Derenzy, Evans, Holcroft, Williams, in Sutherland, *His Majesty's Gentlemen*, 122,123, 138, 194 and 379. Militia and District General Orders, 24 and 25 October 1812, *DHC*, 4:161-3.Robinson biography, *DCB*, 9:668. Benn, *The Iroquois in the War of 1812*, 99-102. General Order, 15 November 1812, by Baynes, *DHC*, 4:214.
65. Sheppard, *Plunder, Profit, and Paroles*, 4-5. Sheppard, "Deeds Speak." Stacey, "The War of 1812 in Canadian History." Stanley, "The Contribution of the Canadian Militia during the War.

**Epilogue: "May its effects not be lost upon the rising generation."**

1. Cruikshank, "A Sketch of the Public Life and Services of Robert Nichol …," 37.
2. Report of the Commissioners …, 1 December 1821, NAC, RG 5, A1, 71:37715. Clark to Hillier, 13 January 1824, *ibid.*, 65:34146. Nichol to Hillier, 25 February 1824, *ibid.*, 34519. Proposed Arrangements for the 13th October, 1824, Broadside Series, Baldwin Room, Toronto Reference Library. Martineau, *Retrospect of Western Travel*, 1:100.
3. *St. Catharines Journal and Welland Canal General Advertiser*, 30 April 1840. *Niagara Chronicle*, 13 July 1853. *Daily Globe*, 14 October 1859.
4. *The* [Niagara] *Mail*, 20 July 1853.
5. *The* [Niagara] *Mail*, 20 October 1853.
6. *Niagara Mail*, 20 October 1853. Brock's current monument was completed in 1857 and commemorated on 13 October 1859, Malcomson, *Burying General Brock*, 26-44

**Appendix A: The Last Words of Isaac Brock**

1. Tupper, H. *Who was Isaac Brock? Short Summary of the Life of Major-General Sir Isaac Brock, K.B*, 20.
2. Ridout to his father, 14 October 1812, newspaper account, NAC, MG 13, WO 44:245.
3. McLean to unknown, 15 October 1812, *Quebec Mercury*, 27 October 1812.
4. Robinson, "Account of the Battle of Queenston Heights," 14 October 1812, OA, F44, John Beverley Robinson Papers.
5. Smith to Procter, 18 October 1812, USNA, RG 59, M588, 7:115.
6. *The Niagara Bee*, 24 October 1812, OA, John Fisher Papers, MU 4198.
7. Sutherland, *Merritt Journal*, 3.
8. Of the biographies reviewed for this project, Brock's order to "Push on" was featured in: Tupper, H. *Who was Isaac Brock? Short Summary of the Life of Major-General Sir Isaac Brock, K.B*, 20; Symons, *The Battle of Queenston Heights being a narrative of the Opening of the War of 1812 with notices of the life of Major-General Sir Isaac Brock, K. B.*, 1859, 11.
9. Glegg to W. Brock, 14 October 1812, DHC, 4:83. Glegg's version (with an appeal by Brock to be remembered to his sister, added) appeared in F. B.Tupper's first work about Brock, *Family Records; containing Memoirs of Major-General Sir Isaac Brock, K. B*, (1835), 18, and has been frequently repeated: Nursey, *The Story of Isaac Brock*, 181; Symons, *The Battle of Queenston Heights*, 11; Fraser, *Brock Centenary, 1812-1912*, 19; Read, *Life and Times of Major-General Sir Isaac Brock*, 219.
10. Eayrs, *Sir Isaac Brock*, 92.

11. Among those who portrayed Brock's silent death are: Carnochan "Sir Isaac Brock;" Goodspeed, *The Good Soldier*, 145; Marquis, *Sir Isaac Brock*, 31; Adams, *General Brock and Niagara Falls*, 160; Lamb, *The Hero Of Upper Canada*, 25; Berton, *The Death of Isaac Brock*, 66; Edgar, *General Brock*, 304; and Marquis, *Brock: The Hero of Upper Canada*, 127.
12. Kosche, "Relics of Brock: An Investigation."
13. Jarvis narrative, DHC 4:116.

**Appendix B: Brock's Monuments and Queenston Heights Today**

1. "Architectural Notices: The Brock Monument," *The Canadian Journal*,.1852, 1:41-2. Progress Reports: by William Thomas, 15 October 1855, OA, MU 296, The Brock Monument Papers, 1840-1857; by Building Committee, 22 October 1857, *ibid.* May 1856, *The Canadian Journal*, 203-4. *The Daily Globe*, 14 October 1859. For a description of this monument and more details about the monuments, see Malcomson, *Burying General Brock: A History of Brock's Monuments.*
2. *The Daily Globe*, 14 October 1859.

**Appendix D: New York State Militia and Volunteer Personnel in the American Army on the Niagara River, 1812**

1. This number is based upon the 6714-man strength of Van Rensselaer's army at the time of the battle (see Appendix E) plus the strength of the units and companies which served only temporarily during the summer, (Section D of this appendix). This latter strength totals 766 officers and men. The grand total is 7480.
2. Organization of the New York Militia is presented in Hugh Hastings, ed., *Military Minutes of the Council of Appointment of the State of New York, 1783-1821*, 2:1400-9. The best available report on the size of the New York Militia showed the 1809 figures in Return of the Militia of the United States, by Eustis, 15 February 1811, *ASP:MA*, 1:298-301.
3. An Act to authorize a detachment from the Militia of the United States, 10 April 1812, Twelfth Congress, Session 1, Chapter 55. Quotas of Militia from the Several States, by Eustis, 28 May 1812, *ASP:MA*, 1:319.
4. General Order by Paulding, 18 June 1812, *DDT*, 1:336.
5. As examples: Elijah Clarke was the only company commander in Allen's Twentieth Detached that had been in Allen's Twenty-Second Infantry from 1810 (Hastings, *Military Minutes of the Council of Appointment*, 2:1146). Prior to joining Allen's detached regiment, James Bogert and Abraham Dox (light company) were in the Forty-Second Infantry from Geneva, Ontario County (*ibid.* 1311, 1190), Joel Hart was in the One Hundred Third Infantry, also from Ontario County (*ibid.*, 1312) and Salma Stanley was in Major William H. Cuyler's battalion of riflemen (*ibid.*,1312). The other detached regiments were formed in the same way.
6. Hall to Tompkins, 13 August 1812, DHC, 3:173.
7. Twelfth Congress, Session 1, Chapter 21.
8. Tompkins to Van Rensselaer, 9 September 1812, *DDT*, 3:108.
9. John Compston was a captain of militia artillery from Aurelius in the Cayuga County (Hastings, *Military Minutes of the Council of Appointment*, 2:1387) that was mobilized in September, but rolls for his subunit were not found in the archival records. For that reason no other officers but him are listed. According to Miller's Diary, (Pennsylvania State Archives, MG 6) Compston arrived at Buffalo on 6 October 1812 with twenty men and two pieces of artillery.
10. This regiment was originally formed of 600 infantry detached from Major General Amos Hall's Seventh Division in April 1812 and appears to have become a regiment of volunteers under the Act of 6 February 1812. On 23 August, however, Swift wrote to Tompkins for confirmation of the arrangement, stating that his 470 officers and men were willing to serve as volunteers, DHC, 3:202. The regiment's category was clearly shown in the Weekly Return of Lieutenant Colonel Philetus Swift's Regiment of United States *Volunteers* (author's italics) stationed at Black Rock ... 2 October 1812, SVRMP, Box 12, F10.
11. Francis McClure had been in command of a battalion of rifles in 1809, General Order by Paulding, 17 April 1809, *DDT*, 1:209. His battalion earned compliments in 1810 for its "appearance, equipment and discipline," General Order by Livingstone, 5 November 1810, *ibid.*, 274. Charles Moseley had commanded a company of rifles in 1809 with Leonard Kellogg as his lieutenant and Charles Bristol as his ensign, General Order by Paulding, 19 September 1809, *ibid.*, 229.
12. Lieutenant Jacob Miller states in his diary (Pennsylvania State Archives, MG 6) that his company under Captain Allison arrived at Buffalo on 2 October 1812 and that the companies of Captain Collins and Philips arrived there on 7 October. All three companies were ordered by Stephen Van Rensselaer to take post at Buffalo. Miller referred to the three companies as "volunteers."
13. Tompkins referred to the status of McClure and Gaylord's battalions as volunteers under the Act of 6 February in Tompkins to Dearborn, 29 September 1812, *DDT*, 3:153. McClure's battalion was also formally attached to the Eighth Brigade of Detached Regiments under Brigadier General George McClure of the town of Bath, Steuben County and, therefore, part of Stephen Van Rensselaer's Division, General Order by Paulding, 18 June 1812, *DDT*, 1:336. Moseley's advancement to major was conditional upon him forming the companies as volunteers under the Act of 6 February, Tompkins to Moseley, 27 April 1812, *DDT*, 2:563.

14. Camp's squadron was referred to as a "Volunteer Cavalry" under the Act of 6 February, General Order by Solomon Van Rensselaer, 15 September 1812, SVRP, General Orders, Box 12, F7.
15. Wadsworth to Tompkins, 6 July 1812, DHC, 3:101.
16. The strength of Davis's Regiment was 328 officers and men. This number is based upon rolls found in NYSA, Adjutant General's Office – Transcriptions of War of 1812 Payrolls for New York State Militia Units, 1812-1815, B0811 [hereafter NYSA, AGO, B0811], Box 6, F4, F5.
17. The strength of Churchill's Regiment was 132 officers and men. This number is based upon rolls found in NYSA, AGO, B0811, Box 5, F20, F22.
18. The strength of the independent companies was 306 officers and men. This number is based upon rolls found in NYSA, AGO, B0811, Box 5, F2, F3, F5, F22; Box 6, F2, F3.

**Appendix E: Van Rensselaer's Army on the Niagara River, October 1812**

1. Porter to Tompkins, 9 July 1812, *DDT*, 3:117.
2. Dearborn to Eustis, 14 September1812, USNA, RG 107, Letters Received by the Secretary of War, Registered Series, Sept. 1811–Dec. 1812, (C, D).
3. Hitsman, *Incredible War*, 92, used the 6000-strong figure (unattributed), although he clearly used figures from the return that Solomon Van Rensselaer published, Table One. Hickey, *The War of 1812*, 86, states the American force was stronger than 6000 as does Turner, *The War of 1812*, 50, and Mahon, *The War of 1812*, 76, claims a strength of 6300. None refers to a definite source for their numbers. Elting, *Amateurs to Arms*, 40, shows 2650 militia in total, 1650 regulars at Buffalo and 1300 regulars around Fort Niagara, without attribution.
4. Return of the troops under the command of Major General Stephen Van Rensselaer of the New York Militia, Head Quarters, Lewiston, October 12th, 1812, *The Affair of Queenstown*, 19.
5. This number represent nominal strength. Some of the returns show the number of men absent due to illness, desertion, etc. The strength of the units was diminished by an average of about 20% , leaving in this case almost 5400 men available for active duty.
6. The best return of the regular force posted at Fort Niagara is the Morning Report of the Garrison of Fort Niagara ..., 30 September 1812, SVRMP, Box 12, F11. It includes all the companies from the artillery and infantry at Fort Niagara. Musters of individual companies show nominal strength from one month to another, but do not state strength on specific dates as the above report does. They are useful in identifying names and casualties, etc. See pay or muster rolls in USNA, RG 94, Records of the Adjutant General's Office, Muster Rolls of the Regular Army, 1780-1917 [Hereafter: USNA RG 94], 1st Regiment of Artillery, Box 38A; 3rd Regiment of Artillery, Box 49A; Regiment of Light Artillery, Box 101.
7. USNA RG 94, 6th Regiment of Infantry, Box 262, 262C; 13th Infantry, ca 1812-1815, Box 340; 23rd Infantry, ca 1812-1815, Boxes 360D, 361.
8. Chrystie mentions that he brought "nearly 400" men to Niagara, Chrystie to Cushing, 22 February 1813, Chrystie to Cushing, Armstrong, *Notices of the War*, 1:207 and that, if asked, he could have marched 380 men to Lewiston on 12 October, Chrystie to Gallatin, 11 March 1813, Albert Gallatin Papers, Lockwood Library, SUNY, Buffalo, Roll 26, F84. USNA, RG94, 13th Infantry, ca 1812-1815, Boxes 338, 339B.
9. USNA, RG94, Regiment of Light Artillery [James Gibson, August-October 1812], Box 101.
10. USNA, RG94, Second Regiment of Artillery [James N. Barker, August-October 1812], Box 43 and [Nathan Towson, September-December 1812], Box 46A.
11. Smyth described the strength of his brigade with, "They shall march, to the number of 1200 effective men, but imperfectly disciplined," Smyth to Stephen Van Rensselaer, 12 October 1812, *The Affair of Queenstown*, 72. An analysis of the muster and pay rolls for each of these regiments was not undertaken since the activities of Smyth's brigade figure only slightly in this account.
12. The strength of the Sixth Brigade of Detached Militia is based upon the rolls of the individual companies (not listed here) in NYSA, AGO, B0811-85, Sixteenth Regt. Box 7, F9, 19, 20, 21; Seventeenth Regt., Box 12, F15, 16. A second primary source was USNA, RG 94, Office of the Adjutant General, Volunteer Organizations and State Militia, War of 1812: Sixteenth and Seventeenth Regt., Box 126.
13. The strength of the Seventh Brigade of Detached Militia is based upon Report of Troops under the Command of Brig. General Wadsworth, 6 October 1812, SVRMP, Box 12, 11. As with the Sixth Brigade the other sources were the rolls for individual companies (not listed here) in NYSA, AGO, B0811, Eighteenth Regiment, Box 5, F11, 12, 15, 20, Box 6, F14, 17, 18, Box 7, F24; Nineteenth Regiment, Box 5, F13, 14, 23; Twentieth Regiment, Box 5, F 6, 7, 25 and USNA, RG 94, Eighteenth Regiment, Boxes, 126, 127; Nineteenth Regiment, Box 128; Twentieth Regiment, Box 129.
14. Spalding's company was listed as being at Lewiston with a strength of sixty-six officers and men on the Report of Troops under the Command of Brig. General Wadsworth, 6 October 1812, SVRMP, Box 12, 11. A roll for Spalding is in NYSA, AGO, B0811, Box 5, F14.
15. Rolls for Parkhurst and Clough, NYSA, AGO, B0811, Box 5, F14.
16. According to Report of Troops under the Command of Brig. General Wadsworth, 6 October 1812, SVRMP, Box 12, F11, the strengths of the following battalions were "Moseley, 99; Granger, 91, Ireland and Bacon, 94." The other companies were not ac-

counted for. Rolls for all the militia and volunteer rifle companies are found in NYSA, AGO, B0811, Box 5, F4, F5, F15, F19, F20, F21; Box 6, F2, F3. Beyond this group of rifle companies and the volunteer rifle companies, there were also rifle companies included in the detached regiments of infantry. For example, Salma Stanley's unit in Peter Allen's Twentieth Detached was a rifle company.

17. According to Report of Troops under the Command of Brig. General Wadsworth, 6 October 1812, SVRMP, Box 12, F11, the total light infantry strength was 149. No specific companies were accounted for. Rolls for all the light infantry companies are found in NYSA, AGO, B0811, Box 5, F4, F5, F13, F22.
18. According to Report of Troops under the Command of Brig. General Wadsworth, 6 October 1812, SVRMP, Box 12, F11, the total artillery strength was 140. No specific companies were accounted for. Rolls for all the artillery companies are found in NYSA, AGO, B0811, Box 5, F5, F20, F23; Box 6, F3; Box 7, F24. John Compston was a captain of militia artillery from Aurelius in the Cayuga County (Hastings, *Military Minutes of the Council of Appointment*, 2:1387) that was mobilized in September, but rolls for his subunit were not found in the archival records. For that reason no other officers but him are listed. According to Miller's Diary, (Pennsylvania State Archives, MG 6) Compston arrived at Buffalo on 6 October 1812 with twenty men and two pieces of artillery.
19. According to Report of Troops under the Command of Brig. General Wadsworth, 6 October 1812, SVRMP, Box 12, F11, the total cavalry strength was 63. No specific companies were accounted for. Rolls for all the troops are found in NYSA, AGO, B0811, Box 5, F3, F4, F6; Box 6, F4.
20. The Weekly Return of Lieutenant Colonel Philetus Swift's Regiment of United States Volunteers stationed at Black Rock, and of a Battalion under the command of Lieutenant Colonel Silas Hopkins, detached from Brigadier General Hopkins Brigade, stationed in the village of Buffalo, 2 October 1812, SVRMP, Box 12, F10, shows Hopkins's strength as 121. No specific companies were accounted for. Rolls for all Hopkins's companies at Black Rock are found in NYSA, AGO, B0811, Box 5, F15.
21. L. Powers's company was part of the volunteer battalion commanded by Major Francis McClure, NYSA, AGO, B0811, Box 5, F8, stationed at Buffalo. It appears that Powers's company was the first one from McClure's Battalion to appear on the Niagara River.
22. The Weekly Return of Lieutenant Colonel Philetus Swift's Regiment of United States Volunteers stationed at Black Rock, ..., 2 October 1812, SVRMP, Box 12, F10 shows Swift's strength as 440. No specific companies were accounted for. Rolls for all Swifts's companies at Black Rock are found in NYSA, AGO, B0811, Box 5, F10, F11, F15. A roll for S. Jenning's company for October was not located and so the strength of his company (71) was not included here.
23. Lieutenant Jacob Miller states in his diary (Pennsylvania State Archives, MG 6) that his company under Captain Allison arrived at Buffalo on 2 October 1812 and that the companies of Captain Collins (sixty-two men) and Philips (forty-five men) arrived there on 7 October. Miller did not identify the size of Allison's company, but it is assumed to have been at least fifty-strong. All three companies were ordered by Stephen Van Rensselaer to take post at Buffalo. Miller referred to the three companies as "volunteers."

**Appendix F: American Order of Battle, 13 October 1812**

1. Sheaffe to Prevost, 13 October 1812, NAC, MG 11, CO 42, 147:225.
2. Stephen Van Rensselaer to Dearborn, 20 October 1812, DHC, 4:143. Return of killed, wounded and prisoners of war, by Evans, 15 October 1812, NAC, MG 11, CO 42, 147:19.
3. This number includes the 610 known to have crossed, plus Lieutenant Colonel Scott, Lieutenant Isaac Roach and Engineer Joseph Totten.
4. This number shows the 105-man strength of the Second Artillery reduced by Scott and Roach's absence.
5. Chrystie to Gallatin, 11 March 1813, Albert Gallatin Papers, Roll 26, 84.
6. Journal of John Mullany.
7. Company musters for this period show that Captain Nathan Towson had fifty-six officers and men and Captain James Barker had forty-nine officers and men, USNA, RG94, Records of the Adjutant General's Office, Muster Rolls of the Regular Army, 1780-1917 [hereafter: USNA, RG94], 2nd Regiment of Artillery, Box 46A and Box 43.
8. Solomon Van Rensselaer noted that "forty picked men from Capt. Leonard's old company of artillery" went with him in the first wave of the attack. It is assumed here that this detachment included some men from James McKeon's Third U.S. Artillery; both company records show participation in the battle. James Gibson's unit of light artillery numbered sixty-nine men. See pay or muster rolls in USNA, RG94, 1st Regiment of Artillery, Box 38A; 3rd Regiment of Artillery, Box 49A; Regiment of Light Artillery, Box 101.
9. This number includes the total of each detached regiment, Spalding's Regiment and the independent companies and Stephen and Solomon Van Rensselaer, William Wadsworth and their aides Lovett, Spencer and Lush.
10. NYSA, AGO, B0811, Box 7, F19, 20, 21. USNA, RG94, Box 126.
11. NYSA, AGO, B0811, Box 12, F15, 16, 17. USNA, RG94, Box 126.
12. NYSA, AGO, B0811, Box 5, F11, 12, 20; Box 6, F14, 15, 17, 18; Box 7, F24. USNA, RG94, Box 126, 127.

13. The archival sets of muster and pay rolls for the Eighteenth New York under Lieutenant Colonel Henry Bloom indicate that no individuals from that unit were killed, wounded or captured, NYSA, AGO, B0811, Box 5, F13, 14, 23; USNA, RG94, Box 128. The number (11) shown here derives from a list of prisoners indicating that Henry Bloom was wounded and that Captains Henry Brinkeroff, Daniel Eldridge and Peley Ellis, Lieutenants John Daniels, Elisha Holcomb, Frederick Kisher Alexander Price and Ensigns William Cobb, Philo Sperry and George Waldroft were captured. With that number of officers involved, there is no doubt that at least fifty of the Eighteenth crossed into Canada, List of American officers killed, wounded or taken prisoner at Queenston, 13 October 1812, DHC 4:76.
14. NYSA, AGO, B0811, Box 5, F6, 7, 24, 25. USNA, RG94, Box 129.
15. Spalding: NYSA, AGO, B0811, Box 5, F15.
16. Bristol, NYSA, AGO, B0811, Box 7, F18; Ireland, Box 6, F2; Kellogg, Box 5, F5, 9: Parke, Box 6, F3; Westfall, Box 6, F3.
17. It is speculated here that Ellicott and Pierce's companies of New York artillery served the guns in Fort Gray and the mortar near the embarkation point. No anecdotal information supports this, but the rolls for their companies show them mustered at Lewiston from September to November, NYSA, AGO, B0811, Box 5, F20, F23.
18. Lovett to Alexander, 14 October 1812, SVRMP, Box 18, F5. Stephen Van Rensselaer to Eustis, 14 October 1812, *The Affair of Queenstown*, 62. Roach, "Journal of Major Isaac Roach, 1812-1824."

**Appendix G: British Army Personnel Involved at Queenston Heights**

1. These figures are based on an examination of the "District General Orders of Maj.-Gen. Sir Isaac Brock from June 27th, 1812–Oct. 16th 1812." Casualties and prisoners for the 41st Foot are shown in Return of British Casualties at Queenston, by Evans, 15 October 1812, NAC, MG 11, CO 42, 148:19 and in Return of NCOs, Drummers, Fifers and Privates of the 49th Foot died, transferred or missing, September to November 1812, PRO, WO 25, 1728 and are enclosed with Smith to Procter, 18 October 1812, USNA, RG 59, M588, 7:115. Casualty returns done by Smith and Evans show two killed and ten wounded, but the other records (including the pay lists) show three killed and sixteen wounded. Chambers was mentioned in Extract from the Diary of General T. Evans while serving as an officer on staff of General Brock at Queenston, War of 1812–1814, Government House, Fort George, 15 October 1812, NAC, MG 24, Hellmuth Papers.
2. Danford was recognized in Sheaffe to Prevost, 17 October 1812, "Letter Book of Gen. Sheaffe," 283. Casualties and prisoners for the 49th Foot are shown in Return of British Casualties at Queenston, by Evans, 15 October 1812, NAC, MG 11, CO 42, 148:19 and in Return of NCOs, Drummers, Fifers and Privates of the 49th Foot died, transferred or missing, September to November 1812, PRO, WO 25, 1829.
3. Holcroft mentioned casualties in a report dated 15 October 1812 that appeared in the *Quebec Mercury* on 27 October. These were: Gunner Birch (shown as Birchell on the original muster), killed; Hunt, badly wounded; and Granger, his leg shot off. He also refers to acting Sergeant Ellerton, shown on the muster as a corporal, Bombardier Robinson, (presumably Robertson on the muster) and Bombardier Phernerson whose name, nor any like it (other than Thomas Henderson), does not appear on the muster.

**Appendix H: Upper Canada Militia Personnel Involved at Queenston Heights**

1. 25 June 1812, George to Thomas Ridout, OA, Ridout Family Papers, 1764-1824, MS537.
2. Gray. *Soldiers of the King: The Upper Canadian Militia, 1812-1815.* Among the contemporary records used as references here are: OA, 1812 Military Records; Abraham Nelles Papers; Robert Nelles Papers, NAC, Claus Family Papers, RG 8, I, 1701.
3. This list based upon Gray, *Soldiers of the King, passim* and a private note from A. T. Holden, a respected local researcher.

**Appendix I: Brock's Army on the Niagara Frontier, October 1812**

1. District General Orders by Evans, 27 June and 2 July 1812, "District General Orders of Maj.-Gen. Sir Isaac Brock," 5 and 6.
2. Shaw offered his services to Brock in August and was posted to command Divisions One and Two which had been under the command of Lieutenant Colonel Thomas Clarke since late June, District General Order, by Glegg, DHC, 3:161. Shaw was a major general in the British Army and head of the province's militia. For his service on the Niagara River, he was given the rank of colonel of militia and the pay and allowances of a lieutenant colonel, although the district general orders referred to him as "major general."
3. The best available tally of the forces at Fort Erie is the Distribution of Troops in Canada, 12 November 1812 (RA, RE, 41st, 49th, Glengarry), NAC, RG 8, I, 1707:60. This source is used for all Royal Artillery deployments shown here.
4. Militia numbers appear to have fluctuated from seventy to eighty men per company, among the Lincoln regiments. James Crooks mentioned that a system was in place that allowed one third of each company to be absent at a time, so the strength of the companies appears to have been about fifty men per company, Crooks to Maclear, 17 March 1853, OA, Miscellaneous Collection, MU 2144, 1853, #14. Some militia material is based upon Gray, *Soldiers of the King*.
5. Companies and platoons of the 41st Foot were frequently moved between Divisions One, Two and

Three during the summer and fall. Their numbers at Chippawa and Fort George are based upon an analysis of the "District General Orders of Maj.-Gen. Sir Isaac Brock."

6. 2nd and 5th Lincoln Regiments, Flank and Battalion Companies, pay roll, 25 October–24 November, MU 2036, 1812 Military Records, #11.
7. The strength of the 49th Foot at Queenston is based upon the 49th Regiment of Foot, pay rolls, June to December 1812, PRO, WO 12, 6044. The presence of a group of 41st Foot at Queenston working as engineers is reported in Smith to Procter, 18 October 1812, USNA, RG 59, M588, 7:115.
8. 2nd and 5th Lincoln Regiments, Flank and Battalion Companies, pay roll, 25 October–24 November, OA, MU 2036, 1812 Military Records, #11. Return of Hatt's company, 5th Lincoln, 3 July 1812, NAC, RG 8, 1701:137. Return of Durand's company, 5th Lincoln, 3 July 1812, *ibid.*, 139. The best available information about the size of the 2nd York is a note describing their strength as sixty on the Morning State of the Militia of the 1st Regiment of Lincoln Militia under the Command of Colonel Claus, stationed at Niagara, 6 July 1812, *ibid.*, 27. On 7 July 1812 the Lincoln Artillery was shown to have 14 officers and men, State of the Third Division, 7 July 1812, DHC, 4:19. An addition of thirty men was ordered to be attached to this sub-unit, the men being taken from battalion companies of the Lincoln regiments, Militia General Order by Macdonell, 22 July 1812, DHC, 3:138.
9. Distribution of Troops in Canada, 12 November 1812 (RA, RE, 41st, 49th, Glengarry), NAC, RG 8, I, 1707:60. "District General Orders of Maj.-Gen. Sir Isaac Brock."
10. Forty is speculated as the strength of each of these York flank companies (there was only one flank company from the 1st York present) since these companies appear to have been weaker in strength than the Lincoln companies. Musters for the flank companies of the 3rd York show their strengths as 27 (Cameron) and 51 (Jarvie), 3rd York, Duncan Cameron, muster roll, 29 August 1812, MU 7522, Miscellaneous Military Records, #5; 3rd York, Ridout, muster rolls, 25 November–17 December 1812, MU 2036, 1812 Military Records, #3. 4th Lincoln Flank Company, John Moore, muster roll, 25 July–24 August 1812, OA, MU 2030, 1812 Military Records, #8. 4th Lincoln Flank Company, Abraham Nelles, Muster rolls July–August 1812, OA, MS 502, Abraham Nelles Papers. Roll of 4th Lincoln Battalion Company, Robert Nelles, 25 November–18 December 1812, OA, MS 503, Robert Nelles Papers. Morning State of Militia at Niagara under Claus, 10 July, 1 and 11 August 1812, NAC, RG 8, 1701:37, 49, 80. Rolls of Crooks's company, 1st Lincoln, 4 and 28 June, *ibid.*, 96 and108. Roll of McEwan's company, 1st Lincoln, 4 July 1812, *ibid.*, 158. A muster of Runchey's company, 24 October 1812, *ibid.*, 208.
11. Klinck and Talman, *Norton Journal*, 304-10.

**Appendix J: British Order of Battle, 13 October 1812**

1. 49th Regiment of Foot, pay rolls, June to December 1812, PRO, WO 12, 6044.
2. Smith to Procter, 18 October 1812, USNA, RG 59, M588, 7:115. Smith only mentions "Private Thomas Haynes 41st Regt who was in the Engineers employed at Queenston was kill'd in the Battery" without explanation about their task. Lieutenant William Crowther who served as an acting engineer with the Canadian Command from July 1812 until May 1813 (Sutherland, *His Majesty's Gentlemen*, 112) was probably at Queenston in charge of this squad from the 41st Foot.
3. No specific muster for the men of Captain William Holcroft's company of Royal Artillery at Queenston is available for October. The number shown here is based on what is believed to be Holcroft's account of the battle, published in the *Quebec Mercury* on 27 October 1812, DHC, 4:117. The Distribution of the Forces in Canada, 12 November 1812, NAC, RG 8, I, 1707:60 which shows six members of the RA on command at Chippawa, seven at Lyons Creek and six at Fort Erie while thirty-three were at Fort George. A month later forty-three were at Fort George, three at Queenston, five at Chippawa and six at Fort Erie according to the Distribution of the Troops in Canada, 21 December 1812, *ibid.*, 124. According the Muster Roll for October 1812 for Holcroft's company in the Fourth Battalion of the Royal Artillery (PRO WO10, 912), there were 125 officers and men in his company of whom there were fewer than sixty on the Niagara Frontier at the time.
4. The size of the 5th Lincoln flank companies is based upon Morning State of Three Flank Companies under Claus, Niagara, 5 and 6 July 1812; Morning State of the 1st Regiment of Lincoln Militia under Claus, Niagara, 5, 7 and 10 July 1812; NAC, Claus Family Papers, RG 8, I, 1701: 21, 23, 29 and 37; 5th Lincoln, Samuel Hatt and James Durand, 3 and 5 July 1812, *ibid.*, 137-9. James Crooks mentioned that a system was in place that allowed one third of each company to be absent at a time, so the strength of the companies appears to have been about fifty men per company, Crooks to Maclear, 17 March 1853, OA, Miscellaneous Collection, MU 2144, 1853, #14. These companies had between seventy and eighty officers and men, so it is speculated here that one third of that number was on leave.
5. Captain John Powell of the 1st Lincoln Artillery was absent, leaving Lieutenant John Ball in command. On 7 July 1812 the Lincoln Artillery was shown to have 14 officers and men, State of the Third Division, 7 July 1812, DHC, 4:19. An addition of thirty men was ordered to be attached to this sub-unit, the men being taken from battalion companies of the Lincoln regiments, Militia General Order by Macdonell, 22 July 1812, DHC, 3:138.
6. One source for this company is a remark added to the

Morning State of the ... Militia under ... Claus, 6 July 1812, (NAC, Claus Family Papers, RG 8, I, 1701:27) indicating that the 2nd York flank Companies, numbering sixty men would march to Queenston that evening. In the State of the Third Division, by Chambers, 7 July 1812, (DHC, 4:19), Chisholm's company is shown to have thirty-nine officers and men while Applegarth's has fifty. It is speculated that their individual strength was about forty men each and it is assumed that one third of the men were not on leave at York in the same way that the Lincoln militia allowed a portion of its men to be absent.

7. Robinson, "Account of Queenston Heights."
8. The specific size of the light company of the 41st Foot is not mentioned in the various accounts. The best available muster of this regiment shows only rank and file. A portion of each of the companies stationed at Fort George was on command at Chippawa and above (various detachments, small and large, had been marched back and forth along the river since July as shown in "District General Orders of Maj.-Gen. Sir Isaac Brock"). Company Five was the largest, numbering eight-three Rank and File; sergeants, ensigns, lieutenants and captains excluded. This data was used as the basis for the strength of Derenzy's light infantry.
9. Extract from the Diary of General T. Evans while serving as an officer on staff of General Brock at Queenston, War of 1812-1814, Government House, Fort George, 15 October 1812, NAC, MG 24, Hellmuth Papers.
10. Crooks Account.
11. Robert Runchey (taken from McEwan's 2nd Flank Company of the 1st Lincoln) commanded the Coloured Company from 28 August 1812, District General Order by Evans, "District General Orders of Maj.-Gen. Sir Isaac Brock," 27. Runchey's Coloured Corps, OA, MU2036, #12. Militia musters, 1812, NAC, RG 8, I, 1701:141; 208
12. Crowther's 3-pdrs. were attached to one of the dependencies of Fort George, their precise location unidentified, Return of Iron and Brass Ordnance, 15 December 1812, NAC, RG 8, I, 1701:82; Sheaffe to Prevost, 13 October 1812, NAC, MG 11, CO 42, 147:225.
13. Klinck and Talman, *Norton Journal*, 304-10.
14. This number is shown in the best available source, Robinson, "Account of Queenston Heights."
15. It is assumed that one third of the two companies of militia were available for service at Queenston Heights, as was the Niagara militia, Crooks Account.
16. Gun emplacements are based upon: Return of the Brass and Iron Ordnance Mounted on Traveling and Garrison Carriages at the different Stations in Lower and Upper Canada, Quebec, 15 December 1812, By Glasgow, Major General Royal Artillery, NAC, RG 8, I, 1707:82; Return of Brass and Iron Ordnance at the Several Batteries and Stations between York and Fort Erie in Upper Canada with the number of Rounds of Ammunition attached to each piece, the quantity on reserve and what is required to complete, Quebec, 19 December 1812, *ibid.*, 121; Holcroft's account, *Quebec Mercury*, 27 October 1812, DHC, 4:117; McLean Narrative,1860; Sutherland, *Merritt Journal*, 3; Sheaffe to Prevost, 13 October 1812, NAC, MG 11, CO 42, 147:225.

**Picture captions**

1. Anon., *Some Account of the Public Life of...* Prevost, 18. Anon., *The Letters of Veritas*, 17
2. Byfield, "A Common Soldier's Account," *Recollections of the War of 1812*, 3.
3. Tompkins to Cook, 12 December 1811, cited in Irwin, *Daniel D. Tompkins*, 140.
4. Baldwin to Firth, 22 April 1812, OA, Jarvis-Powell Papers.
5. *Livingston Register*, 13 March 1833.
6. Cited in Fink, *Stephen Van Rensselaer: The Last Patroon*, 76.
7. Blackburn, *Cherry Hill: The History and Collections of a Van Rensselaer Family*, 56.
8. Brock to Gordon, 28 September 1806, Tupper, *Life of Brock*, 38-9.
9. Robinson, *Life of Sir John Beverley Robinson*, 31.
10. Swain, *The Story of Laura Secord and Fanny Doyle.* There is some evidence to support this story, as Andrew Doyle was listed as a prisoner of war in Captain James Leonard's company of the First U.S. Artillery, see Appendix C.
11. Benn, *The Iroquois in the War of 1812.*
12. *The St. Catharines Journal and Welland Canal General Advertizer*, 30 April 1840.

# *Bibliography*

## PRIMARY SOURCES – ARCHIVAL


Archives of Ontario
- 1812 Military Records
  - Various Militia material, MU 2036, 2030, 7522
- Abraham Nelles Papers, MS 502
- John Fisher Papers, MU 4198
  - *The Niagara Bee*, 24 October 1812
- John Beverley Robinson Papers, F44
- Merritt Papers, MS 74
- Miscellaneous Collection, 1797-1802, MU 2100
- Miscellaneous Collection, 1563-1820, MU 2143
- Miscellaneous Collection, 1563-1820, MU 2144
- Municipal Records of the Township of Newark/Niagara, 1793-1899
- Robert Nelles Papers, MS 503
- Niagara Historical Society Collection, MS 193 (3)
- Ridout Family Papers, 1764-1824, MS 537

Buffalo and Erie County Historical Society
- Peter B. Porter Papers, Roll 2: War of 1812, 30 January 1812–April 1814
- War of 1812 Letters and Prisoner List, A64-286, John E. Wool Correspondence

Geneva Historical Society
- Dobbin Family Papers

Historic Cherry Hill, Albany, NY
- Van Rensselaer Papers

National Archives of Canada
- MG 11, CO 42, Original Correspondence, Secretary of State, Lower Canada, volumes 143-165
- MG 13, WO 17, Monthly Returns, Canada, 1808-1812, volumes 1514-1516
- MG 13, WO 25, Registers Various, Isaac Brock (volume 7448), Thomas Evans (volume 798)
- MG 13, WO 44, Ordnance Office, In-Letters, volume 245
  - Account of battle of Queenston Heights (Holcroft), *Quebec Mercury*, 27 October 1812
- MG 13, WO 57, Commissariat Department: In Letters, Canada, 1811-1815, volume 14
- MG 23, K, I, 3, Samuel Jarvis letter, volume 1
- MG 24, Hellmuth Papers, Extract from the Diary of General T. Evans while serving as an officer on staff of General Brock at Queenston, War of 1812–1814, Government House, Fort George, 15 October 1812
- RG 8, I, "C" Series, British Military and Naval Records, United States, War of 1812, 1806-1834, volumes 673-76
  - Claus Family Papers, volume 1701
  - District Troop Returns, volume 1707

New York State Archives, Albany, New York

New York State Library, Albany
John Ellis Wool Papers, Special Collections, 15361
Solomon Van Rensselaer Papers, SC 7079, Box 83

Oneida County Historical Society Library, Box 93, War of 1812 Collections
Joseph Hawley Dwight, Thirteenth U.S. Infantry Regiment, "Journal of an Ensign in the War of 1812"

Ontario County, Canandaigua
Dox (Abraham) Papers

Pennsylvania State Archives
Diary of Jacob Miller, MG 6
Orderly Book of Brigadier General Adamson Tannehill

Public Record Office, Kew, England
WO 10, 912, Muster Rolls.
WO 12, 5416 and 6044, Pay Lists
WO 25, 1768 and 1829, Casualty Returns

State University of New York, Buffalo, Lockwood Library
Albert Gallatin Papers

Toronto Reference Library, Baldwin Room
Broadside Series

United States National Archives
RG 59, General Records of the Department of State – Intercepted Correspondence
RG 94, Records of the Adjutant General's Office, 1780-1917
RG 98, General Orders and Circulars of the War Department and Headquarters of the Army, 1809-1860
RG 107, Records of the Office of the Secretary of War, 1791-1947

## PRIMARY SOURCES – PUBLISHED

Cruikshank, Ernest A., ed. *Documentary History of the Campaigns upon the Niagara Frontier in 1812-1814* (titles vary slightly). Welland: Tribune Press, 1896-1908, 9 vols.

———, ed. *Records of Niagara (No. 42) in the Days of Commodore Grant and Lieutenant-Governor Gore: 1805-1811.* Niagara: Niagara Historical Society, 1931.

Dudley, William S. ed. *The Naval War of 1812: A Documentary History.* Washington: Historical Center, Department of the Navy, 1985, 1992. 2 vols.

Firth, Edith G. *The Town of York: 1793-1815.* Toronto: The Champlain Society: University of Toronto Press, 1962.

Hastings, Hugh, ed. *Military Minutes of the Council of Appointment of the State of New York, 1783-1821.* Albany: J. B. Lyon Company, 1901, 4 vols.

Johnston, Charles M. *The Valley of the Six Nations: A Collection of Documents on the Indian Lands of the Grand River.* Toronto: The Champlain Society, 1964.

Preston, Richard A. *Kingston Before the War of 1812.* Toronto: The Champlain Society, 1959.

Provost, H. *Recensement de la Ville de Québec.* Quebec: La Société Historique de Québec, 1976.

U.S. Congress, *American State Papers: Military Affairs.* Washington, D.C.: Gales and Seaton, 1832, Vol. 1.

U.S. Congress, *Annals of The Congress of the United States.* Washington: Gales and Seaton, 1853, 12th Congress.

U.S. Congress, *Public Statutes at Large...* Boston: Little and Brown, 1845, Vols. 1 and 2.

## PUBLISHED MEMOIRS, DIARIES, JOURNALS AND CORRESPONDENCE

Adams, Henry, ed. *The Writings of Albert Gallatin.* New York: Antiquarian Press, 1960, 3 vols.

Armstrong, John, ed., *Notices of the War of 1812.* New York: General Dearborn & Wiley and Putnam, 1840, 2 vols.

Bonney, Catherine V. R. *A Legacy of Historical Gleanings.* Albany: J. Munsell, 1875, 2 vols.

Campbell, William W. *The Life and Writings of De Witt Clinton.* New York: Baker and Scribner, 1849.
Carnochan, Jane. "Col. Daniel McDougal and Valuable Documents," *Niagara Historical Society*, No. 23 (1912), 26-40.
Claus, William. "An Account of the Operations of the Indian Contingent with Our Forces on the Niagara Frontier in 1812-13," Cruikshank, E. A., ed. *Campaigns of 1812-14.* Niagara-on-the-Lake: Niagara Historical Society, 1902.
Crooks, James. "Recollections of the War of 1812," *Niagara Historical Society*, No. 28 (1916), 31.
"District General Orders of Maj.-Gen. Sir Isaac Brock from June 27th, 1812–Oct. 16th 1812," *Transactions of the Women's Canadian Historical Society.* No. 19 (1920), 5-48.
Fredriksen, John C. ed. *War of 1812 Eyewitness Accounts: An Annotated Bibliography.* Westport, CT: Greenwood Press, 1997.
Glover, Michael, ed. *A Gentleman Volunteer: The Letters of George Hennel from the Peninsular War, 1812-13.* London: Heinemann, 1979.
Hastings, Hugh, ed. *The Public Papers of Daniel D. Tompkins, Governor of New York.* Albany: J. B. Lyon Company, 1898, 1902, 3 vols.
Hopkins, James F., ed. *The Papers of Henry Clay.* Lexington: University of Kentucky Press, 1959. 5 vols.
Hull, William. *Memoirs of the Campaign of the Northwest Army of the United States, A. D. 1812.* Boston: True and Greene, 1824.
Hunt, Gaillard, ed. *The Writings of James Madison.* New York: G.P. Putnam's Sons, 1908, 9 vols.
Klinck, Carl F. and James J. Talman, ed. *The Journal of Major John Norton, 1816.* Toronto: The Champlain Society, 1970.
"Letter Book of Gen. Sir Roger Hale Sheaffe." *Publications of the Buffalo Historical Society*, 17 (1913), 271-381.
Myers, Mordecai. *Reminiscences, 1780-1814, Including Incidents in the War of 1812-14.* Washington: Crane, 1900.
O'Reilly, Miss. "A Hero of Fort Erie: Letters relating to the Military Service, Chiefly on the Niagara Frontier, of Lieutenant Patrick McDonogh," *Publications of the Buffalo Historical Society*, 5 (1901), 63-98.
Roach, Isaac. "Journal of Major Isaac Roach, 1812-1824," *Pennsylvania Magazine*, 17 (1893), 129-315.
Robinson, C. W. *Life of Sir John Beverley Robinson, Bart., C.B., D.C.L., Chief Justice of Upper Canada.* Toronto: Morang and Co., Ltd., 1904.
Spragge, George W., ed. *The John Strachan Letter Book: 1812-1814.* Toronto: Ontario Historical Society, 1946.
Sutherland, Stuart, ed. *"A Desire of Serving and Defending my Country": The War of 1812 Journals of William Hamilton Merritt.* Toronto: Iser Publications, 2001.
Tupper, Ferdinand Brock. *The Life and Correspondence of Major-General Sir Isaac Brock, K. B.* 2nd ed. London: Simpkin, Marshall & Co., 1847.
Willson, Jared. "A Rifleman of Queenston," *Publications of the Buffalo Historical Society*, 9 (1906), 373-6.
Wood, William C. H., ed. *Select British Documents of the Canadian War of 1812.* Toronto: Champlain Society, 1920-28, 3 vols.
Wool to Stone, 13 September 1838, "Major-General John Ellis Wool to W. L. Stone on the Battle of Queenston Heights in October, 1812," *New York Public Library Bulletin*, 9 (1905), 120-2.
Wool to the editor of the *Herald*, 30 November 1865, *Historical Magazine*, 2 (1867), 283-5.

## BIOGRAPHICAL ENCYCLOPEDIAS, REGISTERS, DICTIONARIES, MILITARY UNIT AND MEDAL SOURCES

*American National Biography.* New York: Oxford University Press, 1999, 24 vols.
Birkhimer, William E. *Historical Sketch of the Organization, Administration, Matériel and Tactics of the Artillery, United States Army.* New York: Greenwood Press, 1968, original publication James J. Chapman, 1884.
Carter-Edwards, Dennis. *At Work and Play: The British Junior Officer in Upper Canada, 1796-1812.* Ottawa: Parks Canada, 1985.
Chichester, Henry Manners and George Burges-Short. *The Records and Badges of Every Regiment and Corps in the British Army.* London: Gale and Porden, Ltd., 1900.
*Dictionary of American Biography.* New York: Scribner, 1958-1964, 22 vols.
*Dictionary of Canadian Biography.* Toronto: University of Toronto, 1976-1988, vols. 5-9.

Duncan, Major Francis. *History of the Royal Regiment of Artillery.* London: John Murray, (3rd ed.), 1879, 2 vols.

Gray, William. *Soldiers of the King: The Upper Canadian Militia, 1812-1815.* Erin, Ontario: The Boston Mills Press, 1995.

*Harper's Encyclopedia of United States History.* New York: Harper & Brothers, 1905, 10 vols.

Heitman, Francis B., ed. *Historical Register and Dictionary of the United States Army from its Organization, September 29, 1789 to March 2, 1903.* Washington: 1903; reprint, Baltimore: Genealogical Publishing Co., Inc., 1994, 2 vols.

James, Charles. *A New and Enlarged Military Dictionary, or, Alphabetical Explanations of Technical Terms…* London: T. Egerton, 1802.

McAlexander, U. G. *History of the Thirteenth Regiment United States Infantry.* Regimental Press, Frank D. Gunn, 1905. (Place of publication not in original)

Petre, F. Loraine. *The Royal Berkshire Regiment (Princess Charlotte of Wales's), 49th Foot and 66th Foot.* Reading: 1925, 2 vols.

Riling, Joseph R., ed. *Baron Von Steuben and his Regulations.* Philadelphia: Ray Riling Arms Books Co., 1966.

Smyth, Alexander. *Regulations for the Field Exercise, Manoeuvres and Conduct of the Infantry of the United States: Drawn Up and Adapted to the Organization of the Militia and Regular Troops.* Philadelphia: Anthony Finley, 1812.

*Statement Showing the Name, Age and Residence of Militiamen of 1812-15…* Ottawa: Maclean, Roger and Co., 1876.

Summers, Jack L. and René Chartrand. *Military Uniforms in Canada: 1665-1970.* Ottawa: Canadian War Museum, 1981.

Sutherland, Stuart. *His Majesty's Gentlemen: A Directory of Regular British Army Officers of the War of 1812.* Toronto: Iser Publications, 2000.

## SECONDARY SOURCES – PUBLISHED

### Books

Adams, Samuel Hopkins. *General Brock and Niagara Falls.* New York: Random House, 1957.

Allen, Robert S. *His Majesty's Indian Allies: British Indian Policy in the Defence of Canada, 1774-1815.* Toronto: Dundurn Press, 1992.

Armstrong, John. *Notices of the War of 1812.* New York: George Dearborn, 1836, 2 vols.

Barnard, Daniel D. *A Discourse on the Life, Services and Character of Stephen Van Rensselaer Delivered Before the Albany Institute, April 15, 1839.* Albany: Hoffman & White, 1839.

Begamudré, Ven. *Isaac Brock: Larger than Life.* Montreal: XYZ Publishing, 2000.

Benn, Carl. *The Iroquois in the War of 1812.* Toronto: University of Toronto Press, 1998.

Bennett, Geoffrey. *Nelson the Commander.* London: B.T. Batsford Ltd., 1972.

Berton, Pierre. *The Death of Isaac Brock.* Toronto: McClelland and Stewart, 1991.

Blackburn, Roderic H. *Cherry Hill: The History and Collections of a Van Rensselaer Family.* Albany: Historic Cherry Hill, 1976.

Bobbé, Dorothie. *De Witt Clinton.* Port Washington, N. Y.: Ira J. Friedman (reprint), 1962.

Brant, Irving, ed. *James Madison: Commander in Chief, 1812-1836.* New York: Bobbs-Merrill, 1961. 6 vols.

[Brenton, E. B.] *Some Account of the Public Life of the late Lieutenant-General Sir George Prevost, Bart,…* London: T. Cadell and T. Egerton, 1823.

Chartrand, René. *Uniforms and Equipment of the United States Forces in the War of 1812.* Youngstown, New York: Old Fort Niagara Association, 1992.

Chazanof, William. *Joseph Ellicott and the Holland Land Company: The Opening of Western New York.* Syracuse: Syracuse University Press, 1970.

Clausewitz, Carl Von. *On War.* Michael Howard and Peter Paret, translators and editors, New York: Everyman's Library (Alfred A. Knopf), 1993.

Coffman, Edward M. *The Old Army: A Portrait of the American Army in Peacetime, 1784-1989.* New York: Oxford University Press, 1986.

Coles, Harry L. *The War of 1812.* Chicago: University of Chicago Press, 1965.

Cooke, J. *The Battle of Queenston Heights, Oct. 13, 1812.* Niagara Falls, NY: Courier Press, 1901.

Cooke, Jacob E. *Tench Coxe and the Early Republic.* Chapel Hill: University of North Carolina Press, 1978.

Crackell, Theodore J. *Mr. Jefferson's Army: Political and Social Reform of the Military Establishment, 1801-1809.* New York: New York University Press, 1987.

Cruikshank, E. A. *The Battle of Queenston Heights.* Niagara Falls: Lundy's Lane Historical Society, 1891.

Darling, Anthony D. *Red Coat and Brown Bess.* Alexandria Bay, NY: Museum Restoration Services, 1991.

Desloges, Yvon. *Structural History of Fort George.* Ottawa: National Historical Parks and Sites Branch, Parks Canada, 1980.

Dickason, Olive Patricia. *Canada's First Nations: A History of the Founding Peoples from Earliest Times.* 3rd edition. Toronto: Oxford University Press, 2002.

Dunnigan, Brian Leigh. *The British Army at Mackinac, 1812-1815.* Mackinac: Mackinac State Historic Parks, 1980.

Dunnigan, Brian Leigh and Patricia Kay Scott. *Old Fort Niagara in Four Centuries: A History of its Development.* Youngstown, N. Y.: Old Fort Niagara Association, 1991.

Eayrs, Hugh S. *Sir Isaac Brock.* Toronto: Macmillan, 1918.

Edgar, Lady. *General Brock.* London: Oxford University Press, 1928.

Elting, John R. *Amateurs, To Arms! A Military History of the War of 1812.* Chapel Hill: Algonquin Books of Chapel Hill, 1991.

Errington, Jane. *The Lion, the Eagle and Upper Canada: A Developing Colonial Ideology.* Kingston: McGill-Queen's University Press, 1987.

Fox, Dixon Ryan, *The Decline of Aristocracy in the Politics of New York, 1801-1840.* New York: Harper and Row, 1919; reprint, 1965.

Fraser, Alexander, ed. *Brock Centenary, 1812-1912: Account of the Celebration At Queenston Heights, Ontario, on the 12th October 1812.* Toronto: William Briggs, 1913.

Fredriksen, John C. *Officers of the War of 1812 with Portraits and Anecdotes: The United States Army Left Division Gallery of Honor.* Lewiston: Edwin Mellen Press, 1989.

Glover, Michael. *Warfare in the Age of Bonaparte.* London: Cassell, 1980.

Gooding, S. James. *An Introduction to British Artillery in North America.* Alexandria Bay, NY: Museum Restoration Service, 1986.

Goodspeed, D. J. *The Good Soldier: The Story of Isaac Brock.* Toronto: Macmillan, 1964.

Graves, Donald E. *Where Right and Glory Lead! The Battle of Lundy's lane, 1814.* Toronto: Robin Brass Studio,1997.

Gray, Hugh. *Letters from Canada, Written During a Residence there in the Years 1806, 1807 and 1808....* London: Longman, Hurst and Company, 1809.

Halliday, Hugh A. *Murder Among Gentlemen: A History of Duelling in Canada.* Toronto: Robin Brass Studio, 1999.

Hammond, Jabez D. *The History of Political Parties in the State of New-York.* Cooperstown: H. & E. Phinney, 1846, 3 vols.

Handel, Michael I. *Masters of War: Classic Strategic Thought.* London: Frank Cass, 3rd edition, 2001.

Hatch, Alden. *The Wadsworths of the Genesee.* New York: Coward-McCann, inc., 1959.

Hatzenbuehler, Ronald and Robert L. Ivie, ed. *Congress Declares War: Rhetoric, Leadership, and Partisanship in the Early Republic.* Kent, Ohio: Kent State University Press, 1983.

Haythornthwaite, Philip J. *The Napoleonic Source Book.* New York: Facts on File, 1990.

———. *Weapons and Equipment of the Napoleonic Wars.* London: Arms and Armour, 1979.

Hickey, Donald R. *The War of 1812: A Forgotten Conflict.* Chicago: University of Illinois Press, 1990.

Higginson, T. B. ed. *Major Richardson's Major-General Sir Isaac Brock and the 41st Regiment.* Burks Falls: Old Rectory Press, 1976.

Hitsman, J. Mackay. *The Incredible War of 1812: A Military History.* Toronto: University of Toronto, 1965; reprint, Toronto: Robin Brass Studio, 1999.

Holmes, Richard. *Redcoat: The British Soldier in the Age of Horse and Musket.* London: HarperCollins, 2002.

Horsman, Reginald. *The Causes of the War of 1812.* New York: A.S. Barnes and Company, 1962.

Hosack, David. *Memoir of De Witt Clinton.* New York: J. Seymour, 1829.

Houlding, J. A. *Fit For Service: The Training of the British Army, 1715-1795.* Oxford: Clarendon Press, 1981.

Irwin, Ray W. *Daniel D. Tompkins: Governor of New York and Vice President of the United States.* New York: The New-York Historical Society, 1968.

Jackson, John N. *St. Catharines, Ontario: Its Early Years.* Belleville: Mika Publishing, 1976.

Kalbach, Warren E. and Wayne W. McVey. *The Demographic Bases of Canadian Society.* Toronto: McGraw-Hill, 1971.

Lamb, W. Kaye. *The Hero Of Upper Canada.* Toronto: Rous and Mann Press, 1962.

Lankevich, George J. and Howard B. Furer. *A Brief History of New York City.* Port Washington, N. Y.: National University Publications, 1984.

Lynn, John A. *The Bayonets of the Republic: Motivation and Tactics in the Army of Revolutionary France, 1791-94.* Urbana: University of Illinois Press, 1984.

Mahan, Alfred T. *Sea Power in its Relations to the War of 1812.* London: Sampson Low, Marston and Company, 1905, 2 vols.

Mahon, John K. *The War of 1812.* New York: Da Capo Press, 1972.

Malcomson, Robert. *The Battle of Queennston Heights.* Niagara-on-the-Lake: The Friends of Fort George, 1994.

———. *Burying General Brock: A History of Brock's Monuments.* Niagara-on-the-Lake: The Friends of Fort George, 1996.

———. *Lords of the Lake: The Naval War on Lake Ontario, 1812-1814.* Toronto: Robin Brass Studio, 1998.

———. *Warships of the Great Lakes: 1754-1834.* London: Chatham Publishing, 2001.

McConnell, David. *British Smooth-Bore Artillery: A Technological Study.* Ottawa: Parks Canada, 1988.

McKenna, Katherine M. J. *A Life of Propriety: Anne Murray Powell and Her Family, 1755-1849.* Montreal: McGill-Queen's University Press, 1994.

Marquis, T.G. *Sir Isaac Brock.* Toronto: Ryerson Press, 1929.

Martineau, Harriet. *Retrospect of Western Travel.* New York: Saunders and Otley, 1838, 2 vols.

Melish, John. *Travels through the United States of America in the Years 1806, 1807, 1809, 1810 and 1811.* Belfast: J. Smyth, 1818.

Merritt, Richard, Nancy Butler, and Michael Power, eds. *The Capital Years: Niagara-on-the-Lake, 1792-1796.* Toronto: Dundurn Press, 1991.

Middleton, Jesse Edgar and Fred Landon. *The Province of Ontario: A History, 1615-1927.* Toronto: Dominion Publishing Company, Ltd., 1927, 2 vols.

Moffat, Riley. *Population History of Eastern U.S. Cities and Towns, 1790-1870.* Metuchen, N. J.: Scarecrow Press, 1992.

Nettels, Curtis. *The Emergence of a National Economy, 1775-1815.* New York: Holt, Rinehart and Winston, 1962.

North, Douglass C. *The Economic Growth of the United States, 1790-1860.* Englewood Cliffs, N. J.: Prentice-Hall, Inc., 1961.

Nursey, Walter R. *The Story of Isaac Brock, Hero, Defender and Savior of Upper Canada, 1812.* Toronto: McClelland and Stewart, 1923.

Owen, David A. *Fort Erie (1764-1823) An Historical Guide.* Niagara Falls: The Niagara Parks Commission, 1986.

Perkins, Bradford. *Prologue to War: England and the United States, 1805-1812.* Los Angeles: University of California Press, 1963.

Pope, Dudley. *The Great Gamble: Nelson at Copenhagen.* New York: Simon and Schuster, 1972.

Read, J.B. *The Life and Times of Major-General Sir Isaac Brock, K. B.* Toronto: Briggs, 1894.

[Richardson, John.] *The letters of Veritas: republished from the* Montreal Herald; *containing a succinct narrative of the military administration of Sir George Prevost, during his command in the Canadas; whereby it will appear manifest, that the merit of preserving them from conquest, belongs not to him.* Montreal: W. Gray, 1815.

Riley, Moffat. *Populations History of Eastern U.S. Cities and Towns, 1790-1870,* Metuchen, NJ: Scarecrow, 1992, reprint.

Risch, Erna. *Quartermaster Support of the Army: The History of the Corps, 1775-1939.* Washington: Office of the Quartermaster General, 1962.

Schlesinger, Arthur M. *History of American Presidential Elections, 1789-1968.* New York: Chelsea House Publishers, 1971, vol 1 of 4.

Scott, Stuart D. *An Archeological Survey of Artpark.* Lewiston, N. Y.: Edward Mellen Press, 1993.

Scott, Winfield. *Memoirs of General Scott, Written by Himself.* New York: Sheldon, 1864, 2 vols.

Sears, Louis Martin. *Jefferson and the Embargo.* New York: Octagon Books, Inc., 1966.

Seibel, George A. *The Niagara Portage Road 200 Years 1790-1990.* Niagara Falls: City of Niagara Falls, 1990.
Sheppard, George. *Plunder, Profit and Paroles: A Social History of the War of 1812 in Upper Canada.* Montreal: McGill-Queen's University Press, 1994.
Skeen, C. Edward. *Citizen Soldiers in the War of 1812.* Lexington: University of Kentucky, 1996.
Spafford, Horatio Gates. *A Gazetteer of the State of New York.* Albany: H.C. Southwich, 1813.
Stagg, J.C. A. *Mr. Madison's War: Politics, Diplomacy and Warfare in the Early American Republic, 1783-1830.* Princeton: Princeton University Press, 1983.
Stone, William L. *Life of Joseph Brant – Thayendanegea.* New York: Blake, 1838, 2 vols.
Symons, John, Ed. *The Battle of Queenston Heights being a narrative of the Opening of the War of 1812 with notices of the life of Major-General Sir Isaac Brock, K. B. and description of the Monument Erected to his Memory.* Toronto: Thompson and Sons, 1859.
Tupper, H. *Who was Isaac Brock? Short Summary of the Life of Major-General Sir Isaac Brock, K.B.* Guernsey: Clarke, circa 1919.
Turner, Wesley. *The War of 1812: The War that Both Sides Won.* Toronto: Dundurn Press, 1990.
———. *British Generals in the War of 1812: High Command in the Canadas.* Montreal: McGill-Queen's University Press, 1999.
Van Rensselaer, Florence. *The Van Rensselaers in Holland and in America.* New York: The American Historical Company, Inc., 1956.
Van Rensselaer, Solomon. *A Narrative of the Affair of Queenstown: In the War of 1812.* Boston: Leavitt, Lord & Co., 1836.
Wilkinson, James. *Memoirs of My Own Times.* Philadelphia: Abraham Hall, 1816, 3 vols.
Wilson, Bruce G. *The Enterprises of Robert Hamilton: A Study of Wealth and Influence in Early Upper Canada, 1776-1812.* Ottawa: Carleton University Press, 1983.

**Articles**

Aimone, Alan. "West Point's Contribution to the War of 1812," *Military Collector and Historian*, 54 (2002), 7-15.
British Army. "The Assault Crossing of Water Obstacles," Military Training Pamphlet no. 20, London: War Office (WO 8213), 1947.
Burghardt, Andrew F. "The Origin and Development of the Road Network of the Niagara Peninsula, Ontario, 1770-1851," *Annals of the Association of American Geographers*, 59 (1969), 417-40.
Cain, Emily. "Building the Lord Nelson," *Inland Seas*, 41 (1985), 121-129.
Carnochan, Jane. "Sir Isaac Brock," *Niagara Historical Society*, No. 15 (1913), 1-22.
Casey, Richard P. "North Country Nemesis: The Potash Rebellion and the Embargo of 1807-09," *The New-York Historical Society Quarterly*, 64 (1980), 31-49.
Cruikshank, E.A. "Battle-Fields of the Niagara Peninsula During the War of 1812-15," *Selected Papers from the Transactions of the Canadian Military Institute* (1890-91), 25-48.
———. "Record of the Services of the Canadian Regiments in the War of 1812, Part IX, The Lincoln Militia," *Selected Papers from the Transactions of the Canadian Military Institute*, 13 (1903), 11-41.
———. "A Sketch of the Public Life and Services of Robert Nichol...," *Ontario Historical Society Papers and Records*, 19 (1922), 37-63.
———. "A Study of the Disaffection in Upper Canada in 1812-15," *Transactions of the Royal Society of Canada*, 6 (1912), 11-40.
Douglas, W.A.B. "The Anatomy of Naval Incompetence: The Provincial Marine in Defence of Upper Canada Before 1813," *Ontario History*, 71 (1979), 3-25.
Gero, Anthony F. and Philip G. Maples. "Notes on the Dress of the 13th Regiment, United States Infantry, 1812-1813," *Military Collector and Historian*, 38 (1986), 167-8.
Graves, Donald E. "'Dry Books of Tactics': US Infantry Manuals of the War of 1812 and After, Part I," *Military Collector and Historian*, 38 (1986), 50-61.
———. "'Dry Books of Tactics': US Infantry Manuals of the War of 1812 and After, Part II," *Military Collector and Historian*, 38 (1986), 173-7.
———. "Field Artillery of the War of 1812: Equipment, Organization, Tactics and Effectiveness," *Arms Collecting*, 30 (1992), 39-48.
———. "American Ordnance of the War of 1812: A Preliminary Investigation," *Arms Collecting*, 31 (1993), 111-20.

Green, Ernest. "The Niagara Portage Road," *Ontario History*, 22 (1926), 260-311.

Hatzenbuehler, Ronald L. "The War Hawks and the Question of Congressional Leadership in 1812," *Pacific Historical Review*, 45 (1976), 1-22.

Hickey, Donald R. "The War of 1812: Still a Forgotten Conflict?" *The Journal of Military History*, 65 (2001), 741-69.

Hitsman, J. Mackay. "Sir George Prevost's Conduct of the Canadian War of 1812," *The Canadian Historical Association*, (1962), 34-43.

Kimball, Jeffrey. "The Fog and Friction of Frontier War: The Role of Logistics in American Offensive Failure During the War of 1812," *Old Northwest*, 5 (1979-80), 323-43.

Koke, Richard J. "The Britons who Fought on the Canadian Frontier: Uniforms of the War of 1812." *The New-York Historical Society Quarterly*, 45 (1961), 141-194.

Kosche, Ludwig. "Relics of Brock: An Investigation." *Archivaria*, 9 (1979), 33-103.

———, "Contemporary Portraits of Isaac Brock: An Analysis," *Archivaria*, 20 (1985), 22-66.

Lord, Philip Jr. "The Mohawk/Oneida Corridor: The Geography of Inland Navigation Across New York," in David Curtis Skaggs and Larry L. Nelson, ed. *The Sixty Years' War for the Great Lakes, 1754-1814.* (East Lansing: Michigan State University Press, 2001), 275-90.

Mahon, John K. "British Command Decisions in the Northern Campaigns of the War of 1812," *Canadian Historical Review*, 46 (1965), 219-37.

McBarron, H. Charles and Kochan, James L. "22nd U.S. Infantry Regiment, 1812-1813," *Military Collector and Historian*, 36 (1982), 164-165.

Malcomson, Robert. "Upper Canada Preserved: Isaac Brock's Farewell to Arms, Queenston Heights, 1812," *The Beaver*, 73 (1993), 4-15.

———. "Little Gained at Great Cost: A Canadian View of the War of 1812," *Command: Military History, Strategy and Analysis*, 48 (1998), 18-36.

———. "'It remains only to fight:'" The Battle of Queenston Heights, 13 October 1812, Donald E. Graves, ed. *Fighting for Canada: Seven Battles, 1758-1945.* Toronto: Robin Brass Studio, 2000.

———. "'Not Very Much Celebrated:' The Evolution and Nature of the Provincial Marine, 1755-1813," *The Northern Mariner/Le Marin du Nord*, 11 (2001), 25-37.

Murray, J.M. "John Norton," *Ontario History*, 37 (1945), 7-16.

Palmer, Richard F. "James Fenimore Cooper and the Navy Brig *Oneida*," *Inland Seas*, 40 (1984), 90-9.

Potter, J. "The Growth of Population in America, 1700-1860," in Glass, D. V. and Eversley, D. E. C., ed. *Population in History.* London: Edward Arnold Ltd., 1965.

Redway, Jacques W. "General Van Rensselaer and the Niagara Frontier," *Proceedings of the New-York State Historical Association*, 8 (1909), 14-22.

Risford, Norman K. "Election of 1812," in Arthur M. Schlesinger, ed., *History of American Presidential Elections, 1789-1968.* New York: McGraw-Hill Book Co., 1971, 4 vols, 1:249-72.

Sheppard, George. "Deeds Speak: Militiamen, Medals and the Invented Traditions of 1812," *Ontario History*, 83 (1990), 207-32.

Skelton, William B. "High Army Leadership in the Era of the War of 1812: The Making and Remaking of the Officer Corps," *William and Mary Quarterly*, 51 (1994), 253-74.

Stacey, C.P. "The War of 1812 in Canadian History," *Ontario History*, 50 (1958), 153-9.

Stagg, J.C.A. "Between Black Rock and a Hard Place: Peter B. Porter's Plan for an Invasion of Canada in 1812," *Journal of the American Republic*, 19 (1999), 385-422.

———. "Enlisted Men in the United States Army, 1812-1815: A Preliminary Survey," *William and Mary Quarterly*, 48 (1986), 615-45.

———. "Soldiers in Peace and War: Comparative Perspectives on the Recruitment of the United States Army, 1802-1815," *William and Mary Quarterly*, 57 (2000), 79-120.

Stanley, G.F.G. "Contribution of the Canadian Militia during the War," Philip Mason, ed. *After Tippecanoe: Some Aspects of the War of 1812.* Toronto: Ryerson Press, 1963, 28-48.

Strum, Harvey. "A Gross and Unprovoked Outrage: Niagara Incident," *Inland Seas*, 48 (1992), 284-90.

Van Rensselaer, Kiliaen. "The Van Rensselaers of Rensselaerwyck," *The New-York Historical Society, Quarterly Bulletin*, 39 (1945), 17-37.

Weaver, Sally M. "Six Nations of the Grand River, Ontario," Sturtevant, William C., ed. *Handbook of North American Indians.* Washington: Smithsonian Institute, 1978-2002, 15:525-536, 18 vols.

Whitfield, Carol. "The Battle of Queenston Heights," *Occasional Papers in Archeology and History*, No. 11, Parks Canada, 1974, 9-59.

## SECONDARY SOURCES – UNPUBLISHED

Coombe, Suzanne E. "The War of 1812 Losses Claims in the Niagara Peninsula." Bachelor of Arts Thesis, Brock University, 1972.

Couture, Paul Morgan. "A Study of the Non-Regular Military Forces on the Niagara Frontier, 1812-1814." Parks Canada, Manuscript Report, March 1985.

Dimitroff, Terry Curtis. "The Portage Era of the Niagara River Region and the Development of Queenston, 1678-1812." Bachelor of Arts Thesis, Brock University, 1968.

Fink, William B. "Stephen Van Rensselaer: The Last Patroon." Ph.D. Thesis, Columbia University, 1950.

Graves, Donald E. "Joseph Willcocks and the Canadian Volunteers: An Account of Political Disaffection in Upper Canada During the War of 1812." Master of Arts Thesis, Carleton University, 1982.

Hendry, Douglas L. "British Casualties Suffered at Several Actions during the War of 1812." Ottawa: Directorate of History, 1994.

La Croix, Mina B. "Solomon Van Rensselaer: His Career as Political Spoilsman." 1987, Historic Cherry Hill, Albany.

McLean, James M. "A Survey of Some ... Activities in the Life of Solomon Van Rensselaer." 1966, Historic Cherry Hill, Albany.

Malcomson, Robert. "Management of Batteaux by the British in the War of 1812." Project Report for Parks Canada (Fort George) and the Friends of Fort George, 1996.

Snow, Elizabeth M. "Salvage Archaeology at the Redan Battery, Queenston Heights, Ontario, 1975." I-33, in "Miscellaneous Salvage Archaeology Reports." Parks Canada, Manuscript Report, March 1985.

Strum, Harvey Joel. "New York and the War of 1812." Ph.D. Dissertation, University of Syracuse, NY, 1978.

Walden, Isaac. "Isaac Brock: Man and Myth. A Study of the Militia Myth of the War of 1812 in Upper Canada, 1812-1912." Master of Arts Thesis, Queen's University, 1971.

## NEWSPAPERS

*Daily Globe*
*Kingston Gazette*
*Livingston Register*, N.Y.
*Niagara Bee*
*Niagara Chronicle*
*Niagara Mail*
*Northern Whig*, Hudson, N.Y.
*The Oracle of Dauphin*, Harrisburg, Penn.
*Quebec Gazette*
*Quebec Mercury*
*St. Catharines Journal and Welland Canal General Advertiser*
*Western Star and Harp of Erin*, N.Y.

# Index

## BY THE SAME AUTHOR

# Lords of the Lake

### The Naval War on Lake Ontario, 1812-1814

Of all the struggles that took place along the border between the United States and the British provinces of Canada during the War of 1812, the one that lasted the longest was the crucial battle for control of Lake Ontario. Because the armies depended on it for transportation, control of the lake was a key element in American invasion attempts and the defensive actions of the British. Both nations worked feverishly to build vessels with which to gain mastery of the waterway.

*Lords of the Lake*, the first full-length study of this aspect of the war, tells the story of the contest from the days of the incompetent Provincial Marine to the launch of the 104-gun ship *St. Lawrence.* The narrative features battles and raids, shipwrecks, chases and blockades, treachery and heroism. The book is illustrated with maps, illustrations and diagrams.

Winner of the 1998 John Lyman Prize for Best Work in Canadian Naval and Maritime History.

"All in all, this is an outstanding book, beautifully produced, and it should be read by anyone interested in the War of 1812." *The Mariner's Mirror.*

**432 pages • 6 x 9 inches • about 100 pictures, maps • published in U.S.A. by Naval Institute Press and in Canada by Robin Brass Studio**